CENTURY OF THE CHILD

GROWING BY DESIGN 1900–2000

JULIET KINCHIN | **AIDAN O'CONNOR**

With contributions by

TANYA HARROD, PABLO HELGUERA, MEDEA HOCH, FRANCIS LUCA, MARIA PAOLA MAINO, AMY F. OGATA, DAVID SENIOR, AND SARAH SUZUKI

The Museum of Modern Art, New York

Published in conjunction with the exhibition *Century of the Child: Growing by Design, 1900–2000* at The Museum of Modern Art, New York, July 29–November 5, 2012, organized by Juliet Kinchin, Curator, and Aidan O'Connor, Curatorial Assistant, Department of Architecture and Design.

Major support for the exhibition is provided by Lawrence B. Benenson.

Additional funding is provided by the Nordic Culture Fund, Lily Auchincloss Foundation, Inc., the Barbro Osher Pro Suecia Foundation, and Marimekko.

Support for the publication is provided by The International Council of The Museum of Modern Art and the Jo Carole Lauder Publications Fund of The International Council of The Museum of Modern Art.

Edited by Emily Hall and Libby Hruska
Designed by McCall Associates, New York
Production by Marc Sapir
Printed and bound by Asia One Printing Limited, Hong Kong

Medea Hoch's essay "Performing the Modern: Swiss Puppets" was translated from the German by Catherine Schelbert.

Maria Paola Maino's essay "Italy: The Unruly Child" was translated from the Italian by Marguerite Shore.

This book is typeset in FF Kievit and Alright Sans. The paper is 157gsm Gold East matt.

Library of Congress Control Number: 2012937353
ISBN: 978-0-87070-826-8

Published by The Museum of Modern Art
11 West 53rd Street, New York, New York 10019
www.moma.org

Distributed in the United States and Canada by ARTBOOK | D.A.P.
155 Sixth Avenue, 2nd Floor, New York, New York 10013
www.artbook.com

Distributed outside the United States and Canada by Thames & Hudson Ltd
181A High Holborn, London WC1V 7QX
www.thamesandhudson.com

Cover: Boys in a Glasgow back court show off their Christmas presents, which include astronaut suits and Space Hoppers. 1970. Published in *The Scotsman*. Photograph by Gordon Rule. Licensor SCRAN, Glasgow. See p. 187

Front endpapers: Harry Callahan. *Untitled*. c. 1953. Gelatin silver print, 5⁵/₁₆ x 8¹/₈" (13.5 x 20.6 cm). The Museum of Modern Art, New York. Gift of the photographer. See p. 27
Clarence H. White. *Drops of Rain*. 1903. Platinum print, 7⁵/₈ x 6" (19.4 x 15.2 cm). The Museum of Modern Art, New York. Gift of Mrs. Mervyn Palmer

Page 1: Toyen (Marie Cerminová). Newsboy with paper and rotary press, original drawing for plate 17 from *Náš svět* (Our world), a collection of poems for children by Zdenka Marčanová. c. 1934. Ink and watercolor on paper, 10 x 9" (25.4 x 22.9 cm). Cotsen Children's Library, Princeton University Library

Page 2: Tadanori Yokoo. *NFC*. 1997. Silkscreen, 39⁹/₁₆ x 28³/₄" (103.1 x 72.8 cm). Published by NFC, Tokyo. The Museum of Modern Art, New York. Gift of the designer

Page 248: Pikotron Electronic Circuit toy. 1971. Various materials, 2³/₁₆ x 13³/₄ x 9¹/₁₆" (5.5 x 35 x 23 cm). Manufactured by PIKO, Sonneberg, Germany (est. 1949). The Museum of Modern Art, New York. Gift of Christian Zoellner

Back endpapers: Detail from *Stahlrohmöbel* (Tubular steel furniture), loose-leaf sales catalog for Thonet Company showing Marcel Breuer's B341/2 chair and B53 table. 1930–31. Lithograph, gravure, and letterpress, 8³/₈ x 6¹/₈" (21.3 x 15.6 cm). Published by Thonet International Press Service, Cologne. The Museum of Modern Art, New York. Department of Architecture and Design Study Center. See p. 96
Jens S. Jensen. *Boy on the Wall, Hammarkullen, Gothenburg*. 1973. Gelatin silver print, 9⁷/₁₆ x 11³/₄" (24 x 29.8 cm). The Museum of Modern Art, New York. Gift of the artist. See p. 27

Back cover: Roger Limbrick. Space Station and Space Rocket cardboard toys. 1968. Fluted cardboard, with silver foil and flexographic print design, rocket: 59 x 38" (150 x 96 cm). Manufactured by Polypops Products Ltd, London. Photograph by Timothy Quallington. Design Council/University of Brighton Design Archives. See p. 185

Printed in Hong Kong

CONTENTS

CHILDREN HAVE HAD A PLACE at The Museum of Modern Art from almost the very beginning. The Museum's first exhibitions and acquisitions in design and architecture, in the early to mid-1930s, were soon followed by the launch of the Educational Project in 1937 and the enfolding within the Museum of the Young People's Gallery in 1939. MoMA's distinguished exhibition history has since included unique presentations that explore the ways that these areas overlap and inform each other. Exhibitions of art and design both by and for children were especially numerous and diverse in the 1940s and '50s, including *Modern Architecture for the Modern School* (1942), *Original Illustrations of Children's Books* (1946), and *Teaching Elements of Design to Children* (1954).

Having all been — if not having helped to raise — children ourselves, we find design for children to be a subject that resonates universally, yet this rich area has been underrepresented in scholarly inquiry and exhibition — until now. *Century of the Child: Growing by Design, 1900–2000* represents the first large-scale and synthetic effort to investigate the many intersections of children and design, including toys and games, furniture and nursery interiors, playgrounds, school architecture and pedagogy, political propaganda, and urban planning. With its own renowned collections complemented by vital loans from generous institutions and individuals, MoMA is uniquely suited to presenting such a project. The Museum has always embraced characteristics shared by modernist artists, designers, and children — liberated innovation, unbridled creativity, even disobedience — and its dedication to the interconnectedness of the arts is mirrored in the interdisciplinary perspective of this publication and the corresponding installation of works by both celebrated designers and lesser-known figures.

Century of the Child also extends MoMA's commitment, foregrounded in the recent Modern Women's Project, to highlighting the contributions of women as architects, designers, teachers, critics, and social activists. I am grateful to the partners in research and lending who have made possible the formulating of new dimensions for familiar material and public recognition for the unfamiliar. Thanks to them, MoMA now has the honor of exhibiting works that have never before been seen in this country, from Germany, the Czech Republic, Hungary, Switzerland, and South Africa.

Juliet Kinchin, Curator in the Department of Architecture and Design, and Aidan O'Connor, Curatorial Assistant, have demonstrated great ambition in pursuing the scale and scope of this unprecedented exhibition, as well as a tenacity and freshness of perspective entirely appropriate to the subject of youth. I am grateful to them and to their many colleagues at the Museum and collaborating supporters for their contributions to this multifarious project. On behalf of the staff and trustees of the Museum, I would like to especially thank Lawrence B. Benenson, for his major support in funding this exhibition, as well as the Nordic Culture Fund, Lily Auchincloss Foundation, Inc., the Barbro Osher Pro Suecia Foundation, and Marimekko, and for support for the publication, The International Council of The Museum of Modern Art and its Jo Carole Lauder Publications Fund.

Glenn D. Lowry
Director, The Museum of Modern Art, New York

IN ACCORDANCE with its title, *Century of the Child* has been both a long and demanding project. Its successes have been absolutely dependent on a large number of people who have awakened us to new ideas and possibilities, facilitated international arrangements, and helped us fit together the many pieces of this large, complex puzzle.

With half of the exhibition made up of loans, we must first and foremost express sincere thanks to our lenders. These individuals and institutions from all over the world have enlightened us about their wonderful materials and in some cases allowed us to deprive them of multiple items for the sake of this unique presentation. We are incredibly grateful for their patience, responsiveness, and flexibility. Our international lenders include Ivan Adamovič; Archivio Randone, Rome; Klassik Stiftung, Bauhaus-Museum, Weimar; Canadian Centre for Architecture, Montreal; Glasgow Life (Glasgow Museums) on behalf of Glasgow City Council; Danish National Art Library, Copenhagen; Design Museum Finland, Helsinki; Designmuseum Danmark, Copenhagen; Aldo van Eyck Archive, Loenen aan de Vecht, the Netherlands; Fondazione Biagiotti Cigna, Rome; Estate of Abram Games, London; Gödöllő Town Museum, Hungary; gta Archives, ETH Zürich; The Hunterian, University of Glasgow; Roger Limbrick; Maurizio Marzadori; Musée des Arts Décoratifs, Paris; Musée National d'Art Moderne, Centre Georges Pompidou, Paris; Museum Boijmans van Beuningen, Rotterdam; Museum für Gestaltung Zürich; Museum of Decorative Arts, Prague; Die Neue Sammlung–The International Design Museum Munich; Peter Opsvik; Alasdair Peebles; John and Sue Picton; RIBA Library Drawings and Archives Collection, London; Rovereto MART–Museo di Arte Moderna e Contemporanea di Trento e Rovereto, Italy; Andrea Schito; Stadt Soest, Stadtarchiv, Soest, Germany; Stokke AS, Ålesund, Norway; Universität für angewandte Kunst Wien, Kunstsammlung und Archiv, Vienna; Vandkunsten Architects, Copenhagen; Victoria and Albert Museum, London; Victoria and Albert Museum of Childhood, London; Vitra Design Museum, Weil am Rhein, Germany; and Wolfsoniana–Fondazione Regionale per la Cultura e lo Spettacolo, Genoa.

Domestic lenders include The Art Institute of Chicago; Norman Brosterman; Susanna Carlisle and Bruce Hamilton; Collection Daddy Types, Washington, D.C.; Cotsen Children's Library, Princeton University Library; Joan Wadleigh Curran; Herman World, Encino, California; Imre Kepes and Juliet Kepes Stone; Minneapolis Institute of Arts; Price Tower Arts Center, Bartlesville, Oklahoma; Space Age Museum/Kleeman Family Collection, Litchfield, Connecticut; Walt Disney Imagineering, Glendale, California; Winnetka Historical Society, Winnetka, Illinois; The Mitchell Wolfson Jr. Private Collection, Miami; The Wolfsonian–Florida International University, Miami Beach; Frank Lloyd Wright Foundation, Taliesin West, Scottsdale, Arizona.

In New York our lenders include Architectural Playground Equipment, Inc.; Artek USA Inc.; Avery Architectural and Fine Arts Library, Columbia University; Brooklyn Museum; Daniela Chappard Foundation; Jane and Ivan Chermayeff; Elaine Lustig Cohen; Cooper-Hewitt, National Design Museum, Smithsonian Institution; Mia Curran;

Richard Dattner; Mike Gibbons; Maharam; Pam and Charles Meyers; Zesty Meyers and Evan Snyderman/R 20th Century; Mondo Cane; The Museum at the Fashion Institute of Technology; Petr Nikl; The Isamu Noguchi Foundation and Garden Museum; Sharing to Learn; Bruce Sterling Collection; Mariana Uchoa; U.S. Fund for UNICEF; John C. Waddell; and Margot Weller. Additional thanks go to the individuals who have anonymously provided material from their private collections, in New York, Rome, Stockholm, and elsewhere.

We warmly thank those friends of the exhibition who provided special assistance with both research and loans; their efforts have been vital. Thank you to Greg Allen; Einat Amitay, Museum of Art, Ein Harod, Israel; Claudia Balla; Christian Brändle, Museum für Gestaltung Zürich; Ning de Coninck-Smith; Joe Earle, Japan Society, New York; Sharon and Peter Exley, Architecture Is Fun, Chicago; Sarah Ferrari and Ilaria Cavallini, Reggio Children, Reggio Emilia, Italy; Ninetta Ferrazzi, Archivio Randone; Matteo Fochessati, Wolfsoniana; Ania Frąckiewicz, National Museum Warsaw; Naomi Games; Larry Giacoletti, Noguchi Museum, New York; Susanne Graner, Vitra Design Museum; Colin and Laurie Greenly; Michael Joaquin Grey; Hervé Halgand, Vilac, Moirans-En-Montagne, France; Karen Hewitt; László Kiss Horvath; Catherine Howell, Lucy Tindle, and Ieuan Hopkins, Victoria and Albert Museum of Childhood; Michael Jusko, Walt Disney Imagineering; Katalin Keserü; John, Veronica, and Peter Kleeman; Helena Koenigsmarkova, Iva Knobloch, and Marie Míčová, UPM Prague; Minna Lee; Cathy Leff, Marianne Lamonaca, Kimberly Bergen, and Whitney Richardson, The Wolfsonian; Elizabeth Legge, University of Toronto; Maria Paola Maino; Maurizio Marzadori; Ellen McAdam, Alison Brown, and Fiona McKellar, Glasgow Museums; Cara McCarty and Sarah Coffin, Cooper-Hewitt, National Design Museum, Smithsonian Institution, New York; Zesty Meyers; Achim Moeller; José Netto, Museu de Arte de São Paulo; Pavla Niklová and Kristyna Milde, Czech Center New York; Jennifer Komar Olivarez, Minneapolis Institute of Arts; Nicholas Olsberg; Alfred Pacquement, Jean-Claude Boulet, Françoise Guichon, and Olivier Cinqualbre, Musée National d'Art Moderne, Centre Georges Pompidou, Paris; Patrick Parrish, Mondo Cane, New York; Carlos Pérez, Museo Valenciano de la Ilustracíon y la Modernidad, Valencia; Paul Reubens and his associates at Herman World, Encino, and Team Services, Woodbury, New York; Beatrice Salmon and Dorothée Charles, Musée des Arts Décoratifs, Paris; Kristian Seier and Jens Thomas Arnfred, Vandkunsten, Copenhagen; Tom-Arne Solhaug and Fredrik Brodtkorb, Krabat, Hvalstad, Norway; Susan Solomon; José Lebrero Stals, Museo Picasso Málaga; Carl Steinitz, Harvard University, Cambridge, Massachusetts; Janos Stone; Josef Strasser, Die Neue Sammlung Munich; Árpád Szabados; Himanshu Tayal, Hole-In-The-Wall Education Limited, New Delhi; Mienke Simon Thomas, Museum Boijmans van Beuningen; Cecilia de Torres; Ildikó Várnagy; Simone Vingerhoets-Ziesmann, Artek USA, New York; Daniel Weiss, gta Archives; Tess van Eyck Wickham; Christopher Wilke and Hannah Kaufmann, Victoria and Albert Museum, London; Micky Wolfson and Lea Nickless; Andrzej Wolski; Hideki Yamamoto; and

Yuval Yasky, Bezalel Academy of Art and Design, Jerusalem. For daily doses of support and laughter, thank you also to Liz McLawhorn.

The additional writers for this book were critical to our identification and research of diverse materials from around the world. They have generously shared their expertise above and beyond their contributions to this book: Kate Carmody, Curatorial Assistant, Department of Architecture and Design, MoMA; Tanya Harrod, art and design historian, London; Medea Hoch, art historian and curator, Zurich; Frank Luca, Adjunct Professor of History and Chief Librarian, The Wolfsonian–Florida International University, Miami Beach; Maria Paola Maino, Director of Archivi delle Arti Applicate Italiane del XX secolo and design historian, Rome; Amy F. Ogata, Associate Professor and Chair of Academic Programs at Bard Graduate Center, New York; David Senior, Bibliographer, The Museum of Modern Art Library; and Sarah Suzuki, Associate Curator, Department of Prints and Illustrated Books, MoMA. They delivered under brutal deadlines and word limits and we could not have completed this book without them. We also extend our most grateful thanks to Pat Kirkham, whose expertise and peerless guidance have benefited this book immensely.

At The Museum of Modern Art, New York, this project has involved every department. Our foremost thanks go to Glenn D. Lowry, Director, whose support has allowed this exhibition to thrive despite its challenges. Ramona Bannayan, Senior Deputy Director for Exhibitions, Collections, and Programs, and Peter Reed, Senior Deputy Director for Curatorial Affairs have provided fundamental and enthusiastic oversight. We truly appreciate the support of all of the chief curators here at MoMA, who have allowed us to deepen our interpretation of design for children by associating the idea with works of art: Ann Temkin, in the Department of Painting and Sculpture; Sabine Breitwieser, in the Department of Media and Performance Art; Raj Roy, in the Department of Film; Christophe Cherix, in the Department of Prints and Illustrated Books; and Connie Butler, in the Department of Drawings. We also extend sincere thanks to the colleagues in these departments who have directly assisted with internal loans and research, to Charles Silver, Sarah Meister, Anne Morra, Ron Magliozzi, Josh Siegel, Cora Rosevear, Doryun Chong, Barbara London, Starr Figura, Kathy Curry, Judy Hecker, Lilian Tone, Erica Papernik, Martin Hartung, Nancy Lim, Marina Chao, Katherine Alcauskas, Ashley Swinnerton, Lily Goldberg, Katie Trainor, Peter Williamson, and Iris Schmeisser.

The variety of materials gathered for this exhibition from many sources and in many states of condition has meant significant conservation work. Special thanks to Erika Mosier, lead Conservator for this exhibition, and her top-notch colleagues: Jim Coddington, Chief Conservator; Lee Ann Daffner, Photography Conservator; Roger Griffith, Associate Sculpture Conservator; Karl Buchberg, Senior Conservator; Scott Gerson, Associate Conservator; Hanako Murata, Assistant Conservator of Photographs; and Brenna Campbell, Mellon Fellow.

Many of our colleagues have become intimately familiar with the details and guiding spirit of this project in order to find it suitable funding, broadcast it to the public, assist with a wide range of external inquiries, and craft the exhibition's visual aspects. For their sensitivity and zeal we are grateful, in the Department of Development, to Todd Bishop, Director; Hallie Hobson, Associate Director; Lauren Stakias, Associate Director, Exhibition and International Fundraising; Heidi Speckhart, Manager, Exhibition Funding; and Sylvia Renner, Development Officer, International Funding. In Marketing and Communications we thank Kim Mitchell, Chief Communications Officer; Margaret Doyle, Director of Communications; Daniela Stigh, former Assistant Director; and Paul Jackson, Senior Publicist, and in Graphic Design, Julia Hoffmann, Creative Director; Brigitta Bungard, Assistant Creative Director; and Claire Corey, Production Manager.

At the time of this writing, the actual installation of *Century of the Child* is an adventure still on the horizon, but many colleagues have already contributed their expertise in the general guidance and detailed execution of every aspect of the planning process. In the Department of Exhibitions, Maria DeMarco Beardsley, Coordinator; Jennifer Cohen, Associate Coordinator; and Jessica Cash, Department Coordinator, have brought incredible knowledge and diplomacy to a project with numerous contributors. Patty Lipshutz, General Counsel; Nancy Adelson, Deputy General Counsel; and Dina Sorokina, Paralegal and Department Manager, have provided important advice. Although we have thrown at them a shocking number of works to comprehend and manage, our extraordinary colleagues in the Department of Collection Management and Exhibition Registration have kept apace at every stage: Jennifer Wolfe, Associate Registrar; Corey Wyckoff, Senior Registrar Assistant; Steven Wheeler, Assistant Registrar; Jeri Moxley, Manager, Collection and Exhibition Technologies; Ian Eckert, Coordinator, Collection and Exhibition Technologies; and Kat Ryan, Coordinator, Collection and Exhibition Technologies. We are grateful for the essential support of our colleagues managing operations, in-house art transportation, installation, and security during the run of the exhibition, including James Gara, Chief Operating Officer; Tunji Adeniji, Director of Facilities and Safety; and LJ Hartman, Director of Security, as well as, in Art Handling and Preparation, Rob Jung, Manager; Steve West, Assistant Manager; Sarah Wood, Assistant Manager; and Steve Burkhart, lead Preparator for this exhibition.

We appreciate the outstanding commitment and creativity of our colleagues in the Department of Exhibition Design and Production, including Jerry Neuner, Director; Michele Arms, Department Manager; and especially the wonderful Betty Fisher, Production Manager and the exhibition designer for *Century of the Child*. We would also like to recognize the superior talents of Peter Perez, Foreman, with his team in the Frame Shop; Allan Smith, Foreman, with his team in the Carpenter Shop; and the AV crew, including Mike Gibbons, Lucas Gonzalez, Bjorn Quenemoen, Howie Deitch, and Charlie Kalinowski.

Such a complex exhibition about children but not expressly for them relies heavily on quality interpretation and related programming. We are very grateful to our colleagues in the Department of

Education for their creative and diligent assistance: Wendy Woon, The Edward John Noble Foundation Deputy Director for Education; Pablo Helguera, Director, Adult and Academic Education; Laura Beiles, Associate Educator, Adult and Academic Programs; Kirsten Schroeder, Coordinator, Community and Access Programs; Sarah Kennedy, Associate Educator, Lab Programs; Sara Bodinson, Director, Interpretation and Research; Stephanie Pau, Associate Educator; Liz Margulies, Assistant Director, Family Programs; Cari Frisch, Assistant Educator, Family Programs; and Carrie McGee, Associate Educator, Community, Access, and School Programs.

Our research and checklist selection drew heavily on the Museum's Library and Archives, adding purchasing, research, and cataloguing tasks to their already impressive operations. We warmly thank Milan Hughston, Chief of Library and Museum Archives; Jennifer Tobias, Librarian; David Senior, Bibliographer; Lori Salmon, Library Assistant; Michelle Elligott, The Rona Roob Museum Archivist; and Michelle Harvey, Archivist. Our colleagues in Imaging Services not only provided important existing images for this book but also expeditiously managed the production of numerous new photographs with characteristic care and patience. Cheers to Erik Landsberg, Head of Collections Imaging; Robert Kastler, Production Manager; Roberto Rivera, Production Assistant; and Collection Photographers Thomas Griesel and John Wronn.

The Department of Publications, operating with its characteristic professionalism and perspicacity, has made this book a reality. We offer profound thanks to Christopher Hudson, Publisher; Kara Kirk, Associate Publisher; David Frankel, Editorial Director; Marc Sapir, Production Director; and Hannah Kim, Marketing and Book Development Coordinator. Emily Hall and Libby Hruska, our intrepid editors, have demonstrated utmost diligence in this process. They have waded, side by side with us, through a vast amount of information originating from multiple authors and states of mind and helped distill it into pithy publishable texts over an intense few months. We have been so grateful for their accessibility, flexibility, enthusiasm, and humor, and we would also like to thank their children for helping to make them so patient before we got to them. We also thank intern Makiko Wholey for her thoughtful and thorough work on the book's index. Mark Nelson of McCall Associates is the designer of this book, and his talents have repeatedly been admired in this process as "magic." We thank him for *getting it*, from the very beginning, and for elegantly achieving the impossible task of squeezing what we wanted to say and show into the space available. As proofreader, Susan Richmond deserves recognition for sparing our readers from inevitable flubs.

On the home team of our own department, we are immensely grateful for the enduring support of Barry Bergdoll, The Philip Johnson Chief Curator of Architecture and Design, as well as the bountiful wisdom of Paola Antonelli, Senior Curator. Invaluable encouragement and assistance have been provided by Paul Galloway, Cataloguer and Study Center Supervisor; Margot Weller, Curatorial Assistant; Pamela Popeson, Preparator; Emma Presler, Department Manager; and Colin Hartness, Assistant to the Chief Curator. Whitney May, Department Assistant, has been critical in expertly managing everything from travel arrangements and invoices to special research and work flow. Heartfelt thanks are due to Kate Carmody, who not only contributed two essays to this book but also merrily and heroically took on the burden of many exhibition-planning tasks and is to thank in large part for the maintenance of our collective sanity.

Several department interns have contributed their time and efforts and cheered us on behind the scenes. We thank Luke Baker, Craig Lee, Jenny Florence, and Jonatan Jahn for their steadfast support. A very special thanks goes to our twelve-month intern Mia Curran, without whom this book would simply not have been possible. With her professional, meticulous, and graceful navigation of image rights and management, caption wrangling, research, checklist development, and lender correspondence, she has shown remarkable dedication both to this project and to us.

We are deeply grateful for the extraordinary generosity and enthusiasm of the exhibition supporters. Even before becoming a major supporter of the exhibition, Lawrence B. Benenson made possible our acquisition of kindergarten materials, displayed at MoMA for the first time as an exhibition highlight. We express gratitude also to the Lily Auchincloss Foundation, Inc., the Barbro Osher Pro Suecia Foundation, and Marimekko. This project has benefited greatly from the sustained and multifaceted support offered by Sarah Peter. And this book was funded by The International Council of The Museum of Modern Art and the Jo Carole Lauder Publications Fund of The International Council of The Museum of Modern Art.

Our earliest cheerleaders in this project were a group of individuals representing the consulates, foreign ministries and various arts agencies of the Nordic countries. They have provided tremendous support for our research and travel over these past three years, culminating in the sponsorship of the exhibition by the Nordic Culture Fund. Among these friends are Maiken Tandgaard Derno, Ane Asløv, Marc Jacobsen, Aslaug Nygård, Ingrid Moe, Kajsa Guterstam, Niklas Arnegren, Elisabeth Halvarsson-Stapen, Magdalena Herrgård, Kati Laakso, Ilkaa Kalioma, Riitta Gerlander, and Paula Parviainen. *Tack så mycket* to Jens S. Jensen, who has been delightfully supportive in our use of his photography.

To Paul and Drew, our champions, you know.

Juliet Kinchin and **Aidan O'Connor**

IN SEARCH OF THE MODERN CHILD

Speaking solemnly to the camera in 1995 as part of the fictionalized documentary film *Children's Video Collective*, a young boy predicts, "In the future, children will cease to exist. As a social category, we will simply become irrelevant. My generation is likely the last generation of children. Or, rather, the last generation to experience childhood. That doesn't necessarily mean that now is the time to put away childish things. Instead it may mean that the use of childish things may be extended indefinitely, until death."[1] Children — we are reminded by the ambivalent twist at the end of this statement — have the potential to turn the hegemony of the adult world upside down. Could it be that the imprint of childish things on twentieth-century culture has been so profound that ultimately it is not children but adults who will cease to exist?

Childhood is not a fixed concept but has been constantly redefined, in legal as well as cultural terms. Starting with Philippe Ariès's pioneering study, *Centuries of Childhood: A Social History of Family Life*, in 1962, which claimed that "in medieval society, the idea of childhood did not exist," historians have been locating paradigmatic shifts in the way we think about children in various centuries and cultures.[2] Nevertheless, the case for the twentieth century as *the* century of the child is a compelling one, and the starting point for this book and exhibition is the timely publication, on New Year's Day of 1900, of *Barnets århundrade* (published in English in 1909 as *The Century of the Child*), by the perceptive Swedish design reformer and social theorist Ellen Key.[3] Brimming with both aspiration and dread, this prescient manifesto for change — social, political, aesthetic, and psychological — presented the universal rights and well-being of children as the defining mission of the century to come. Key enfolded this cause within multiple agendas for reform, arguing that the time had come to put an end to child labor, to stop "murdering souls in schools," to counter international conflict and the materialistic spirit of the age with a new spiritualism, to attend to the environmental degradation of the world's modern cities, to halt the meaningless consumption of poorly designed and manufactured goods, and to extend suffrage to women and the working classes.[4]

Key identified the search for new languages of form and style, which reached a critical peak around 1900, as having a crucial role in shaping this constellation of ideas. The reawakening of an artistic culture would start with children and with the natural unfolding of their development at home. Her essay "Beauty for All," published in 1899, promoted an aesthetic ideal of simplicity that would endow the child's experiences of a rapidly changing world with a greater sense of visual and spatial coherence.[5] Like many of the progressive intellectuals and artists with whom she was associated, such as Carl and Karin Larsson, leading exponents of the Arts and Crafts movement in Sweden, Key viewed the quality of the spaces where children's physical and mental development took place as highly influential in the delicate process of personal growth. Carl Larsson's *Ett Hem* (*A Home*, 1899), a book later published in ten countries, set the tone for idealistic views of the designed childhoods that would flourish in the twentieth century, showing his children at play, developing unhampered in light, airy spaces, close to the natural world, and protected from the cares and corrupting influences of adult life (no. 1).[6]

There were other modern childhoods of which Key was also keenly aware, such as those recorded by the American photographer and sociologist Lewis Hine on behalf of the National

1 CARL LARSSON (Swedish, 1853–1919)
Mammas och småflickornas rum (Mamma's and the small girls' room) from the book *Ett Hem* (*A Home*). 1899
Watercolor on paper, 12 5/8 x 16 15/16" (32 x 43 cm)
Nationalmuseum, Stockholm

Child Labor Committee (no. 2).[7] A source of cheap labor then, as they are now, children in factories and sweatshops assisted in the process of churning out goods designed for markets that included their middle-class peers. Key felt that children growing up in an industrial, competitive, and future-oriented culture required adult protection and stimulation that could be assisted by design. And by 1900 modern types of dedicated objects and spaces had begun to delineate the newly sacralized concept of childhood, as on Théophile-Alexandre Steinlen's advertising billboard *La Rue* (The street) (no. 3), printed in Paris in 1896, in which the most vivid figure is a girl in a smart red dress, clutching a hoop. Standing at the center of a cavalcade of modern urban types, including street vendors, workmen, clerks, housewives, and bourgeois promenaders, she signals the importance of children in the expanding consumer economies of the century to come (no. 4).[8] Elastic and powerful, the symbolic figure of the child has masked paradoxical aspects of the human predicament in the modern world and enabled irreconcilable sets of beliefs, which are reflected in the material forms of modern design.

GROWING, OR WILTING, BY DESIGN?

Key's prediction was correct: thinking about and designing for children would become a preoccupation in the twentieth century as never before, amounting to a virtual "cult of childhood," as philosopher George Boas called it in 1966.[9] Throughout the century the aesthetic, material, and technical innovations in design for children were remarkable, closely paralleling, and at times directly influencing, other areas of visual culture. Ideas about creative play catalyzed major iterations of modern design teaching and practice — from Franz Cižek's revolutionary teaching methods at the Vienna Kunstgewerbeschule (School of applied arts) and Joaquín Torres-García's exploration of abstraction through toy design to the Bauhaus workshops (no. 5); and from the urban innovations of Aldo van Eyck and CoBrA artists in postwar Amsterdam (no. 6) to Victor Papanek's ethical design. In 1990 some 1,500 professionals from around the world gathered in Aspen for "Growing by Design" (no. 7), the fortieth (but first child-themed) International Design Conference, to take stock and to fashion an agenda for the future of design that would support "the needs of children and, by extension, the needs of the community — and all of us."[10] Children also participated in discussions and workshops and created their own exuberant environment, a Micropolis, with the help of adult "slaves." In this respect the conference reflected a growing recognition of children as design activists in their own right, pushing against imaginative and physical limitations and constantly re-creating the world as they see it, using whatever equipment they happen to have at hand.

But the mood in the plenary session oscillated between optimism and gloom. In lively debates about design for schools, parks, television programs, play spaces, and psychological spaces, participants expressed concern about the contraction of childhood in disadvantaged communities, child labor, poverty, the slow attrition of space for play in cities all over the world, uneven access to inspiring design, and the obsessive adult concern with security and safety, at the expense of adventure and learning. Indeed, in such areas it was questionable how much progress had been made in addressing many of Key's concerns and aspirations. CBS correspondent Robert Krulwich summarized the proceedings, reporting that "people agreed much more

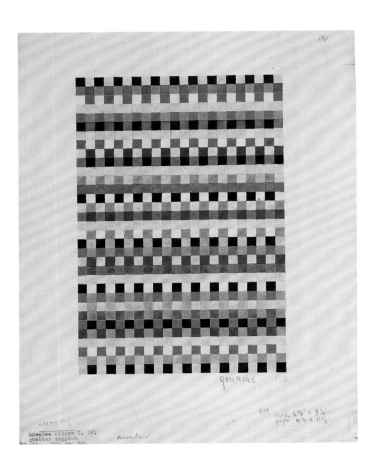

5 ANNI ALBERS
(American, born Germany. 1899–1994)
Rug design for child's room. 1928
Gouache on paper, 13⁷/₁₆ x 10⁷/₁₆" (34.1 x 26.5 cm)
The Museum of Modern Art, New York. Gift of
the designer

6 *Experimental Art*, CoBrA exhibition at the
Stedelijk Museum, Amsterdam, 1949, designed
by Aldo van Eyck. 1949
Aldo van Eyck Archive, Loenen aan de Vecht,
the Netherlands

than disagreed. I can report that we agreed that the environment we have created for children is getting worse.... Not only in America, but when we mention the rest of the world it seems to be getting worse there, too."[11] This sense of an impending crisis was also echoed throughout the last two decades of the century in numerous cultural commentaries and contemporary artworks that referred to the "disappearance" or "end" of childhood, not least in *Children's Video Collective*, the artwork by the Canadian artist Steve Reinke with which this essay opened.[12]

From *The Century of the Child* in 1900 to "Growing by Design" in 1990 we have been periodically reminded how the forces of modernity shape design and childhood in ways that are extraordinary and exhilarating yet also complex and contradictory. What has remained consistent, however, is the faith among designers in the power of aesthetic activity to shape everyday life. As an embodiment of what might be, children help us to mediate between the ideal and real: they propel our thoughts forward. Their protean nature encourages us to think in terms of design that is flexible, inclusive, and imaginative.

THE CENTURY OF THE CHILD, REVISITED

In this book we track the fascinating confluence, unique to the twentieth century, between the cultures of modern design and childhood, using a kaleidoscopic narrative of innovative ideas, artifacts, and people. Like "childhood," "modern" is a mercurial term. By its own definition what is up-to-the-minute and aesthetically or conceptually innovative in a certain decade or in one particular context should not, indeed cannot remain so, any more than a child can remain a child.

Certain themes recur, at different times and in different parts of the world: creative play as a paradigm of learning and creativity not only for children but for adults; children as a source of social and aesthetic renewal and as the citizens of tomorrow; concern about protecting and nurturing some of the most vulnerable individuals in society as the impetus to create critical design interventions, new pedagogies, and social policies; children as consumers of an ever-widening range of products and environments, both physical and virtual; and children as viewers and subjects of new forms of advertising and ideological persuasion. The examples of objects and ideas throughout the book are the result of creative discussions that took place over a period of one hundred years, among educators, designers, manufacturers, social reformers, medical specialists, psychologists, and children themselves. Together they show how diverse perspectives have intertwined in meaningful and modern design.

Although the book is international in range, we could not hope to provide a comprehensive survey of the most widely available or popular design for children. Nor did we set out to propose new approaches to any one designer or area, such as toys, playgrounds, children's furniture, or clothing, each of which already has, or deserves, a major publication devoted to it.[13] Instead the emphasis is on the interrelationship of all these design phenomena at particular moments throughout the century, a synoptic approach that posits modern children and modern design as an unfolding relationship in the context of mass society in regional, national, and transnational settings. Through children we may follow the socially dynamic, forward-looking trajectory of innovative design in the twentieth century.

Despite being ubiquitous and the focus of intense concern and profound thought, children remain one of the most underevaluated subjects in the historical analysis of modern design. What, we may ask, explains their relative invisibility in narratives of pioneering design in the twentieth century? One answer lies in the overlay of adult nostalgia, sentiment, and angst onto anything to do with children, which inhibits dispassionate and rigorous analysis; another, perhaps, in our work-centric culture, in a deep-rooted sense of play as trivial — just messing about, with no serious rationale or quantifiable outcomes — and of children and childcare as part of predominantly domestic and therefore lesser worlds. The humorous design that children have inspired is rarely accorded serious critical attention, despite, or perhaps because of, the universal demand for works that delight, humanize, and emotionally connect us to our surroundings. The stereotypical perception of children as sensual and intuitive sits uneasily with the critical discourse of intellectualism and rationality that surrounds heroic modernist architecture, but with the advent of postmodern and psychoanalytic approaches to academic studies, beginning in the 1970s, many innovations in children's design have begun to attract the critical attention they deserve, particularly in relation to comics, animation (no. 8), and video games—new types of products initially developed for the young but soon taken up by adults and artists in avant-garde visual practices.

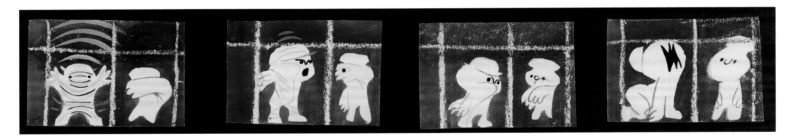

The diminutive scale and ephemeral quality of most design for children is by its very nature the antithesis of the monumental, and it resists critical aggrandizement (no. 9). Partly for this reason, the fascination with children of many iconic figures of modernism, such as Charles Rennie Mackintosh, Marcel Breuer, Ernő Goldfinger, Charles Eames, and Ladislav Sutnar, is rarely discussed. In the case of male designers in particular, the experience of engaged parenting and teaching is often treated as a sideline or aberration — not least by the designers themselves — and downplayed as a formative influence on their more publicly appraised work, or omitted altogether. Only recently has due acknowledgment been given to the early career of modernist designer Piet Zwart, a pioneer of Constructivist graphics, as a schoolteacher and designer of children's artistic, reformed dress.[14] The once anomalous position of toy design and pedagogy in the oeuvre of Torres-García is currently undergoing similar revision; these activities, far from being simply the means of sustaining his main practice as a fine artist, have been revealed to be the generative impulse behind his masterful exploration of abstraction.[15]

A focus on children also enriches the narrative of modern design in the twentieth century, adding to it other, less familiar names, many of them women's, who made contributions not only

Seltener Besuch in der Kinderrepublik

35

8 JOHN HUBLEY (American, 1914–1977) and
FAITH HUBLEY (American, 1924–2001)
Storyboard for the film *Adventures of an **. 1957
6 x 26⁵/₈" (15.2 x 67.6 cm)
The Museum of Modern Art, New York. Hubley
Collection, Special Collections

9 JOHN ROMBOLA (American, born 1933)
Alice in Wonderland wallpaper. 1968
Screenprint on vinyl, 30⁵/₈ x 29⁵/₁₆" (77.8 x 74.5 cm)
Manufactured by Piazza Prints, Inc., New York
Cooper-Hewitt, National Design Museum,
Smithsonian Institution. Gift of The Museum
at The Fashion Institute of Technology, New York

10 NIELS BRODERSEN (German, 1895–1971)
and RICHARD GRUNE (German, 1903–1983)
Page from the book *Die rote Kinderrepublik*
(Red children's republic), by Andreas Gayk. 1930
11⁷/₁₆ x 9³/₁₆" (29 x 23.3 cm)
Published by Arbeiterjugend Verlag, Berlin
The Museum of Modern Art Library, New York

as designers, but as teachers, philanthropists, art therapists, and critics. The critical fortunes of women and children have been closely linked throughout the century, during which time women's access to professional training, accreditation, and paid employment steadily increased. Women were identified persistently as the most effective educators (by Friedrich Froebel and Key, for example) and as biologically more attuned than men to the psychological, emotional, and physical needs of children (although it is ironic that many of the women who made a significant impact on child-centered design — from Key, Jane Addams, and Maria Montessori to Grete Lihotzky and Friedl Dicker — had no children of their own). Women, like children, were perceived as having a natural affinity for color, detail, and pattern and for the tactile, sensual, and more imaginative attributes of design.[16] The closeness of this association with children was often used to infantilize or patronize women in the critical discourse about modernist design; a term like "little" can quickly assume pejorative overtones.[17] Since the 1970s, however, feminist and postmodern approaches to theory and practice have served to validate qualities seen as stereotypically feminine or childlike, a development reflected in the emergence of women's studies and childhood studies as academic disciplines in their own right.

As empires crumbled in the postwar decades, many ethnic minorities began to articulate their political and cultural independence in ways that critiqued, in a similar fashion, the dominance of a Western canonical view of modernism. Children had long been implicated in this process by virtue of their identification with the primitive — a label that encompassed folk, vernacular, and popular material culture, as well as the arts of African, Oceanic, Native American, and Indian peoples and design by children (no. 10). As early as 1856 Owen Jones wrote in his influential book, *The Grammar of Ornament*, "If we would return to a more healthy condition we must

even be as little children or as savages," a link that persisted well into the twentieth century: in 1959, the anthropologist Douglas Newton could still describe "the world-wide fraternity of children" as "the greatest of savage tribes, and the only one which shows no sign of dying out."[18] This cultural phenomenon was, at various points during the century, a metaphor for artistic spontaneity.[19] The association was made explicit in Frank Lloyd Wright's design for the Rosenwald-Whittier School for Negro Children in Hampton, Virginia (1928), whose decoration reflected the architect's belief that African Americans had a keener perception and appreciation of color, geometry, pattern, and abstraction.[20] A similar confluence of child art and primitivism was found in the design of Van Eyck and the CoBrA group of artists in the 1950s and in the ethnic-design references of countercultural movements in the late 1960s and '70s. Modernism's involvement with the primitive also had pronounced negative effects, such as the trope of primitive peoples as childish or childlike, used to justify imperial domination by "adult" Europeans and North Americans, which was made evident in many toys and children's books.

In the world's preeminent collections of modern design, not least at The Museum of Modern Art, children's toys, books, and clothing have historically had a low profile. This has been true despite the personal fascination that design for children has held for several legendary museum directors, an interest that formed a significant factor in their intellectual makeup and their approach to their institutions' educational missions. Henry Cole, a prominent design reformer, produced a number of children's books and toys before he took up his role as the first director of the South Kensington Museum of Art and Design (now the Victoria and Albert Museum) in London.[21] Alfred H. Barr, Jr., amassed a personal collection of Soviet children's books (no. 11) during a formative visit to the Soviet Union in 1927–28, prior to his appointment as The Museum of Modern Art's founding director (see "'Colorful, Specific, Concrete': Soviet Children's Books," p. 79).[22] René d'Harnoncourt, who joined MoMA in 1944 as director of the Department of Manual Industries and was appointed Museum director in 1949, designed and wrote several children's books in the 1930s and gathered one of the largest collections of Mexican toys in the world.[23] Both Barr and d'Harnoncourt had a keen sense of MoMA's educational role, which was to foster creativity and innovation in children and adults, and were responsible

11 VLADIMIR LEBEDEV (Russian, 1891–1967)
Cover of *Slonenok* (Elephant), by Rudyard Kipling. 1922
Book with 12 letterpress illustrations,
10 ^{1}/$_2$ x 8 ^{1}/$_8$" (26.7 x 20.7 cm)
Published by Epokha, St. Petersburg
Edition: 1,500
The Museum of Modern Art, New York. Gift of
The Judith Rothschild Foundation

for encouraging many exhibitions, workshops, and lectures that featured design by and for children. This dedication had little impact on the permanent collection, however, despite both directors' generous gifts in various mediums, and their own collections of child-related material instead reside in the MoMA Archives.

Bringing children from the periphery to the forefront of our attention cuts across geographical, political, and stylistic demarcations in the mapping of modern design: following in the footsteps of Lihotzky, for example, in the 1920s to 1940s — moving from Vienna, Frankfurt, and Moscow to Tokyo, Ankara, and Sofia — leads us to locations both familiar and unexpected, where engagement with modernism and children was at its most intense. In a similar fashion, the multiple trajectories leading out from Cizek's teaching in Vienna suggest new continuities and connections between artistic centers and areas of design practice, taking us in one direction toward Johannes Itten's *Vorkurs* (introductory course) at the Bauhaus and to children's art classes in the concentration camp at Theresienstadt; in another toward the design of adventure playgrounds on World War II bombsites and the manufacture of developmental toys in London by Paul and Marjorie Abbatt; and in yet another to the worlds of art therapy and mid-century modern design in the United States (no. 12). Children bring into focus how modern design has straddled high and low cultural practices, from comics to architecture and urban planning. They enable us to follow threads throughout the century that connect the most disparate and apparently contradictory of tendencies.

12 JOHN FOLLIS (American, 1923–1994) and REX GOODE (American, dates unknown) Covers from the magazine *Everyday Art* (top row and bottom left: Spring 1953, Summer 1953, and Fall 1953 [edited by Emmy Zweybrück-Prochaska]; bottom right: Winter 1960–61 [edited by Edward Mattil]) Each: 9 1/16 x 6 1/8" (23 x 15.5 cm) Published by American Crayon Company, Sandusky, Ohio (est. 1890) Universität für angewandte Kunst Wien, Kunstsammlung und Archiv, Vienna

13 GODTFRED KIRK CHRISTIANSEN
(Danish, 1920–1995)
Lego building bricks. 1954–58
ABS plastic, dimensions variable, largest:
$^7/_{16}$ x 1 $^1/_4$ x $^5/_8$" (1.1 x 3.2 x 1.6 cm)
Manufactured by Lego Group, Billund, Denmark
The Museum of Modern Art, New York. Gift of
the manufacturer

CREATIVE PLAY FOR CHILDREN AND DESIGNERS: CONSTRUCTING THE UNIVERSE

Rudolf Steiner claimed in 1909 that "the world is built by thought," meaning thought not formulated as an abstract idea but experienced as a living, creative energy that creates and supports forms.[24] This was the kind of spiritualized, form-giving creativity that Theo van Doesburg observed in the design of Torres-García in 1929: "He touches dead things and ordinary materials, and they come to life. He places before you a small sculpture in painted wood or a simple toy he has created, and they seem to breathe in some miraculous fashion."[25] Designers, like children, find patterns and make connections. The importance of pattern making and creative play with material things, for children and adults, as a route to understanding spatial relations and problem solving, as well as creating a sense of the individual in relation to larger cosmic harmonies, comes up again and again in the twentieth century.

Breuer, the Hungarian-born designer and architect who was associated with the Bauhaus and then found his way to the United States in the late 1930s, was one of many modernists who maintained a lifelong interest in the principles of constructive play. In 1970, in an acceptance speech for an honorary degree from the university in Pécs, his childhood home, he invoked play in a description of the process of becoming an architect: "When children play with building blocks, they discover that they fit together, because they are square.... Then, the child discovers that the blocks are empty, that the sides turn into walls, and that there is a roof and a structure.... That is when the child will indeed become an architect. Manager of voids and spaces, priest of geometry."[26] And the idea of play as a means of exploring imaginative space and building worlds in microcosm has continued with the introduction of a slew of new construction toys, from Lego blocks, in 1954–58 (no. 13), to Michael Joaquin Grey's Zoob system, in 1993–96 (no. 14). In 1974 the Hungarian architect Ernő Rubik came up with his famous cube (no. 15) — widely considered the best-selling toy of all time — by experimenting with geometric shapes with his students at the Budapest Academy of Applied Arts.[27]

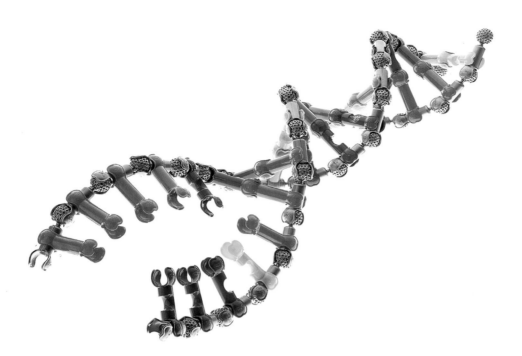

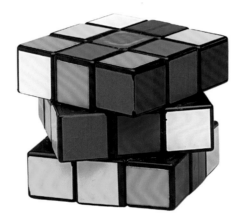

There were strong links between forward-looking education specialists and the directors of leading design schools and museums in the twentieth century, so much so that several of the most progressive schools of art and design have borne the imprint of the modern child in their architectural design, educational philosophy, and student culture. Mackintosh's design for the Glasgow School of Art (1899–1909) was closely related to the spatial organization and architectural symbolism of that for Scotland Street Public School (1904–06), just as Walter Gropius's design for the Bauhaus in Dessau (1925), Eliel Saarinen's for the Cranbrook Academy of Art, in Bloomfield Hills, Michigan (1925), and Wright's for Taliesin, in Spring Green, Wisconsin, all reflected their respective architects' interest in the new pedagogy for young children and concurrent design for kindergartens and schools. Both Cranbrook and the first Bauhaus in Weimar were conceived as part of larger educational communities that included facilities for children, although these connections have been consistently underplayed in historical accounts of the institutions.[28] The childlike student culture in twentieth-century design schools has been a hallmark of their modernity, with pranks, joyous experimentation, and uninhibited socializing merging with a playful approach in the studio. Anni Albers, recalling the Weaving Workshop at the Bauhaus in the early 1920s, described how "they began amateurishly and playfully, but gradually something grew out of their play, which looked like a new and independent trend."[29]

14 MICHAEL JOAQUIN GREY
(American, born 1961)
Zoob play system. 1993–96
ABS plastic, each: 2¹/₂ x ⁷/₈ x ³/₄" (6.4 x 2.2 x 1.9 cm)
Manufactured by Infinitoy, San Mateo, California
The Museum of Modern Art, New York. Gift of
the designer

15 ERNŐ RUBIK (Hungarian, born 1944)
Rubik's Cube. 1974
Plastic, 2¹/₄ x 2¹/₄ x 2¹/₄" (5.7 x 5.7 x 5.7 cm)
Manufactured by Ideal Toy Corporation, New York
The Museum of Modern Art, New York. Gift of
the manufacturer

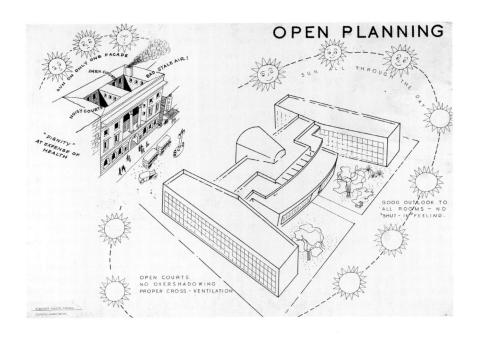

UTOPIA–DYSTOPIA

16 BERTHOLD LUBETKIN (Russian, 1901–1990)
and TECTON (England, est. 1932)
Explanatory drawing for the Finsbury Health
Centre, London. 1936
Printed ink on paper pasted to board,
19 1/2 x 26 7/16" (49.5 x 67.2 cm)
RIBA Library Drawings & Archives Collection, London

17 KIJO ROKKAKU ARCHITECT AND
ASSOCIATES (Japan, est. 1969)
Zasso Forest School (Zasso-no-mori Playschool
and Soyokaze Kindergarten), Tuzuki-gum,
Kyoto-fu, Japan. 1975–77
Rooftop sculptures designed by Susumu Shingu
(Japanese, born 1937)
Photograph by Osamu Murai
The Museum of Modern Art, New York. Architecture
and Design Study Center

Children, with their perception uncluttered by the baggage of social and cultural conventions, have long symbolized the visionary modernist focus on the future. In this respect they belong at the heart of utopian thought, and they inspire us to demand a different, better, brighter future. For anyone wanting to create a new world, the well-being of children has been a good place to start. Belief in architecture and design as catalysts for progress and as active partners in the shaping of society has been fundamental to design for children throughout the century, in the form of toys, schools, orphanages, medical facilities (no. 16), and entire communities with children as their raison d'être. The poetic structure of the hilltop Zasso Forest School (no. 17), by Kijo Rokkaku, is an example that brings architectural form and children into alignment with the natural world: the complex is enlivened by the natural elements and the energy of children at play, with propeller-like sculptures at different heights that move according to the wind and activate several play mechanisms inside the school's playroom.

MILITARIZATION OF CHILDREN

"We begin with the child when he is three years old. As soon as he begins to think he gets a little flag put in his hand. Then follows the school, the Hitler Youth, the S. A. and military training. We don't let him go until he dies, whether he likes it or not."
Dr. ROBERT LEY, *Leader of Nazi Labor Front (Education in Nazi Germany)*

However dazzling the visions of utopia may be, the specter of social engineering is never far away (no. 18). In the tradition of Aldous Huxley's *Brave New World* (1932) and George Orwell's *1984* (1949), Thomas Pynchon described, in *Gravity's Rainbow* (1973), Zwölfkinder, a sinister utopia apparently run by children but in reality manipulated by invisible adult authorities:

> In a corporate State, a place must be made for innocence, and its many uses.
> In developing an official version of innocence, the culture of childhood has proven invaluable.... Over the years it had become a children's resort, almost a spa.
> If you were an adult, you couldn't get inside the city limits without a child escort.
> There was a child mayor, a child city council of twelve. Children picked up the papers, fruit peelings and bottles you left in the street, children gave you guided tours through the Tierpark... child police reprimanded you if you were caught alone, without your child accompanying. Whoever carried on the real business of the town — it could not have been children — they were well hidden.[30]

Utopian worlds can ultimately never be realized, and the failure of many modernist projects is particularly poignant when it comes to children. Designer Svetlana Boym, on returning in the 1990s to her childhood haunts in Leningrad (now St. Petersburg), described how she found herself wandering around the miniature rockets that "crash-landed" in the playgrounds in the 1960s and were now rusting there. These relics were made in the euphoric era of Soviet space exploration, "when the future seemed unusually bright and the march of progress triumphant. Soon after the first man flew into space, Nikita Khrushchev promised that the children of my generation would live in the era of communism and travel to the moon. We dreamed of going into space before going abroad, of travelling upward, not westward. Somehow we failed in our mission. The dream of cosmic communism did not survive, but the miniature rockets did."[31]

18 "Militarization of Children," part of the exhibition *Nature of the Enemy*, Office of War Information (OWI), Rockefeller Plaza, New York. 1943
Photograph by Arthur S. Siegel
United States Holocaust Memorial Museum, Washington, D.C.

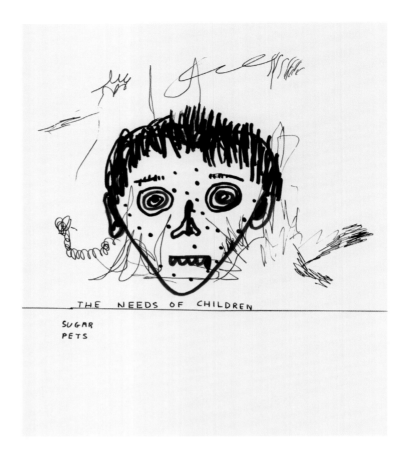

THE NEEDS OF CHILDREN

SUGAR
PETS

ADULTS AND CHILDREN: THE STRUGGLE IS ON

Childhood has in many ways been prolonged, and children now have a higher status and greater agency both in the family and in society at large. Left to their own devices would children define their needs as sugar and pets, as artist David Shrigley implies (no. 19)? At "Growing by Design," Krulwich described the friction between adult desire for control and the childhood need for independence as an apparently irresolvable tussle (no. 20): "On the one hand is the adult culture, which has a design for children and knows how children should grow. It knows what they should become.... On the other hand, there is the private world of a child, who is at first, all potential. This child, this little boy or girl, could be anything...the child says, let me be me. So the contest begins and the struggle is on, and it's the right struggle."[32]

Children are controlled by, yet also take control of, the world around them. Although living in a world constructed by adults, they are social actors in their own right, using and interpreting modern design on their own terms, employing the materials at hand (no. 21). But the agency of children has inevitably been circumscribed by their dependence on adults, and despite attempts to enshrine their universal rights, they remain even more powerless and inarticulate than other marginalized groups. In recent decades the power of adults has squeezed out children from public spaces and limited their physical freedom through legislation that reinforces risk-averse attitudes. Even more controversial is the debate over the ultimate form of adult design: the possibility of prepackaging children's genetic makeup.

Another facet of the contest between adult and child is the complex, discursive debate about child sexuality and the apparently unstable boundaries between childhood and sexual maturity, particularly when considered in relation to class and gender. From the outcry that greeted Oskar Kokoschka's *Die träumenden Knaben* (*The Dreaming Boys*) at the Vienna *Kunstschau* in 1908 to the fetishistic adornment of the Lolita fashions adopted by many Japanese girls and young women in the 1990s, the shifting constructs of childhood and sexual desire have created a great deal of adult unease. Much of the fashion for tweens (children between the ages of about

19 DAVID SHRIGLEY (British, born 1968)
Untitled (The Needs of Children). 2002
Felt-tip pen on paper, 9 1/2 x 8 1/4" (24.1 x 21 cm)
The Museum of Modern Art, New York. The Judith Rothschild Foundation Contemporary Drawings Collection Gift

20 JOHN HUNTER (American, born 1934)
The Day the Kids Finally Took Over. 1969
Lithograph, sheet: 24 $^1/_{16}$ x 35" (61.1 x 89 cm)
Printed by Tamarind Lithography Workshop,
Los Angeles
The Museum of Modern Art, New York. Gift of
Kleiner, Bell & Co.

21 JENS S. JENSEN (Swedish, born 1946)
*Boy at the Junk Playground, Hammarkullen,
Gothenburg*. 1973
Gelatin silver print, 9 $^7/_{16}$ x 12" (24 x 30.5 cm)
Courtesy of the artist

nine and fourteen) at the end of the century has visibly eroded the differences between adults and children and challenged the notion of a definable end of childhood, providing clothes for the knowing child who may or may not be in control of her appearance and sexuality.

The new imaginative freedom granted to children via access to digital technology and the Internet has to some degree compensated them for increased physical constraints in public urban space, but it has come at the cost, to adults, of new fears about the effects of unregulated exposure to media content. Anxieties about new technology and control are nothing new, but they have a particular resonance when children are involved, as Sarah Kember, lecturer in new technologies of communication at Goldsmiths, University of London, has suggested. "Children are perceived not only to be more computer literate than most adults," she has written, "but to be perpetrators of computer crime and other excesses including addiction...in relation to technology, children are seen not as being innocent but as worrying, dangerous and out of control."[33] But the present can also be seen as an extraordinary time for children, with digital technologies giving them access to an infinite artistic palette and an enormous range of cultural references with which to build—whatever. Plenty of evidence points to a process of massive cultural empowerment, catapulting us toward an explosion of creativity as the current generation assumes control of the world.[34]

INTO THE TWENTY-FIRST CENTURY

In a time of acute economic, ecological, and political uncertainties, the utopian promises that played so large a part in modern design for children in the twentieth century have plenty of nostalgic allure and fascination, but they also offer a critical tool for analyzing the present and an inspiration for addressing the challenges that continue to engage designers. It is our aim in this sweeping, admittedly partial view of children and modern design to provoke renewed consideration of the larger question of the position of the child in society today (no. 22). As Key observed in *The Century of the Child*, "The development of the child...answers in miniature to the development of mankind as a whole."[35]

It now seems as urgent to drastically shift our conception of education and modern design as it did in 1900.[36] What is necessary for this to happen, as educator Christian Long has argued, is a new generation equipped with new ways of thinking. "Our children must master systems-thinking," he has written, "to envision multiple methods for addressing complex challenges like renewable energy, world hunger, climate change, and ultimately, the design of a better world."[37] The need to foster the young child's innate capacity for divergent thinking—the ability to come up with lots of different answers—brings us back to the early-twentieth-century pioneers of the kindergarten movement and the concept of open-ended play as a strategy for learning and design innovation, an idea echoed in the mantra of musician and cultural commentator Pat Kane: "Play will be to the 21st century what work was to the industrial age—our dominant way of knowing, doing and creating value."[38] If there is one lesson that adults should learn from children, it is that at a time of environmental and economic crisis, play is a crucial point of connection to the physical and imaginative world (no. 23). We need to give ourselves time and space for play, space in which the unpredictable can happen.

NEW CENTURY, NEW CHILD, NEW ART

INTRODUCTION

The child is innocence and forgetting, a new beginning, a game, a self-propelled wheel, a first movement, a sacred "yes." For the game of creation, my brothers, a sacred "yes" is needed: the spirit now wills its own will.
— Friedrich Nietzsche, 1883[1]

FOR MANY designers, writers, and reformers in the years on either side of 1900, children were the living symbol of the sweeping changes that ushered in the birth of the modern. At the beginning of the new century, children bore the brunt of millennial fears and utopian dreams, and in emergent artistic centers in Europe and the United States — from Glasgow and Chicago to Rome, Budapest, and Vienna — the leading designers and intellectuals of the day, many of them women, were addressing children's rights, welfare, and educational reform.

Paradoxically, children were both the targets of an expanding consumer culture and exploited as a source of cheap industrial labor. The experience of modernization was always uneven. While many families could afford to indulge their offspring, countless other children at the beginning of the century suffered from malnutrition, disease, and squalid living conditions in rural and urban areas. At the same time, children, more than any other social group, appeared to offer a redemptive role for modern design, a mission that was morally and spiritually uplifting for all concerned, promising progress and social cohesion. For designers seeking to reconcile in their work the tensions and ambiguities of modern life, children seemed an inexhaustible source of renewal, evoking both a paradise lost in the remote past and the future possibility of an ideal city or state. Evolutionary models of thought and metaphors of organic processes abounded, not only in relation to progressive design but also to child development, such as American psychologist G. Stanley Hall's idea that the maturation

of children recapitulated human evolution.[2] "The child is older than the adult," he wrote in 1907, "in the sense that its traits existed earlier in the world than those that characterize the mature man or woman."[3] In other contexts, children's development was perceived as analogous to the organic development of the modern city, community, and nation.

A fresh conception of design — loosely termed the New Art — that drew on the Arts and Crafts movement, Art Nouveau, and National Romantic style was catalyzing the creation of a new culture. In progressive circles this reformed design language was applied to all areas of children's experience in ways that reflected an integrated approach to their education, playtime, and employment both prospective and actual. Children's dress, for example, was reformed to allow for freedom of movement, liberating young bodies from the tyranny of tight-fitting, elaborately tailored clothes. Artistic homes, schools, and communities demonstrated a more liberal and inclusive approach to the "new child," with spaces and objects designed to stimulate the imagination and physical well-being of the young.

The international design-reform tendencies that coalesced around a social, democratizing concept of art had much in common with the principles and values of the kindergarten movement. In directing their attention to children, many educators and designers sought to recover an authenticity of expression that they felt had been lost with the innovations of modern life. Both the New Art and the new pedagogy emphasized authentic expression, the inspiration of the natural world, and the creative potential of every individual, every child. In the design studio and the classroom a new emphasis was placed on the enjoyment of the creative process and an empirical, intuitive investigation of materials.

Juliet Kinchin

See page 54

1 GUSTAV KLIMT (Austrian, 1862–1918)
Hope II. 1907–08
Oil, gold, and platinum on canvas, 43 $^1/_2$ x 43 $^1/_2$" (110.5 x 110.5 cm)
The Museum of Modern Art, New York. Jo Carole and Ronald S. Lauder and Helen Acheson Funds, and Serge Sabarsky

Play is the highest stage of the child's development...the purest, the most spiritual product of man at this stage, and it is at once the prefiguration and imitation of the total human life — of the inner, secret, natural life in man and in all things. It produces, therefore, joy, freedom, satisfaction, repose within and without, peace with the world.
— Friedrich Froebel, 1826[1]

KINDERGARTEN WAS NOT a twentieth-century invention, but it was only around the turn of the century that the movement's wider international impact triggered both avant-garde artistic experimentation and a decisive shift in educational theories and methods. Inspired by late-eighteenth- and early-nineteenth-century educational theorists, above all Johann Heinrich Pestalozzi and Friedrich Froebel (no. 2), a new way of thinking about the child was taking hold, one that questioned rigid discipline in the classroom and the mind-numbing traditional methods of learning by rote. In progressive educational circles a general consensus was emerging that children were active, rather than passive, learners, and that they were best educated by women, using kindness and encouragement rather than rebuke and corporal punishment (no. 3). Most educators agreed that singing, dancing, direct observation of nature (no. 4), and, above all, open-ended play with real objects stimulated the most effective learning, although opinions differed about how directed this process should be. As often happens during a transfer of ideas, these progressive educators and designers were often selective in their adaptation of Pestalozzi's and Froebel's theories, and the widespread commercialization and production, by various manufacturers, of kindergarten materials by the end of the nineteenth century further undermined any uniform interpretation of the concepts. But the underlying philosophy and methods, like those subsequently developed by Maria Montessori and Rudolf Steiner, have continued to inform educational theory and inspire modern design to this day.

The philosophy of kindergarten drew on a blend of eighteenth-century natural history, social theory, and Romantic spirituality. Pestalozzi, acknowledging the influence of Jean-Jacques Rousseau, transformed the idea of the Romantic child spontaneously exploring the natural world into a practical model of early-childhood education at his model schools in Frankfurt and Yverdon, Switzerland, established in 1805 and 1808, respectively. Inspired by Pestalozzi, the Scottish industrialist Robert Owen embarked on a utopian experiment at New Lanark, a modern, industrial community with education at the core of its philosophy (no. 5). The children of New Lanark, gleaned from the orphanages of Glasgow and Edinburgh, made up the bulk of the workforce in the community's cotton mills, but these children were also educated, starting at two years old, at the Institute for the Formation of Character, a school built just for that purpose and opened in 1816; it was run on the play principle, with daily song and dance and direct contact with nature and art rather than books.

Froebel had taught under Pestalozzi at his schools in Frankfurt and Yverdon and worked from 1814 to 1816 with the influential crystallographer Christian Samuel Weiss at the Mineralogical Museum of the University of Berlin, cataloging minerals and crystals according to their internal structure, geometry, and symmetry. In 1826 he published *Die Menschenerziehung* (*The Education of Man*), in which he outlined his own understanding of how a child's development should proceed, by learning to observe, reason, and create through the sacred language of geometry (see "The Crystal Chain and Architectural Play," p. 60). In 1837 he founded his first school in order to put his ideas into practice, a play and activity institute in Bad Blankenburg, Germany. He also

2 Froebel Gift No. 2: Sphere, Cylinder, and Cube.
c. 1890
Wood and string, 11 1/4 x 10 1/4 x 3" (28.6 x 26 x 7.6 cm)
Manufactured by J. L. Hammett Co., Braintree,
Massachusetts (est. 1863)
The Museum of Modern Art, New York. Gift of
Lawrence Benenson

3 FRANCES BENJAMIN JOHNSTON
(American, 1864–1952)
Kindergarten Children Washing and Ironing.
1899–1900
Platinum print, 7 9/16 x 9 1/2" (19.2 x 24.2 cm)
The Museum of Modern Art, New York. Gift of
Lincoln Kirstein

4 FRANCES BENJAMIN JOHNSTON
(American, 1864–1952)
Primary Class Studying Plants: Whittier School.
1899–1900
Platinum print, 7 1/2 x 9 9/16" (19 x 24.3 cm)
The Museum of Modern Art, New York. Gift of
Lincoln Kirstein

5 G. HUNT (British, dates unknown)
Dance class at Robert Owen's Institute for the
Formation of Character
in New Lanark, Scotland, with the animal mural
by Catherine Vale Whitwell in the background. 1825
Hand-colored engraving
New Lanark Trust, Scotland

6 Kindergarten teacher's workbook produced by
Ella Steigelman, founding member of the California
Kindergarten Training School. c. 1890
Folded: 8 1/4 x 10 3/4" (21 x 27.3 cm)
The Museum of Modern Art, New York. Gift of
Lawrence Benenson

established a training school for women, whom he saw as ideal educators of infants, and coined the term *Kindergarten* (literally, "children's garden") for his model of early-childhood education.

Like Pestalozzi, Froebel emphasized *things* rather than words, and *doing* rather than talking or memorizing. To this end he devised a system of twenty play objects for kindergarten students, which he called Gifts — a radical system of abstract design activities developed to teach recognition and appreciation of natural harmony (no. 6). Gifts one through ten, which were intended to remain in their original forms, included crocheted balls in different colors, wooden building blocks, parquetry pieces for pattern making, and steel rings (no. 7). Gifts eleven through twenty provided the materials for occupations — focused activities that involved modification, such as cutting, weaving, and folding with multicolored sheets of paper (no. 8). The Froebel Gifts anchored sessions of play both directed by teachers and instigated by the children themselves; as tools for exploring and understanding the fundamental structure and interconnectedness of the natural world and fostering the creativity and curiosity of developing young minds, they formed the core of Froebel's pioneering educational model, which exploded in popularity after his death in 1852. By the late-nineteenth century the Gifts were being exhibited at world's fairs and adopted in progressive schools in Europe, the United States, and Japan, where they had an undoubted impact on many of the designers and artists who later made radical experiments with abstraction, such as the architect-designer Arthur Heygate Mackmurdo, who remarked that since he was "not allowed to read till I was seven, I found my delight in building structures with wooden bricks."[2]

In the opening decades of the twentieth century the agendas of educational reform and design reform converged in fascinating ways, initially around the concept of play and of kindergarten teaching materials. The methods were often picked up by specialist and independent schools with a focus on manual craft skills and industrial art, where there was interest in children's natural pattern making and the relationship between physical, emotional, and intellectual development, and such institutions set the pace for wider reform in general education. New developments in child psychology were applied to teaching methods, for example, in the classes of Franz Cižek in Vienna and Marion Richardson in England before and after World War I, and in the work of William Hailmann, head of the department of psychology at the Chicago Normal School in the early 1900s and a leading exponent of Froebel's methods. James Liberty Tadd's *New Methods in Education:*

Art, Real Manual Training, Nature Study (1899) emphasized blackboard drawing (no. 9) with large freehand movement as a means of conserving vitality and developing "a union of thought and action…a process that unfolds the capacities of children as unfold the leaves and flowers; a system that teaches the pupils that they are in the plan and part of life, and enables them to work out their own salvation on the true lines of design and work as illustrated in every natural thing."[3] Montessori and Steiner (nos. 10, 11) also believed in humanistic educational methods as part of a holistic or cosmological worldview, and they emphasized the importance of well-designed teaching materials and learning environments and their roles as active agents in the educational process (see "Rome: Modern Arts, Crafts, and Education," p. 47). Steiner established his first school in 1919 for children of employees at the Waldorf-Astoria cigarette factory in Stuttgart and subsequently extended his educational philosophy to a wide range of educational initiatives, including kindergartens. Within a decade Steiner schools had been established not only in Germany but in Switzerland, the Netherlands, Britain, Norway, Hungary, the United States, and Austria.

Associating progressive education with child's play and female teachers may have contributed to the marginalization of the kindergarten movement in conventional histories of modern design, but in more recent scholarship the role that kindergarten may have played in developing an abstract sensibility in the arts — in particular in modern architecture and design — has begun to intrigue historians of modernism.[4] On a formalist level, Froebel's distillations of natural forms often bear a striking resemblance to the most abstract modes of artistic expression, a relationship sometimes reinforced by an individual designer's experience of kindergarten. In the case of Steiner, progressive education and innovative design practice were inextricably connected. His own work as an architect directly tied his innovative pedagogy and anthroposophical belief with modernism in the performing arts and architecture: his Expressionist designs for the First and Second Goetheanums (no. 12) in Dornach, Switzerland, the location of Steiner's Anthroposophical Society, included theater spaces and the School for Spiritual Science, thus reflecting the importance to his educational method of imagination, performance, and the integration of practical, artistic, and conceptual elements.

Juliet Kinchin

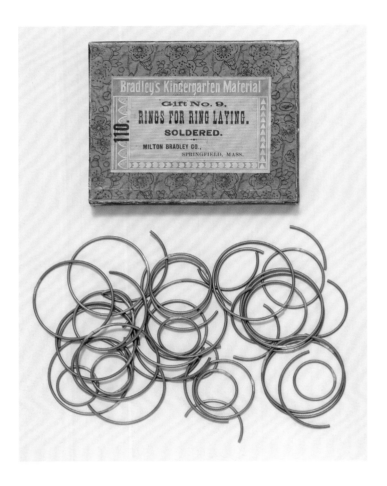

7 Froebel Gift No. 9: Rings for Ring Laying. c. 1880
Cardboard and steel, box: 4 1/4 x 5 1/4 x 1 3/8"
(10.8 x 13.3 x 3.5 cm)
Manufactured by Milton Bradley, Springfield,
Massachusetts (est. 1860)
The Museum of Modern Art, New York. Gift of
Lawrence Benenson

8 Froebel Gift No. 13: Cutting Papers. c. 1920
Paper, 9 1/4 x 6 1/8" (23.5 x 15.6 cm)
Manufactured by Milton Bradley, Springfield,
Massachusetts (est. 1860)
The Museum of Modern Art, New York. Gift of
Lawrence Benenson

9 Freehand drawing exercise, as reproduced in
New Methods in Education: Art, Real Manual
Training, Nature Study, by James Liberty Tadd
(New York: Orange Judd Company, 1899). 1899
The Museum of Modern Art Library, New York

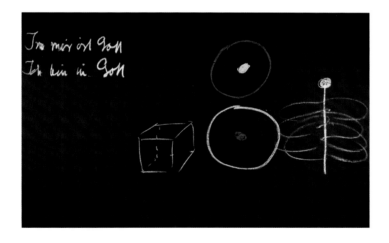

10 Teaching materials conceived and commissioned by Maria Montessori. 1920s
Wood, dimensions variable
Manufactured by Baroni e Marangon, Gonzaga, Italy (est. 1911)
Collection of Maurizio Marzadori, Bologna

11 RUDOLF STEINER (Austrian, 1861–1925)
In mir ist Gott—Ich bin in Gott (God is in me—I am in God), one from a series of drawings produced during Steiner's lectures on anthroposophy. 1924
Chalk on paper, 40 ³/₁₆ x 59 ¹³/₁₆" (102 x 152 cm)
Rudolf Steiner Archiv, Dornach, Switzerland

12 RUDOLF STEINER (Austrian, 1861–1925)
Second Goetheanum, Dornach, Switzerland. 1924–28
Rudolf Steiner Archiv, Dornach, Switzerland

BY 1900 Glasgow had made a spectacular transformation from medieval city and classical mercantile center into an industrial powerhouse of the British Empire, a process of modernization that engendered shocking dislocations, both social and visual, with children as its beneficiaries and victims (no. 13). The name Glasgow (from the Gaelic *Glaschu*) signifies a "dear green place." But was Glasgow "a green flowery world," asked Thomas Carlyle, one of Scotland's dourer prophets, or rather "a murky simmering Tophet," a biblical term that conjured associations of child sacrifice?[1] The challenge for progressive designers was to reawaken a sense of Glasgow as a "dear green place," infusing the city's industrial culture with a mystical sense of nature and tapping into the remote Celtic past in much the same way that the Glaswegian anthropologist James George Frazer was doing in *The Golden Bough: A Study in Magic and Religion* (an expanded edition of which was published in 1900), his monumental and ongoing study of ancient belief systems underpinning modern scientific thought. Children were implicated in this aesthetic and social renewal in ways both symbolic and practical, at the receiving end of acclaimed innovations in school architecture, educational publishing, artistic interiors, and dress reform.

The designers Charles Rennie Mackintosh and Margaret Macdonald won international attention for a series of collaborative projects, including the design of their own home and, in 1900, the year they were married, their participation in the *Haus eines Kunstfreundes* (House for an art lover) competition sponsored by the German publisher Alexander Koch (no. 14). Their entry's playroom emphasized the notion, widely held in reform circles, that the cultivation of an artistic sensibility began at home, with organic imagery particularly effective for children, themselves like plants in a garden. Here, electric light fittings took the form of stylized trees, enhancing a fairytale atmosphere as well as a sense of the psychological interiority particular to children. The dreamlike scheme, never realized, embodied the milieu, spiritual but not religious, in which artistic types aspired to raise their children.

The Mackintoshes had no children of their own but struck up close relationships with those of other artistic couples and clients. Hamish, the son of their client William Davidson, for whom Mackintosh designed a toy cupboard and schoolroom furniture, later recalled how "Uncle Tosh," a keen gardener, had deliberately evoked the outdoor world with the furniture's green-stained finish (no. 15).[2] The furniture was designed in a robust and simple style that, according to ideals of the Arts and Crafts movement, honestly expressed its means of construction. Its forms were derived from vernacular Scottish types, offering a visual education in national traditions as well as in aesthetic, moral, and spiritual values.[3]

Glasgow's enlightened school-building program, a central part of a vigorous program of civic improvements, was in part a pragmatic response to concerns about the health and moral welfare of working-class children. Scotland had a long-established reputation as one of the best-educated societies in the world, thanks to the Calvinist emphasis on self-improvement and reading the Bible, along with the holistic approach, developed during the Scottish Enlightenment, to knowledge, culture, and the environment. Mackintosh had designed his first school while still an assistant in the architectural firm Honeyman & Keppie, but it was not until Scotland Street Public School, his last complete building in Glasgow (no. 16), that he most brilliantly articulated a modern and aesthetically stimulating environment for children.[4] The exterior of this school expressed "simply and directly, the natural form and purpose of the plan" and an educational philosophy aimed at developing the body and spirit of the child in as healthy and harmonious a manner as possible.[5] There were separate entrances for boys and girls and one for infants in the center of the building; it was equipped with spacious cloakrooms on each floor, advanced heating and ventilation systems, an airy exercise hall (no. 17), and light-filled classrooms along spinal corridors on three floors, all planned in an elegantly simple solution to the Glasgow School Board's brief.

But Mackintosh struggled to stay within his budget. He deviously tried to circumvent the Board's financial restrictions by circulating two

13 Children breaking sticks for firewood,
from a series of photographs showing Glasgow
backlands and slums. c. 1900
Glasgow City Archives and Special Collections

14 CHARLES RENNIE MACKINTOSH (British,
1868–1928) and MARGARET MACDONALD
(British, 1865–1933)
Der Spiel-Raum der Kinder (Children's playroom)
from the folio *Haus eines Kunstfreundes*
(House for an art lover). 1902
Lithograph, 15 9/16 x 20 13/16" (39.6 x 52.9 cm)
Published by Alexander Koch, Darmstadt, Germany
The Museum of Modern Art Library, New York

15 CHARLES RENNIE MACKINTOSH
(British, 1868–1928)
Design for a toy cupboard for Windyhill,
Kilmacolm. 1901
Pencil and watercolor on paper, 10 3/8 x 14 5/16"
(26.4 x 36.4 cm)
The Hunterian, University of Glasgow

16 CHARLES RENNIE MACKINTOSH
(British, 1868–1928)
Perspective drawing for Scotland Street Public
School, Glasgow. 1904
Ink and pencil on thick wove paper, 21 5/16 x 43 3/8"
(54.2 x 110.2 cm)
The Hunterian, University of Glasgow

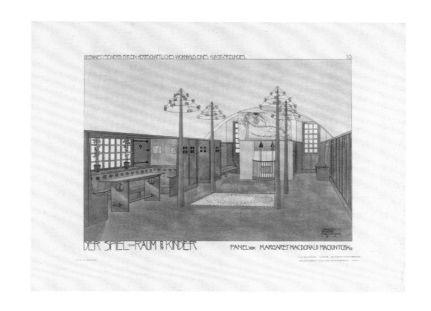

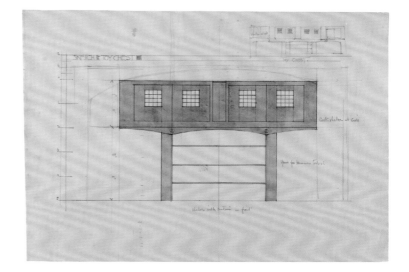

17 Exercise Hall in Scotland Street Public School, Glasgow. c. 1916
Photograph commissioned by the Glasgow School Board
Glasgow City Archives and Special Collections

18 TALWIN MORRIS (British, 1865–1911)
Cover of the book *Shorter Fables*, by Jean de La Fontaine, no. 26 from Blackie's Little French Classics. c. 1902
6 1/2 x 4 1/4" (16.5 x 10.8 cm)
Edited by Arthur H. Wall
Published by Blackie & Sons Ltd, London and Glasgow
Private collection, New York

19 JESSIE M. KING (British, 1876–1949)
Dollhouse. 1912
Painted wood and leather, 18 1/2 x 28 1/16 x 11 1/2" (47 x 71.2 x 29.2 cm)
Victoria and Albert Museum of Childhood, London

20 JESSIE M. KING (British, 1876–1949)
"The Frog Prince" nursery wall panel. c. 1910
Oil on panel, with frame: 20 11/16 x 33 7/16 x 2 3/16" (52.5 x 84.9 x 5.5 cm)
Glasgow Life (Glasgow Museums) on behalf of Glasgow City Council, purchased with the support of the Heritage Lottery Fund

21 Daisy McGlashan and her daughters in reform dress. c. 1915
The Glasgow School of Art Archives and Collections

22 MARGARET A. R. WILSON (British, 1887–?)
Child's coat, needlecraft study piece executed by Wilson as a schoolgirl following exercises in *Educational Needlecraft* (1911), by Ann Macbeth and Margaret Swanson. c. 1912
Linen and thread, 22 1/2 x 31" (57.2 x 78.7 cm)
Glasgow Life (Glasgow Museums) on behalf of Glasgow City Council, gift of Mrs George Innes

sets of drawings: one for the Board and another for the contractors, with more expensive materials and elaborate decoration. The Board managed to rein him in, but he was able to retain the refined architectural details and references that made Scotland Street School a veritable palace of education for working-class children. The twin stair towers were derived from his studies of Falkland Palace, built 1501–41, during the Scottish Renaissance, and the fourteenth-century cathedral in Orvieto, Italy. Instead of the thick walls and small windows of the originals, Mackintosh sheathed the towers in curtains of glass that let the light stream in, giving body to his idea that entering good modern architecture should be "like an escape into the mountain air from the stagnant vapours of a morass."[6] The "etherialization" of architecture, as Frank Lloyd Wright had called it in 1901, was a defining feature of the developing modern movement.[7] An almost mystical sense of structure is emphasized, with pupils as part of a larger natural organism, and highly stylized stems, leaves, and flowers ornament the building both inside and out, so that it appears symbolically rooted in a manner that echoes the children's spiritual and physical growth.

The unified visual language characterizing the New Art in Glasgow was applied to all branches of knowledge and all aspects of modern life, including the design of cheap textbooks and children's books. The most striking of these were the spare linear designs of Talwin Morris for Blackie & Sons (no. 18), a Scottish company specializing in educational and religious publications that were distributed on a massive scale throughout the British Empire. Children's-book illustration and graphic design was an area in which many women excelled, chief among them Jessie M. King, who attended the Glasgow School of Art and from 1899 taught design and bookbinding and subsequently embroidery and ceramic decoration. Her childlike vision and understated technical brilliance in many mediums attracted the attention of *The Studio*, a leading international arts magazine, which went on to frequently publish her work; at the 1902 *Prima esposizione internazionale d'arte decorativa moderna*, in Turin, she won a gold medal for her binding of *L'Évangile de l'enfance*. In 1913 *L'Exposition de l'art pour l'enfance*, a major exhibition of design for children, was held at the Musée Galliera in Paris, and King contributed an entire nursery, including a dollhouse in a modernized

vernacular style (no. 19) and a panel illustrating an episode from "The Frog Prince" (no. 20). By using fairy-tale iconography, she encouraged children to enter and share her make-believe world; in other works, including batik textiles and ceramics, she involved them as active participants in the processes of design and production.

Many women designers were inspired by the radical approach of Jessie Newbery, whose teaching in the department of embroidery at the Glasgow School of Art established embroidery as a specialist subject linked to other arts. Newbery felt strongly that embroidery was a utilitarian art form available to all social classes and age groups, and she attempted to develop the individual creativity of each student. King and Daisy McGlashan were among her students, and they went on to make loose-fitting, highly individual clothes, for themselves and their children, using basic stitches and cheap materials (no. 21). Newbery's methods were brought to a German audience by Anna Muthesius, the wife of the influential German architect and writer Hermann Muthesius, in her book *Das Eigenkleid der Frau* (Do-it-yourself women's dress, 1903), and were critically acclaimed when shown in international exhibitions of the period. Even more influential in disseminating the Glasgow design philosophy were the School of Art's Saturday-morning classes for schoolteachers, started in 1899, and later run by Ann Macbeth, one of Newbery's most talented pupils, who succeeded her as head of the department of embroidery. Macbeth, with Margaret Swanson, wrote *Educational Needlecraft* (1911), a textbook, used in schools throughout Britain and the Empire into the 1950s, that led girls through a curriculum of carefully graduated exercises designed to hone both aesthetic sensibility and manual skills, from simple to more elaborate work, that paralleled the way older art students were being taught at the School of Art (no. 22). The teaching was both practical and stimulating to individual creativity, equipping women and girls with the means to express themselves artistically and to shape their everyday surroundings.

Juliet Kinchin

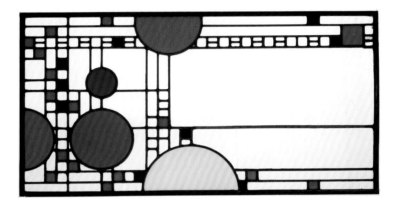

FRANK LLOYD WRIGHT described the vibrant stained-glass windows of the Avery Coonley Playhouse (no. 23), the addition he designed in 1912–13 for the suburban Chicago estate of the industrialist and his wife, Queene Ferry Coonley, as a "kinder-symphony."[1] Like Wright's mother and his first wife, Catherine, Mrs. Coonley was drawn to Friedrich Froebel's educational system (see "The Kindergarten Movement: Building Blocks of Modern Design," p. 30), and she commissioned the playhouse as a kindergarten for her youngest daughter and neighborhood children. The building, which featured a stage and a child-proportioned kitchen (no. 24), was encircled by a band of windows composed of brightly col-ored geometric motifs, inspired by a parade, which playfully suggest from the exterior that the school is filled with balloons, confetti, and flags. With this gesture, Wright paid homage to the basic forms of Froebel's Gifts, which he described as an epiphany, and departed from his established decorative motif of abstract plants to one of pure shapes.[2] He also demonstrated a remarkable capacity for childlike joy at a time when he was being ostracized for leaving his own family — including six children — to be with his mistress, Mamah Borthwick Cheney.[3]

Early-twentieth-century Midwestern manifestations of the Prairie School were rarely so whimsical, but they did regularly incorpo-rate design for children, as the architects associated with that primarily residential momement sought to unify buildings and interiors, including their own homes (no. 25). Children were a spiritual inspiration for these architects, as they were in contemporary movements in other countries. In his "Kindergarten Chats," a series of articles published from 1901 to 1902, Louis H. Sullivan, champion of "form follows function," explicitly encouraged a childlike interpretation of nature and form as the pure source for a modern, organic, and uniquely American architecture.[4] "The kindergarten has brought bloom to the mind of many a child," he

observed. "But there is, alas! no architectural kindergarten — a garden of the heart wherein the simple, obvious truths, the truths that any child might consent to, are brought fresh to the faculties."[5] At the helm of one of the most prestigious architectural firms in Chicago, Sullivan became Lieber-Meister to the young Wright, still fresh from his native Wisconsin when he was hired in 1888. In 1901–03 Wright built the rural Hillside Home School complex (no. 26) for his aunts Ellen (Nell) and Jane Lloyd Jones, the teachers who had given him John Ruskin's Seven Lamps of Architecture (1849) and other formative texts.[6] In sandstone structures on his family's sloping land near Spring Green, Wisconsin, Wright created grand spaces for an assembly hall, gymnasium, physics laboratory, and art studio, in addition to standard classrooms.

In 1901 Wright delivered a lecture, "The Art and Craft of the Machine," at Chicago's Hull House, a settlement house established in 1889 and the site of the founding of Chicago's Arts and Crafts Society. Hull House was a pioneering force in a local modern phenomenon: a network of Progressive Era reform efforts in Chicago with children as their overarching concern. Chicago, the second largest city in the United States, was a hotbed of muckraking and activism and in the first decades of the twentieth century was both socially and physically redesigned to benefit its youngest residents. Hull House became famous for its various local activities, including providing social services for the poor (no. 27), organizing labor groups and ethnic clubs for imigrants, and agitating for improvements in sanitation, housing, working condi-tions, and health care.[7] But its first organized undertaking was, in fact, a kindergarten, run by volunteers in the drawing room.[8] Cofounder Jane Addams never had children of her own, but she argued passionately for them and became a national authority on child labor. Hull House also provided a number of clubs whose purpose was "arousing a higher imagination" in children, primarily through handwork, which public schools rarely offered, and then only for older students.[9]

This kind of handwork (sewing, for example), sympathetic both to contemporary Arts and Crafts sensibilities and the exigencies of Hull House's working-class residents, was one of the defining characteristics of a new educational system pioneered a few miles away at another landmark of Progressive Era Chicago: John Dewey's Laboratory School. In 1896 Dewey, chairman of the department of philosophy, psychology, and pedagogy at The University of Chicago, began the school as an experiment, which continues today. Believing that "education is the fun-damental method of social progress and reform," he rejected traditional curricula, based on memorization, recitation, and strict discipline,

23 FRANK LLOYD WRIGHT
(American, 1867–1959)
Clerestory window from Avery Coonley
Playhouse, Riverside, Illinois. 1912–13
Clear and colored glass in zinc matrix,
$18\frac{5}{16}$ x $34\frac{3}{16}$" (46.5 x 86.8 cm)
The Museum of Modern Art, New York.
Joseph H. Heil Fund

24 FRANK LLOYD WRIGHT
(American, 1867–1959)
Kitchen of Avery Coonley Playhouse. 1912–13
Photograph attributed to Wayne Andrews
The Museum of Modern Art, New York.
Department of Architecture and Design
Study Center

25 WILLIAM EUGENE DRUMMOND
(American, 1876–1946)
High chair designed for the architect's
residence in River Forest, Illinois. 1902
Stained oak and leather, 39 x 17 x $15\frac{1}{4}$"
(99.1 x 43.2 x 38.7 cm)
Price Tower Arts Center, Bartlesville, Oklahoma

26 FRANK LLOYD WRIGHT
(American, 1867–1959)
Hillside Home School, Spring Green,
Wisconsin. 1901–03
The Frank Lloyd Wright Foundation,
Taliesin West, Scottsdale, Arizona

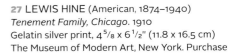

27 LEWIS HINE (American, 1874–1940)
Tenement Family, Chicago. 1910
Gelatin silver print, 4⅝ x 6½" (11.8 x 16.5 cm)
The Museum of Modern Art, New York. Purchase

28 Manual training at the University
Elementary School, Chicago. c. 1904–06
Special Collections Research Center,
University of Chicago Library

29 Diagrammatic representation based on
John Dewey's ideal visions for school building,
reproduced in his book *School and Society* (1923)

30 Lawn Swing at the Women's Gym, Mark White
Square, South Park System Chicago. c. 1905
Photograph by the George R. Lawrence Co.
Chicago Park District Special Collections

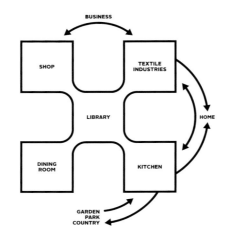

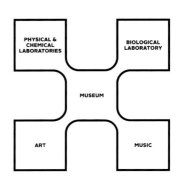

and instead conceived of a school as a lively, cooperative community.[10] In accordance with this idea, Dewey promoted manual education to keep children alert and active and encourage teamwork. Young Lab pupils — boys and girls together — practiced woodworking, basketry, cooking, sewing, clay modeling, printing, and bookbinding, thus learning practical life skills and achieving sensory, aesthetic, and expressive growth (no. 28). With the building of the University's Belfield-Blaine complex (1901–04), Dewey's ideal visions (no. 29) became concrete. Advanced facilities on multiple levels, including workshops, kitchens, laboratories, art and music studios, and an industrial museum, belied the buildings' elaborate historicist facades with their maximum natural light and ventilation, red cement floors, and gray brick walls.

Playgrounds (no. 30) were central to the missions of both Hull House and the Laboratory School, and the former gave Chicago its first public playground, on Halsted Street, in 1893. In 1890 only a single public playground existed in the United States, and in the early 1900s they were still not widely available. As concern grew about the safety, physical and moral health, and delinquency of urban children, dovetailing with an increased national fervor for physical culture, reformers began to rally. Chicago was not the birthplace of America's playground movement, but it was there that the movement's ideals reached their fullest expression, with an ambitious system of public parks and neighborhood playgrounds that provided a model for cities across the country as well as in Europe and Japan.[11] This revolution began in the late 1890s, when the Municipal Science Club began studying the need for breathing spaces in Chicago, where rapid urbanization, industrialization, and immigration were causing unprecedented overcrowding and health concerns. Affluent neighborhoods benefited from large parks and boulevards, but most children played in streets and prairies (empty lots). "While this has been called the children's age," wrote Sadie American, an activist, "they have not yet been accorded their full rights. Place to play is one of these."[12] In 1898 the club hosted the photojournalist Jacob Riis, who showed its members flash-lit photos of squalid urban tenement interiors.[13] The club took these images to heart, along with warnings by advocates such as Joseph Lee ("The child without the playground is father to the man without a job"), and petitioned the city for play spaces and equipment.[14] The following year, Mayor Carter Harrison established a special parks commission, and soon President Theodore Roosevelt was holding up Chicago's South Park system as "one of the most notable civic achievements of any American city."[15]

In June 1907 the Playground Association of America gathered two hundred "playmates" (a term used in opening remarks by Frederick Greeley, president of the association's Chicago chapter) from thirty cities in Chicago for its first national convention.[16] The event confirmed and made a model of the city's commitment to children. "Chicago forgot its commercialism," one attendee reported. "The tense and earnest onrush of its life paused for the brief space of one day in one corner of its great throbbing hulk."[17] By the time British researcher Walter Wood surveyed the country in 1913, Chicago had spent $11 million over ten years to develop playgrounds, and he confirmed the widely held belief that "the parks and playgrounds in Chicago are the finest in the United States."[18] Chicago's playgrounds, with swings, slides, seesaws, sand heaps, shaded areas, and paddling pools, were integrated in the extensive network of parks, the acreage and care of which still distinguish this dense city. Celebrated designers, including Daniel Hudson Burnham, Jens Jensen, Frederick Law Olmsted, Jr., and Dwight H. Perkins, helped direct a renaissance of natural and manicured spaces, vitalizing a city devastated only a few decades before by the Great Fire. This combination of progressive activism and design for children also transformed Chicago's adults, creating a change in the general urban spirit that did not go unnoticed by Wood. "The spectacle of the people of an industrial city like Chicago at play in the parks through the summer evenings," he wrote, "is the spectacle of a city working out its own salvation."[19]

Aidan O'Connor

ALTHOUGH COMICS AND ANIMATION, two art forms initially created for children, are rooted in earlier forms of visual narrative and popular culture, it wasn't until the twentieth century that they began to have a profound and global impact on modern visual culture. In the space of just a few years during the 1890s, the modern mass-circulation comic appeared in Europe and the United States. Generally following the adventures of an individual or small group of characters, their distinctive features were a narrative sequence of framed panels supported by supplementary text or speech bubbles. It was the younger, anti-establishment characters with a marked disrespect for adult authority that became most popular. The characters in *The Yellow Kid* and *The Katzenjammer Kids* were constantly getting into scrapes, which they always survived, even if the laws of physics had to be contradicted. The comics, which drew on folktales and popular vaudeville humor, also established a new childish (or childlike) taste in the mainstream media: a fantasy world of danger and absurdity that was both transgressive and reassuring for children, because shared by many others of their age group.

The drawing style in these early comics was quite bold, but the approach to narrative and layout was fairly conventional. It was precisely this formal aspect that was addressed by Winsor McCay and Lyonel Feininger, the two great illustrators of American comics in the first decade of the twentieth century. In 1905 the *New York Herald* launched McCay's *Little Nemo in Slumberland* and, with it, a design revolution in children's comics. In a dream world Little Nemo ("nobody" in Latin) undergoes the most extraordinary and occasionally frightening experiences, but he always wakes up, in the final scene, in or beside his bed — a trope whose logic is grasped immediately. Although the places that Nemo visits and the fantastic processes that transport him are original, it is the mode of representation and, especially, the striking reorganization of the page layout that established a new standard in popular design. *Little Nemo* had only mixed success, but it prepared the way for a form of graphic narrative in American children's comics that had little, if any, equivalent in Europe.

In 1906 the German-American illustrator Feininger published the first installments of *The Kin-der-Kids* and *Wee Willie Winkie's World* in the *Chicago Sunday Tribune* (no. 31). Like McCay, Feininger conceived of the comic strip as a full-page layout enlivened by radical and inventive experiments in scale, sequence, and format. Feininger announced the style of the comic in a full-page illustration that showed him manipulating puppets, with the caption "Feininger the famous German

artist exhibiting the characters he will create" (no. 32); from here the Kids embarked on a series of absurd and humorous adventures, often in their ocean-going bathtub, as they tried to avoid their formidable Auntie Jim-Jam and her much-feared castor oil. The drawing style of *The Kin-der-Kids* and *Wee Willie Winkie's World* strips (no. 33) has attracted a good deal of attention, largely because Feininger subsequently achieved success as an Expressionist artist in Germany, but many of the devices he later employed in his paintings, including distortions of scale and viewpoint, were already part of his repertoire as a comic artist. Was he a modernist painter applying avant-garde techniques to comics? Or a comic artist whose mastery of physical exaggeration and expressive effects prepared him for a career as an Expressionist painter? Both are equally likely. What is not in doubt is the imaginative gusto that he brought to comics, experimenting with stylistic features more commonly associated with Secessionist book illustration in Germany and Austria.

This sense of fantasy playing out in the illusion of the printed page led directly to early animated cartoons. In 1911 McCay described his animated film *Little Nemo* as "moving comics" in which he enacted the process of drawing on-screen before allowing his characters to take over.[1] The performative aspect was even more evident in *Gertie the Dinosaur* (no. 34), from 1914, in which McCay animated a dinosaur and conversed with it from a lectern on the stage; he then extended the illusion by walking into the screen to climb on its back, a vaudeville-style act that reflects a fascination with the process of animation. Other designers saw the potential for animated films to become an independent medium, but most of the characterization and narrative techniques in early examples were derived from strip cartoons; *Felix the Cat* (1919), *Steamboat Willie* (1928), *Betty Boop* (1929), and *Tom and Jerry* (1940) could have stepped directly from the frames of a children's comic into the new space of the movie screen.

To this day, American animated films produced by mainstream studios are aimed primarily at children, albeit with a nod to adult viewers. But an alternative tradition of experimental animation explored by avant-garde artists and designers is increasingly making an appearance in the mainstream cinema as well as in the wider market of comic books and graphic novels.

Juliet Kinchin

31 LYONEL FEININGER (American, 1871–1956)
Wee Willie Winkie from *Chicago Sunday Tribune*,
November 4, 1906
Lithographed comic strip, 23 3/8 x 17 13/16"
(59.4 x 45.3 cm)
Published and printed by Tribune Company, Chicago
Edition: 215,322
The Museum of Modern Art, New York. Gift of
the artist

32 LYONEL FEININGER (American, 1871–1956)
The Kin-der-Kids from *Chicago Sunday Tribune*,
April 29, 1906
Lithographed comic strip, 23 3/8 x 17 13/16"
(59.4 x 45.3 cm)
Published and printed by Tribune Company, Chicago
Edition: 215,322
The Museum of Modern Art, New York. Gift of
the artist

33 LYONEL FEININGER (American, 1871–1956)
Studies for the comic strip *The Kin-der-Kids*. 1906
Recto: ink, pencil, crayon, and watercolor on
paper; verso: pencil on paper, 12 ³/₈ x 9 ¹/₂"
(31.4 x 24.1 cm)
The Museum of Modern Art, New York. Gift of
Julia Feininger

34 WINSOR MCCAY (American, 1871–1934)
Animation still from *Gertie the Dinosaur*. 1914
35mm print (black-and-white, silent), 7 min.
The Museum of Modern Art, New York

DESPITE POLITICAL UNIFICATION in 1861 and momentum for social change in the years leading up to 1900, Italy remained at the margins of industrialized Europe, lagging far behind in terms of economic, social, and technological development.[1] But a small number of radical artists and educational reformers, eager to break the conservative stranglehold in Rome, were dedicated to addressing the desperate plight of children in the city and surrounding countryside. Although they did not share a common program, the social, aesthetic, and educational agendas of this small group converged at the 1911 *Esposizione internazionale d'arte* in Rome.

Francesco Randone (no. 35), a painter and potter with an idealist mission of providing all children with an artistic education, established La Scuola d'Arte Educatrice in 1890, a studio and small private school that survives to this day. Classes were modeled on principles of the Arts and Crafts movement that encouraged learning by doing and breaking down distinctions between architecture, art, design, and craft. Randone and his pupils were given permission from Italy's minister of education to inhabit and repair a dilapidated section of the Aurelian Walls, which had encircled the ancient heart of Rome since 275 AD (no. 36). Conceived in the belief that art was a medium for unifying, elevating, and consoling — which was reinforced by his theosophical convictions — Randone's project was both practical and visionary: the lives of children (including his own brood of seven) would be enriched by releasing their creative potential through practical arts-and-crafts classes and by involving them directly in the process of urban renewal. With the children he was rebuilding civic culture in microcosm, from within, arresting the physical, psychological, and social degeneration represented by the dilapidated state of the ancient walls. His program, revolutionary in its simplicity, would "teach what is not taught in public schools" by giving children the space and materials to develop their creativity independently.[2] Lessons were free, and a text on the entrance walls read, "No differences exist between children. Paper, crayons, clay will be provided for all." Pupils decorated the furniture (no. 37) and interior walls of the ancient edifice with brilliant colors and created small ceramic bricks and artifacts that were fired on-site (a kiln was added in 1895).

Among the frequent visitors to the school were the Futurist artist-designers Giacomo Balla, Fortunato Depero, and F. T. Marinetti, who

were interested in children's creativity and craftwork despite their technological orientation, and occasionally joined the children in the experimental creation of everyday objects (see "Italy: The Unruly Child," p. 66). In 1906 the school also caught the attention of Maria Montessori, who would establish her first Casa dei Bambini in Rome in 1907. While studying for her medical degree at the Regia Università di Roma Sapienza, the first woman to qualify there, she had developed a particular interest in the creative potential of children categorized as feeble-minded. From systematic analysis of their play, she devised an activity-based teaching method that used material objects to stimulate their senses, and to this she added Randone's way of encouraging infants to work with clay — decorating it, baking it, and appreciating the finished object. "I thought I would experiment in the Casa dei Bambini," Montessori wrote, "with some of the really interesting works that I'd seen being made by an ingenious artist, Professor Randone, in the Scuola d'Arte Educatrice."[3] She openly admired his promotion of civic values by educating young people to be kind toward the environment, "having respect for objects, buildings and monuments."[4] For Randone and Montessori the process of education was dictated not by the teacher but by the teaching materials, which children explored at their own pace (no. 38), and the innovative model of the Casa dei Bambini, outlined in Montessori's 1909 publication about her method, developed an international following.[5]

The situation for the impoverished population in the Roman countryside was particularly dire in those years. Malaria was rife,

35 Francesco Randone with his son Belisario. c. 1906
Archivio Randone, Rome

36 Interior of Francesco Randone's
Scuola d'Arte Educatrice

37 Pupils of Francesco Randone
Painted stool from La Scuola d'Arte Educatrice.
c. 1920–30
Archivio Randone, Rome

and, living in a depressed agrarian economy, the people were largely uneducated, malnourished, and exploited by the landowners whose fields they tended. The high level of illiteracy made many of them unable even to follow simple instructions for taking lifesaving medication. Anna Celli, the wife of an eminent malariologist; the writer Sibilla Aleramo; and several artists and designers, most notably Balla, his brother-in-law Alessandro Marcucci, and Duilio Cambellotti, joined forces to establish schools for the rural poor. Marcucci described their didactic and civil program as "an action of preparation — one might even say the action of an avant-garde. This work precedes the inevitable transformation of rural life and presupposes a new cultural and economic order."[6]

In 1911, at the *Esposizione internazionale d'arte* in Rome, mounted to celebrate the fiftieth anniversary of Italian unification, the committee drew international attention to the cause by exhibiting a rustic *capanna*, or hut. For Cambellotti and Marcucci, this vernacular structure represented both the source of their artistic inspiration and a demonstration of their social commitment to children. They were inspired by personal contact with two Russian champions of the poor and oppressed: Leo Tolstoy, whose portrait by Balla was given pride of place in the *capanna*, and Maxim Gorky, who had visited Cambellotti in his studio. The Rome exhibition was partly a nation-building exercise, the familiar form of the thatched *capanna* intended to mobilize a collective sense of national belonging and renewal through a symbolic return to origins, and it also highlighted the primitive conditions in which the rural population lived, and raised money for new schools by selling peasant and artistic crafts. Marcucci went on to design school desks and chairs (nos. 39, 40) in 1914, using simple plank construction and locally grown wood in an Arts and Crafts style. The patterns were designed to facilitate manufacture by nonprofessionals, and many copies were produced and subsequently remained in use through World War II.

These schools were but one example of the humanitarian work for children that preoccupied Cambellotti and Marcucci over the next two decades; others included the design of teaching materials, toys, and children's books and the collaborative furnishing and decoration of schools. During World War I Cambellotti worked with disabled veterans to manufacture hand-painted children's toys using plywood and cheap timber offcuts. Their radically simplified forms and economic use of materials required little specialized fabrication, thus providing a model for the industrial manufacture of modern and artistic toys.

Juliet Kinchin

38 Montessori School, Arezzano, Italy. 1927
Archivi delle Arti Applicate italiane del XX
secolo, Rome

39 ALESSANDRO MARCUCCI
(Italian, 1876–1968)
Chairs and desk from a school for the rural poor.
c. 1914
Wood, desk: 30 $5/16$ x 38 $3/8$ x 12 $5/8$" (77 x 97.5 x 32 cm);
chairs (each): 30 $5/16$ x 12 $5/8$ x 10 $1/4$" (77 x 32 x 26 cm)
Collection of Maurizio Marzadori, Bologna

40 ALESSANDRO MARCUCCI
(Italian, 1876–1968)
Desk, chairs, and small bookcase from
a school for the rural poor. 1914–15
Archivi delle Arti Applicate italiane del XX
secolo, Rome

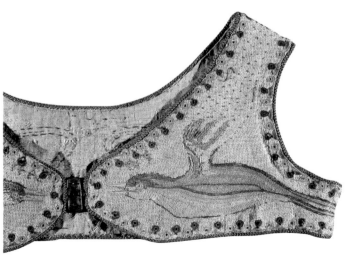

NOSTALGIA FOR the integrity of rural life inspired the artist Aladár Körösfői Kriesch to settle in Gödöllő, Hungary, near Budapest, with his family in 1901. They were soon joined by Kriesch's sister Laura, her husband, Sándor Nagy (no. 41), and other like-minded young artists, designers, and architects in search of a fulfilling and philosophically rich lifestyle. This Arts and Crafts colony, which flourished from 1901 to 1920, was one of many established throughout Europe and the United States during those decades, but it was distinguished both by its emphasis on shaping a national consciousness through modern crafts and by its focus on children at the heart of a utopian vision of shared life and work.[1] Drawing inspiration from the ideal vision of peasant life celebrated by Leo Tolstoy and by British Arts and Crafts designers (above all William Morris and Charles Ashbee), the colony members promoted an egalitarian, cooperative view of social relations and enlightened attitudes toward women and children. A belief in existence as an almost continuous source of joyous affirmation underpinned their approach to life and art. "We love others when we consider ourselves the small offshoots, leaves or flowers of the great common tree of life," proclaimed Kriesch, on the occasion of an exhibition of Gödöllő arts and crafts at the Budapest National Salon in 1909. "What our day-to-day work produces in the light of this jubilant joy in living is our art. We know no other artistic program."[2]

Both the search for totality of expression and the belief in the socially and spiritually transformative power of art was rooted in the concept of the colony as a collaborative *Gesamtkunstwerk*, a unified work of art that would be created by every colony member in every medium, from buildings and stained glass to clothing (no. 42) and toys. The architectural design and decoration of the colony's living spaces encouraged this sort of work, in particular the children's rooms (nos. 43, 44), like those designed by Nagy and Ede Toroczkai Wigand and by Mariska Undi, which provided a space for open-ended interaction between adults and children and, more generally, a model for the reform of domestic design and lifestyle. In these spaces, children's spontaneity and pleasure in learning and their relationships with adults, stifled by urban life, would flourish; they were encouraged to participate in a way of life — working in the craft studios, drawing at home, playing in a natural environment — that would foster self-sufficiency and unhampered development of the individual (no. 45).

By modernizing traditional crafts and adding a heightened focus on the needs of children, the colony was making a conscious attempt to bolster a sense of national belonging and to offset the destabilizing

VIGAND EDE ÉS NAGY SÁNDOR · GYERMEKSZOBA

UNDI MARISKA · GYERMEKSZOBA

41 Sándor Nagy, Laura Kriesch, and their
daughter in reform dress. 1903
Photograph by Elek Lippich, Hungarian
Minister of Culture
Gödöllő Town Museum, Hungary

42 LAURA KRIESCH (Hungarian, 1879–1966)
Child's embroidered bodice. c. 1903
Cotton embroidery on linen, 5 1/8 x 11" (13 x 28 cm)
Gödöllő Town Museum, Hungary

43 SÁNDOR NAGY (Hungarian, 1869–1950)
and EDE TOROCZKAI WIGAND (Hungarian,
1869–1945)
Design for children's room. 1904
Lithograph, 11 5/8 x 16 1/4" (29.5 x 41.3 cm)
Published by the Hungarian Ministry of Culture
in *Mintalapok* (Pattern sheets) (1904),
new folio 2 (X), no. 2, sheet 1
The Museum of Modern Art, New York. Purchase

44 MARISKA UNDI (Hungarian, 1877–1959)
Design for children's room. 1903
Lithograph, 11 5/8 x 16 1/4" (29.5 x 41.3 cm)
Published by the Hungarian Ministry of Culture
in *Mintalapok* (Pattern sheets) (1903),
new folio 1 (IX), no. 1, sheet 2
The Museum of Modern Art, New York. Purchase

45 Gödöllő children in summer. c. 1910
Gödöllő Town Museum, Hungary

46 Children weaving. 1910
Photograph by Rudolf Balogh
Gödöllő Town Museum, Hungary

47 JÁNOS VASZARY (Hungarian, 1867–1938)
The Fair – Gingerbread Stall, wall hanging woven
by children in the Gödöllő Weaving Workshop. 1905
Woven wool, 39 ³/₄ x 64 ¹⁵/₁₆" (101 x 165 cm)
Gödöllő Town Museum, Hungary

48 EDE TOROCZKAI WIGAND
(Hungarian, 1869–1945)
Perspective drawing and plan for church-school,
as reproduced in *Magyar Iparművészet* (vol. 12). 1910
Private collection, New York

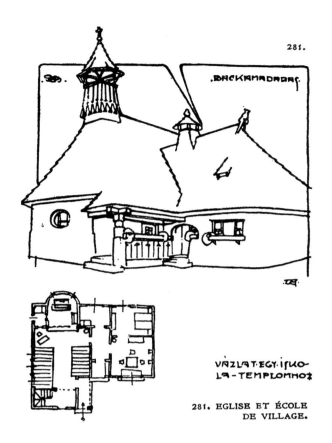

281.

281. EGLISE ET ÉCOLE
DE VILLAGE.

effects of rapid and uneven socioeconomic change by referring to a natural, spiritual order. Yet the Gödöllő project was not simply the romantic escapade of a few Arts and Crafts devotees attempting to live out a rural idyll; in fact it was part of a government-sponsored movement to develop a Hungarian national style that combined colorful, traditional folk culture with technological innovation and a response to international artistic currents. Despite the radical socialism that informed their pronouncements on art and the unconventional aspects of their lifestyle (vegetarianism, sandal wearing, reformed dress, nude bathing, and sleeping outdoors), the activities of the Gödöllő artists had the financial support of the Hungarian Ministry of Education and Culture and were part of larger ambitious programs for craft and design training and school building implemented throughout Hungary. The Gödöllő community supported itself with a weaving school, opened in 1904 and run by a Belgian artist, Leo Belmonte, that in 1907 became a national training center. At its height it employed about forty weavers, many of them children, who were encouraged to draw and experiment with color and pattern as well as working at the looms (no. 46). The most skilled girls executed designs by established artists, such as János Vaszary, that often featured children in them (no. 47). The bold flattened treatment of the figures was a clear reference to Vaszary's own painterly preoccupations and those of the Nabis and other Symbolists, but the medium — wool — was also part of the message; more than oil paint, textile arts in Hungary had the potential to communicate the values of social interconnectedness and continuity that were central to Arts and Crafts ideology.

Several of the colony's leading artists and architects devoted themselves to the design of children's furnishings, clothes, and toys as part of a wider government-sponsored strategy to galvanize the aesthetic development of traditional home industries. Work by the Gödöllő artists was aggressively promoted at international exhibitions before World War I, such as the nursery designed by Undi for the Saint Louis World's Fair, or Louisiana Purchase Exposition, in 1904, in order to highlight the country's progress in educational reform and its development of a modern craft idiom. The Undi scheme, along with many other designs for children, was published in pattern sheets by the Ministry of Culture and distributed around the country for use in elementary and specialist schools as well as in factories and workshops (no. 44). Even subsidized, however, and with a high level of positive exposure at international exhibitions, the finished products were rarely profitable.

At Gödöllő the emphasis on community values, social cohesion, and the integration of art into everyday life had been tested on a small scale, but these ideas were taken to a new level by some colony members' involvement in a spurt of school-building projects throughout Hungary between 1907 and 1913. A national system of schooling and standards of literacy, including the introduction of Hungarian crafts in the curriculum, was seen by the government as critical for the cultural assimilation of a linguistically and ethnically diverse population. István Bárczy, the mayor of Budapest, who had once served in the Ministry of Education, embarked on an ambitious program of architectural commissions, including the construction of fifty-six schools, which would cement Budapest's reputation as a world city run by an enlightened municipal authority. Groups of artists from Gödöllő contributed mosaics, stained glass, ceramics, and architectural sculpture to these schools, while Wigand, far away from Budapest, in rural Transylvania (now part of Romania), designed a series of multifunctional church-schools that were innovative in their planning and reductivist treatment of vernacular sources (no. 48). In addition to responding to the local communities' need for flexible shared space, these National Romantic–style buildings made young pupils aware of their heritage of Hungarian design.

Juliet Kinchin

THEATER SPIEGEL

GUSTAV KLIMT, the artist who led the Viennese Secession — the break, in 1897, from the traditional Künstlerhausgenossenschaft (Association of Austrian artists) — communicated a profound ambivalence about the emerging cultures of modernity and childhood in a painting of a pregnant woman entitled *Hope II* (see p. 28, no. 1). In this composition the gestation of the New Art and the new child is symbolically merged with the modern ornamental language decorating a gown that obscures the mother's swollen belly, but the unborn child as an embodiment of hope is complicated by unsettling allusions to sex and death in the form of a skull attached to her like an incubus. The anxiety suggested by this coupling was mirrored in the intellectual and aesthetic ferment of Vienna at the turn of the century, above all in the emergence of psychoanalysis. Sigmund Freud's theory of child development as a series of psychosexual stages driven by libidinal desires worked in opposition to the relentless mythologizing of children as paradigms of innocence and joy. Although he was primarily concerned with mental excavations that led to healthy adulthood rather than with ameliorating the experience of childhood itself, Freud recognized the distinctiveness of children as individuals, taking seriously their fantasy worlds and mental anguish; in this sense he added an influential, albeit controversial, voice to calls for less repressive childcare and education.[1]

Franz Cižek, a pioneering Viennese educator also intrigued by the child within, started independent art and craft classes for children in 1897. He described his teaching method as a process of liberating internally generated imagery from the child: "I take off the lid, and

other art masters clap the lid on — that is the only difference.... Here they draw things out of their heads, everything they feel, everything they imagine, everything they long for. They have no models, nothing but the bare walls of the schoolroom and the materials."[2] To awaken this spontaneous creativity, children were encouraged to play with materials of their choice, often with background music. Cižek's Secessionist contemporaries were fascinated by the results, and in 1904 his classes for six- to fourteen-year-olds were formally incorporated in the Vienna Kunstgewerbeschule (School of applied arts) (no. 49), thereby embedding progressive arts-and-crafts education for children alongside training for adult designers. Two years later Cižek introduced a related design course for older students on the "theory of ornamental form," from which subsequently emerged the abstract visual language of Viennese Kinetism.[3]

The significance of this intersection between innovative pedagogy and modern design was highlighted in the 1908 *Kunstschau*, a forum and exhibition for the most advanced art and design of the moment, organized by Secessionist artists and designers and timed to coincide with sixtieth anniversary of the accession of the Emperor Franz Joseph I. With his position on the organizing committee, Cižek secured prime placement for his pupils' work at the entrance to the exhibition, where it prepared visitors for the adult refinement of the childlike aesthetic by Secessionist designers in the galleries that lay beyond. An emphasis on newness and youth was signaled by the posters for the exhibition, by Berthold Löffler (no. 50) and his pupil Oskar Kokoschka, which each featured a young girl; the exhibition's major themes — the dismantling of the usual hierarchies of artistic production to include design by and for children, the extension of art into everyday life — were echoed in Klimt's opening speech. "[We are] united in the conviction that no aspect of human life is so trifling, so insignificant as not to offer scope for artistic endeavour," he proclaimed. "In the words of [William] Morris, even the most insignificant object, if perfectly made, helps us to increase the sum total of beauty on this earth."[4]

These ideas were the founding principles of the Wiener Werkstätte, an Arts and Crafts workshop enterprise established in 1903 under the direction of designers Josef Hoffmann and Kolo Moser, both founding members of the Vienna Secession and colleagues of Cižek at the Kunstgewerbeschule. Far from being considered trifling, the production of playthings, books, clothes, and furnishings for children formed a significant part of the workshop's output, and were put on the same footing as fine art. At the 1908 *Kunstschau* the Wiener Werkstätte

49 MARGARETA (GRETE) HAMERSCHLAG
(Austrian, 1902–1958)
Theaterspielen (Theater play), drawing from studies
in Franz Cižek's *Jugendklasse* (Class for children)
at the Vienna Kunstgewerbeschule (School of
applied arts). 1908–14
Graphite, watercolor, and ink on paper, 11 5/8 x 15 3/4"
(29.5 x 40 cm)
Victoria and Albert Museum of Childhood, London

50 BERTHOLD LÖFFLER (Austrian, 1874–1960)
Kunstschau Wien 1908. 1908
Lithograph, 14 3/8 x 19 1/2" (37.5 x 49.5 cm)
The Museum of Modern Art, New York. Gift of The
Lauder Foundation, Leonard and Evelyn Lauder Fund

51 OSKAR KOKOSCHKA (Austrian, 1886–1980)
Schlafende Frau (Sleeping Woman) from
Die träumenden Knaben (The Dreaming Boys).
1907–08 (reissued 1917)
Photolithograph from an illustrated children's book
with eight photolithographs and three line block
reproductions, page: 9 7/16 x 11 9/16" (24 x 29.3 cm)
Published by Kurt Wolff Verlag, Leipzig
Printed by Albert Berger, Vienna
Edition: 275
The Museum of Modern Art, New York.
The Louis E. Stern Collection

52 Raum der Kunst für das Kind (Room of art for children)
at the *Kunstschau*, Vienna (1908), showing works
by students of Adolf Böhm at the Kunstschule für
Frauen und Mädchen (Art school for women and girls),
as reproduced in *The Studio* (vol. 44). 1908
The Museum of Modern Art Library, New York

53 MAGDA MAUTNER VON MARKHOF
(Austrian, 1881–1944)
Kalenderbilderbuch (Calendar picture book). 1905
Woodcut, 4 x 9 1/4 x 1/2" (10.2 x 23.5 x 1.3 cm)
The Museum of Modern Art, New York. Gift of
Jo Carole and Ronald S. Lauder

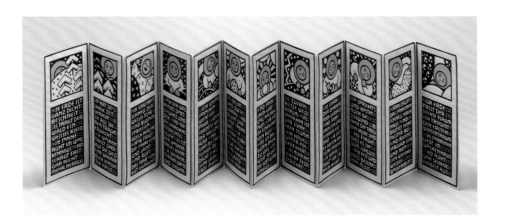

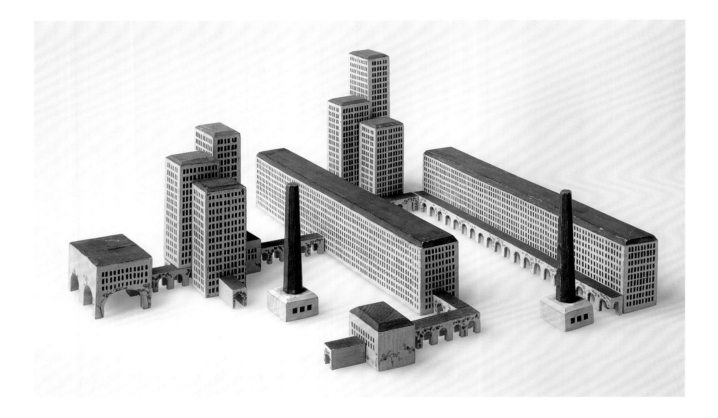

54 MINKA PODHAJSKÁ
(Czechoslovak, born Moravia. 1881–1963)
Devil and Saint Nicholas. 1908
Painted wood, devil: 3 $^{15}/_{16}$″ (10 cm) tall;
Saint Nicholas: 4 $^1/_2$″ (11.5 cm) tall
Museum of Decorative Arts, Prague

55 FANNY HARLFINGER-ZAKUCKA
(Austrian, 1873–1954)
Page from *Schablonen Drucke* (Stencil patterns).
c. 1908
Single page: 9 $^5/_8$ x 8 $^3/_4$″ (24.4 x 22.2 cm)
Cotsen Children's Library at Princeton
University Library

56 JOSEF FRANZ MARIA HOFFMANN
(Austrian, 1870–1956)
Fabrik (Factory), stacking assembly system. c. 1920
Painted wood, various dimensions, built:
20 x 24 $^{13}/_{16}$ x 5″ (50.8 x 63 x 12.7 cm)
Canadian Centre for Architecture, Montreal.
Acquired with the support of Bell Quebec

showed one of its most controversial projects, *Die träumenden Knaben* (*The Dreaming Boys*) (1907–08), a book, supposedly for children, written and designed by Kokoschka (no. 51). With flattened forms, intense colors, and primitivist ornament, the illustrations present an eroticized dream world that Kokoschka described as a "reflection of my spiritual state."[5] The first sheet depicts a mountainous fairy-tale island inhabited by wild beasts and a blonde princess, and thereafter the imagery and text become increasingly brutal and sexualized: "Little red fish/ Red little fish/Let me stab you to death with my three-pronged knife/ Tear you apart with my fingers." "Revolting" was the response of critic Richard Muther in *Die Zeit*, who added "and yet I have to admit that I have not witnessed such an interesting debut for years. This enfant terrible is indeed a child, not an imposter at all."[6] No doting parent was prepared to buy any of the five hundred copies printed for the exhibition, straining the already precarious Wiener Werkstätte finances, and the ensuing scandal cost Kokoschka his job at the Kunstgewerbeschule. Fritz Wärndorfer, the Wiener Werkstätte's financial backer, observed that he could get people to spend two thousand crowns on champagne during a single night at the Cabaret Fledermaus, whereas Kokoschka's book "would not bring in 2000 crowns in 10 years."[7]

Many objects at the *Kunstschau* were designed "to give delight to a child and arouse his aesthetic sense."[8] Adolf Böhm, a professor at the Kunstschule für Frauen und Mädchen, an art school for women and girls, organized a room on the theme of art for children (no. 52), with a frieze designed and decorated by a group of girls from his class. There were toys, picture books (no. 53), and furnishings, almost all of them created by women connected with the Kunstgewerbeschule and Wiener Werkstätte, such as Minka Podhajská (no. 54), Fanny

Harlfinger-Zakucka (no. 55), and Marianne Roller, who drew on their knowledge of regional design and craft traditions and vernacular toy making in the Austrian Crown lands. An imposing dollhouse by Magda Mautner von Markhof (Moser's sister-in-law) stood in the middle of the room, a miniature *Gesamtkunstwerk* detailed throughout in a Secessionist style. Although established male designers like Hoffmann and Carl Otto Czeschka were bringing their talents to bear on design for children — a field generally not perceived to be remunerative or high status — it was women who made the more substantive contribution to Viennese toy design. "[Women] see here a congenial outlet for their fantasy and a new and important field of art," wrote Amelia Levetus. "It is, indeed, essentially suited to women, for they better understand child nature than men; they are nearer to them in thought, and sympathise with them in a way that men rarely do."[9]

Here as on subsequent occasions modern Viennese design was criticized as modern art for the rich. Indeed, with one or two exceptions, most notably color postcards and the bentwood children's furniture mass-produced by the companies Thonet and Jacob & Josef Kohn, Secessionist designers were associated with the production of luxury objects. The only reference to industrial production was Hoffmann's 1920 set of construction blocks, called Factory (no. 56), although the actual pieces were handmade. Of longer-term significance than such decorative arts was the impact of Cižek's teaching (nos. 57, 58) and the spread of his approach by former pupils — including Friedl Dicker, Margarete Hamerschlag, and Emmy Zweybrück-Prochaska — in their own careers as designers and educators.[10]

Juliet Kinchin

57 BELLA VICHON (nationality and dates unknown)
Food Distribution in Austria, linocut made in Franz Cižek's *Jugendklasse* (Class for children) at the Vienna Kunstgewerbeschule (School of applied arts). c. 1916
Linocut, 8 1/4 x 16 9/16" (21 x 42 cm)
Victoria and Albert Museum, London. Gift of Professor Cižek

58 Unknown pupil of Franz Cižek
Group in Movement II. 1921
Terracotta, 6 5/16 x 3 15/16 x 3 15/16" (16 x 10 x 10 cm)
Universität für angewandte Kunst Wien, Kunstsammlung und Archiv, Vienna

INTRODUCTION

True artists have never lost their childlike soul. That is the secret whereby the artist can remain a child with children.
   —Otto van Tussenbroek, 1925[1]

"In style play is the goal" — *"In play the goal is style"* — *"The goal reached, play and style are one."*
   —Paul Scheerbart, 1920[2]

DURING AND IMMEDIATELY after World War I, the modern movement was brought into being by groups of designers working simultaneously in different countries, with a growing interchange between them. For many such avant-gardists, an idealistic engagement with the everyday began with aspiring to recapture the "innocent eye" of the child.[3] To this end, designers delved into basic forms of culture and experience to find something so fundamental that its appeal could be universal. Touring exhibitions of arts and crafts, especially those produced by pupils of Franz Cižek in Vienna, of Marion Richardson in Britain, and of Alfredo Ramos Martinez in Mexico, further stimulated the international fascination with "untutored" design by children. As British avant-garde artist Wyndham Lewis pointed out in 1927, "I suppose there is no one who has not noticed…the prevalence of what now amounts to a cult of childhood and of the Child. This irresponsible Peter Pannish psychology is the key to the Utopian of the 'revolutionary' Rich…it is connected with the cult of the primitive and the savage."[4]

Personal experiences, whether as parents or teachers, tend to be sidelined in accounts of the intellectual formation of modernist pioneers. Yet observing children's aesthetic preferences and characteristic patterns of thinking, feeling, and behaving can be an important form of empirical research. Indeed, it seems likely that Gerrit Rietveld in the Netherlands, Hermann Finsterlin in Germany, and Giacomo Balla in Italy, among others, found such observation — and the creation of furniture and toys for their families — a vital inspiration for their own practices.

Two avant-garde tendencies in particular can be seen to connect concepts of childhood and the modern. One represented an attempt to recapture a childlike, untutored, and undisciplined attitude toward the world, while the other sought to establish essentialist, basic concerns, stripping away extraneous elements to get back to the purest forms of human experience and language. The interplay of these two tendencies resulted in a variety of formal vocabularies and approaches to creative experimentation, each justified in terms of relevance and applicability to childhood experience. Children's innocently subversive mode of questioning the world around them offered artists a means of probing social conventions or revealing the absurd; this kind of playful and unpredictable attitude to cultural norms brought out the uncanny or sinister dimensions of experience that Expressionists and Surrealists were keen to exploit (no. 1). Puppets became an important vehicle for design innovation, from the modest scale of those by Sophie Taeuber-Arp to the giant inflatables seen in the Macy's Thanksgiving Day Parade, which began in 1924. The latter, by referencing figures from children's comics and animation, injected the childlike into an important arena of modern popular and consumer culture.

The artistic, social, and educational reform movements that had opened the twentieth century set the tone for these avant-garde explorations. Ellen Key, whose *Century of the Child* continued to circulate in multiple languages, had written presciently in 1900, "For success in training children the first condition is to become as a child oneself, but this means no assumed childishness, no condescending baby-talk…. It means to treat the child as really one's equal."[5] For modern design, the process was two-way; adults could refresh their creativity through opening themselves up to children's perceptual universe, but they could also design for children in ways that might release youthful energy and imagination, and thereby help shape the society of the future.

Juliet Kinchin

1 GIOVANNI PRINI (Italian, 1877–1958)
Skittles. 1916
Painted wood, largest: 11 x 1 3/8 x 1 3/8"
(28 x 3.5 x 3.5 cm)
Private collection, Rome

2 BRUNO TAUT (German, 1880–1938)
Alpine Architektur. 1919
Book with lithographed illustrations,
15 3/4 x 13 3/8" (40 x 34 cm)
Published by Folkwang Verlag, Hagen
The Museum of Modern Art Library, New York

3 HERMANN FINSTERLIN (German, 1887–1973)
Play objects. c. 1919
Painted wood, each: approx. 4 5/16 x 4 5/16 x 2 15/16"
(11 x 11 x 7.5 cm)
Die Neue Sammlung–The International
Design Museum, Munich

4 HERMANN FINSTERLIN (German, 1887–1973)
Study for a House of Sociability, project. c. 1920
Polychromed plaster and paint, 10 1/4 x 12 3/16 x 15 1/2"
(25.4 x 31 x 39.4 cm)
The Museum of Modern Art, New York.
Gift of D. S. and R. H. Gottesman Foundation

"TODAY THERE IS ALMOST NOTHING TO BUILD.... Let us consciously be 'imaginary architects'! We believe that only a total revolution can guide us in our task.... Break up and undermine all former principles!"[1] With these words, Bruno Taut initiated a correspondence with a small group of other German architects and artists, including Walter Gropius, which became known as the Crystal Chain (Die gläserne Kette). This project, lasting from November 1919 to December 1920, was not just a call to build on the ruins of German culture following World War I, but an opportunity to go back to a naive, exploratory mode of architectural thought that was seen as being more harmonious, natural, and spiritualized. Dreaming his way toward a utopian future, Taut advocated "floating, impracticable models: stars and absolute fantasy.... Probably the most important starting-point for the new architecture. A frivolous world!" (no. 2).[2]

Repeated references to child's play and imaginative fantasy in the Crystal Chain letters epitomized a conscious rejection of the more militaristic and regimented culture of prewar Wilhelmine Germany. Hans Scharoun urged, "Shouts of disagreement on all sides! Like arguments in the nursery. Intoxication of the senses and the circulation. Punch the spiritual eye so that images bubble and spray out, as original and lovely as cascading sparks."[3] Wenzel Hablik exclaimed, "Children!

What magnificent materials our earth still has as 'material for our building games'! Just think: We have rock! Metal and diamonds! And many beautiful sands! And water! Fire and air! We can blow — suck — hit — bore — lift — press — smelt — and soon we shall also be able to fly! We can live in the air!"[4] Hermann Finsterlin, another correspondent, was so intent on retaining his childlike vision that he resisted formal architectural training altogether, preferring to develop his ideas through play with his two children, or with fantastical drawings and models of colorful abstract forms.

At a time of severe material shortages and inactivity in the building industries, more modest undertakings such as construction toys and children's books stood a better chance of being realized. These also enabled children to "build" free of real-world constraints, using their imagination and artistic intuition. For several of the Crystal Chain correspondents, including Taut and Finsterlin, toy design reflected the same quasi-religious quest for spiritual enlightenment and open-ended speculation as their visionary architectural projects on paper. Finsterlin's colorful play objects (no. 3) complemented his sense of architecture as a living organism assembled from basic shapes and emotional impulses (no. 4).

In 1919–20 Taut designed Dandanah – The Fairy Palace, a set of colored glass building blocks (no. 5) manufactured by the Luxfer-Prismen-Gesellschaft in Berlin.[5] This company was a leading producer

of architectural glass and prisms and had previously sponsored the construction of Taut's Glass House (no. 6), a domed multifaceted pavilion made of colored glass bricks, shown at the 1914 Deutscher Werkbund exhibition in Cologne. Both the Glass House and the Dandanah blocks used slack factory capacity and effectively advertised the use of glass in modern architecture. Taut was fascinated by the material qualities of glass: "I have here on my table a thick piece of yellow glass. Heavy as a building brick, constantly changing in appearance," he wrote in a letter to the Crystal Chain in 1920, going on to observe how its prismatic form was constant, "but there is an ever-changing life in it. It's simply fantastic what effects the light produces, and yet within a fixed form. The vessel of the new spirit that we are preparing will be like this."[6]

Apart from expressing Taut's interest in sensory experience, the Dandanah blocks embodied pragmatic constructive values. The simple shapes could be reconfigured endlessly (the set came with six colored sheets showing a variety of assemblages). This malleability fit with Taut's conception of the new spirit in architecture as dynamic and mobile. Children could create structures equivalent to his proposal for a flexible house published in *Die Auflösung der Städte* (The dissolution of the city, 1920). Finsterlin described how his daughter would build fairy palaces, playing with the glass blocks by candlelight in a darkened room.

As suggested by their adoption of the name "Crystal Chain," glass had a spiritual quality for Taut and his contemporaries. A central text for German Expressionist architecture was *Glasarchitektur* (Glass architecture), published by the utopian poet Paul Scheerbart in 1914. This book was dedicated to Taut, who returned the compliment by inscribing aphorisms from Scheerbart around the base of his Glass House dome at the Werkbund exhibition, including: "Coloured glass destroys hatred"; "Without a glass palace life is a burden";

and "Glass brings us a new era, building in brick only does us harm."[7] Taut expressed a comparable sense of glass as a carrier of spiritual transformation and political metamorphosis in his illustrated architectural fantasy *Alpine Architektur*, published in 1919. In this volume, the viewer is led on a metaphoric journey through sublime shimmering landscapes before arriving at a house made of glass. The illustrations, with their sparkling color, imaginative forms, and dislocations of scale, are reminiscent of a fantastical children's adventure tale (no. 2).

Such a mystical view of glass was deeply rooted in German Romanticism, resonating with Friedrich Froebel's view of crystals as the design of a higher power. In 1814–16 Froebel had spent two years organizing samples in the collection of Berlin University's Mineralogical Museum, observing systematic variations in the planes, forms, and symmetries of crystals, "and thereafter my rocks and minerals served me as a mirror wherein I might descry mankind, and man's development and history.... Nature and Man now seemed to me mutually to explain each other through all their numberless various stages of development."[8] Nearly a century later, Wassili Luckhardt extemporized in a similar vein on a crystal geode lying in front of him: "Many many pyramids and prismatic forms have, as it were, grown out of the earth's crust, and radiate in the sunshine. All are varied in size and shape, but each one is built according to the same constructional law. Doesn't one already have the impression here of architectonic creation — don't these structures seem to demand the creating hand of man to shape a meaningful entity out of the chaos of these elemental forms?"[9] Finsterlin too studied the natural sciences before turning to art and architecture, and subscribed to a biological concept of form as a mystical reconciliation of mind and matter. In this respect, his play objects, and Taut's Dandanah blocks, represented nothing less than utopian environments in microcosm, a means of comprehending larger architectural and cosmic structures.

Juliet Kinchin

5 BRUNO TAUT (German, 1880–1938)
Dandanah – The Fairy Palace. 1919–20
Colored cast glass, box: 1 9/16 x 10 15/16 x 10 13/16"
(4 x 27.8 x 27.5 cm)
Patented by Blanche Mahlberg
Manufactured by Luxfer-Prismen-Gesellschaft,
Berlin (est. 1907)
Canadian Centre for Architecture, Montreal.
Phyllis Lambert Collection

6 BRUNO TAUT (German, 1880–1938)
Glass House (pavilion of the
Luxfer-Prismen-Syndikat),
Deutscher Werkbund exhibition, Cologne. 1914
Gelatin silver print
Foto Marburg

IN HIS 1853 ESSAY "Morale du joujou," Charles Baudelaire aphorizes that playthings are a child's first initiation into art.[1] His observation applied literally to the marionettes — a long-established popular cultural form — that introduced avant-garde art and design to children. Modernism's active espousal of puppet theater was motivated by an interest in folk art and a desire to unite art and life. The Deutscher Werkbund, an association of designers and manufacturers founded in early-twentieth-century Germany, fostered the modern tradition of puppetry primarily for educational purposes, but also in the belief that the simple turned-wood forms of vernacular puppets lent themselves to industrial production. As an alternative to theater and to movies — the latter still viewed by many at the time as kitsch — puppet shows for both children and adults were organized at large Werkbund exhibitions of the 1910s. Reform-oriented schools of arts and crafts discovered the potential of the puppet show as a Gesamtkunstwerk project involving various disciplines, and for artists to engage in innovative, transdisciplinary experiments in design. Avant-garde movements in the 1910s and '20s devised their own distinctive theater projects: in Futurism, it was Fortunato Depero's *Balli plastici* (Plastic dance) and Enrico Prampolini's *Matoum et Tevibar*; in Constructivism, productions by Ladislav Sutnar, Vladimir Sokoloff, Natalia Goncharova, Mikhail Larionov, and Alexandra Exter; in the Bauhaus, Oskar Schlemmer's *Das Triadische Ballett* (The triadic ballet), Ilse Fehling's stick puppets, and Alma Siedhoff-Buscher's construction of a cupboard containing a puppet theater (see "Bauhaus Play and Pedagogy," p. 74); and in Dada, Sophie Taeuber-Arp's *König Hirsch* (The stag king) (no. 7) and Otto Morach's *La Boîte à joujoux* (The toy box).

The Swiss Puppet Theater was founded in 1918, on the occasion of the Swiss Werkbund (Schweizerischer Werkbund) exhibition in Zurich.[2] Werner Reinhart, a Winterthur businessman and patron of modernist music, was the chairman of the puppet committee. Of the nine pieces in the program, Reinhart was particularly interested in the premiere of Claude Debussy's ballet *La Boîte à joujoux* (1913), for which he engaged Dadaist Hans Heusser to play the piano. Taeuber-Arp, the only woman on the committee, had long been interested in puppets and also had experience as a dancer at Rudolf von Laban's school of movement in Zurich

7 SOPHIE TAEUBER-ARP (Swiss, 1889–1943)
Sentry puppet from *König Hirsch* (The stag king). 1918
Wood, oil paint, and metal, 15$^{15}/_{16}$ x 7$^1/_{16}$ x 7$^1/_{16}$"
(40.5 x 18 x 18 cm)
Museum für Gestaltung Zürich,
Kunstgewerbesammlung

and as a performer at Dada soirées. The young dancers who attended Laban's school often expressed themselves through fairy tales (no. 8). In his 1926 publication *Des Kindes Gymnastik und Tanz* (Gymnastics and dance for the child), Laban describes how he began his lessons by telling fairy tales that spontaneously led to a diversity of movement that far exceeded anything found in traditional *varietés*. Under Suzanne Perrottet's direction, in December 1917 the children performed the production *Ein Weihnachtstraum* (A Christmas dream), featuring familiar fairy-tale figures, as well as the dolls delivered by Santa Claus.

In *König Hirsch*, the miraculous insinuates itself into everyday reality: King Deramo chooses a bride with the aid of a magical statue whose smile betrays whether or not the hopeful candidates are sincere. In Taeuber-Arp's version, produced in Zurich, the figure of Freudanalytikus, as deus ex machina, ensures a happy denouement. This character, whose name parodied the intellectual vogue for psychoanalysis, was the work of René Morax and Werner Wolff, who directed and wrote

dramas for marionettes. Taeuber-Arp's modern marionettes mark a sea change from their predecessors. Their basic elements, pieces of wood that have been turned rather than carved, are round and sculptural, while the stage set — a pioneering work of Constructivist design — is radically flat (no. 9). The mechanics of her puppets are not concealed. Their extremities, mostly monochromatic in color, have ringbolt joints, making them unnaturally limber and allowing movement in many directions. A variety of formal, chromatic, and material features characterize the relations between the typified figures. King Deramo, his bride, Angela, and the Stag King have golden pupils; Pantalon and his children wear conical hats; Freudanalytikus and his alter ego, the parrot, share the same pastel color scheme; and the would-be king, Tartaglia, and his daughter are distinguished by the cinnabar color of the throne. *König Hirsch* managed three performances in September 1918 despite the outbreak of the Spanish influenza epidemic that forced the cancellation of some other performances. Euphorically received by the avant-garde, it became a Dada icon. Taeuber-Arp reproduced the figure of Freudanalytikus in the Dada journal *Der Zeltweg* in 1919.

The Dadaists treated marionettes primarily as sculptures, as demonstrated by Gabrielle Buffet-Picabia placing marionettes side by side with sculptures by Aleksandr Archipenko, Marcel Duchamp, Man Ray, Francis Picabia, and Pablo Picasso,[3] while showing little interest in the innovative technology of their production. Discussion of such technicalities is first found in the catalogue accompanying Marcel Duchamp's London exhibition of 1939, *Contemporary Sculpture*: "At the Zurich Exhibition in 1918, [Buffet-Picabia's] marionettes in turned wood were the starting point for a new technique in decorative art." Art historians have tended to ignore the importance of these technical developments as a vital impetus for abstraction, unlike Walter Benjamin, who noted in his 1928 essay "Old Toys" that traditional playthings provided inspiration for new forms. The technique of turning wood, which had long been used to make toys, was indeed an innovation when it came to puppetry.

The characters in *La Boîte à joujoux*, which tells the story of figures in a toy box that come to life one night in Paris, are themselves toys. André Hellé, the writer of the production's libretto and also a maker of wooden toys, had had a children's ballet in mind, but Debussy preferred the idea of using marionettes. In preparation for the premiere at the Swiss Puppet Theater, Taeuber-Arp proposed commissioning her Werkbund colleague Johanna Fülscher for the special challenge of creating a ballet for dolls. Fülscher had been awarded second prize for her charming wooden figures in the 1915 toy competition of the Swiss Werkbund. She passed the commission on to Morach, however, who designed Cubist marionettes boasting angular and sweeping movements that recall Archipenko's *Medrano* sculptures. Carved out of wood by Carl Fischer, they were painted in monochrome colors with light and dark contrasts and have mostly directional joints. Some show geometrical surfaces; others simultaneously show elements head-on and in profile (no. 10). It was these figures that animated the story's very human tales: a wooden soldier falls in love with a doll (no. 11), who is in turn in love with a jumping jack. The two male characters engage in a fight during which the soldier is wounded. Abandoned by the villainous jumping jack, the doll nurses the soldier back to health. They get married and have many children.

Medea Hoch

8 Pupils of Suzanne Perrottet at the School for Movement (formerly the Laban School), Zurich, as reproduced in Rudolf von Laban's *Des Kindes Gymnastik und Tanz* (Gymnastics and dance for the child) (Oldenburg: Gerhard Stalling, 1926)

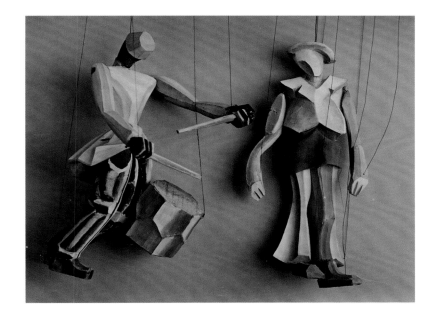

9 SOPHIE TAEUBER-ARP (Swiss, 1889–1943)
"In the Forest," scene from the Zurich production
of *König Hirsch* (The stag king). 1918
Photograph by Ernst Linck
MIZ Zürcher Hochschule der Künste, Zurich

10 OTTO MORACH (Swiss, 1887–1973)
Puppets from *La Boîte à joujoux* (The toy box). 1918
Photograph by Ernst Linck
MIZ Zürcher Hochschule der Künste, Zurich

11 OTTO MORACH (Swiss, 1887–1973)
The doll with the rose from *La Boîte à joujoux*
(The toy box). 1918
Painted wood, $14^{3}/_{16}$ x $7^{7}/_{8}$ x $5^{1}/_{8}$" (36 x 20 x 13 cm)
Museum für Gestaltung Zürich,
Kunstgewerbesammlung

12 GIACOMO BALLA (Italian, 1871–1958)
Child's wardrobe. 1918
Painted wood, 62 13/16 x 51 3/4 x 15 15/16" (159.5 x 131.5 x 40.5 cm)
Rovereto MART — Museo di Arte Moderna e Contemporanea
di Trento e Rovereto, Italy. Long-term loan

The Futurist toy will be very useful to the adult too, because it will keep him young, nimble, joyful, carefree, ready for anything, tireless, instinctive and intuitive.

— Giacomo Balla and Fortunato Depero, March 1915[1]

IN 1910 GIACOMO BALLA exhibited a painting in Rome titled *Affetti* (Affections). In it a woman sits at the center of a sparsely furnished room while a young girl, resting on the woman's knees, reads a book — a touching image of familial affection. This work, which portrays Balla's first daughter, Luce (born in 1906), and his wife, belongs to his Symbolist period. By the time his second daughter, Elica, was born in 1914, Balla had joined the Futurist movement, though his devotion to his family did not diminish. While it is well known that the Futurists wanted to revolutionize and reconstruct not only art but all of society — they abhorred the bourgeoisie and fine sentiments, moonlight and museums — when it came to their families, they often led largely conventional lives.

Balla is known as a great painter, but he also produced furniture (no. 12), clothing, lamps, tablecloths, and numerous other design objects. One of the best examples of this aspect of his work is the room he had built for Elica ("propeller" in Italian). The room, with its bright colors and forms taken from childish morphologies, was conceived during the height of his involvement with Futurism. It was built around the idea that children's personalities develop largely through play — a visionary concept at the time. It consisted of, among other items, specially designed chairs and table, two cabinets, and a child's bed.[2] The chairs, for example, were small enough that children could move them without assistance (no. 13) — a fundamental principle of Maria Montessori, who intended for young children to be able to rearrange their furniture on their own.[3] One of the seven full-scale preparatory drawings (no. 14), intended for a carpenter, clearly shows that the bed's bars represent Futurist force lines; the shapes that support the bars resemble children, with triangles for bodies and ring-shaped heads. In the watercolor drawing that shows the layout for the room (no. 15), the little chairs have the same dynamic silhouette as the vividly colored panel also meant for the room (no. 16), which depicts two children at play. One little girl plays with a hoop while the other is bent over a bucket, and a large curved line against the background of a Futurist landscape connects them. Many elements of this room have been lost over the years, probably during moves from one house to another, and today only the small and large cabinets remain.

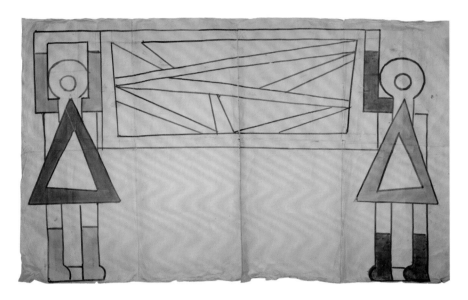

13 GIACOMO BALLA (Italian, 1871–1958)
Children's furniture, as reproduced in
Maurizio Fagiolo dell'Arco, *Futur-Balla*
(Rome, 1970). c. 1920

14 GIACOMO BALLA (Italian, 1871–1958)
Full-scale plan for child's bed. 1917/18
Ink and watercolor on paper, 37 x 50" (94 x 127 cm)
Private collection, Rome

15 GIACOMO BALLA (Italian, 1871–1958)
Design for children's bedroom. 1917/18
Pencil and watercolor on paper, 17 1/2 x 22 13/16"
(44.5 x 58 cm)
Private collection, Rome

16 GIACOMO BALLA (Italian, 1871–1958)
Decorative panel. c. 1918
Gouache and ink on panel, 14 $^3/_8$ x 26 $^9/_{16}$"
(36.5 x 67.5 cm)
Fondazione Biagiotti Cigna, Guidonia, Italy

17 ANTONIO RUBINO (Italian, 1880–1964)
Skittles representing Ciccio, Arcibaldo, Signor
Bonaventura, and Fortunello, four characters from
a cartoon by Sergio Tofano published in *Corriere
dei piccoli* children's weekly cartoon. c. 1910
Painted wood, 19 $^5/_{16}$ x 18 $^7/_8$ x 16 $^1/_8$" (49 x 48 x 41 cm)
Collection of Maurizio Marzadori, Bologna

18 ANTONIO RUBINO (Italian, 1880–1964)
Il bimbo cattivo (The bad child), bedroom
panel. c. 1924
Tempera on canvas, 6' 1 1/4" x 65 3/4" x 9/16"
(186 x 167 x 1.5 cm)
Wolfsoniana–Fondazione regionale per la
Cultura e lo Spettacolo, Genoa

Some years after the completion of this first child's room, Balla designed others; one was similar to the first, only the bed had different supporting elements, which now depict children with full, rounded bodies and heads, less Futurist and more naturalistic. (This bed, like the cabinets from the first room, survive.) Nearly all of the pieces that furnished the various children's rooms ended up being destroyed or given away when the children outgrew them, and even the few works that remained were handed on, first to the daughter of F. T. Marinetti, founder of the Futurist movement (like Balla's older daughter, this girl was also named Luce, or "light"), and then to the daughter of another painter, Sante Monachesi, who was also named Luce, in whose family they have remained until now. In 1932 Balla created yet another little room with a few pieces of small furniture, this time for the daughter of a friend; Balla used a completely different palette for the furnishings of this room compared to earlier rooms, and in design they are closer to those that the artist had commissioned for his own residence over the years.

Antonio Rubino is another figure from the early decades of the twentieth century who is known for his contributions to design for children. Rubino wore many hats, including poet, graphic designer, writer, director, founder of children's magazines, and set decorator, among others, but he is perhaps best remembered for his work as a preeminent children's illustrator. In 1908 he was a founder of one of the most influential children's magazines in Italy, *Corriere dei piccoli*,[4] for which he created unforgettable characters and story lines (no. 17).

A self-taught artist who eludes classification, Rubino is often associated with the Futurists. Though this is not entirely accurate, he did share that movement's embrace of rupture with the past, interest in machine culture, deconstruction of traditional syntax, phobia of clichés, and sense of transgression—this last being perhaps his most obvious affinity with the Futurists. He buries the world of fine sentiments epitomized by the more sentimental work of Edmondo De Amicis,[5] which until then had dominated childhood literature in Italy. Rubino's graphic works are nurtured by irony, sarcasm, and a taste for the grotesque, the bizarre, and the fantastic. His popular 1919 book *Viperetta* (Little viper), the fanciful story of a nasty little girl, offered a compelling alternative to the dominant representation of girls as wide-eyed and sweetly submissive; as a testament to its lasting influence, its last edition, from 1975, includes commentary by esteemed writer Italo Calvino.

During the 1920s Rubino founded and edited various magazines for children, including, in 1929, *Il mondo bambino*, which was published by the largest Italian department store, La Rinascente. The store's

archives were destroyed during World War II, but it is likely that the children's rooms designed by Rubino and produced by a company in Venice were marketed by the department store, which was then at the forefront of middle- and upper-middle-class taste.[6] The only room we know of that has been entirely preserved consists of eleven elements, including cabinets, nightstands, chests, a bed, and three decorative panels (signed by the artist). The surprising little armchairs with feet, arms, and a human head are a toy transformed into a functional object, a sort of animated bowling pin or perhaps the room's fortunate inhabitant, transformed into a presence made of wood—a masterpiece of its genre. The room's decorative panels have titles: *La città dei sogni* (City of dreams), *Il bimbo buono* (The good child), and *Il bimbo cattivo* (The bad child) (no. 18). Looking at them, the artist's empathy for "bad" children—that is, for transgression—is only too obvious, and it is also clear that the cliché of the good child is a pretext for revealing its other, disturbing face. In fact, *Il bimbo cattivo*, with its treacherous path leading to a dark castle, flanked by throngs of witches, scarecrows, monstrous elves, donkeys, and policemen, is arguably more interesting than the angels and good little mommies in the panel for the "good" child. Processions of elves, fairies, putti, and characters from Italian children's literature, including Pinocchio, crowd this unique work of decorative art, which is an homage to children's fantasy and imagination without serious pedagogical pretexts.

Maria Paola Maino

THE TRANSLATION of Ellen Key's book, *The Century of the Child*, into Dutch in 1903 was soon followed in the Netherlands by international exhibitions and conferences on subjects ranging from children's toys, dress, and drawings to developments in child psychology and educational reform.[1] De Stijl, the avant-garde group of architects and artists that coalesced around the journal of that name published from 1917 to 1931, embraced this tendency, focusing attention on modern design for children, and ideas of exploratory, constructive play associated with the kindergarten movement (see "The Kindergarten Movement: Building Blocks of Modern Design," p. 30).

Gerrit Rietveld, an early participant in the group, applied the austere and rectilinear aesthetic of De Stijl to his furniture design. As with other modern designers, the experience of fatherhood undoubtedly contributed to a period of radical creativity for Rietveld, which encompassed a lot of work for children. Between 1913 and 1924, Rietveld and his wife had six children — two girls and four boys. Space and money were in short supply, particularly in the lean war years, when they had to move between modest homes around Utrecht. For a number of years, home life and work were particularly intertwined since the couple lived on the premises of the designer's furniture workshop on Adriaanstraat. In 1919 he tackled a familiar childhood object, the high chair (no. 19). Like an inquisitive child, he went through a process of breaking it down into basic shapes and then rearranging and reconstructing them into something new. This quest for the unadorned purity of fundamental forms also reflected a tradition of Calvinist morality and spirituality in Netherlandish culture.

For several years, Rietveld had been experimenting with ways of creating a furniture joint from three intersecting battens to form a structural node, a process that paralleled the kind of constructive play with blocks and sticks encouraged by Friedrich Froebel and Maria Montessori. The clarity of the chair's elemental structure, resembling scaffolding, differed radically from conventional furniture of the day. The distinctive crisscrossing joints were strong, easy to assemble, and had great spatial and conceptual logic. Not only did the composite form of the chair have a clearly defined presence, but each component part was readily distinguished. In extending past the point of junction, the pieces of timber created a sense of dynamic extension into the surrounding space, rather like an exploded diagram. The same overlapping joint was repeated in the structure of various unique pieces of furniture and lighting, most famously in the 1918 prototype (unpainted) of the iconic Red Blue Chair, but also children's chairs, cradles, and buggies. The pri-

mary colors and geometric planar forms of a 1923 child's wheelbarrow (no. 20) were the result of a similar reductive process. Although made for family and friends, Rietveld's designs for children were circulated among a wider avant-garde audience through the publication of several pieces in *De Stijl* magazine, edited by Theo van Doesburg.[2]

Beginning in 1923, Rietveld collaborated with Truus Schröder, recently widowed, on the design of a new house that was to become the most complete expression of De Stijl principles in architecture and design. In this project, consideration of new and unconventional adult-child relationships determined the open plan of the first floor. Schröder, who had strongly disagreed with her husband about child-rearing, was anxious to create a space in which she could have more interaction with her son and two daughters. "After my husband died and I had full custody of the children, I thought a lot about how we should live together," she explained in an interview years later. "So when

19 GERRIT RIETVELD (Dutch, 1888–1964)
High chair. 1919
Wood and leather, 35 7/16 x 17 15/16 x 16 3/4"
(90 x 45.5 x 42.5 cm)
Die Neue Sammlung–The International
Design Museum, Munich

20 GERRIT RIETVELD (Dutch, 1888–1964)
Child's wheelbarrow. 1923 (manufactured 1958)
Painted wood, 12 1/2 x 11 3/8 x 33 1/2"
(31.8 x 28.9 x 85.1 cm)
Manufactured by Gerard van de Groenekan
The Museum of Modern Art, New York.
Gift of Jo Carole and Ronald S. Lauder

Rietveld had made a sketch of the rooms, I asked, 'Can these walls go too?' To which he answered, 'With pleasure, away with those walls!'... and that's how we ended up with one large space."[3] Flexible partitions gave the bedrooms an element of privacy but could also be opened up to accommodate social activity during the day. On Rietveld's axonometric plan, these vertical floating screens are related to similar rectangular planes of color on the floor, extending the logic of his hallmark furniture construction to interior space and creating a coherent composition of supporting and supported parts. The notion of structural "honesty" and spatial transparency became a metaphor for modern family relationships that broke with bourgeois convention. As such, the aesthetic and social rupture that the Schröder house represented was difficult for some neighbors to accept. Living in such a strange abode, the Schröder children were taunted by schoolmates, some of whom were prohibited from playing with them.[4]

A process of playful deconstruction and synthesis also informed the design of several landmark children's books from other De Stijl artists. Van Doesburg's answer to the radical abstraction of El Lissitzky's *Pro dva kvadrata. Suprematicheskii skaz v 6-ti postroikakh* (*Of Two Squares: A Suprematist Tale in Six Constructions*) (p. 79, no. 35), from 1920, was *Die Scheuche* (The scarecrow) (no. 21), a collaboration with German artists Käte Steinitz and Kurt Schwitters.[5] The pages are composed almost entirely of typographic elements, used expressively to stand for human figures, animals, and emotions rather than to create conventional text. The story narrates a farmer's annoyance at the inability of his scarecrow to frighten off the birds eating his seed. By the end of the book, the scarecrow has been broken down into its constituent parts as the former owners of the items from which he was made come to reclaim their property. The book's anarchic composition seems the antithesis of the orderly graphic style and compressed page layouts of Bart van der Leck, another founding member of the De Stijl group. Van der Leck reduced letter forms to their most basic until arriving at an alphabet of capital letters formed from straight and diagonal lines. He used this system consistently throughout the interwar years and beyond, most comprehensively for a 1941 translation of *Het Vlas* (The flax) by Hans Christian Andersen (no. 22).

Typographer and designer Piet Zwart worked directly with the De Stijl circle in the early 1920s, but was nonetheless critical of aspects of Van der Leck's work as overly formulaic. While maintaining a severely Constructivist aesthetic, Zwart experimented with photomontage and overlaid colored inks. In 1938 he designed the endearing paper figure of Mr. Post in *Het Boek van PTT* (The PTT book) (no. 23), to teach children about the Dutch postal service and modern telecommunications network. The gentle humor of both text and image gives this national corporation a family-friendly aspect that still feels fresh.

The synthesis of aesthetic and educational reform principles was a feature of several interwar initiatives in the Netherlands. The company ADO, for example, developed out of a philanthropic venture at a tuberculosis sanatorium where, as part of their therapy, patients created simple wooden toys (no. 24) inspired by Montessori's philosophy and by progressive teaching materials such as Het Teekenuur (no. 25).[6] Designer-critic Otto van Tussenbroek described the abstract forms of ADO toys as "permeated by the concepts that grown-ups just don't want to hear about."[7] Also in the 1920s, Cor Alons set up the design and manufacturing firm Plateelbakkerij Duinvoet (1923–27), in The Hague, which translated simple planar structures and bold colors to furniture for adults and children (no. 26). The designs of ADO, Alons, Van der Leck, and Rietveld were promoted through Metz & Co., an enlightened furnishing emporium in The Hague with a particular interest in children. Catharina de Leeuw-Schönberg, wife of the store's owner, was a supporter of modern pedagogy, particularly Franz Cižek's method in Vienna, and encouraged her husband to stock a wide range of artistic and educational toys. She herself wrote a magazine column, "Educational Letters," about raising her own children, as well as a children's book illustrated by Cižek pupil Herta Zuckerman.[8] A further Cižek spin-off was Metz & Co.'s production of textiles that were designed by his pupils and sold alongside those of established artists such as Van der Leck and Paris-based Sonia Delaunay-Terk.

Juliet Kinchin

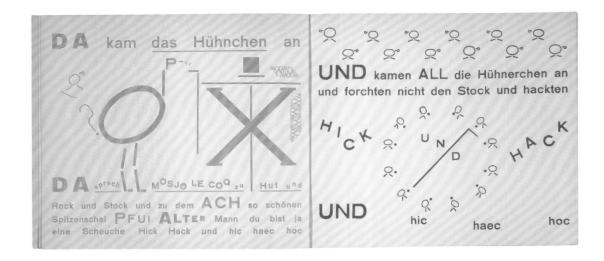

21 KURT SCHWITTERS (German, 1887–1948)
Double-page spread from *Die Scheuche*
(The scarecrow), a typographic fairy tale
published in *Merz* (nos. 14/15). 1925
8 x 9 1/2" (20.3 x 24.1 cm)
Published by Aposs Verlag, Hanover
Cotsen Children's Library, Princeton
University Library

22 BART VAN DER LECK (Dutch, 1876–1958)
Single page from *Het Vlas* (The flax)
by Hans Christian Andersen. 1941
9 13/16 x 7 1/16" (25 x 18 cm)
Published by N. V. de Spieghel, Amsterdam
Cotsen Children's Library, Princeton
University Library

23 PIET ZWART (Dutch, 1885–1977)
Het Boek van PTT (The PTT book). 1938
Rotogravure, 9 7/8 x 7" (25.1 x 17.6 cm)
Printed by Nederlandsche Rotogravure Mij.,
Leiden, the Netherlands
The Museum of Modern Art, New York.
Jan Tschichold Collection, Gift of Philip Johnson

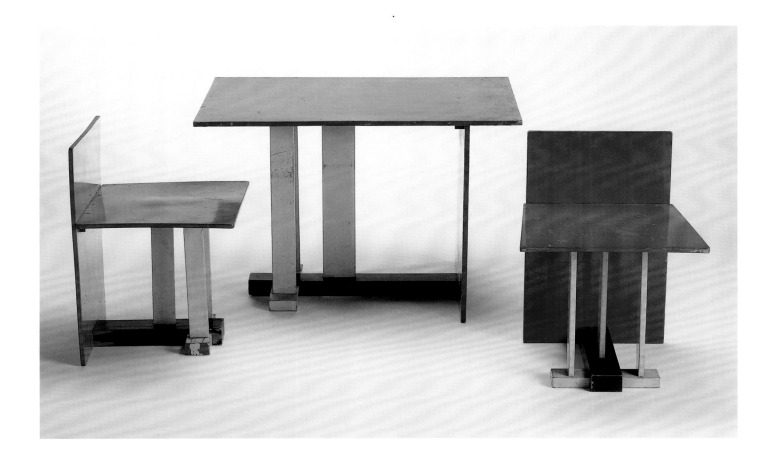

24 KO VERZUU (Dutch, 1901–1971)
Blocks. c. 1930
Painted wood, 11 7/16 x 11 7/16 x 13/16" (29 x 29 x 2 cm)
Manufactured by ADO (Arbeid door onvolwaardigen),
Apeldoorn, the Netherlands (est. 1925)
Collection Daddy Types, Washington, D.C.

25 W. M. JUTTE (Dutch, dates unknown)
Het Teekenuur, set of geometric play shapes to
accompany seven-stage teaching materials. c. 1930
Printed tin and card, 4 1/2 x 4 3/8 x 1/2"
(11.4 x 11.1 x 1.3 cm)
Published by De Boekcentrale, Amsterdam
The Museum of Modern Art, New York. Gift of
Lawrence Benenson

26 COR ALONS (Dutch, 1892–1967)
Children's furniture. 1926–27
Lacquered wood, table: 17 11/16 x 25 9/16 x 16 15/16"
(45 x 65 x 43 cm), chair (each): 17 11/16 x 13 3/8 x 12"
(45 x 34 x 30.5 cm)
Manufactured by Winterkamp en Van Putten,
The Hague
Museum Boijmans van Beuningen, Rotterdam

27 JOHAN NIEGEMAN (German, 1902–1977)
Untitled (Hans Volhard, Johan Niegeman,
and Alma Siedhoff-Buscher in a playhouse mirror). 1926–29
Gelatin silver print, 4 1/8 x 2 15/16" (10.5 x 7.5 cm)
The Museum of Modern Art, New York.
Thomas Walther Collection. Gift of Thomas Walther

*Marshalling the play of forces within us — outside of us — in work oblivious
to all else, as a festive act — means creating in the fashion of children.*
— Johannes Itten, 1919[1]

RECENT SCHOLARSHIP has revealed that the Bauhaus, especially in
the early Weimar years (1919–25), was much more playful and anarchic
than its subsequent reputation for rational design would suggest
(no. 27).[2] Walter Gropius, the founding director, preferred to downplay
this early history, notably in the 1938 Bauhaus exhibition at The Museum
of Modern Art, which he co-organized with Herbert Bayer.[3] Nonetheless,
we are now coming to appreciate the extent to which Bauhaus masters
and students were drawn to experimental play and the free flow of the
unstructured imagination in both their workshop practice and social
lives (no. 28). Many of the masters had experience of the kindergarten
movement, and it is significant that in 1924 Gropius was commissioned
to design a "Friedrich Froebelhaus" — containing a kindergarten, day
care center, youth center, and training school for mothers — at Bad
Liebenstein to mark the seventy-fifth anniversary of Friedrich Froebel's
death. Gropius planned to use a prefabricated slab construction system
for the main building and eight smaller play pavilions.[4] Though never
built, elements of the plan for an integrated educational complex were
incorporated into the new Bauhaus buildings when the school moved
to Dessau in 1925.

The master most clearly linked to the Froebel system was
Johannes Itten, who had been a kindergarten teacher before taking
up his post as director of the Bauhaus's *Vorkurs*, or preliminary course.
Itten's teaching aimed for a radical intervention in the students' mental
outlook, advocating movement, breathing exercises, and meditation
to cleanse the mind of conventional patterns of thinking. In this, he was
inspired by the unstructured approach to play and child development
championed by Froebel and Franz Cižek, his former colleague in Vienna
at the Kunstgewerbeschule (School of applied arts). As he wrote to a
friend at the start of his Bauhaus career, "I proposed that we should
prepare all sorts of games for the coming weeks. Thus in one stroke,
I have knocked out the traditional life-drawing academic approach by
leading back all creative activity to its roots in play. Those who fail at
this in my book fail as artists or students."[5] Just as a young child is
encouraged to explore and find his or her own sense of being in relation to the wider world, so were Itten's students expected to divest
themselves of older ways of thinking in order to discover a new approach
to design and creativity. Like Cižek, Itten had no specific goal in mind —

28 ALBRECHT HEUBNER (German, 1908–1945)
Thematische (nicht nur optische) Kontrastierungen
(Thematic [not just visual] contrasts), photo-
montage study for Bauhaus design course with
Joost Schmidt. c. 1928
Ink and photocollage, 16 x 23³/₈" (40.6 x 59.4 cm)
The Museum of Modern Art, New York. Acquired
through Walter Gropius

29 OSKAR SCHLEMMER (German, 1888–1943)
Poster for the *Grosse Brücken Revue*
(Great Bridge Revue). 1926
Lithograph, 44³/₁₆ x 36¹/₈" (112.3 x 91.8 cm)
Published by Städtische Bühnen, Frankfurt
Printed by Kunstanstalt Gebrüder Fey, Frankfurt
The Museum of Modern Art, New York. Abby Aldrich
Rockefeller Fund, Jan Tschichold Collection

only the sense that, by discovering something within themselves, his students would develop into imaginative individuals ready to confront the great task of designing for a new society.

Bauhaus students responded to this challenge in a number of ways that Itten could hardly have anticipated; quite apart from the diverse political and mystical sects that had been taking hold among the student body,[6] they also took to playful and experimental, even juvenile, modes of socializing. The games, fancy-dress parties, kite-flying expeditions, dances, and, judging from the many photographs of the students at leisure, a bohemian familiarity with one another, demonstrate the emergence of what we might now describe as a youth culture. As Lou Scheper, a student in the mural painting workshop, recalled, "In the early days games went hand in hand with the objective nature of the task in this Workshop as everywhere else in the school. It was like this when the canteen was being painted. Its walls and ceiling, whose furthest corners could only be reached by colour-soaked sponges thrown into the air, served as a playground for the creation of lively ornamentation of the smallest size and in the brightest colours. Working together, we painted and sprayed with both delight and a bad conscience for we knew that what we were doing was entirely non-functional."[7] This was unlike the student culture in equivalent institutions. In addition, the Bauhaus had a thriving theater design department that actively encouraged many of the more experimental performances put on at the school.

Running throughout this expressive and performative tendency in the Bauhaus was the ever-present metaphor of the child, and of children's toys as a means of encouraging adult creativity. Oskar Schlemmer's *Das Triadische Ballett* (The triadic ballet), much as it aimed to develop a new choreography based upon a limited range of movements, relied specifically on primary colors and abstracted body shapes whose paradigm lay in children's wooden dolls and puppets (no. 29). In the Bauhaus

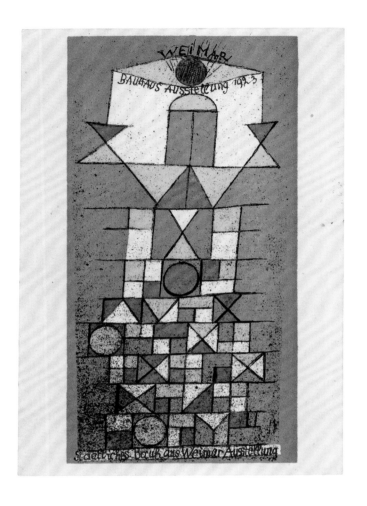

32 LUDWIG HIRSCHFELD MACK
(German, 1893–1965)
Optical Color-Mixer. 1924
Wood and cardboard, discs (each): 4"
(10.2 cm) diameter
Manufactured by Fabrikation
Spiel-Naef, Basel (est. 1954)
The Museum of Modern Art, New York.
Given anonymously

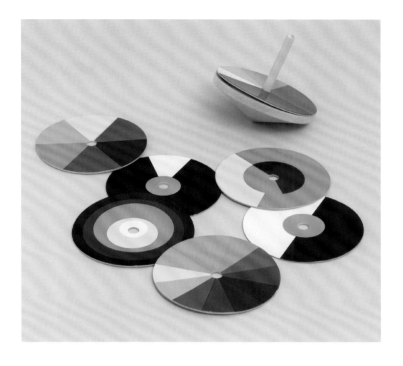

manifesto of 1923, Schlemmer emphasized that the line between puppets and human play was blurred, since "Man, self-conscious and perfect being, [is] surpassed in accuracy by every puppet."[8] In 1916, before the Bauhaus was established, Paul Klee found an escape from the horrors of war by making puppets for his beloved son Felix. It was only one of many aspects of Klee's work that sought out the pure and uncorrupted idealism of a child's vision, something he aimed to preserve in his own painting through the study and emulation of children's drawings and their re-creation of the world through stylized forms (no. 30). Klee designed and made more than fifty puppets with which he and Felix could experiment, creating miniature theater performances in their home. Puppets featured throughout the history of the Bauhaus, some growing out of studio projects and others conceived within groups of friends as both a playful diversion and an outlet for new ideas on design, drama, and performance.

Many Bauhauslers had serious views about how toys in general should be designed and how they could be used to promote a new sensibility. Experience with toy design, often as a result of idealistic attempts to bring up their own children in a new and creative manner, was common. Lyonel Feininger, one of the first appointments to the school's printmaking workshop, designed a great many toys for his son. His townscapes of carved and painted wooden houses and churches (no. 31) had a counterpart in Expressionist art and film of the time, and they were central to his own work. For example, the jagged spire of a Gothic church first carved in miniature for his son reappeared in paintings and prints, including the famous herbpiece to the first Bauhaus manifesto of 1919. Toys made for the school's Christmas market in 1919 sold well, and were felt to be a potential source of income for the new institution. As a result, masters and students from both the woodworking and theater workshops were engaged in designing toys — all of which adhered to the emerging Bauhaus aesthetic of simple geometric forms and unmodulated primary colors — throughout the next decade and beyond. Eberhard Schrammel's twirling marionette and Ludwig Hirschfeld Mack's spinning top (no. 32) and dollhouse, all from 1925, were among the most successful.

The individual most closely associated with the challenges of design for children was Alma Siedhoff-Buscher, whose career at the school takes us into some of the most problematic and contradictory aspects of the Bauhaus myth. Trained in the weaving workshop — women were at first not allowed to participate in the traditionally male crafts — she was eventually permitted to study furniture design, a field in which she went on to make her greatest contribution. Initially, however, she was restricted to designing toys for external sales, achieving some success for her toy theaters, ship models, and spinning tops. She had an ambitious conception of the importance of design for children and the potential of this area to effect change in society at large, as well as in the individual child or family. It was she who reinterpreted the principles of Bauhaus design for the nursery, creating the furniture and toys for the children's room in the Haus am Horn (no. 33), an experimental house featured in the Bauhaus exhibition of 1923. Widely regarded as the first true manifestation of the Bauhaus's modernist principles in furniture construction and domestic design, Siedhoff-Buscher's furniture exemplifies the modern aesthetic of elemental, multipurpose forms with the potential for mass production (no. 34). After the exhibition closed, the nursery furniture was purchased by a young museum curator, Nikolaus Pevsner, who was just beginning to appreciate the promise of fledgling modernism to offer a spiritual rebirth of architecture and design. Pevsner went on to place the Bauhaus at the climax of his influential history of modern design, *Pioneers of the Modern Movement*, first published in 1936 and in print ever since.[9]

Juliet Kinchin

33 ALMA SIEDHOFF-BUSCHER
(German, 1899–1944)
Haus am Horn nursery furniture. c. 1923–24
Painted wood, overall 59 1/16 x 61 x 35 7/16"
(150 x 155 x 90 cm)
Klassik Stiftung, Bauhaus-Museum, Weimar

34 HERBERT BAYER
(American, born Austria. 1900–1985)
Kinderspielschrank im Gebrauch (Children's
cabinet in use), page from *Katalog der Muster*
(Catalog of designs), sales catalog of
Bauhaus objects showing Haus am Horn
nursery furniture (cat. no. TI 24) designed
by Alma Siedhoff-Buscher. 1925
Letterpress, 8 1/4 x 11 3/4" (21 x 30 cm)
The Museum of Modern Art, New York. Jan
Tschichold Collection, Gift of Philip Johnson

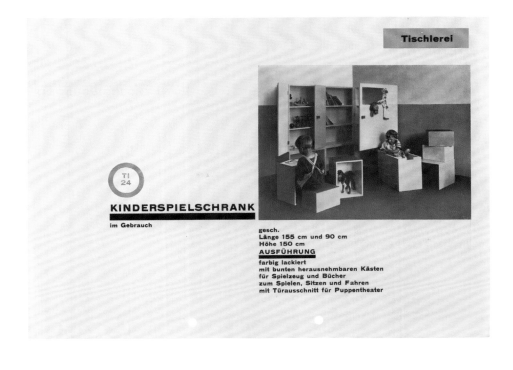

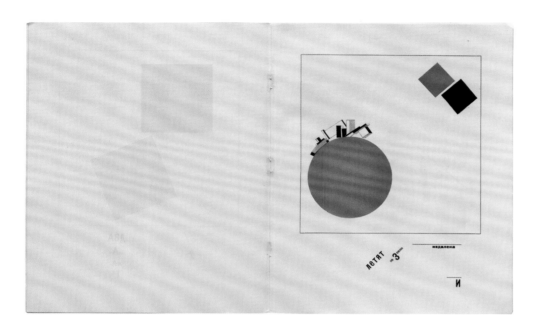

THE 1910S AND '20S in the Soviet Union, and in the city of Petrograd (Leningrad after 1924, now St. Petersburg) in particular, represent a golden age for children's books, when practitioners at the highest level of both art and literature came together in an effort to produce volumes to nurture and challenge young minds.

The universe of childhood and children's art was of broad interest within avant-garde circles of the period. Literary giants such as Aleksei Kruchenykh absorbed misspellings and transpositions, reminiscent of children's language, into poetic experiments and the development of *zaum*'s transrational structure. Artist Mikhail Larionov both collected children's drawings and included them alongside work of his contemporaries in exhibitions he organized. The Revolution of 1917 ushered in the desire to create a modern New Man, with an attendant ideology that touched all aspects of contemporary life, from the economy to education to the production of children's books. Some of the most significant artists of the day responded to the challenge, applying avant-garde artistic tactics to the creation of stimulating works for children.

In 1920 El Lissitzky created the landmark children's volume *Pro dva kvadrata. Suprematicheskii skaz v 6-ti postroikakh (Of Two Squares: A Suprematist Tale in Six Constructions)* (no. 35). Several years later, Lissitzky described the waxing power of the book, stating "[it] has become the most monumental work of art; it is no longer something that is caressed by the hands of bibliophiles; on the contrary, it is

something handled by hundreds of thousands."[1] In a book intended "for all, all children" — which appears as a dedication at the beginning — Lissitzky made the radical gesture of applying the nonobjective visual language of Suprematism to a loose narrative. The images comprise his signature vocabulary of reduced geometric forms, surging planes and vectors, and a palette of red, black, and white. Using only the sparest text, laid out in the dynamic typographic style for which he was already famous, Lissitzky tells the story of two squares, one red and one black, sent from the cosmos to battle it out and bring order to chaos. At the end of the tale, "on the black settled redly clearly," in what is often considered an allegorical retelling of the victorious Bolshevik Revolution. Though *Of Two Squares* offers an incredibly sophisticated aesthetic statement from one of the artistic pioneers of this period, in the end, the obtuse poetic terseness of Lissitzky's agitprop prose and his abstract visual language, unfamiliar to children's eyes, didn't connect with its target audience.

35 EL LISSITZKY (Russian, 1890–1941)
Double-page spread from *Pro dva kvadrata. Suprematicheskii skaz v 6-ti postroikakh (Of Two Squares: A Suprematist Tale in Six Constructions)*. 1920
Book with letterpress illustrations and typographic designs, 10 $^{15}/_{16}$ x 8 $^{7}/_{8}$" (27.8 x 22.5 cm)
Published by Skify (Scythians), Berlin
The Museum of Modern Art, New York. Jan Tschichold Collection, Gift of Philip Johnson

36 BORIS ENDER (Russian, 1893–1960)
Cover of *2 tramvaia* (2 trams) by Osip
Mandel'shtam. 1927
Book with lithographed illustrations,
10 ⁵/₁₆ x 7 ⁷/₈" (26.2 x 20 cm)
Published by Gosudarstvennoe izdatel'stvo,
Leningrad
Edition: 10,000
The Museum of Modern Art, New York.
Gift of The Judith Rothschild Foundation

37 NIKOLAI KUPREIANOV
(Russian, dates unknown)
Double-page spread from *Spor mezhdu
domami* (A dispute between buildings) by
Nikolai Agnivtsev. 1926
Book with lithographed illustrations,
10 ¹⁵/₁₆ x 8 ³/₄" (27.8 x 22.2 cm)
Published by Raduga, Leningrad
Edition: 10,000
The Museum of Modern Art, New York.
Gift of The Judith Rothschild Foundation

38 EVGENIIA EVENBAKH (Russian, 1889–1981)
Double-page spread from *Stol* (Table) by
Boris Zhitkov. 1926
Book with lithographed illustrations,
8 ⁵/₁₆ x 6 ⁷/₁₆" (21.1 x 16.3 cm)
Published by Gosudarstvennoe izdatel'stvo,
Leningrad
Edition: 10,000
The Museum of Modern Art, New York.
Gift of The Judith Rothschild Foundation

Many projects resulted from joint efforts between avant-garde
artists and writers and touched on a range of subjects, including
transportation in a volume by painter Boris Ender and populist poet
Osip Mandel'shtam (no. 36); life in a humming city by Nikolai Kupreianov
and Nikolai Agnivtsev (no. 37); and the journey of manufacturing
by the prolific team of Evgeniia Evenbakh and Boris Zhitkov (no. 38).
One of the most esteemed of such collaborations was to be between
Sergei Treti'akov, an acclaimed poet, playwright, and journalist, and
Constructivist photographer Aleksandr Rodchenko. The basis of their
planned—but never realized—children's book, *Samozveri* (Autoanimals),
was a poem by Treti'akov that described animals in whimsical detail,
addressing their physical characteristics, and ascribing to them anthropomorphized traits:

> Busy with affairs quite important,
> Carrying a burden is the elephant.
> He has a collected character
> As he pumps water and hauls lumber.
> The elephant's life is very long,
> For three hundred years he goes on strong.
> Go ahead, try and see
> If the elephant with his knee
> Picks
>   his
>   trunk[2]

Rodchenko was known for his radical experiments with photomontage and cinema, studies of light and shadow, and dramatic cropping and perspectives. But together with his wife, artist Varvara
Stepanova, he responded to Treti'akov's work with charming cardboard
dioramas: three-dimensional depictions of broadly smiling boys, girls,
and beasts, built of a simple geometry of circles, squares, cylinders,
and rectangles (no. 39). Photographed in black-and-white, the sets
show the influence of the artist's photographic work, with the cast
shadows of his cardboard figures as integral to the compositions
as the constructions themselves.[3] Alfred H. Barr, Jr., then a young
art historian and professor who would later become the director of
The Museum of Modern Art, saw this volume on a visit to Treti'akov's
home in 1927. The very next day, December 29, Barr bought the first
of more than forty-five Russian children's books he collected during
his three-month trip.

Some of the most lasting monuments of children's books from
this period come from the team of artist Vladimir Lebedev and author
Samuil Marshak. Lebedev's artistic ideas were highly cultivated and
politically engaged, and his philosophy about children's books was clear:
they should be, in his words, "colorful, specific, concrete,"[4] and find
a balance between sophistication and accessibility, high and low.
He drew on Cubism and Suprematism, but never fully abandoned figu-
ration, offering a familiar anchor to children while introducing them
to new visual modes, an approach visible in *Bagazh* (*Baggage*) (no. 40).
Likewise, Marshak's goal was to create a new literature, one that
nourished the intellectual and visual imagination. The two began collaborating in 1924, with books so popular that they were often issued
in massive editions of 10,000 with reprints not far behind.

In *Vchera i segodnia* (Yesterday and Today) (no. 41) Lebedev
and Marshak create contrasts in both form and content. On the cover,
sketchy monochromes show the hunched, overburdened figures of
the past set against the bright, upright, stencil-like forms of the ever-

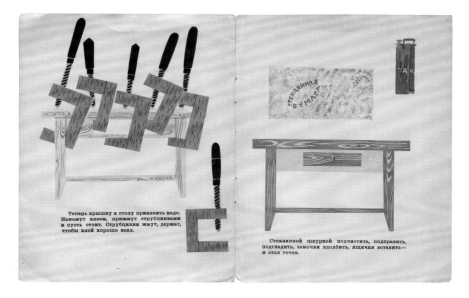

advancing present. Inside, new technologies are championed over old: an outmoded pen-and-ink manuscript page dotted with messy ink blotches, for example, juxtaposed with a neatly typed serif font, below which appears an image of that wondrous new machine, the typewriter. This gentle advocating for revolutionary ideals in the name of progress can be seen in a number of their other works. *Morozhenoe* (*Ice Cream*) (no. 42) tells the story of an insatiable businessman who eats so much ice cream that he turns into a snowman, illustrated with reduced geometric forms — its flatness and syncopated repetition calling to mind a more easily digestible version of Lissitzky's Suprematism.

By the late 1920s, the Stalinist crackdown had begun, and the government was soon censoring many more publications than they approved. With Lebedev pushed away from his modernist aesthetic experiments and toward state-sponsored Social Realism, this short-lived golden era drew to a close. However, the influence of these children's volumes reverberated in international avant-garde circles. In 1929, the venerable Swiss-born French poet Blaise Cendrars, whose own

artistic collaborations included volumes with Fernand Léger and Sonia Delaunay-Terk, organized an exhibition of Russian children's books. Held in Paris, *Exposition le livre d'enfant en U.R.S.S.* included books and posters made during the preceding years by Lebedev and his colleagues. Along with other foreign exhibitions, Cendrars's show provided an international platform by which the volumes found broad exposure. The result was generations of reprints and translations in multiple languages, establishing these examples as monuments of the era, the product of artistic collaboration at the highest level intended to stimulate the eyes and minds of young comrades.

Sarah Suzuki

39 ALEKSANDR RODCHENKO
(Russian, 1891–1956)
Elephant, illustration for the unpublished
children's book *Samozveri* (Autoanimals)
by Sergei Treti'akov. 1926–27
Gelatin silver print, 8^{15}/$_{16}$ x 6^{11}/$_{16}$" (22.7 x 17 cm)
The Museum of Modern Art, New York. Gift of
Anne Ehrenkranz in honor of Philip Johnson

40 VLADIMIR LEBEDEV (Russian, 1891–1967)
Double-page spread from *Bagazh* (*Baggage*)
by Samuil Marshak. 1926
Book with lithographed illustrations,
7^{1}/$_{2}$ x 5^{7}/$_{8}$" (19 x 15 cm)
Published by Raduga, Leningrad
Edition: 30,000
The Museum of Modern Art, New York.
Gift of The Judith Rothschild Foundation

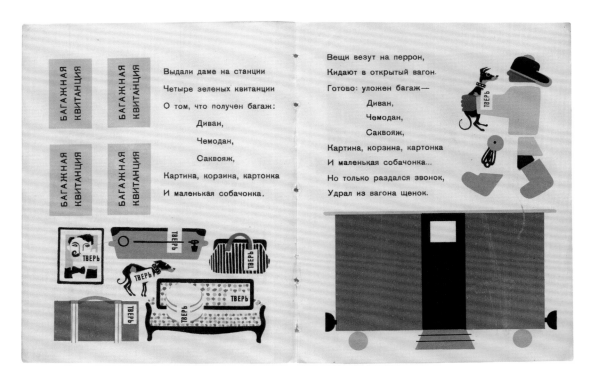

41 VLADIMIR LEBEDEV (Russian, 1891–1967)
Cover of *Vchera i segodnia* (Yesterday and today)
by Samuil Marshak. 1925
Book with lithographed illustrations,
11 x 8 3/8" (28 x 21.3 cm)
Published by Raduga, Leningrad
Edition: 10,000
The Museum of Modern Art, New York.
Gift of The Judith Rothschild Foundation

42 VLADIMIR LEBEDEV (Russian, 1891–1967)
Double-page spread from *Morozhenoe* (Ice Cream)
by Samuil Marshak. 1925
Book with lithographed illustrations,
10 7/8 x 8 9/16" (27.7 x 21.7 cm)
Published by Raduga, Leningrad
Edition: 10,000
The Museum of Modern Art, New York.
Gift of The Judith Rothschild Foundation

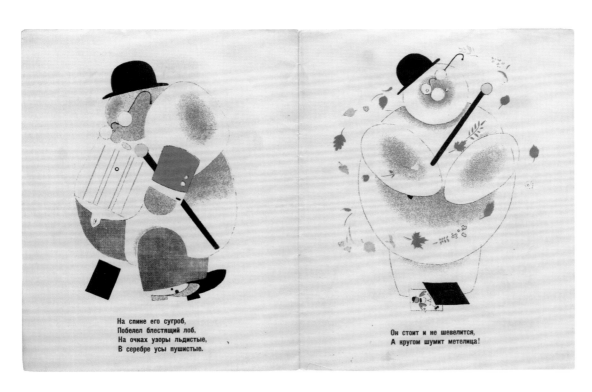

43 JOAQUÍN TORRES-GARCÍA
(Uruguayan, 1874–1949)
Three Figures. c. 1925
Painted wood, twelve interchangeable pieces,
dimensions variable
Daniela Chappard Foundation

AS CASE STUDIES, the modernist toys of Joaquín Torres-García and Ladislav Sutnar embody a combination of utopian aspiration and commercial failure between the two World Wars. While not personally connected, these two designers (Uruguayan and Czechoslovak, respectively) shared a modernist belief in the social value of art, and viewed well-designed toys as an important means of shaping the values of a new generation living in a modern world. "As the First World War ended, we who had returned from the front — the new, war-matured generation — brought with us a firm will to rethink, re-evaluate, and alter the principles and hopes that the war had proven to be false," wrote Sutnar in 1961.[1] In his later years, Torres-García would call children's education his destiny.[2] The pursuit of their beliefs involved the two men in a long chain of efforts to manufacture, package, advertise, and sell the toys they designed. But in practice, the political and commercial reality of the times circumscribed the realization of each of their visions.

Like many avant-garde artists in desperate financial straits after World War I, Torres-García complemented his sculptural practice of experimental abstractions in wood with play objects, which he viewed as a valid form of artistic expression. It is perhaps ironic that toy design, teaching art, and the education of children were to inform the majority of his professional life, when as a child in Montevideo he had run away from school so often that his parents were forced to allow him to be homeschooled. During his tenure as a teacher of art and handicrafts

in a progressive kindergarten in Barcelona, Torres-García would formulate some of his most enduring theories on education, creativity, and interactive play. He laid particular stress on the importance of supplying the child with abstract components rather than ready-made or fully constructed copies of objects found in daily life or in nature, believing instead that it was from combining and building with such shapes — which did not inspire preconceived notions as to a "correct" combination— that the child would most fully benefit creatively.

Both as a teacher and a parent, Torres-García had observed that a majority of children, when given a toy car or train, immediately attempted to remove the wheels of the toy, at times even breaking the object, an occurrence that frequently elicited a sense of guilt in the child. Realizing this, he began making a series of robust wooden figures (both humans and animals) that could be pulled apart and easily reassembled (nos. 43, 44). The creative potential inherent in such toys, with their interchangeable torsos, feet, and heads, is likewise present in his Numerario, which allowed the child to order, stack, disassemble, and reassemble the buildings, bridges, and other elements of a village streetscape (no. 45).

After moving to New York City in 1921, Torres-García set up the Aladdin Toys company to manufacture his *"juguetes transformables"* (transformable toys). During the short life of this company, he wrote and published his own catalogs, in which each toy was illustrated on

44 JOAQUÍN TORRES-GARCÍA
(Uruguayan, 1874–1949)
Birds. 1927–28
Painted wood, eight interchangeable pieces,
dimensions variable
Daniela Chappard Foundation

45 JOAQUÍN TORRES-GARCÍA
(Uruguayan, 1874–1949)
Village with Numbers. 1928
Painted wood, ten interchangeable pieces,
dimensions variable
Private collection, New York

46 LADISLAV SUTNAR (American, born
Bohemia [now Czech Republic]. 1897–1976)
Toy rhinoceros. c. 1930
Turned and painted wood, $3\,^1/_8$ x $3\,^1/_8$ x $6\,^5/_{16}$"
(8 x 8 x 16 cm)
Manufactured by State Institute for
Home Industry, Prague
Museum of Decorative Arts, Prague

47 MINKA PODHAJSKÁ (Czechoslovak, born Moravia [now Czech Republic]. 1881–1963) Series of personifications of childhood misdeeds. 1930 Painted wood, largest: 5 1/8" (13 cm) tall Museum of Decorative Arts, Prague

48 LADISLAV SUTNAR (American, born Bohemia [now Czech Republic]. 1897–1976) Poster for the exhibition *Mezinárodní výstava hraček a učebných pomůcek* (International toys and teaching aids), Prague. 1930 Letterpress, 18 1/8 x 24 13/16" (46 x 63 cm) Museum of Decorative Arts, Prague

two sheets — one laid out as parts in its box and the other displaying multiple combinations of the parts. He received important international orders from Paul & Marjorie Abbatt Ltd in London, and the Dutch furnishing store Metz & Co., among others, which encouraged him to begin searching for a European base and new, cheaper methods for producing his toys. Following a disastrous fire in the Aladdin factory in 1925, Torres-García decided to leave New York for good, eventually settling in Paris in 1926. When the Parisian department store Au Printemps placed an order for seven hundred sets of his toys for Christmas in 1927 (eight thousand pieces total), Torres-García enlisted a local carpenter to cut out the basic shapes, which he and a group of family and friends then finished by painting and boxing. In the end, despite continued efforts to perfect his toys and to market them to ever wider groups of consumers in the United States and Europe, large-scale manufacture never proved financially viable for the designer. Turning increasingly to painting from about 1929–30, Torres-García's work would, however, continue to display references to his wooden toy figures and their abstract, interchangeable parts for years to come.

Like Torres-García, Sutnar maintained a compulsive interest in the world of children throughout his career. In 1921, while still a student at the School of Applied Arts in Prague, he began designing sets and puppets for marionette theaters in a radical abstract manner. This first venture into theater design would inspire his interest in performance and, above all, in the role of creative play as the mainspring of his aesthetic thinking. At the same time he began designing wooden toys — like puppets, part of a long tradition in the region (no. 46). These early toys also relied on simple woodworking techniques. For Sutnar, these basic, elemental forms — rectangles and cylinders — were more than a convenience. He deplored the naturalistic toys that dominated the international market but that did little to stimulate a child's imagination or develop basic sensory, motor, and intellectual skills. In this he was not alone. Minka Podhajská, who had established a reputation for artistic toy design before World War I, was similarly committed to the modern treatment of traditional Czech toys (no. 47).

The Prague-based Artel Cooperative, established in 1908 along the lines of the Wiener Werkstätte, produced handmade toys based on the designs of both Podhajská and Sutnar, but the latter dreamed of competing in the mass market. Only then could he envisage a revolution in the consciousness of children, for which toys would be catalysts of the new age that most modernists believed was waiting to be born. The poster he designed for the 1930 *Mezinárodní výstava hraček a učebných pomůcek* (International toys and teaching aids exhibition) in Prague (no. 48) reaffirmed his identification of the modern world with design for children. Here, within the geometric forms of the so-called New Typography, a photograph of one of Sutnar's toy trains, viewed from a dynamic angle, stands for the tempo of modern life and the future development of the national toy industry in the newly formed state of Czechoslovakia. In a related advertisement featuring the same photograph, the selling points of Sutnar's toys in an international market — and by association modern Czechoslovak toys in general — were identified as "simple, cheap, beautiful, artistic" (*einfach*, *billig*, *schön*, *künstlerische*).[3]

49 LADISLAV SUTNAR (American, born Bohemia [now Czech Republic]. 1897–1976)
Build the Town building blocks. 1940–43
Painted wood, thirty pieces of various dimensions, largest smokestack: 7 3/8 x 2" (18.7 x 5.1 cm)
The Museum of Modern Art, New York. Gift of Ctislav Sutnar and Radoslav Sutnar

50 LADISLAV SUTNAR (American, born Bohemia [now Czech Republic]. 1897–1976)
Promotional print for Build the Town building blocks. c. 1943
Silkscreen, 8 1/2 x 11 1/16" (21.6 x 28.1 cm)
The Museum of Modern Art, New York. Gift of Radoslav Sutnar

In 1922 Sutnar had designed a set of painted wooden building blocks, the first in a series of construction toys that he would come to regard as central to his larger ideas about design and modern life. Like many educational reformers of the previous century, Sutnar believed in the cognitive power of a visual language rooted in elemental shapes and colors, and in 1926 he designed another set of blocks called Factory Town (Tavern most) that was inspired by contemporary American factories and their attendant planned communities. For Sutnar, building entire cities with blocks gave the child an awareness of form and structure that made direct reference to modern functionalist architecture, but also a sense of the forces that shape a community. Sutnar described these lessons as "mental vitamins necessary for the right development of a child."[4] Through them, he hoped to stimulate bold spatial experimentation, encourage patience, and instill a sense of the planning necessary for fast-growing urban areas.

Unfortunately, Factory Town was not a commercial success. Nor was his next effort, titled American, from 1930. Even after he emigrated to the United States in 1939, Sutnar kept his ideas for a popular building toy alive, and between 1940 and 1943 he produced a series of prototypes for a set that would be called Build the Town (no. 49). Sutnar went so far as to design promotional silkscreen prints, in his most elegant graphic manner (no. 50). But he could not find a reliable manufacturer for the blocks, and retailers passed on the project. Sutnar continued to work successfully in the field of graphic design, becoming both one of the leading advocates of modernist principles in commercial design and a pioneer of information graphics. The failure to bring his construction toys to a mass market, however, seems to have haunted his later years. "Toys are selected by adults and given to children,"

he wrote in his 1961 book *Visual Design in Action: Principles, Purposes*. "For merchandising reasons, they are often made to appeal more to the childishness of an adult than to the child. Only the vitality of an imaginative toy design of high standards can help a child's creativity to grow and be fun to the adult as well."[5]

Juliet Kinchin

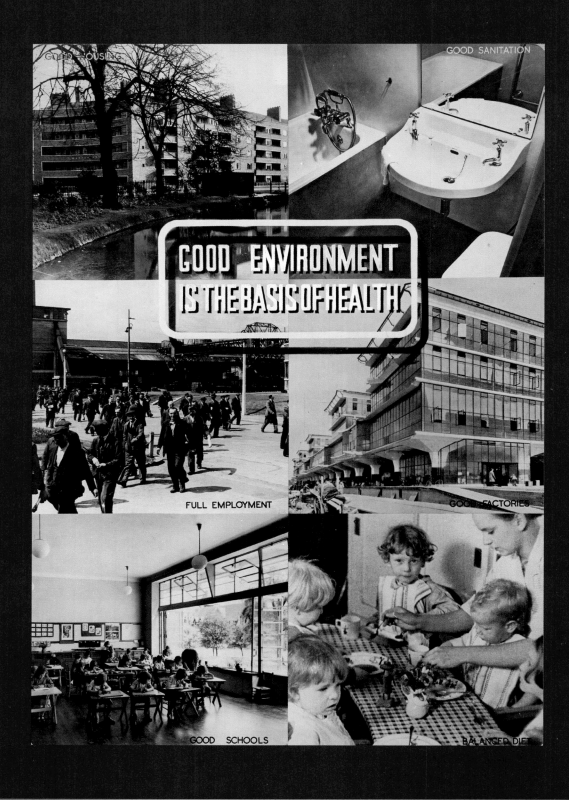

INTRODUCTION

The protection of health is of equal importance to the protection of life. It is rank injustice to children in this age to permit them to suffer from lack of ample light, good air, sufficient heat, cleanliness and comfort.
    —Samuel A. Challman, 1921[1]

Let us bring up a generation with a desire for cleanliness of the deeper things of life and they will cleanse society of all its dirt!
    —Dr. Benzion Liber, 1927[2]

MODERNISM, as a reforming social project, revealed its greatest idealism and its most practical application in design for children between the two world wars. Children were already well-established symbols of an optimistic future, but the modernists united a concern for health and safety in the child's environment with a determination to transform society. There was a core belief in the idea that modern architecture could address the problems of overcrowded housing, unsanitary conditions, and the limited prospects of poorer children.

Despite massive economic obstacles, modernist architects and designers committed themselves to building a new society and looked to schools, health centers, playrooms, toys, books, and clothing as agents of social change. Working in collaboration with a new generation of education and health-care specialists, they highlighted the need for "science" and "rationalism" combined with systematic analysis of the wider social and economic factors that impacted children's lives. According to a number of psychological studies, for example, children possessed a heightened appreciation of simple geometric forms, smooth surfaces, and bold color, which made them potentially more receptive than adults to modern design.

Both educational and design reformers believed that modern essentials of light and air, hygiene and fitness should permeate all aspects of a child's early environments. Physical education, delivered through schools and clubs, encouraged children to participate in modern forms of dance, gymnastics, sport, and play, whether as a means of inculcating collective values, teamwork, and conformity or of promoting individualism, health, and self-expression. School buildings in particular were viewed as crucial to the absorption and spread of modernist values. Harnessing the language of abstraction as well as new materials and industrial production, the new modern schools were simple, light, and flexible: a tabula rasa upon which the modern child could inscribe his or her identity. The utopian society of the future, it was argued, would have the same dynamic curiosity, openness, and unaffected simplicity as children themselves. Children would become the agents of a systematic modernization of traditional culture, the front line in the assault on bourgeois taste and values, and the heralds of the new way of life.

If the built environment was central to shaping the larger awareness of modern society, the mental environment of the child also required attention. Interactive play with picture books and artistic toys led children on spatial, temporal, and imaginative journeys into the wider world of modern things and ideas, preparing them to function as members of an industrialized society and mass culture. Through addressing mind, body, and the physical environment, modern design for children was to lay the foundations for lives of constructive work and healthy leisure.

Juliet Kinchin

See page 113

1 ERNŐ GOLDFINGER (British, born Hungary. 1902–1987)
Good Environment Is the Basis of Health, photomontage
panel for the exhibition *Health*, organized by the Army Bureau
of Current Affairs, London. 1943
Photolithograph, 26 3/4 x 18 15/16" (68 x 48.1 cm)
RIBA Library Drawings and Archives Collection, London

IN THE OPENING CHAPTER of her book *The Century of the Child* (1900), Ellen Key pictured the advent of the twentieth century as "a small naked child, descending upon the earth, but drawing himself back in terror at the sight of a world bristling with weapons."[1] That tiny figure was invested with the potential of physical and psychical transformation, "of a closer reciprocal action between the external and internal world; of the mastery over disease, of the prolongation of life and youth."[2] In little more than a decade, the world surveyed by Key's emblematic child would be engulfed in a modern war of global proportions waged with foot soldiers, mechanized weapons, and poison gas. The loss of human life and the extent of human mutilation and suffering was unprecedented in what came to be known as the war to end all wars.

The social and psychological results of that conflict were profound, affecting how people thought about the future and about children. The poor health of many young army recruits, together with the influenza pandemic of 1918–19 that took more lives than the war (estimated to be between twenty and forty million), triggered an almost obsessive concern with children's health. This preoccupation led to a new emphasis on physical culture, the design of healthier clothing, medical products for children, and graphic propaganda about new lifestyles, promoting everything from diet to exercise. As a symbolic entity, the child's body was inscribed with the paradoxical pressures of modernity, signifying on the one hand a connection with nature, primal emotion, and unrestrained psychic energy, and on the other the concept of a perfectible human machine that could be conditioned to function within a utopian, modern world.

Expressive, natural movement was an important part of new education methods developed in the early twentieth century. James Liberty Tadd, for example, emphasized the physical nature of drawing and talked about "speaking through the fingertips" in a manual that was widely read in Europe and the United States; "I am firmly convinced that the better and firmer the union of each hand with its proper hemisphere of the brain...the better the brain and mind and the better the thought, the reason and the imagination will be" (see "The Kindergarten Movement: Building Blocks of Modern Design," p. 30).[3] Another key figure, Rudolf Steiner, included eurythmic exercises — in which pupils inscribed increasingly complex forms on surrounding space, occasionally with the aid of rods or balls, creating a kind of visible speech through their bodies — in the curriculum of the first German Waldorf school (established 1919) as a way to develop powers of concentration and

coordination. Eurythmy was a cornerstone of Steiner's anthroposophy, connecting an individual with the creative forces of nature, "an inexhaustible source of the infinite."[4] A similar quasi-mystical belief in the psychological and therapeutic power of expressive movement inspired pioneers of modern dance education in Europe and the United States, among them Isadora Duncan, Émile Jaques-Dalcroze, Rudolf von Laban, and Margaret Morris, all of whom established private schools for children (no. 2). Classes were frequently conducted outdoors, and emphasized a natural athleticism. Touring troupes of scantily clad girls trained by Isadora Duncan — the Isadorables — and Margaret Morris's Dancing Children performed with bare feet and loose hair, causing a public sensation before and after World War I.

With medical experts and educators endorsing the beneficial effects of modern dance and gymnastics on academic performance as well as general physical and psychological health, a growing number of schools took up the new approaches to body and exercise, offering improved gym facilities and classes that departed from regimented, militaristic drills in favor of expressive movement (no. 3). Girls in particular benefited from the increased mobility and encouragement to participate in sport or dance; the liberation from self-conscious body inhibition

2 TIMES WIDE WORLD PHOTOS
(American, active 1919–1941)
"A Famous School of Dance Has a Birthday,"
class at an Isadora Duncan dance school. c. 1929
Gelatin silver print, 4 $^{13}/_{16}$ x 6 $^{7}/_{8}$" (12.2 x 17.5 cm)
The Museum of Modern Art, New York. The New
York Times Collection

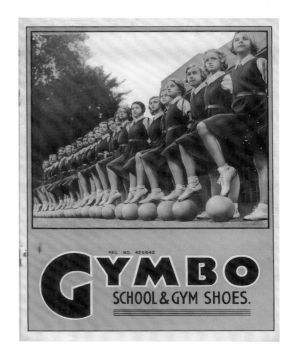

3 JOSEF SUDEK (Czechoslovak, 1896–1976)
Kindergarten exercise. 1934–35
Gelatin silver print, 5$^{1}/_{4}$ x 3$^{1}/_{3}$" (13.4 x 8.5 cm)
Museum of Decorative Arts, Prague

5 LADISLAV SUTNAR (American, born
Bohemia [now Czech Republic]. 1897–1976)
Design for a cover of the magazine *Žijeme*
(We live). 1931
Collage on board, 23$^{5}/_{8}$ x 16$^{1}/_{8}$" (60 x 41 cm)
Museum of Decorative Arts, Prague

4 Advertisement for Gymbo School &
Gym Shoes. c. 1930
Letterpress and photogravure, 12$^{5}/_{16}$ x 9$^{1}/_{2}$"
(31.2 x 24.2 cm)
Published by Ashworths Ltd, Bury, UK
Printed by Shepherd and Markham Ltd, London
Alasdair Peebles, London

6 ALEKSANDR RODCHENKO
(Russian, 1891–1956)
Physical-culture Parade. 1936
Gelatin silver print, 11$^{1}/_{8}$ x 19$^{1}/_{8}$" (28.2 x 48.6 cm)
The Museum of Modern Art, New York. David H.
McAlpin Fund

7 JOHN RIDEOUT (American, 1898–1951) and
HAROLD VAN DOREN (American, 1895–1957)
Skippy-Racer. c. 1933
Steel, paint, wood, and rubber, 31³/₄ x 43³/₁₆ x 6¹/₂"
(80.6 x 109.7 x 16.5 cm)
Minneapolis Institute of Arts. Gift of funds from
Don and Diana Lee Lucker

8 ISAMU NOGUCHI (American, 1904–1988)
Playground equipment for Ala Moana Park, Hawaii
(unrealized). 1939
Painted metal and tape, slide: 4⁵/₈ x 10¹/₄ x 8¹/₂"
(11.7 x 26 x 21.6 cm); jungle gym: 4⁵/₈ x 3 x 3"
(11.7 x 7.6 x 7.6 cm); swing: 7¹/₈ x 12 x 6³/₈"
(18.1 x 30.5 x 16.2 cm)
The Isamu Noguchi Foundation and Garden
Museum, New York

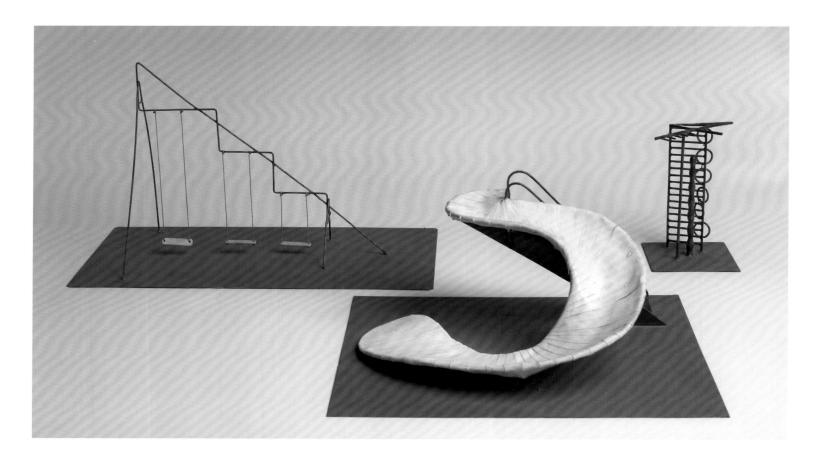

9 Children during a light-therapy session,
as reproduced in *Le Visage de l'enfance*
(The face of childhood). 1937
Published by Horizons de France, Paris
The Museum of Modern Art Library, New York

and timid behavior perceived as conventionally feminine was more pronounced than for boys. After World War I, teaching physical education in schools also opened up to women as a new career field.[5]

Innovations in children's clothing were initially applied to activewear to accommodate the new emphasis on movement. A British advertisement for "Gymbo, the happy shoes" (no. 4) emphasizes the "absolute freedom" given to every part of the foot by the rubber-soled canvas shoes that were required for all pupils in 1930s schools.[6] For children in Britain and elsewhere, modern activewear also meant minimal use of trimmings and decorative fabrics (such as the ubiquitous gym slip as worn by girls in the Gymbo advertisement), and often consisted of interchangeable parts. Dress reformers highlighted the rationality and versatility of playsuits and T-shirts for boys and girls as suited to modern life. Dutch modernist architect Jan Duiker drew a parallel between the new spirit in 1920s architecture and light hygienic clothing such as T-shirts that are "popular among young people"; clothing, like architecture, could help to shape a new "functional society."[7] Similarly, a boy on the 1931 cover of the Czechoslovak magazine *Žijeme* (We live), designed by Ladislav Sutnar, wears a playsuit (no. 5), signifying the spirit of modernization and progress.

The new state of Czechoslovakia (created 1920) placed great emphasis on modern forms of physical culture, highlighting how children's movement and clothing could sometimes be seen as an extension of political beliefs or systems. From age six, most boys and girls participated in Sokol, a sports and gymnastics movement initially founded as part of a wider resistance to imperial Hapsburg domination. A French commentator described in 1937 how "the smallest village has its *soklovna*, containing a gym, a theatre and a library for the rational cultivation of the body and spirit. The Sokols consider everyone like brothers and sisters and teach themselves.... Children are put through movements, often holding flags or hoops that they move together rhythmically.... This organization embodies the spirit of the nation."[8]

The spectacle of massed, smiling children moving in unison made a powerful statement about national efficiency and strength, and in all countries, children were on occasion involved in massed displays that subjugated individual difference in statements of group allegiance. This was particularly so in the Soviet Union, where displays of collective, military-style discipline helped to homogenize an ethnically diverse population (no. 6). The Skippy-Racer (no. 7), on the other hand, mass-produced in Toledo, Ohio, was expressive of a material culture of personal freedom, mobility, and consumer choice. Advertising emphasized

its stylish modern streamlining, speed, and new features like ball-bearing wheels. Priced at $4.95, it was nevertheless beyond the reach of many children still living in abject poverty during the Depression — and thus a reminder of the uneven reach of modern design.

Advances in medical knowledge and behavioral psychology contributed to a sounder understanding of the environmental conditions needed for the proper physical and mental development of young children (see "Urban Health: Two Centers," p. 118). There was general consensus that access to plenty of fresh air, sunlight, and water was a route to health.[9] One strategy was to remove children from cities altogether, at least temporarily (see "To the Mountains and the Sea," p. 114); another was to improve public access to swimming pools and playgrounds (no. 8).

In terms of product design, new artificial sunlamps were introduced to treat malnutrition, rickets, and tuberculosis (no. 9), all scourges of children among the urban poor. There was also a belief in medical circles that arrested development, both mental and physical, could be rectified by proper feeding (no. 10). The industrial manufacture of artificial proteins like Nutricia, a Dutch powdered milk substitute, helped to extend the shelf life of perishable food in homes without refrigeration. Nutricia was one of a new generation of products used to battle malnutrition and high levels of infant mortality. Modern graphic design assisted in the promotion of such brands while also helping to allay consumer suspicions. Paul Schuitema's photomontage of smiling children and a mass society (no. 11) suggested both the widespread appeal and the modernity of the product. The question of children's nutrition, however, was also political. In 1930s Vienna, Friedl Dicker produced a poster about child starvation for the local Communist party (no. 12), using photomontage and statistical graphics to make a compelling case for the measurable impact of inflation and spiraling unemployment on children's health. In this poster, a process of social degeneration is starkly imprinted on the interwar child's body, rather than progress toward a sunny utopia.

Juliet Kinchin

10 LEWIS HINE (American, 1874–1940)
Boy with glass of milk, classroom. 1931
Gelatin silver print, 19 7/8 x 15 1/2" (50.5 x 39.4 cm)
Avery Architectural and Fine Arts Library,
Columbia University, New York

11 PAUL (GEERT PAUL HENDRIKUS) SCHUITEMA
(Dutch, 1897–1973)
Nutricia, le lait en poudre (Nutricia, powdered milk).
1927–28
Letterpress, 14 1/2 x 11 13/16" (36.8 x 30 cm)
The Museum of Modern Art, New York. Jan
Tschichold Collection, Gift of Philip Johnson

12 FRIEDL DICKER (Austrian, 1898–1944)
Die Lösung der Probleme der Ernährungswissenschaft ist
(The solution to nutrition problems). c. 1933
Photomontage and collage, original size
approx. 47 1/4 x 39 3/8" (120 x 100 cm)
Universität für angewandte Kunst Wien,
Kunstsammlung und Archiv, Vienna

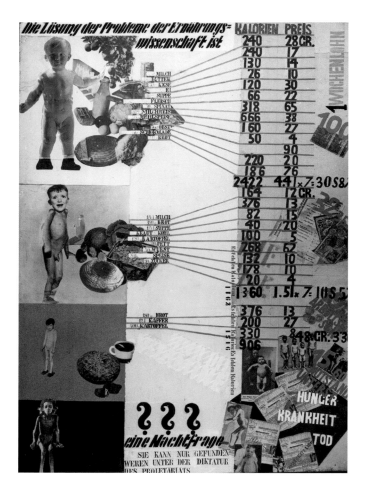

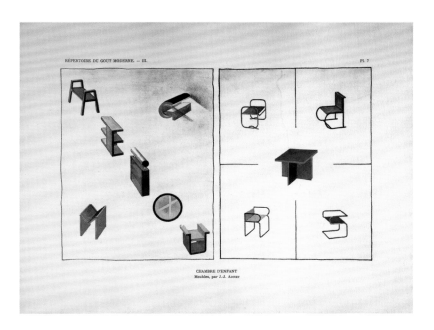

13 J.-J. ADNET (Jacques Adnet [French, 1900–1984]; Jean Adnet [French, 1900–1995]) *Chambre d'enfant: Meubles* (Child's room: furniture), plate 7 from *Répertoire du goût moderne III* (Compendium of modern taste III). 1929
Pochoir by Jean Saudé
Pochoir, 10 ¹/₄ x 13 ³/₈" (26 x 34 cm)
Published by Éditions Albert Lévy, Paris
The Mitchell Wolfson Jr. Private Collection, Miami

"TO MAKE EVERY WALL a copy book and every corner a lesson appeared at one time to be the ideal," wrote design critic John Gloag of the modern nursery in 1922.[1] He preferred simple hygienic and practical schemes considered from a child's point of view, using modern materials and bold uncluttered forms to provide "good light, good colour and living interest."[2] In the 1920s and '30s the shift away from a severely didactic approach paralleled developments in progressive education that emphasized child-centered perspectives and learning through play. Gloag believed the nursery should be "an adaptable background and never too purposeful. The walls must not say: 'We are here to interest you,' they must be able to cooperate with all the varied range of fancy, and say: 'We're here to back up any game you like to play.'"[3] Such sentiments were echoed in literature on household taste in Europe and the United States, a genre closely tied to a tradition of design reform since the late nineteenth century, in which the home was constantly described as a formative influence on children's health, morality, and spiritual growth. Modernist designers set out to reshape the middle-class home, stressing functional beauty and cutting through what was characterized as a suffocating accumulation of things. Simple schemes, it was thought, would release children's energy and encourage mobility.[4]

As the principal guardians of children's education and well-being in the home, middle-class women were bombarded with advice from designers, medical experts, psychologists, and educators, whose interests converged around the topic of hygiene and fresh air. As Dr. Benzion Liber wrote in 1927, "Everyone hears and reads much these days about the importance of fresh air for the health of the body, but very few people will have the courage to admit that they spend most of their time indoors.... Room-bred children, no matter how much they have learned in schools and books, are ignorant, have a narrow horizon, are more inclined to homocentrism and egocentrism than others. They suffer not only from blood anaemia, but also from moral anaemia.... Children of all ages will profit from being kept outside a great deal.... Let the child be where he is happiest. We owe it to him."[5] On behalf of their children, interwar mothers were pressured to keep up with medical knowledge, and to manifest that knowledge through new standards of cleanliness in children's spaces.[6] "Hygiene is the basis of room arrangements these days," wrote French critic Henri Clouzot in 1934, adding, "This does not necessarily mean encasing our infants in steel and glass like laboratory specimens, but making everything fresh and clear. First and foremost, that means eliminating anything that traps germs and dust."[7] Le Corbusier's famous diatribe against dust, dirt, and ornament in *Towards a New Architecture* (1923) included the injunction, "Teach your children that a house is only habitable when it is full of light and air, and when the floors and walls are clear. To keep your floors in order eliminate heavy furniture and thick carpets" (no. 13).[8]

Arch. Marcel Breuer

A scientific approach to domestic modernism drew on new trends in "biological" psychology, which suggested that children's behavior could be shaped and controlled by a process of reinforcing natural reflex responses to an external stimulus. The so-called Little Albert study, conducted in 1920 by John B. Watson and his assistant Rosalie Rayner, was a landmark and widely reported experiment in this field (one that would not be repeated today). Watson was able to produce a conditioned response of fear in an eleven-month-old child by repeatedly associating white, furry animals and objects with a very loud noise, and emphasized the manipulation of the child's environment as the critical mechanism for learning.[9] In his dystopian novel *Brave New World* (1932), however, Aldous Huxley explored the wider ethical implications of cultural conditioning through design, describing working-class children as being conditioned by the state to dislike books and flowers or natural objects in order to fit into preassigned future roles. Scientific method was also often used to normalize gender relations and occupations. Starting with the assumptions that there is "a natural evolution of taste" and that the evolution could be fostered and developed, a study conducted by John Littlejohns in 1933 systematically tested and quantified the responses of children, aged eleven to fifteen, to varied examples of "good" (modern and/or modernist) and "bad" (decorative and/or historicist) design.[10] Of the sixteen hundred children tested in seven different schools, the majority of boys showed preferences for plain, simple forms and good proportion, dismissing "weaknesses of illogical construction and vulgarity of flamboyant elaboration."[11] By contrast, the study found that girls were seduced by "prettiness," color, and

ornament. What is more, girls' taste appeared to "deteriorate" the older they got. The authors did conclude that this disparity could be addressed by improvements in the design of the school environment and teaching of crafts in the national curriculum.

Modernist architects and designers did not have a monopoly on concepts of hygiene and practicality, but their use of simple, minimalist schemes, built-in features, and washable surfaces stood up to the wear and tear of boisterous young people. Recessed lighting, for example, avoided the possibility of pendant fittings being knocked out during rowdy play. Unglazed pictures pasted to the wall were less liable to be dislodged than those that were hung, and had the virtue of retaining the visual integrity of the wall as a flush surface. Washable paints, tiling, or plain "sanitary" wallpapers (the commercial term for those that could be wiped clean) were recommended on grounds of hygiene. Blackboard panels encouraged self-expression, and troublesome chalk dust was easily cleaned from floors and tabletops covered with linoleum or cork tiles — materials that associated the appearance of the nursery with that of the modern kitchen and bathroom.

The easy-to-clean principle was extended to simple, undecorated furniture and toys. Glass, plywood, enamel-painted wood, and chromed steel — all of them modernist materials of choice —could be kept absolutely spotless. This pursuit of visual hygiene and literal cleanliness appeared in modernist designs for children's furniture like those by Marcel Breuer and Gerrit Rietveld (nos. 14, 15). The lightness of tubular steel, bentwood, and plywood and the rounded edges of the forms made the furniture easy for children to handle, as Alvar Aalto's

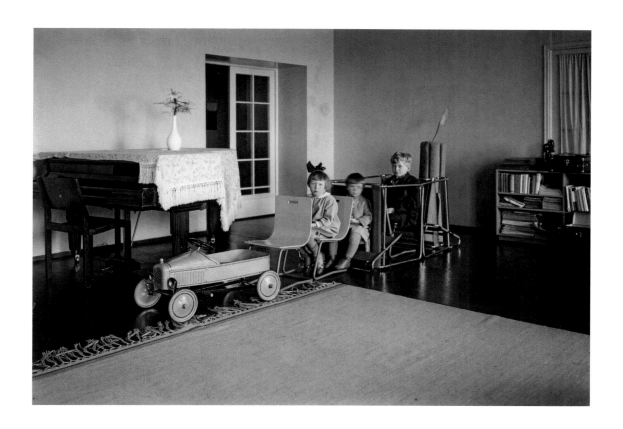

14 Detail from *Stahlromöbel* (Tubular steel furniture), loose-leaf sales catalog for Thonet Company showing Marcel Breuer's B341/2 chair and B53 table. 1930–31
Lithograph, gravure, and letterpress,
$8^3/_8 \times 6^1/_8$" (21.3 x 15.6 cm)
Published by Thonet International Press Service, Cologne
The Museum of Modern Art, New York. Department of Architecture and Design Study Center

15 GERRIT RIETVELD (Dutch, 1888–1964)
Child's chair. c. 1928
Painted bentwood and tubular steel,
$23^1/_4 \times 15^9/_{16} \times 23^1/_2$" (59.1 x 39.5 x 59.7 cm)
Manufactured by Metz & Co., Amsterdam (est. 1740)
The Museum of Modern Art, New York. Gift of Jo Carole and Ronald S. Lauder

16 Hanii and Hamilkar, the Aalto children, with a friend in their house in Turku, Finland. c. 1929
Photograph by Aino Aalto
Alvar Aalto Museum, Jyväskylä, Finland

17 GIO PONTI (Italian, 1891–1979)
Glass desk. 1939
Glass, metal, and wood, $29^3/_4 \times 27^9/_{16} \times 15^3/_4$"
(75.5 x 70 x 40 cm)
Manufactured by Vitrex, Sassuolo, Italy
Collection of Maurizio Marzadori, Bologna

18 BARBARA BRUKALSKA (Polish, 1899–1980)
Child's chair. 1932
Wood, 30 5/16 x 14 3/4 x 16 9/16" (77 x 37.5 x 42 cm)
National Museum, Warsaw

19 Ultra Modern Dolls' House. 1938
Painted wood and metal, 18 x 23 x 13"
(45.7 x 58.4 x 33 cm)
Manufactured by Lines Bros. Ltd, London
(est. 1919), under the Tri-ang Toys trademark
Victoria and Albert Museum of Childhood, London

children demonstrated by playfully upending two Breuer chairs to form a makeshift train (no. 16). Gio Ponti's desk of reinforced glass emphasized an aura of optical hygiene and the free flow of light and air in the modern child's room (no. 17).

Although many modernists were interested in producing standardized, affordable furniture for working-class children, in practice they usually ended up designing for immediate friends and family (no. 18), or for a relatively circumscribed, fashion-conscious elite. With the exception of companies like Thonet or Artek, few manufacturers were prepared to produce such children's furniture on a scale that would make it economically viable, and retailers were wary of being left with unsaleable stock, whereas the mass production of modernist toys like the Lines Bros. dollhouse was a less risky proposition (no. 19).

Perhaps the most logical expression of the modern movement's social program in relation to children's home environments was housing designed for collectivized childcare, an approach pursued most vigorously in the Soviet Union (see "Grete Lihotzky: From Vienna to Ankara," p. 108).

Another innovative example was the Swedish Kollektivhus (Collective house) model pioneered by social reformer Alva Myrdal with architect Sven Markelius in Stockholm in 1935. Like the Soviet examples, this project was undertaken with a view to easing the burden of childcare on working women and giving children more peer-group contact.[12] This high-rise block, set near parkland, contained a central kitchen, a community nursery equipped with safe, pedagogically correct playthings, and a hygienic crèche for infants under the age of two, staffed twenty-four hours a day by professionals. Though the Kollektivhus model was not widely adopted, Myrdal's views on childcare and children's play were influential in the development of the Swedish welfare state and the international play movement after World War II.

Juliet Kinchin

WRITING IN 1942 with a pungent sense of revulsion, Austrian author and intellectual Stefan Zweig looked back on his 1890s school in Vienna as the metaphorical and physical "dungeon" of his generation's youth:

> "As soon as we entered the hated school building we had to keep our heads down, so to speak, to avoid coming up against the invisible yoke of servitude.... To this day I have not forgotten the musty, mouldy odour clinging to that building.... We sat in pairs, like convicts in their galley, on low wooden benches that made us bend our backs, and we sat there until our bones ached.... The century of our youth had not yet discovered that young, still-developing bodies need fresh air and exercise.... The sole purpose of school in the spirit of those times was not so much to bring us on as to hold us back, not to help us to shape our minds but to fit us into the established mould with as little resistance as possible, not to enhance our energies but to discipline them and level them out."[1]

By the late 1920s, however, there had been a paradigmatic shift in the design of schools as architecture was seen increasingly as an active agent in the educational process. The more welcoming, airy, and flexible spaces of the "new school," like the educational philosophies it expressed, were seen by progressive educationalists and design reformers as instruments for social change, and as embodiments of the more equitable and open society to which they aspired. In his essay "The New Building Art as Educator," German art critic Fritz Wichert observed: "New people create new buildings, but new buildings also create new people."[2] In a similar vein, Beatrice Ensor, who initiated the international New Education Fellowship in Britain in 1921, described the "new education" of the interwar period as "primarily a thing of spirit, the fruits of which are new relationships between child and teacher, and between child and child, new attitudes towards learning, towards authority, and one might also say between life itself."[3] Much of the new thinking about school buildings was also based on the relationship between children's education and health, specifically the need for schools to compensate for the lack of hygienic facilities in many children's homelives.

20 WALTER KÄCH (Swiss, 1901–1970)
Ausstellung der neue Schulbau (Exhibition of new school building), poster for an exhibition at the Kunstgewerbemuseum, Zurich. 1932
50 x 35⁷/₁₆" (127 x 90 cm)
Museum für Gestaltung Zürich, Plakatsammlung

The interdisciplinary convergence between progressive pedagogy, medical expertise, and a high modernist architectural and design ideal was showcased in the didactic 1932 exhibition *Der neue Schulbau* (The new school building), held in Zurich, which represented an international selection of notable new schools (no. 20). Organized by a group of architects active in the Congrès Internationaux d'Architecture Moderne (CIAM) together with health reformer Wilhelm von Gonzenbach and pedagogue Willi Schohaus, the show endorsed the pavilion-style school featured on the exhibition poster as the most effective in balancing questions of space, hygiene, light, and pedagogy. The Wiedikon Kindergarten (no. 21) in Zurich was a typical example. Designed by Hans Hofmann and Adolf Kellermüller, this complex of a kindergarten, after-school care facilities, and a community center was housed in eight pavilions, with glass sides and skylights to make maximum use of natural lighting, ventilation, and easy access to the outdoors. Inside, airy classrooms could accommodate different activities simultaneously, with furniture reconfigured for individual or informal group-based learning (no. 22). The abstract clarity of the spatial composition was carried through to the modernist treatment of details such as signage and clocks. It also resonated with the design of new school primers like Tom Seidmann-Freud's 1931 *Hurra, wir rechnen weiter!* (Hurray, we keep counting!) (no. 23).[4] Swiss critic Peter Meyer extolled the child-friendly

21 HANS HOFMANN (Swiss, 1897–1957) and
ADOLF KELLERMÜLLER (Swiss, 1895–1981)
Exterior perspective drawing, Wiedikon
Kindergarten, Zurich, plan no. 43. 1928–32
Ink on tracing paper, 16 9/16 x 33 7/8" (42 x 86 cm)
gta Archives, ETH Zürich. Hans Hofmann Bequest

22 HANS HOFMANN (Swiss, 1897–1957) and
ADOLF KELLERMÜLLER (Swiss, 1895–1981)
Classroom in the Wiedikon Kindergarten. 1932
gta Archives, ETH Zürich. Hans Hofmann Bequest

23 TOM SEIDMANN-FREUD (German, 1892–1930)
Cover of the book *Hurra, wir rechnen weiter!*
(Hurray, we keep counting!). 1932
Single page: 9 15/16 x 8 1/8 x 1/4" (25.3 x 20.6 x 0.7 cm)
Published by Herbert Stuffer Verlag, Berlin
The Museum of Modern Art Library, New York

24 JAN DUIKER (Dutch, 1890–1935)
Cliostraat Openluchtschool voor het Gezonde
Kind (Open-air school for the healthy child),
Amsterdam. 1927–30
The Museum of Modern Art, New York. Department
of Architecture and Design Study Center

25 PIET ZWART (Dutch, 1885–1977)
Child's chair designed for Wassenaar Kindergarten,
the Netherlands. 1935
Birchwood and aluminum, 26 x 12 1/2 x 14"
(66 x 31.8 x 35.6 cm)
Minneapolis Institute of Arts, The Modernism
Collection, gift of Norwest Bank Minnesota

perspective of the Zurich exhibition: "A markedly modest attitude,
one of human goodness and that eschews all pompous falseness,
seems the only right one to teachers and architects concerned today
with the question of school construction."[5]

Jan Duiker's Cliostraat Openluchtschool voor het Gezonde Kind
(Cliostraat open-air school for the healthy child) in Amsterdam (no. 24),
completed in 1930, was also highlighted in the exhibition. Expansive
pavilion-style schools were difficult to accommodate in inner-city locations where land was at a premium, but by deploying a repertoire of
modern structural techniques and materials — large areas of glazing,
cantilevered concrete structures, and steel frames, as well as new
fittings such as sliding doors, adaptive ventilation systems, and flexible
lighting — Duiker designed a compact building flooded with light and
air. Whereas open-air schools earlier in the twentieth century had been
focused on sickly children (the first such institution was established
outside Berlin in 1900), Duiker's school was for the healthy, the first
step in a campaign to harness a "strong hygienic power" in society at
large: "Our approach towards life in the fresh air will be on a different
plane," he wrote. "Modern techniques enable us to keep the material
used in the building to a minimum and to heat these almost entirely
open spaces without any difficulty so that children need only wear light
clothing, as is medically recommended."[6]

Dutch designer Piet Zwart visited Duiker's school when thinking
about the design of a Montessori kindergarten environment in Wassenaar,
a school his own children would attend. Maria Montessori recommended
"light furniture which is correspondingly simple and economical in the
extreme."[7] In 1935 Zwart designed an appropriately simple chair for
the kindergarten (no. 25), which he wanted to develop as an affordable
flat-pack kit but could not interest a manufacturer.

29 Installation view of French tubular-steel
school furniture (attributed to Barret, Cravoisier,
Gascoin, Herbst, and Meyer) at the 1937 Salon
des Arts Ménagers, as reproduced in the
magazine *Acier*. 1938
Photograph by Lacheroy
The Museum of Modern Art Library, New York

Other expressions of the modernist obsession with hygiene, sunlight, and fresh air included the twenty-eight primary schools designed
by Juan O'Gorman for the Mexican Ministry of Culture by 1932 (no. 26)
and the open-air school at Suresnes, near Paris, designed by Eugène
Beaudouin and Marcel Lods (no. 27). The latter project was instigated
by the city's Socialist mayor, Henri Sellier (later the Minister of Health),
and supervised by Louis Boulonnois, a former primary school teacher
and tuberculosis sufferer. Set in a sloping woodland park, the school
had eight pavilion-style classrooms with under-floor heating and folding glass doors on three sides that could be retracted for cross ventilation or shaded with external canvas blinds. Outside each classroom
was a graveled area for outdoor teaching or afternoon rest. There was
also a main building with communal facilities (dining room, kitchen,
playrooms, and showers) and a health-care wing linked to the classrooms
by connecting walkways. Beaudouin and Lods designed many of the
innovative furnishings used in the school, such as metal cupboards
on wheels that made moving books and teaching equipment easier.
Furthermore, all the furniture was light enough for pupils to move
themselves, including tubular steel recliners (no. 28) that could be carried outside for a siesta beneath a shady tree.

The development of such architect-designed metal furniture for
schools was actively encouraged by the Office Technique pour l'Utilisation
de l'Acier (OTUA), an organization established in 1929 to promote use of
steel in France. The results of an OTUA competition for school furniture —
including designs by René Herbst and Robert Mallet-Stevens, and a
Jean Prouvé desk-chair unit originally for Suresnes — were exhibited
at the 1936 Salon d'Automne and again at the 1937 Salon des Arts
Ménagers (no. 29). Hygienic, light, robust, and fireproof, such designs
exemplified a modernist marriage of form and function.

Among the many foreign visitors to Suresnes was Danish architect
Kaj Gottlob, a professor at the Royal Danish Academy of Fine Arts,
perhaps best known for his Skolen ved Sundet (School by the sound)
in Copenhagen, designed in 1938.[8] Gottlob was a communist who
believed — as a sociopolitical principle and because he thought that school
was boring — that children deserved better architectural environments,[9]
and in this example he created two school buildings: closest to the
water was the open-air school for sickly children (no. 30), who inhabited
a bright, open space with eight octagonal classrooms and south-facing
windows, modeled closely after Suresnes. Washing facilities were important at a time when most children had no running water at home. Steps
away, the second building — oval-shaped with glazed classrooms on three
stories around a large atrium — offered a central gathering space for
the entire school, complete with a stage. A brightly colored linoleum
map covered the whole floor (no. 31), setting the school at its very center,
with the roads and railroads of Copenhagen radiating outward. Above,
a giant compass dominated the ceiling and connected to a weather vane
on the roof. With these features, Gottlob not only placed the schoolchildren literally at the center of their world but also made sure that they
could always tell which way the wind was blowing — a gesture with
strong metaphorical implications in 1938.

Juliet Kinchin

30 KAJ GOTTLOB (Danish, 1887–1976)
South-facing rest area in Svagbørnsskolen
(School for weak children) at the Skolen ved Sundet
(School by the sound), Copenhagen. 1935–38
Photograph by Jonals Co.
The Museum of Modern Art, New York. Department
of Architecture and Design Study Center

31 KAJ GOTTLOB (Danish, 1887–1976)
Atrium at the Skolen ved Sundet (School by
the sound), Copenhagen. 1938

WHILE EUROPEAN ARCHITECTS drove a new school revolution in the 1920s and '30s — fostering healthy minds and bodies through modernist structures — American and émigré architects were producing outstanding corollaries in the United States. Schools from both sides of the Atlantic were featured prominently in The Museum of Modern Art's landmark 1932 exhibition *Modern Architecture: International Exhibition*, which firmly linked modern design with children.[1] "The international style in architecture is especially adapted to school buildings," said curator Philip Johnson, "because functional planning, the fundamental principle of the new architecture, is exactly what schools need to develop in sympathy with modern trends in scientific education."[2] In conjunction with the exhibition, the Museum organized conferences for public school teachers and promoted the freedom of school plans that were no longer subordinate to historicist exteriors.[3]

In the 1932 exhibition, American projects by William Lescaze (of Geneva) and Richard Neutra (of Vienna), both of whom had settled in the United States by the early 1920s,[4] were featured alongside European exemplars, such as Ernst May and his associates' Friedrich Ebert School in Frankfurt. Lescaze joined with his business partner George Howe in 1929, and their first commissioned project, Oak Lane Country Day School (no. 32), near Philadelphia, established Lescaze's reputation as a modernist architect in the United States. The two refined their school-building skills with the Hessian Hills School in Croton-on-Hudson, New York (1931), which became the most noted early example of American modernist school design.[5] MoMA's exhibition also highlighted Neutra's Ring Plan School concept, which proposed classrooms as individual units radiating from an inner circle of green lawn.

Neutra soon developed a new model for public schools in southern California, where the mild climate and abundant space rendered unnecessary the traditional East Coast multistory brick and stone buildings, and where a destructive earthquake on March 10, 1933, foregrounded safety concerns that would favor lightweight, single-story construction.[6] Neutra's ideas for more modern and regionally appropriate school design became popular in California, particularly around Los Angeles, where he lived. He produced his first prototype informed by these ideas through a commission from Nora Sterry, principal of

32 GEORGE HOWE (American, 1886–1955) and
WILLIAM LESCAZE (American, born Switzerland. 1896–1969)
Classroom in the Oak Lane Country Day School,
Philadelphia. 1929
Photograph by Ralph Steiner
The Museum of Modern Art, New York. Department
of Architecture and Design Study Center

Corona Avenue School, who (with the support of the League of Women Voters) hired him in 1934 to design an addition to the public elementary school in Bell, a city in Los Angeles County. The result was a single-story L-shaped wing with seven classrooms (two kindergarten, five elementary) for two hundred and fifty children.

Neutra, who had seen Jan Duiker's famous open-air school (1927–30; see no. 24) in Amsterdam, achieved in the Corona Avenue design a dynamic flow between interior and exterior environments as well as between the students' daily activities. The classrooms were lit and ventilated bilaterally: on one side by clerestory windows connecting to a covered outdoor hallway, and on the other by structurally innovative sliding glass walls that opened onto individual garden patios (no. 33). These patios, divided by low hedges, kept the children engaged with the natural world and extended the teaching space for each classroom. Flexible furniture could be arranged indoors as well as out, and was

33 RICHARD NEUTRA
(American, born Austria. 1892–1970)
Corona Avenue School, Bell, California. 1935
Photograph by Julius Shulman
The Museum of Modern Art, New York. Department
of Architecture and Design Study Center

34 RICHARD NEUTRA
(American, born Austria. 1892–1970)
"Typical Classr[oo]m Activity Train[in]g," interior
perspective drawing of the experimental unit of
the Corona Avenue School, Bell, California. 1935
Graphite and pastel on board, 14 1/2 x 19"
(36.8 x 48.3 cm)
Private collection

35 ELIEL SAARINEN (Finnish, 1873–1950)
and EERO SAARINEN (American, born Finland.
1910–1961) with PERKINS, WHEELER, AND WILL
(USA, est. 1936)
Exterior wall detail of the Crow Island
Elementary School, Winnetka, Illinois. 1940
Photograph by Hedrich-Blessing
The Museum of Modern Art, New York. Department
of Architecture and Design Study Center

36 ELIEL SAARINEN (Finnish, 1873–1950)
and EERO SAARINEN (American, born Finland.
1910–1961) with PERKINS, WHEELER, AND WILL
(USA, est. 1936)
Classroom in the Crow Island Elementary School,
Winnetka, Illinois. 1940
Photograph by Hedrich-Blessing
The Museum of Modern Art, New York. Department
of Architecture and Design Study Center

pleasantly shaded by trees and adjustable awnings. All of these features epitomized Neutra's belief in design as an organic life force that could create beauty with positive psychological impact.[7] He dedicated a drawing depicting a typical Corona classroom —vibrant and harmonious — to his own son Richard, who had a developmental disability (no. 34). Once completed, in 1935, this radical design was widely publicized and described as everything from a "test-tube school" to a "penthouse on Mars," but it was also celebrated (especially by educators) as the ideal setting for John Dewey's "learning by doing,"[8] and ultimately proved extremely influential.

Perhaps the most important modern school of this period in the United States (conceived in 1937, built in 1940) was Crow Island in the Chicago suburb of Winnetka. The primary designer of this fourteen-classroom elementary school for three hundred pupils was Lawrence Perkins, son of architect Dwight H. Perkins (with famous local schools to his own name) and Lucy Fitch Perkins, a successful children's book author and illustrator. Perkins's firm, established only three years prior with E. Todd Wheeler and Phil Will, was hired with the requirement that they collaborate with a more established architect. Carleton Washburne, superintendent of the reform-minded Winnetka school board,[9] selected his personal favorite, Finnish-born Eliel Saarinen, who rounded out the team with his son Eero and Eero's wife, Lily Swann Saarinen. The commission was shared equally, with Perkins, Wheeler,

and Will guiding the interior of the school and the Saarinens the exterior and landscaping.[10] To satisfy the ambitious superintendent, Perkins read Washburne's complete pedagogical writings and acted as a sounding board for his plans to make Crow Island a beacon of modern education: "Larry...This is to be our dream school," he said. "We want it to be the most functional and beautiful school in the world. We want it to crystallize in architecture the best educational practices we can evolve."[11] Perkins spent weeks interviewing Winnetka parents, teachers, and children before proposing a school model organized completely around the child-friendly classroom unit. The resulting plan was permanently honored in brick relief on the school's exterior (no. 35).

Each L-shaped classroom had its own bathroom, work sink, wall of windows, and private courtyard. Larger spaces for outdoor play included a jungle gym and open-air stage. Inside, ceilings were nine feet high instead of the standard twelve, and other elements (blackboards, windowsills, light switches, doorknobs) were scaled to the height of children (no. 36). Lily designed bright print curtains for the windows and glazed ceramic animal tiles for the exterior walls. Ergonomic bent plywood furniture was designed by Eero Saarinen with Cranbrook colleague Charles Eames and produced by the WPA's Illinois Craft Project and Milwaukee Art Project.[12] An atmosphere of organic warmth was enhanced throughout by materials such as brick, limestone, clay tile, Japanese grass cloth, and white oak and pine.

Essential to the success of Crow Island, which maintains the love of adults and children today, was the cooperative spirit that produced it. Perkins and the rest of the team considered the professional and emotional appeals of teachers (including physical education and art instructors) and even the school janitor (who suggested skylights for the hallways and heating coils in the front steps to melt snow).[13] Inspiring guidance came from activities director Frances Presler, whose demands for the school were published as a letter to the architects:

All the architecture shall be a setting for childlife...a place which permits the joy in small things of life, and in democratic living....The building must not be too beautiful, lest it be a place for children to keep and not one for them to use....Above all the school must be childlike — not what adults think of children. At the same time it should be dignified and playful....It must be warm, personal and intimate, that it shall be to each of these thousands "My school."[14]

Crow Island's designers achieved the secure, nurturing, and stimulating qualities requested, and the new school was held up as an ideal by Joseph Hudnut, dean of Harvard's Graduate School of Design, who described it as an affirmation of "that liberating spirit which is making the art of teaching (the greatest of all arts) articulate in the art of architecture." "If I could," Hudnut concluded, "I would transport the educational authorities of New York, by force if that should be necessary, to Winnetka...they should yet discover, I think, the spirit which gives life to architecture."[15]

Aidan O'Connor

KINDER, KÜCHE, KIRCHE (children, kitchen, church): if "the three Ks," a popular German expression in the nineteenth and twentieth centuries, could be taken to define women's roles in society, by the end of World War I this conventional pattern was under assault. While Grete Lihotzky became identified strongly with design for both children and kitchens, it was as a pioneering, fully qualified architect rather than in the traditional sense of a woman's domestic duties. She was the first woman to become an architect in Austria, graduating from the Vienna Kunstgewerbeschule (School of applied arts), and quickly moved to the center of European modernism, producing outstanding designs in Germany, the Soviet Union, China, Turkey, Bulgaria, and Austria.

Her interest in shaping the daily lives of women and children was always part of a politically committed and comprehensive vision for creating a healthier, more equitable society. While studying architecture with Oskar Strnad and Adolf Loos in Vienna, from 1917 to 1919, her work on emergency housing projects introduced her to the day-to-day struggle of working-class women raising families in the most desperate of circumstances. Starvation and tuberculosis were rife among local children, many of them war orphans, and after qualifying as an architect in 1919, Lihotzky and her sister accompanied a troop of sickly children to recuperate in the Netherlands. Her awareness of illness, in particular tuberculosis (a disease that she herself contracted

and that also killed her parents), sensitized her to health issues and the needs of women and children, and galvanized her politically. In the course of her peripatetic architectural career, and in her lectures and writings, Lihotzky repeatedly returned to the shortage of childcare facilities, which she saw as a hindrance to women of all classes wishing to lead fuller lives and work outside the home.[1] She involved herself with social and political aspects of design for children as well as questions of education, and of the practical realization of schools, children's clubs, homes, and furniture through the application of new materials and methods of production. Her pragmatism and idealism were clear reflections of her belief in progress—architectural, social, technological, and political.

In 1926 Lihotzky joined the international, interdisciplinary team assembled by City Architect Ernst May to work on the comprehensive modernization of Frankfurt am Main, Germany. Using simple, prefabricated forms, the group of architects, engineers, and planners effectively housed an astonishing ten percent of the population in little more than five years, in fifteen new housing estates around the city. In this "New Frankfurt," schools were underlined as the most important public building type in publications and publicity produced by May's office (no. 37).[2] Architect Wilhelm Schütte, whom Lihotzky would marry in 1928, was in charge of the school-building program, and pavilion-style designs by

199

37 ERNST MAY (German, 1886–1970)
Reform School on the Bornheimer Hang
housing estate. 1926–30
Photomontage as reproduced in *Das neue Frankfurt*, vol. 4 (no. 9) (September 1930)
Photograph by Dr. Paul Wolff
The Museum of Modern Art Library, New York

38 MARGARETE (GRETE) LIHOTZKY
(Austrian, 1897–2000)
Model for a pavilion-style kindergarten on the Praunheim estate, Frankfurt am Main. 1929
Designed under the auspices of the City Architecture Department, Frankfurt am Main
Universität für angewandte Kunst Wien, Kunstsammlung und Archiv, Vienna

39 MARGARETE (GRETE) LIHOTZKY
(Austrian, 1897–2000) and HANS SCHMIDT
(Swiss, 1893–1972)
Wall elevation for Standardized Housing Units. 1934–36
Watercolor on paper, $7^{1}/_{16}$ x $15^{3}/_{8}$" (18 x 39 cm)
Designed under the auspices of the Moscow Architecture Academy
Universität für angewandte Kunst Wien, Kunstsammlung und Archiv, Vienna

40 MARGARETE (GRETE) LIHOTZKY
(Austrian, 1897–2000)
Design for a bookcase with blackboard and writing surface. 1935–36
Watercolor on tracing paper, $8^{1}/_{4}$ x $11^{13}/_{16}$"
(21 x 30 cm)
Designed under the auspices of Moscow Architecture Academy
Universität für angewandte Kunst Wien, Kunstsammlung und Archiv, Vienna

May and Franz Schuster attracted international attention. Although best known for the design of mass-produced, standardized kitchens, Lihotzky also made an innovative contribution in this area at the time of the Congrès Internationaux d'Architecture Moderne (CIAM) meeting in Frankfurt in 1929. Her design for a cruciform kindergarten on the Praunheim estate (no. 38) was conceived along open-air school principles (see "The New School," p. 99). Three single-story classrooms opened onto sheltered gardens for outdoor teaching and play, and, following Maria Montessori's recommendation, there was a central playroom to be shared by the three groups of pupils. With Germany in the throes of economic depression, however, the Praunheim kindergarten was only realized in a modified form in 1961, after Lihotzky's eventual return to Vienna.[3]

In 1930, as the political situation in Weimar Germany continued to deteriorate, she and her husband accompanied May to the Soviet Union as members of the so-called May Brigade, charged with planning large industrial towns as part of the First Five-Year Plan (1928–32). The new settlements were organized around the incorporation of women in the workforce, made possible in part by the enhanced provision of state-run children's clubs, kindergartens, and nursery facilities, for which Lihotzky was responsible (Schütte continued to focus on school building). Heading up a team of approximately thirty draftsmen and engineers (a multilingual group including people from different

parts of the Soviet Union necessitating the constant use of interpreters), she organized classes on new building materials, drawing techniques, and the detailing of windows and doors for workers in her section to encourage the consistent adoption of standardized forms. As in Frankfurt, she was able to draw on the expertise of doctors, pedagogues, sociologists, and psychologists in considering how best to accommodate appropriate methods of teaching and circulation patterns that would assist children in building social relationships and working groups while also designing layouts to limit the spread of infections.

The need for childcare facilities was so great that her team worked almost exclusively on standardized "type" designs that could be adapted for different numbers of children and the varied climatic conditions found throughout the Soviet Union (no. 39). Plans were dispatched from the office to countless locations, though not necessarily erected; the huge distances created problems of communication, compounded by the number of languages and dialects in areas where the facilities were built, lack of transportation infrastructure, and material shortages. Steel, glass, and cement were nearly all commandeered for industrial use, so Lihotzky used locally grown timber wherever possible.

She approached the design and production of children's furniture with the same clarity, rationalism, and economy of means as in her architectural designs. Because there was no tradition of specialized furniture for children in the Soviet Union, she issued tabulated dimensions,

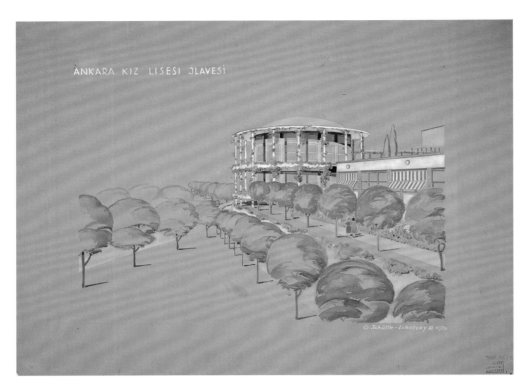

ANKARA KIZ LİSESİ İLAVESİ

Köy ve okulu

guidelines for construction and use, and age-group specifications, allowing her designs to be disseminated widely. The furniture — all of which was easy to assemble, stack, and transport — was characterized by visual and physical lightness geared to children's physiques and dexterity, while being robust and hygienically finished with washable paint and smooth surfaces (no. 40). While still based in the Soviet Union, she and her husband visited Bruno Taut and his wife in Japan, where Lihotzky drew up kindergarten plans for the Japanese Ministry of Education, and went on to tour schools in many different areas in China.

Forced to leave the Soviet Union in 1937 because of the Stalinist purge of foreign experts, it was through Taut that the couple eventually found work at the Istanbul Académie des Beaux-Arts, designing schools for the Ministry of Education. Led by Mustafa Kemal Atatürk, Turkey was a young republic undergoing radical modernization, a process being given architectural form by German-Austrian professionals — representatives of international modernism like Taut and Ernst Egli (head of architecture at the Académie).[4] In her 1938 design for an extension of Egli's school for girls in Ankara, the new capital, Lihotzky combined the simple geometric volumes and rational layout advocated by the New School movement with reference to Ottoman monuments in a double-story glazed rotunda (no. 41). By contrast, her "type" plans for rural schools in Anatolia were moderated by her respect for simple vernacular materials and forms (no. 42). In December 1940 her intensive productivity was stalled when she returned to Vienna as a member of the Austrian Communist resistance and was promptly arrested by the Gestapo. After four years in a Nazi prison in Aichach, Germany, she went to work in Sofia, Bulgaria (1945–47), where she established a central architectural institute for children's facilities, built various schools, and developed a design manual for schools and children's furniture. Anti-communist sentiment in Vienna, where she lived from 1947 until her death in 2000, meant that no major commissions were forthcoming, although she continued to work as a consultant for child-related design in Soviet bloc and other communist states, including Cuba and China.

Juliet Kinchin

43 ERNŐ GOLDFINGER (British, born Hungary. 1902–1987) and MARY CROWLEY (British, 1907–2005)
Design for an expanding nursery school, commissioned by the Nursery Schools Association. 1934
Pencil and colored crayon on tracing paper, 12 3/8 x 19 7/8" (31.5 x 50.5 cm)
RIBA Library Drawings & Archives Collection, London

HUNGARIAN-BORN ARCHITECT Ernő Goldfinger made design for children a key theme in his early career. When he first moved from Paris to London in 1934, there was general hostility to the modern movement both inside and outside the British architectural profession, and limited opportunities for realizing the kind of large-scale project — a twenty-three-story slab block with communal facilities, including a nursery and school — he had submitted to the 1933 Congrès Internationaux d'Architecture Moderne (CIAM) meeting in Athens.[1] The birth of his first son in 1933, however, also had shifted his focus toward children, reinforced by new encounters with British idealists interested in progressive education, child development, and modernist design, chief among them Marjorie and Paul Abbatt.

The Abbatts, who were in the process of establishing a company for the sale of developmental and construction toys, were to become Goldfinger's close friends and principal clients in the 1930s and '40s. They were typical British "moderns" — highly educated, relatively affluent, liberal, and internationalist. Their passion for children's well-being was intellectually grounded: on leaving Cambridge University, Paul had worked as a tutor and teacher, including at the open-air school established by the Order of Woodcraft Chivalry, a progressive Scouting-like movement.[2] Marjorie, an Oxford University graduate, whose doctoral research combined her interests in psychoanalysis and speech

therapy for children, was conversant with the pioneering work of Maria Montessori and educational experiments in Vienna and Soviet Russia that she and her husband were able to experience firsthand during an extended honeymoon in the early 1930s.

In Vienna, the Abbatts sat in on Franz Cižek's classes and visited the inspirational Montessori kindergartens designed by the Atelier Singer-Dicker and Franz Schuster. They also met Milan Morgenstern and Helena Löw-Beer, who had been developing teaching methods for children with physical and learning disabilities, and who would later design toys for the Abbatts. On returning to London in 1932, Paul and Marjorie organized an exhibition in their Bloomsbury apartment featuring the experiential toys and teaching aids they had gathered. Such was its success that they registered a mail-order business as toy designers, manufacturers, and retailers, renting a room in the same building as the Froebel Institute, the Home and School Council, and the Nursery School Association. Paul Abbatt articulated the shared mission of this progressive enclave in 1933: "We are now beginning to realise that it is the child who has had plenty of opportunity for play who will later work with better will and efficiency: and we are concerned that all children, even the poorest, shall be provided with a rich and happy playtime." Play and playthings, he continued, were "just as necessary for the child as food and clothes."[3]

44 Cover of *25 Best Toys for Each Age*, mail-order catalog for Paul & Marjorie Abbatt Ltd. 1938
Produced by Paul & Marjorie Abbatt Ltd
Company logo designed by Ernő Goldfinger
8⁷/₁₆ x 5¹/₂" (21.5 x 14 cm)
Victoria and Albert Museum of Childhood, London.
Paul and Marjorie Abbatt Archive

45 Posting Box, developed in association with Milan Morgenstern. c. 1933 (this example produced 1965)
Varnished wood and plywood, 5⁷/₈ x 5¹/₈ x 5¹/₈"
(15 x 13 x 13 cm)
Manufactured by Paul & Marjorie Abbatt Ltd, 1965
Victoria and Albert Museum of Childhood, London

46 Children's section in the British Pavilion at the *Exposition internationale des arts et techniques dans la vie moderne*, Paris, designed by Ernő Goldfinger in association with Paul and Marjorie Abbatt. 1937
Photograph by Millar and Harris
RIBA Library Photographs Collection, London

Advised by the Abbatts, the Nursery Schools Association commissioned a prototype nursery school from Goldfinger and Mary Crowley in 1934 (no. 43). The brief was to design a stimulating environment that could be economically manufactured and adapted for different numbers of children. Crowley, one of the few fully qualified female architects in Britain, was well versed in the arguments for progressive school design through her father, Ralph H. Crowley, senior medical officer at the Board of Education, who had campaigned vigorously for healthier schools and free school meals.[4] Goldfinger and Crowley's concept was modular, flexible, and — unusually for schools at this time — designed for prefabrication. Each base unit could accommodate forty children, with an optional glass-covered veranda. Goldfinger's internal perspective shows an open-plan activity space with full-length doors opening to the outdoors. The equipment supplied by the Abbatts offered opportunities for climbing, sliding, and sandpit play to vivify mind and body. Anticipated demand from local authorities for new kindergartens did not materialize and the prototype was not put into production, but Goldfinger implemented the ideas in the prefabricated schools that he designed after World War II.

Every aspect of the Abbatts' enterprise reflected their commitment to modernist design, from their mail-order catalogs (no. 44) and the presentation of their showrooms and exhibition stands to their actual toys. They largely turned to Goldfinger for design work, but also helped out other Jewish émigré friends fleeing fascist Europe with small commissions.[5] In 1936 Goldfinger designed their first shop, at 94 Wimpole Street. Children were encouraged to play on the cork-tiled floor or read in the book section. The Abbatts took pride in selling

simple, sturdy toys for active, purposeful play, stocking designs from elsewhere in Europe, such as Czechoslovak toys by Ladislav Sutnar, but also commissioning children's furniture and toys from Goldfinger. Like Morgenstern's system of developmental toys (no. 45), Goldfinger's expandable table responded to the need for furniture to grow with children. Such designs were prototyped in the nursery Goldfinger created for his own children as part of his modernist family home in Hampstead (1936–39). All Goldfinger's work for the Abbatts was tackled with the same thoughtful rationalism, classical simplicity, economic yet robust construction, and sensitivity to materials and scale that he brought to bear on his larger architectural projects.

Goldfinger's 1935 logo for the Abbatts' company communicated a modernist ethos of simplicity, standardization, and gender neutrality. The latter was especially true for the under-fives, with the company's catalog emphasizing how all young children love hammering and messing around in water and sand. But toys aimed at older children reflected more conventional gender stereotyping, as evidenced in the Goldfinger-Abbatt playroom in the British Pavilion at the 1937 Paris *Exposition internationale des arts et techniques dans la vie moderne* (no. 46). Paul Abbatt's script for the installation highlighted adult expectations of the male child: "One day he is to be a man — already

he creates a man's world in his nursery. Aeroplanes fly, trains shunt, ships sail, huntsmen ride.... Later also he uses tools — a carpenter's bench, fretsaw, things for clay-modelling, crayons, pencil, ruler, setsquare. His nursery presents means to ends, equips him for school and life, makes him resourceful, understanding, confident." No such attributes are ascribed to his sister, who is perfunctorily described as "already a mother with dolls, kitchen, a little house of her own."[6]

With the onset of hostilities in 1939–40, Goldfinger, Crowley, and the Abbatts pooled their energies to promote a practical response to the war effort, feeling, with some justification, that the needs of mothers and young children were being ignored in the design of temporary housing and evacuation camps being built by the National Camps Corporation. With many mothers being recruited for jobs previously filled by departing soldiers, there was a growing need for communal childcare facilities in these camps, and areas where children could safely play.[7] To highlight such concerns, the Abbatts organized an exhibition of alternative designs for temporary housing by Goldfinger and Crowley. Looking to the future, the architects proposed compact, economic, prefabricated units that could be visually integrated with the surrounding neighborhood and adapted to postwar use. Despite the practical and innovative aspects of these designs, like the Expanding Nursery School, they were not implemented. Nevertheless, the overall concepts and philosophical approach would be recapitulated after World War II, when Crowley assumed a defining role in the acclaimed Hertfordshire school-building program, Goldfinger realized two prefabricated schools, and the Abbatts became linchpins of the international "good toy" movement (see "Back to School," p. 166, and "Good Toys," p. 171).

During World War II, Goldfinger presented a strong visual polemic about the future development of Britain's cities after the predicted end of the war in a series of exhibitions for the Army Bureau of Current Affairs. On the issue of health, for example, he created contrasted views of the old and the new, prewar and postwar, in which children featured prominently. In a panel on the "good environment" (no. 1), the eye is automatically drawn to photographs of an airy classroom and a close-up view of well-fed children eating around a table. This photomontage was contrasted with a panel on the "bad environment" that included children in a slum street, an outside toilet, a dirty, poorly ventilated classroom, and a close-up of an appallingly undernourished child. The presence of children in these different contexts added to the already powerful arguments for modernization. By visualizing social change in this way, Goldfinger helped to mobilize public opinion in a direction that few would argue with — advocating for full employment, good housing, good schools, well-nourished children — and linked this agenda to modernist design. As Paul Abbatt had written in 1937, "A significant index of the culture of a country is its understanding and care of children."[8]

Juliet Kinchin

OFTEN LOCATED in remote coastal or mountainous sites, the huge number of holiday and rehabilitation centers for children built throughout Europe in the 1920s and '30s included some of the most progressive achievements of modern architecture, and were widely admired as such at the time. Like the related phenomenon of the open-air school, these projects embodied an essentially modernist belief in sunlight, fresh air, and hygiene. Also in the 1930s, international luminaries of progressive tendencies in architecture associated with the Congrès Internationaux d'Architecture Moderne (CIAM) joined forces to evolve principles for reshaping urban environments in a rapidly changing world; only by creating opportunities for everyone, above all children, to lead healthier lives, it was argued, could the contemporary city resist entropic forces of stagnation and regression. There were those within CIAM who considered many cities too chaotic and ideologically flawed to survive, and advocated instead designing new communities from scratch that would reconfigure adult-child and city-country relationships. At a time of intense political tension and economic uncertainty, however, sweeping master plans for cities and their regions proved difficult to implement.

Since the late nineteenth century, statistical data had been gathered in many different countries documenting the impact of decayed urban housing stock, polluted air, and ineffectual waste management on public health.[1] Yet despite the growing level of official and public concern, diseases like tuberculosis, rickets, whooping cough, and diphtheria — all experienced most acutely by the very young — continued to ravage Europe's inner cities in the 1920s and '30s. Perhaps the most telling, and quantifiable, indicator of an unhealthy city was infant mortality among the urban poor, as suggested in the forceful visualization of Barcelona by architect Josep Lluís Sert (no. 47). His team's analytical study, part of a larger international survey of contemporary cities and their surrounding regions conducted under the auspices of CIAM, drew attention to the city's slum children, many of whom suffered ill health and malnutrition in congested streets that often led to a rapid propagation of disease. Within CIAM, these urban studies were the prelude to the members' formulation of international, supra-political principles, by which modernist architects aspired to guide the process of future urban development around the world. Discussions focused on four closely connected "functions": housing, industry, recreation, and transportation. With support from the Catalan authorities, Sert's team proposed a master plan that would transform Barcelona into a model Functional City (the theme of the

fourth CIAM conference). On the subject of recreation, the group proposed a rapid transit link to a new coastal resort for rest and relaxation south of the city (no. 48), a vision that foundered with the Spanish Civil War and imposition of General Francisco Franco's fascist regime. Opting for exile in the United States, Sert continued to advance the CIAM understanding of urbanism through his influential book *Can Our Cities Survive?* (1942), and established the first degree in urban planning at Harvard University.[2]

While Sert left Barcelona in 1936, another major modernist architect and former director of the Bauhaus, Hannes Meyer, returned to his native Switzerland following a Stalinist purge of foreign experts from Soviet Russia.[3] One of Meyer's major Swiss commissions — from former colleagues in the national cooperative movement, Dr. Bernhard Jaeggi and his wife — was for a mountain holiday home with convalescent facilities for Swiss children of all classes (no. 49). This project exemplified not only Meyer's radical functionalism but also his socialist mission to broaden access to a socially exclusive type of health care: though Switzerland could be said to have invented sanatorium architecture and winter sports tourism, it was generally on behalf of those of considerable financial means.

Nestled on a hillside above the Alpine village of Mümliswil, Meyer's design comprised two low-rise blocks extending from either side of a solarium, with a roof terrace for communal activities and exercise. Building for Meyer meant the "organization of life processes," including communal life, personal hygiene, and access to sunshine, but he also understood that a community is made out of individuals, and he deliberately laid out the home so that each child could "'retire within themselves' even when living in a community of twenty to twenty-five other children. They should be able to keep their things in a cupboard and write a letter to their parents in a quiet corner."[4] Circular and fully glazed, the solarium gave architectural shape to the belief of Swiss pedagogue Johann Heinrich Pestalozzi in the educational power of the family circle.[5] At mealtimes the children would sit around tables in a horseshoe formation, with panoramic windows framing the drama of the mountains. Uncluttered living spaces were equipped with the barest essentials for the constantly changing groups of children. Using an innovative form of notation on the architectural plan, which revealed his fascination with the modern medium of film, Meyer added cinematic-style "projections" of landscapes that the children would be able to view from various rooms within the building. This emphasis on the way the spaces were *experienced* departed from the conventional

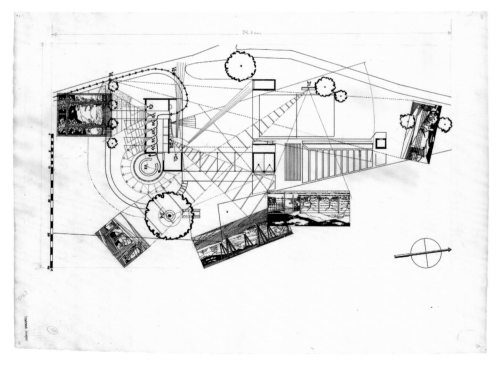

47 JOSEP LLUÍS SERT (Spanish, 1902–1983)
with GATCPAC (Grup d'Arquitectes i Tècnics
Catalans per al Progrés de l'Arquitectura
Contemporània) (Catalonia, est. 1928)
Panel showing the relation between population
density and child mortality in the central districts of
Barcelona, from the CIAM exhibition *The Functional
City*, Amsterdam. 1935
Photographic reproduction on cardboard panel,
39 x 39" (99 x 99 cm)
gta Archives, ETH Zürich. CIAM Archives

48 JOSEP LLUÍS SERT (Spanish, 1902–1983)
with GATCPAC (Grup d'Arquitectes i Tècnics
Catalans per al Progrés de l'Arquitectura
Contemporània) (Catalonia, est. 1928)
Panel showing the Ciutat de Repos i de Vacances
(City of rest and relaxation), public resort
outside of Barcelona, from the CIAM exhibition
The Functional City, Amsterdam. 1935
Collage on cardboard, 39 x 39" (99 x 99 cm)
gta Archives, ETH Zürich. CIAM Archives

49 HANNES MEYER (Swiss, 1889–1954)
View plan of *Kinderferienheim* (Children's holiday
home), Mümliswil, Switzerland. 1937
Ink on paper, 20 1/16 x 27 7/16" (51 x 69.7 cm)
gta Archives, ETH Zürich. Hannes Meyer Bequest

52 Colonia IX Maggio, Bardonecchia, Italy, as reproduced in *PNF: Federazione dei Fasci di Combattimento: Opere costruite maggio XIII–maggio XVII, Torino* (PNF: Federazione dei Fasci di Combattimento: Works built May of the 13th year to May of the 17th year of the Fascist Revolution, Turin). 1938
16 1/8 x 13 3/4" (41 x 35 cm)
Published by Partito Nazionale Fascista (PNF), Turin
Printed by Le industrie grafiche Gros Monti & C., Turin
The Wolfsonian–Florida International University, Miami Beach. The Mitchell Wolfson, Jr. Collection

definition of architectural form as a combination of static, enclosed volumes. Within several years, Hans Thöni's poster promoting healthy outdoor activity for Swiss boys and girls (no. 50) emphasized a different concern, that of maintaining national strength and morale in a time of war.

An even more remarkable architectural and social experiment was the prodigious number of *colonie di infanzia* — holiday camps for children — built in Italy during the fascist regime (1922–45) in remote hill sites or near the seaside (no. 51). An Italian tradition of therapeutic hospices for poor and sickly children originated in the late nineteenth century, supported by charitable organizations, the church, and certain local authorities or employers, but the *colonie* network was gradually subsumed under state control in the 1930s, and the emphasis shifted from curative to preventative measures. Removed from poor or modest homes, the normal life of boys and girls was put on hold and everything revolved around simple daily routines of diet, rest, and exercise in the fresh air and sunshine. Children could be inoculated, examined, and, if necessary, quarantined. Treatment was free for most children, although those who could afford it paid a small fee. In addition to health care, these environments were designed to facilitate the children's socialization and ideological formation. As a social bonding exercise, the camps brought together children from different regions and helped to break down the distinct cultures of town and country. In the absence of parental control, disciplined communal life was used to prepare young bodies and spirits for their future as obedient members of the fascist state.

As a potent form of international propaganda, the *colonie* presented a view of Italy that united progressive architecture with Benito Mussolini's apparently beneficent, humanist interest in children. Even in the context of the regime's already massive public building program, the camps created unprecedented opportunities for many ambitious modern architects, in that they were extensively photographed, published, and exhibited, thereby contributing to the architects' international reputations as well as serving a propaganda purpose (no. 52). The program was driven by a belief in the transformative power of a modernist aesthetic, as described in 1941: "Everything [in the *colonie*], from their abstract lines and volumes to their ground plans, which trace the itineraries of communal life, from the breadth and type of door and window frames and the design of railings, from plaster to floorings, colors and materials; everything combines...to make up the plastic form and visual image with which these children will identify the memories of periods spent in the Colonie...[and] accept the influence of taste."[6]

Many of the *colonie* survive to this day, but in a dilapidated state that reads as a metaphor for the failure of twentieth-century modernism's grand narrative.[7] The utopian and dystopian dreams of modernist architecture appear concentrated in these neglected ruins, made all the more poignant on account of their dedication to children.

Juliet Kinchin

IN LONDON, two pioneering health centers, both icons of interwar British modernism, opened in 1935 and 1938. Health care for the working classes was a pressing issue at this time: high levels of infant mortality among the urban poor, and health issues such as malnutrition, lice, rickets, tuberculosis, whooping cough, diphtheria, and infantile paralysis, remained a cause for concern even in economically advanced nations. Prior to the 1956 Clean Air Act, children were also particularly vulnerable to London's notoriously poor air quality. Radical in terms of architectural style and planning as well as medical philosophy, these centers delivered an innovative range of medical treatments and health-care facilities to working-class children. Health centers were a building type that matched the modernist commitment to functionality and art for all, connecting aesthetic ideology with the interwar cult of health. At the same time, the growing importance of children as a group for targeted health care was becoming visible internationally in new purpose-built facilities, although the outer form of these, if not the planning and technical facilities, was often far from modern.

The Pioneer Health Centre, opened in 1935 in Peckham, a district of southeast London, was a bold experiment in preventative health care. Funded by private donations, this spectacular glass and concrete "factory of health," designed by architect Owen Williams, was built on three floors around a top-lit swimming pool (one of the largest in Britain) and set in two acres of greenery. Additional facilities included a nursery, play area, theater, cafeteria, sun balconies, and gymnasium, and doctors were on hand for medical advice and regular checkups. Interior surfaces were left unadorned, and cork flooring meant that children could wander around barefoot. The center was equipped with standardized plywood furniture designed by Kit Nicholson (no. 53), a rising star of early British modernism. Within the open plan, simple tables and chairs in two sizes — one for adults and one for children — could be clustered and interlocked in a variety of patterns, reflecting the center's experimental ethos and emphasis on social interaction. The chair was economical to produce: two flat pieces of birch plywood (cut from a standard sized sheet to minimize waste) slotted together as a base structure onto which a flat seat and bentwood back panel were fitted. The cruciform shape of the chair's base echoed the section-profile of the building's concrete pillars. At night, the building's shimmering glass exterior blazed with electric light, standing out as a beacon of modernity and optimism in this working-class locality.

Williams's design expressed the radical brief of two doctors, George Scott Williamson and Innes Pearse, who believed that an

individual's social and physical environment could decisively affect his or her long-term state of health.[1] Their ideas were influenced by "biologism" (the study of social behavior according to biological principles that dominated social theory at this time among both health professionals and architects), and by Maria Montessori's theory of learning as a spontaneous process. Viewed this way, the center was a kind of human laboratory, designed to test the doctors' belief that environment and social interaction between free agents, rather than medicine, held the key to the study of health. Rowdy children created mayhem when the center first opened, but Williamson rejected the use of authoritarian discipline to reestablish order, instead trusting that "a sort of anarchy … will permit the emergence of order through spontaneous action."[2] The transparency of the glass-clad structure and its open plan was vital to the doctors' observation of such interactions among the participants. Nine hundred and fifty families signed up for "the Peckham Experiment," paying one shilling a week for access to the center's recreational and medical facilities. The emphasis on preventative health care as well as the voluntary nature of participation was markedly different from the recriminatory and patrician tone of most working-class health care, and despite overtones of social engineering and voyeurism, the center was genuinely popular with locals.

53 KIT NICHOLSON (British, 1904–1948)
Child's chair for Peckham Health Centre. 1935
Lacquered plywood, 14 $^7/_{16}$ x 13 $^3/_4$ x 10 $^5/_8$"
(36.7 x 35 x 27 cm)
Vitra Design Museum, Weil am Rhein, Germany

54 GORDON CULLEN (British, 1914–1994)
Mural at the Finsbury Health Centre, London. 1936
Photograph by Dell & Wainwright
Dell & Wainwright/RIBA Library Photographs
Collection

55 ABRAM GAMES (British, 1914–1996)
Your Britain, Fight for It Now, poster designed for
the Army Bureau of Current Affairs (ABCA),
London. 1942
19 $^{15}/_{16}$ x 29 $^1/_2$" (50.7 x 75 cm)
Estate of Abram Games, London

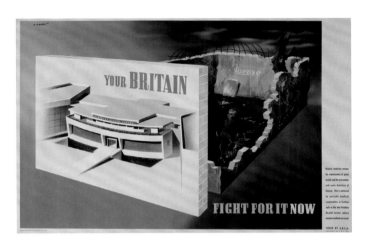

The Finsbury Park Health Centre that opened in 1938 was more focused on curative medicine, but was also a multifunctional facility that made a radical break with traditional access to health care in a borough blighted by tuberculosis and slum housing. It was funded by the local council—known as "the people's republic of Finsbury" for its left-wing radicalism—which turned to the émigré architect Berthold Lubetkin and his group Tecton. Immersed as a student in the revolutionary ethos of Russian Constructivism, Lubetkin had never lost his belief in technology and modern architecture as catalysts for changing people's behavior. "Nothing," declared Lubetkin at the center's opening, "is too good for ordinary people."[3] He wanted to create a welcoming atmosphere completely unlike the forbidding, prisonlike facilities traditionally served up to the poor. While designed to create an informal atmosphere the center was also planned scientifically to function as efficiently and productively as possible. The entrance facade, created of glass blocks for an open, sunlit interior, led to a lobby dotted with modern plywood furniture designed by Alvar Aalto. A mural by Gordon Cullen on the themes of healthy diet, fresh air, and sunshine decorated the entrance to a solarium where children with chronic vitamin deficiency, rickets, or tuberculosis could benefit from artificial sunshine (no. 54).

With its free, integrated services available under one roof—additional offerings included tuberculosis treatment, X-ray and foot clinics, dental surgery, and a disinfecting station for infested bedding and clothing—the center served as a model for the National Health Service that would be founded ten years later. Plans for a national health scheme were already being discussed during World War II, when graphic designer Abram Games produced three posters for the Army Bureau of Current Affairs on the theme of "Your Britain, Fight for It Now." The one dealing with health depicted the radiant entrance to the Finsbury Health Centre standing in front of a dark and blasted landscape, where a sickly child plays in a puddle of muddy water amid total devastation (no. 55). The political implications of health care for all was not lost on the conservative leader Winston Churchill, who ordered the entire issue of this poster to be destroyed on the grounds that it would damage national morale.[4]

Juliet Kinchin

Твой образ будет руководящей звездой.   27

INTRODUCTION

DESPITE ATTEMPTS by educational and design reformers to preserve modern childhood as a time of innocence, children were implicated, both directly and by association, in the major political tendencies of the twentieth century. In the 1920s and '30s some of the best modern designers, finding themselves in controversial times and places, produced work for children that was politically driven or else was politically construed. In the volatile climate of the years between the wars, even educational methods that used nonrepresentational teaching materials and focused solely on the development of the individual child could assume political overtones. To Viennese readers of the *Reichspost* newspaper in 1923, there was a clear correlation between Franz Cižek's innovative style of teaching and the voting preferences of his pupils' parents: "So Pipi, you can tell your parents that if they're staunch Social Democratic voters, you can come back in the next school year to cut up paper again and splash around with paste; but if they vote Christian Democrat, you must learn to read, write and add up."[1]

The new pedagogy and new design of the early twentieth century were in the main linked with liberal, democratic values, but their apparent support for the progressive side of things had little to do with an inherent politics of modernism. The energies feeding into modern design during the tremendous political ferment of the interwar years could go in many different directions. In some cases, great enthusiasm for modern technology and modern forms of architecture and design was coupled with reactionary or totalitarian ideologies. Recent scholarship has also addressed the extent to which modernism in countries like Britain, France, Japan, and the United States was inflected by imperial and colonial values.

As citizens of the future and emissaries of cultural knowledge, children became the focus of patriotic consumption on the part of their parents. This was reflected in a growing demand throughout Europe, the United States, and Japan for products that both were modern and would inculcate the appropriate political beliefs. Children's books, clothing, and toys — often suffused with a combination of humor and violence — became a vehicle for transposing adult politics into fictional worlds of engaged citizenship.

Many politicized modernists were more than willing to use their skills to raise consciousness about the benefits of radical social change, as well as about the collateral damage to children in wartime. As symbols of domestic life, national identity, and the future, children were one of the key motifs in all forms of visual propaganda. The prominent representation of children in posters of the Spanish Civil War and World War II, combined with the use of modern typography and photomontage, exerted a powerful emotional appeal. Modern designers were also recruited to the causes of various state-run and political youth movements, to design uniforms, magazines, and custom-built environments — such as for children's clubs in the Soviet Union and children's colonies in Fascist Italy — that would instill a sense of collective belonging and identification with an ideologically inflected view of the future. The tension between individual development and communal purpose in youth organizations, such as in the Red Falcons in Germany or the activities of the Works Progress Administration for children in the United States, was one also found at the heart of modernist design and educational reform.

This chapter brings into focus a recurrent paradox in twentieth-century design for children: the simultaneous desire to protect the youngest and most vulnerable members of society from the cares of adult existence while also projecting onto them ideological values belonging to that same adult world of partisan politics and unequal power relationships. Children are subjected to a range of forces, from psychological pressure to physical violence, as both victims and perpetrators. Designers have contributed to this process by co-opting children into various forms of propaganda and by providing the props for worlds of play and learning that reflect the larger political and ideological environment. An equally powerful theme emerges, however, in the role of design as a therapeutic agent, which was informed by the unshakable belief of many designers and educators in the power of design to transcend politics.

Juliet Kinchin

See page 122

1 GUSTAV KLUTSIS (Latvian, 1895–1938)
and SERGEI SENKIN (Russian, 1894–1963)
Page from the book *Deti i Lenin* (Children and Lenin).
1924
8 7/8 x 7" (22.5 x 17.8 cm)
Elaine Lustig Cohen, New York

IN 1923 Leon Trotsky declared that "a revolution does not deserve its name if it does not take the greatest care possible of the children — the future race for whose benefit the revolution has been made."[1] Following the 1917 Russian Revolution, which toppled the czarist monarchy, children quickly became the most visible element of Communist propaganda at home and abroad, made into symbols of Soviet modernization and a bright utopian future, despite continuing to suffer the hardship of widespread poverty. Many avant-garde designers in Soviet Russia, including El Lissitzky and Aleksandr Rodchenko, committed themselves to the construction and propagandizing of a radically different society. Despite disagreements among the members of the Constructivist avant-garde about how this was to be achieved and a shift away from radical Constructivism to the more doctrinaire aesthetics of Socialist Realism in the 1930s, what remained consistent in these projects was a focus on children.

Serious and self-assertive, the Pioneer girl photographed by Rodchenko in 1930 (no. 2) stares toward the future — no trace here of childish cheekiness or coy femininity. Instead, her cropped hair and unfrivolous demeanor speak to new concepts of gender equality and active, politically engaged childhood. The Young Pioneers, identified by their white shirts and red neckerchiefs, were a highly organized association established in 1922 for Communist children aged ten to fifteen (also, starting in 1924, known as Young Leninists) (p. 121, no. 1). As part of the cultural revolution these young activists were urged to

exercise leadership of backward or recalcitrant adults. "We compel our parents not to fear fresh air. We fight smoking in the school and the home.... We ask for ourselves our own plates, our own beds."[2] The photograph's close-up cropping and viewpoint from below add to the Pioneer girl's aura of authority, reflecting the importance attached to children, both boys and girls, as combatants in the process of radical political and societal transformation. "This turbulent reality could not be captured within the framework of traditional 'painterly' compositions," wrote Vitaly Zhemchuzhny in 1929; new photographic techniques were required "to reproduce the excerpts from social reality as sharply and precisely as possible."[3]

In 1928 Joseph Stalin introduced the First Five-Year Plan, which set economic goals that would industrially strengthen the Union of Soviet Socialist Republics; the following year, at the sixteenth Communist Party Congress, he emphasized that compulsory primary education was vital to engendering popular support for these policies and the cultural revolution they entailed. As a result, by 1935 the number of children in primary school had risen to 25 million, from 7.5 million in 1914. Reports by the Comintern (the Communist International) and visual propaganda highlighted the state's exemplary attention to children's welfare, social position, and political education, citing them as an index of progress and contrasting them to exploitative practices in the capitalist West or the czarist Russia of old. These claims were supported with data, such as the growth in capacity of city nurseries in 1929–32 (no. 3) or the increase in children's average height and weight, often presented in a visually compelling way and using graphic innovation to create a sense of momentum and make quantitative information understandable to a lay audience. These pictographic images demonstrate a growing emphasis on physiological and psychological conformity in Soviet culture, directed at breaking down differential markers of class, wealth, and ethnicity (no. 4).

From an early age, children were to be taught self-discipline and hygienic habits and inducted into adult roles as productive, politically aware workers (no. 5). It was also Communist Party policy to involve them in management, decision making, and political discussion by giving them representation on committees in schools, factories, clubs, and other institutions. Elizawieta Ignatowitsch's poster from 1931 (no. 6), proclaiming, "The struggle for the polytechnic schools is the struggle for the Five-Year Plan, and for a Communist education of the body politic," demonstrates the prevailing emphasis on industrial achievement, placing a girl at the forefront of the drive to spread modern, rational efficiency

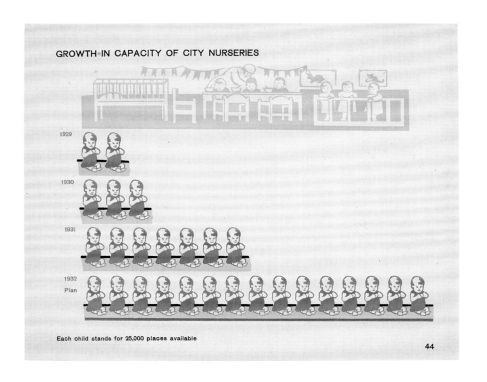

GROWTH IN CAPACITY OF CITY NURSERIES

1929

1930

1931

1932
Plan

Each child stands for 25,000 places available

44

2 ALEKSANDR RODCHENKO
(Russian, 1891–1956)
Pioneer Girl. 1930
Gelatin silver print, 19 $^1/_2$ x 14 $^9/_{16}$" (49.6 x 37 cm)
The Museum of Modern Art, New York. Gift of Alex
Lachmann and friends of the Rodchenko family

3 *Growth in Capacity of City Nurseries*, from the portfolio
The Struggle for Five Years in Four. c. 1932
Lithograph, 7 $^1/_2$ x 9 $^1/_{16}$" (19 x 23 cm)
Published by State Publishing House of Fine Arts, Moscow
The Wolfsonian–Florida International University, Miami Beach.
The Mitchell Wolfson, Jr. Collection

4 ELENA AFANAS'EVA (Russian, 1904–1973)
and I. KULESHOV (Russian, dates unknown)
Cover of the book *Deti sovetov* (Children of the Soviets),
by Osip Kolychev. 1931
9 $^1/_{16}$ x 7 $^7/_8$" (23 x 20 cm)
Published by Molodaia Gvardiia, Moscow
Printed by Obraztsovaia, Moscow
The Wolfsonian–Florida International University,
Miami Beach. The Mitchell Wolfson, Jr. Collection

5 FRANCISZKA THEMERSON
(British, born Poland. 1907–1988)
Cover of the book *Nasi Ojcowie Pracuja*
(Our fathers at work), by Stefan Themerson. 1933
9 $^1/_2$ x 7" (24.1 x 17.8 cm)
Published by Naklad Gebethnera i Wolffa, Warsaw
Cotsen Children's Library, Princeton University Library

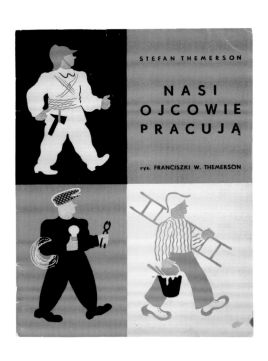

and political consciousness in the factory. She is not enslaved to the machinery but instead wields it with confidence, working to build a new society. Indeed, the state-controlled factory, rather than the family, was, as Lissitzky observed, "the crucible of socialization for the urban population."[4] In the model school of Krasy Bogatyr, which was attached to a rubber-processing factory on the outskirts of Moscow, children started handling tools and working with wood and iron in kindergarten, following the principle that "education is directed from the head to the hands.... Here small tables and chairs for the kindergarten are made by the students themselves, and they even make toys."[5] The toys did not belong to individual children but were borrowed from a centralized depot. When the children turned ten years old, the technical work became more specialized. Krasy Bogatyr was among the modern children's hospitals, schools, nurseries, and clubs that were heavily promoted on official guided tours organized by the Society for Cultural Relations with Foreign Countries, known as VOKS, as operational examples of the utopian world to come. The new Soviet system of craft training in schools was widely admired by progressive educators around the world, including the designer R. R. Tomlinson, who was chief inspector of art for the London County Council; he praised the Soviet integration of teaching for art, craft, and industry, and the aim of giving children a wider cultural outlook by relating design to other subjects in the curriculum and to life outside the school.[6]

6 ELIZAWIETA IGNATOWITSCH
(Russian, 1903–1983)
The Struggle for the Polytechnic Schools Is the Struggle for the Five Year Plan. 1931
Letterpress and lithograph, 20 1/4 x 28 1/4"
(51.4 x 71.8 cm)
The Museum of Modern Art, New York.
Gift of Miss Jessie Rosenfeld

7 EL LISSITZKY (Russian, 1890–1941)
USSR. Die russische Ausstellung (USSR:
The Russian exhibition), poster for exhibition
at the Kunstgewerbemuseum, Zurich, 1929
Gravure, 49 7/8 x 35 5/8" (126.7 x 90.5 cm)
The Museum of Modern Art, New York. Purchase

Ideological superiority and demonstrable progress were also the themes of numerous state-sponsored exhibitions and publications in the late 1920s and '30s, most of them organized through VOKS. In one of his most memorable posters (no. 7), designed for the 1929 *Russische Ausstellung* in Zurich, Lissitzky employed children rather than muscle-bound workers to depict a Socialist future: a boy and a girl photographically fused into a single entity, with the letters USSR emblazoned in red across their conjoined foreheads, making them the embodiment of the international Soviet and its egalitarian, collective consciousness. Their looming over a representation of the actual exhibition installation, a piece of radical functionalism in its own right, further links them to a modern, technologically driven ideal of the Soviet Union. Their open-necked shirts and the girl's breeze-blown hair, silhouetted against an open sky, speak to the children's healthy lifestyle and, by association, the vitality of the state. This poster prefigures many of the conventions that would harden into Socialist Realism, including the relentless optimism and the gigantism that elevates figures to a superhuman scale and power. But Lissitzky's innovations in photomontage and exhibition design combine to make this an effective piece of propaganda that was admired by left-leaning artists around the world, including the avant-garde Swiss typographer Jan Tschichold, who once owned the copy now in the collection of The Museum of Modern Art.

Juliet Kinchin

8 Double-page spread from the book
Deutschland. 1936
13³/₄ x 11" (35 x 28 cm)
Published by Volk und Reich, Berlin
The Wolfsonian–Florida International University,
Miami Beach. The Mitchell Wolfson, Jr. Collection

Unsere Fahne ist die neue Zeit!

IN THE 1920S AND '30S political parties all over Europe and the United States created youth groups in order to develop new constituencies and shore up their legitimacy. This was achieved by providing facilities and a program of playful activities alongside rituals and duties that inculcated a system of values that revered an authority above and beyond that of the family unit. The German Youth Movement was the umbrella term until 1933 for German children's organizations allied with various political or religious creeds; after 1933 all groups except the officially sanctioned Hitler Jugend (Hitler Youth), including rival Nazi ones, were outlawed, and the paramilitary overtones of German youth culture became more pronounced (no. 8).[1]

In its various manifestations, irrespective of alignment with the political right or left, the German Youth Movement embodied a modernist impulse that has been traced back to the Wandervögel (Wandering birds), an open-air movement established in 1896 in revolt against the militarism, rigid discipline, and materialism of middle-class life.[2] Spiritually hostile to bourgeois society and seeking social change, its members created a reform philosophy that emphasized personal development through contact with nature. "Week-end hikes and camps, simpler dress, simpler habits, more spontaneous activities were characteristic of every German youth group," observed Leslie Paul, who was involved with similar activities for children in England, in 1938.[3] This ethos found parallels in several major tenets of the developing modern movement in design: critique of social conventions, celebration of physical health, simpler dress, and uncluttered, minimalist ways of living. It also reinforced new approaches to informal and experiential education, echoing Friedrich Froebel's conviction that "the starting point of all human culture, also of knowledge is doing, action. Action must be the starting point of the real, the developing education."[4]

A modernist agenda was explicit in the visual identity and focus on social transformation of the Rote Falken, or Red Falcons, an organization, established in 1925 in association with the Social Democratic Party, that recruited children from the urban working classes.[5] Like the religious groups that regarded modern capitalist society as corrupt and corrupting, this youth organization sought to create spaces outside that society in which to encourage social activities and attitudes that reflected the party's wider political ideals. In 1927 about two thousand young Falcons, both boys and girls, gathered on a remote lakeside to construct a Rote Kinderrepublik (Red children's republic) that would temporarily create a utopian, socially harmonious community. The event was documented in a book (no. 9) about the children's experiences, illustrated with photomontages and using the cutting-edge New Typography current among Central European avant-gardes — sans serif type, asymmetrical page layouts, bold rules, and photomontage — to reinforce the revolutionary significance and identity of this apparently innocent holiday camp. The book, like the activities it illustrated, was a collaborative project that epitomized the Red Falcons' motto of *gegenseitige Hilfe* (mutual aid): "A book by workers' children, for workers'

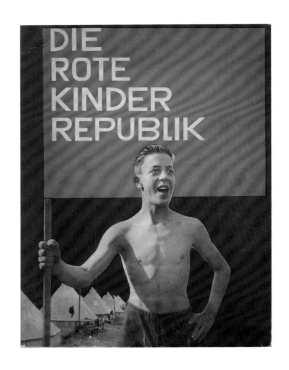

children, drawn from letters, diaries and drawings gathered together and narrated by [well-known left-wing journalist] Andreas Gayk."[6]

The movements to reform both society and design landed on camping as an activity that described a version of a new, ideal world.[7] Gender equality was built into the layout of the Red Falcons' camp as well as the programming of activities and chores, whereas the all-male Hitler Youth camps relegated girls to a separate, more domestically focused organization, the Bund Deutscher Mädel. The Nazi emphasis on military and patriotic training also clashed with the Social Democratic Party's avowed pacifism and internationalist outlook; fearing the potential of groups like the Red Falcons to subvert children's relationships with centralized forms of authority, Adolf Hitler banned all such organizations in 1933.

The culture of militarism was reinforced by Nazi-themed toys, board games, and children's books (no. 10). But in the 1930s, war games were hardly unique to Germany, and one wonders how many American children playing with a miniature zeppelin dirigible (no. 11), sold by J. C. Penney, would have been aware of its German origins and larger political symbolism.

Juliet Kinchin

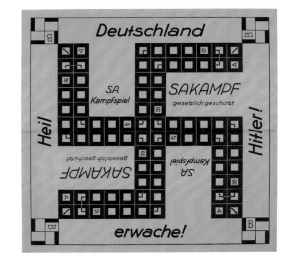

9 NIELS BRODERSEN (German, 1895–1971) and RICHARD GRUNE (German, 1903–1983)
Cover of the book *Die rote Kinderrepublik* (Red children's republic), by Andreas Gayk. 1930
11⁷⁄₁₆ x 9³⁄₁₆" (29 x 23.3 cm)
Published by Arbeiterjugend Verlag, Berlin
The Museum of Modern Art Library, New York

10 SAKAMPF board game. 1933
13³⁄₄ x 13³⁄₄" (35 x 35 cm)
The Wolfsonian–Florida International University, Miami Beach. The Mitchell Wolfson, Jr. Collection

11 Graf Zeppelin. c. 1930
Iron alloy, aluminum, enamel paint, and decals,
7¹⁄₄ x 25" (18.4 x 63.5 cm)
Distribution attributed to J. C. Penney Co., Inc., Plano, Texas
Minneapolis Institute of Arts. The Modernism Collection, gift of Norwest Bank Minnesota

THE ITALIAN DICTATOR Benito Mussolini recognized the importance of winning over the nation's youth in order to ensure the perpetuation of the Fascist ideology and his single-party state. His National Fascist Party browbeat elementary-school instructors into conforming to and teaching the party line and established, in 1926, the Opera Nazionale Balilla (ONB) to organize and exert control over youth groups and extracurricular activities for students younger than eighteen. Under the aegis of the ONB, Italian youth were subjected to Fascist indoctrination and socialization, physical conditioning, and military drills designed to inculcate a spirit of unquestioning obedience and to create generations of ready-trained soldiers who would carry out Il Duce's plans for expanding Italy's empire in North and East Africa.[1]

Six- and seven-year-old Italian boys were enrolled in Figli della Lupa, or the Sons of the Wolf, a group whose name conjured the she-wolf of Rome's founding myth and the glories of the first Roman Empire. At age eight they graduated to the Balillas, named for the stone-throwing Genoese youth said to have initiated the revolt against Italy's Hapsburg occupiers in the eighteenth century.[2] In 1937 the various adolescent groups were reorganized under the umbrella of the Gioventù Italiana del Littorio, with the motto "Credere, obbedire, combattere," or "Believe, obey, fight." Boys of all ages took an oath to "execute the orders of the DUCE and serve with all my strength and, if necessary, with my blood the Cause of the Fascist Revolution."[3] Young girls were enrolled according to age in separate organizations under the auspices of the Fasci Femminili, the women's wing of the party, and encouraged to participate in "doll drill" and other activities that fostered a "cult of the cradle."[4]

While Italian girls were being prepared by the regime for their future reproductive and nurturing roles, boys were encouraged to don uniforms and drill with practice rifles, to prepare them to be soldiers capable of extending the borders of the modern Roman Empire. Dominated by an image of the obelisk in Rome's Foro Mussolini, a poster for Balilla Week (no. 12) positions the viewer as a spectator, standing behind and looking over the shoulder of a Balilla holding a rifle and wearing the organization's uniform of blue neckerchief, black shirt, and khaki shorts. The viewer's eye is drawn toward a shining map of Italy's new East African colonies; at the bottom of the poster are Mussolini's words, in clean, modern letters: "In the Balilla we see the great hope of tomorrow, the dawn that rises at the horizon of the world."[5] As part of a campaign to indoctrinate young Fascists, in 1931 the ONB took control of and continued publishing Il Balilla (1926–43), a weekly newspaper featuring comics illustrated by prominent Italian designers, including

12 C. M. (nationality and dates unknown)
Settimana del Balilla 5–10 Dicembre XIV Genova
(Balilla youth movement week, December 5–10, 1936 Genoa). 1935
Commercial color lithograph, sheet: 55 1/8 x 39 1/2"
(140 x 100.3 cm)
Printed by Barabino & Graeve, Genoa
The Wolfsonian–Florida International University, Miami Beach. The Mitchell Wolfson, Jr. Collection

Antonio Rubino (see "Italy: The Unruly Child," p. 66), Mario Pompei, and Enrico De Seta (no. 13).[6] Rubino eschewed politics and attained fame as a children's book illustrator, while Pompei embraced Fascism and was responsible for the Sons of the Wolf uniforms, which have been described as having "a more 'comic-strip' element, white braces crossed over and linked with a burnished metal M-shaped buckle of essential, modern line."[7] De Seta's contributions to *Il Balilla* included satirical stereotypes of North Africans; with Edizioni d'Arte Boeri, he published racy and racist cartoon postcards of natives during the Ethiopian campaign.[8]

There were opportunities to apply Fascist symbols and ideology to all sorts of everyday items designed for Italian children. In addition to listening to romanticized accounts of combat on the radio and singing the patriotic lyrics of "Faccetta nera" (Little black face), schoolchildren wrote their lessons in notebooks decorated with illustrated covers that invited them to picture themselves in youth-movement uniforms, blurring the distinctions between education and propaganda. Some covers depicted Fascist youths participating in patriotic activities such as waging the "battle for the grain," Mussolini's program for reclaiming and transforming swampland into productive farmland; others pictured them competing in sports events or military marches or drills (no. 14). Still other covers made visual parallels between the military exploits of ancient Rome and the reestablishment of the modern empire by Mussolini across *mare nostrum*, the Latin phrase meaning "our sea," typically used to describe the Mediterranean in Fascist educational media. Outside the classroom, Fascist youth could eat and drink from tableware designed to whet their appetite for future service in the colonies. In the mid-1930s the Richard Ginori porcelain factory manufactured children's plates, cups, and saucers (no. 15), decorated with age-appropriate colonial imagery — the ubiquitous palm tree, camel, pith helmet, rifle, tank, and huts flying the Italian flag — designed to celebrate Italian conquests in North and East Africa.

Games such as La conquista dell'Abissinia (c. 1936) and Tombola di Etiopia: Storica, geografica (no. 16) encouraged children to learn about and vicariously win the contest for Ethiopia. The latter, a game that rewarded knowledge of the history and geography of the Italian Empire, was researched and compiled by Ettore Boschi, the prolific children's author better known by his pseudonym, Nonno Ebe (Grandpa Ebe). Nonno Ebe set an example for the nation's youth by declaring, at age sixty-three, his intention of participating in his fourth war. He also published *Genietti e sirenelle in Africa Orientale* (Little genies and little mermaids in East Africa) (1936), a fairy tale set during the Ethiopia war, in which the imaginary male creatures demonstrated their intelligence, technical prowess, and bravery, while their female counterparts celebrated the army's exploits by singing and draping themselves in the Italian flag.[9]

This gendered division of duties was visually reinforced in other publications promoting Italian colonial efforts in East Africa and aimed at the country's youth. The avant-garde cover design of *Napoli–Addis Abeba*, a book published in 1937 (no. 17), mixes bold, colorful iconography with photomontage to demonstrate the passion of the virile men of Naples serving in Africa. A photographic close-up of the face of a determined Italian male is superimposed atop a bright red *fascio*, an ancient Roman symbol of power revivified by the Fascists; a transport ship enclosed within an arrow connects him across a bright blue dot— symbolizing "our sea," or the globe — to a man taking leave of his wife and baby, while an older boy sporting a pith helmet sits atop his shoulders, suggesting his eagerness to follow his father's example. These and other propagandistic objects and images demonstrate that Mussolini and his regime recognized the importance of psychologically preparing Italy's youth for their future role as soldiers and colonizers, and took every opportunity to remind them of their duty to become active participants in Italy's expanding empire.

Francis Luca

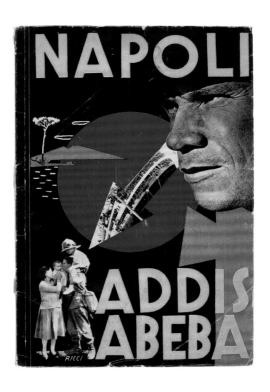

13 ENRICO DE SETA (Italian, 1908–2008)
Back cover of *Il Balilla* weekly cartoon,
February 15, 1934
15 3/8 x 11" (39 x 28 cm)
Published by Presidenza dell'Opera Balilla, Rome
The Wolfsonian–Florida International University,
Miami Beach. The Mitchell Wolfson, Jr. Collection

14 Notebook cover. c. 1939
7 7/8 x 5 7/8" (20 x 15 cm)
Published by Igap, Milan and Rome
The Wolfsonian–Florida International University,
Miami Beach. Gift of Steven Heller

15 Figli della Lupa (Sons of the Wolf) tableware set.
1930s
Manufactured by Richard Ginori, Florence (est. 1775),
Collection of Andrea Schito, Genoa

16 Tombola di Etiopia: Storica, geografica,
strategic board game. c. 1937
Compiled by Nonno Ebe (pseudonym of
Ettore Boschi)
12 1/4 x 8 1/4" (31 x 21 cm)
Manufactured by Carroccio, Milan
The Wolfsonian–Florida International University,
Miami Beach. The Mitchell Wolfson, Jr. Collection

17 RICCI (Italian, dates unknown)
Cover of the book *Napoli–Addis Abeba: Albo
di ferro della passione di Napoli per la fondazione
dell'impero* (Naples–Addis Ababa: Iron register
of the passion of Naples for the foundation
of the empire). 1937
Compiled by Mancuso, Iacobelli, Romei
16 15/16 x 11 13/16" (43 x 30 cm)
Published by A. Caldarola, Naples
The Wolfsonian–Florida International University,
Miami Beach. The Mitchell Wolfson, Jr. Collection

THE GREAT SURGE toward modernity in Japan was shaped as much
by military ambition as by industrial reform. The Meiji ruling elites who
emerged in the wake of Commodore Matthew Perry's gunboat diplomacy of 1853–54 wanted the new state to emulate and surpass its
Western rivals in manufacturing and military organization. The speed
of modernization, along with this determination to establish the nation
as a world power, created tensions in Japan's traditional hierarchical
society that were only held in control by a strict culture that placed a
high premium on virtues such as discipline, loyalty, and respect. These
values were built into the Japanese education system in 1890, when
it was reformed according to the Imperial Rescript for Education, and
schooling became both a tool of the state and the means to fashion the
new society. As a result, the traditional concept of *kokutai*, or personal
identification with the principles of the state and the sovereignty of the
emperor, was frequently combined with allusions to the military in the
worldview and material culture of the modern Japanese child (no. 18).

The pattern of the Norakuro boy's kimono (no. 19), for example,
is a striking assemblage of different themes, including an armored car,
a military plane, and Norakuro, a popular cartoon dog, walking with
a boy scout over a background of Japanese flags and silhouetted battle
scenes with cavalrymen, marching troops, and soldiers, arms raised in
a "Banzai!" gesture, all framed by the sprockets of motion-picture film.[1]
This combination of the popular with the traditional, high with low, and
apparently innocuous figures with powerfully symbolic imagery seems
close to postmodern bricolage, but its juxtapositions — of juvenile and
martial, decorative and nationalistic, the celebration of military technology on a classic item of display clothing — are unquestionably
the product of Japanese modernity. The character Norakuro, created
by Suihō Tagawa and first published in manga in 1931, was as popular
and long-lived in Japan as Mickey Mouse was in the United States.
Norakuro was originally a soldier in a fictitious "fierce dogs brigade"
and participated in battles with obvious parallels to the Japanese
military situation. The year that Norakuro first appeared was also the
year of the Mukden Incident, an alleged Chinese attack on a Japanese-
owned railway, which prompted Japan's invasion of Manchuria and
imperialist campaign to liberate Asia from Western colonial powers.

The process of modernization in Japanese society reached
a high point in the late 1920s and early 1930s, the early Shōwa period,
with the introduction of many of the instruments and symbols of mass
media (Norakuro, for example, appeared in films and newsreels as well
as in comics, as suggested by the sprocket patterns that frame each

scene in the kimono). Despite Western dress being increasingly adopted
in Japan, traditional dress codes continued to be observed especially
for ceremonial occasions and for the young. Fans decorated with
patriotic scenes (no. 20) were still widely used, and in families that
could afford it children would wear the kimono to visit ancestral shrines
such as the Yasukuni shrine in Tokyo, which commemorates soldiers
who died fighting on behalf of the emperor. These rituals make clear
the combined role of war propaganda, familial piety, and the need to
display virtues, such as devotion and respect, that were central to the
modern Japanese ideal. Even the emphasis on constructive play that
formed an important part of the modern school movement was used
to engage young children in the larger imperial effort. Books such as
The Sentiment of Children (no. 21) illustrated everyday children's activities,
but the text and images were tempered by an emphasis on respect for
the military and an appeal for productive work and tributes to be sent
to troops to boost morale during World War II.

Juliet Kinchin

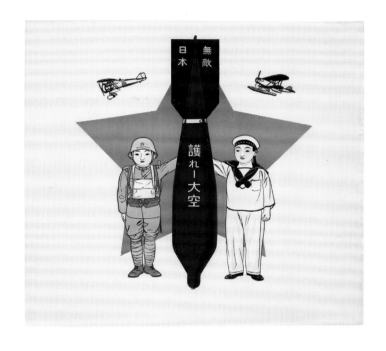

18 Child's kimono with Japanese bomber
planes. c. 1930
Rayon, 27 x 28 1/2" (68.6 x 72.4 cm)
Collection of Norman Brosterman, East Hampton

19 Child's kimono with the manga character
Norakuro the dog. c. 1930
Wool muslin, 34 x 32" (86.4 x 81.3 cm)
Collection of Norman Brosterman, East Hampton

20 Japanese military propaganda illustration
designed to be made into a fan (leaf 4). c. 1940
9 7/16 x 10 1/4" (24 x 26 cm)
The Wolfsonian–Florida International University,
Miami Beach. The Mitchell Wolfson, Jr. Collection

21 *The Sentiment of Children*. 1939
12 3/4 x 9 1/4" (32.4 x 23.5 cm)
Published by Jirou Takachi, Tokyo
Printed by Nakaya Matsuma Printing Company, Tokyo
The Wolfsonian–Florida International University,
Miami Beach. The Mitchell Wolfson, Jr. Collection

22 BEN SHAHN
(American, born Lithuania. 1898–1969)
Children of Destitute Mountaineer, Arkansas. 1935
Gelatin silver print, 6$^{1}/_{2}$ x 9$^{5}/_{8}$" (16.5 x 24.4 cm)
The Museum of Modern Art, New York. Gift of the
Farm Security Administration

23 FRANK SHAPIRO (American, 1914–1994)
A Raising in Early New Jersey, mural study for U.S.
Post Office, Washington, New Jersey (detail). 1939
Tempera and gouache on fiberboard, full study:
25$^{1}/_{4}$" x 6' 3" (64.1 x 190.5 cm)
The Wolfsonian–Florida International University,
Miami Beach. The Mitchell Wolfson, Jr. Collection

IN APRIL 1934, one year after her husband became president of the United States and in the depths of the Great Depression, First Lady Eleanor Roosevelt expressed serious concern for the nation's youth. "I have moments of real terror," she told a crowd of one thousand women, "when I think we may be losing this generation. We have got to bring these young people into the active life of the community, and make them feel that they are necessary."[1] The Roosevelts had good reason for such trepidation; in the years that followed the devastating stock market crash of 1929, thousands of schools had closed, and twenty percent of the country's children were hungry and lacking proper clothing.[2] Rural life in this period was especially difficult, as chronicled by photographers working for the Farm Security Administration, such as Walker Evans, Dorothea Lange, and Ben Shahn (no. 22). They captured bleak documentary images of impoverished families, the most enduring of which include children. Although the political climate in the United States in the 1930s and '40s was markedly different from authoritarian Germany, Italy, and the Soviet Union, American children found themselves the subject of considerable national attention in much the same way that their European counterparts were, and efforts to help them were inseparable from their being used for propagandistic ends.

President Franklin Delano Roosevelt's vast and progressive New Deal programs, implemented between 1933 and 1936, endeavored to unite a desperate country, provide stability and security, and foster hope for the future. "We face the arduous days that lie before us in the warm courage of national unity," the president said in his first inaugural address, "with the clear consciousness of seeking old and precious moral values; with the clean satisfaction that comes from the stern performance of duty by old and young alike."[3] Although primarily associated with putting American men back to work and modernizing national infrastructure, the New Deal launched significant initiatives for children and teenagers, including the National Youth Administration (NYA) and the youth-oriented programs of the Works Progress Administration (WPA). With support from Mrs. Roosevelt, the NYA was established in June 1935 and helped millions of young people stay in school with work-study grants, particularly teenagers not yet eligible for the Civilian Conservation Corps (a public work-relief program that employed only unmarried males over eighteen). The ideological goal was to protect democratic values by shielding at-risk youth from the totalitarian appeals of racist and Fascist groups.

Through the Federal Art Project, the WPA's visual-arts division, artists and designers produced thousands of paintings, prints, sculptures, and, most famously, murals, which fused distinctive modern design with existing architecture. The mural artists enlivened both public buildings (schools, hospitals, libraries) and federal buildings (courthouses, post offices), and many of them were inspired by politically engaged Mexican muralists, such as Diego Rivera. For the most part their designs celebrated American history, diversity, agriculture, industry, and technological progress, using bold forms and bright colors to

extoll the modern, liberal agenda that sponsored them. Children figured prominently and powerfully in these artistic and political statements, as in Frank Shapiro's 1939 study for a mural for a post office in New Jersey (no. 23), with its idealistic scenes of cooperative education and a happy family unit gathered around an open doorway suggesting possibility and prosperity.[4] On the conspicuousness of children in murals around the city, the *New York Times* commented, "The first leit-motif that strikes the observer is a preoccupation with the quieter, gayer sides of life in this city.... Children, trees, dogs and flowers squeeze in everywhere, like grass cracking through cement."[5]

Lucienne Bloch's design for a mural in the House of Detention for Women in downtown Manhattan (no. 24), in 1935, made a bid for the heartstrings (and possible reform) of its intended audience with a notably diverse group of children innocently playing marbles on the city sidewalk.[6] Her work was supported by Commissioner of Correction Austin H. MacCormick, who believed in "the value of color and decoration as an aid to the readjustment of offenders," and this scene was conceived as part of a series of murals representing The Cycle of a Woman's Life, a subject approved by the inmates themselves.[7] In the first completed section of this series, for the recreation room, Bloch included a similar element of quiet play, here accompanied by more dynamic activities (running, swinging, sliding), with supportive adult figures in the foreground and skyscrapers and busy factories in the background.[8] The high-rise jail, designed in 1931 by Sloan & Robertson, the firm that designed the Chanin Building (1929), was once hailed as New York's modern "model prison" but was demolished in 1973–74.[9]

WPA artists also designed posters and books, many of them either aimed at children or featuring them prominently, such as posters advertising free art classes for children — at new art centers, settlement houses, and museums such as the Walker Art Center in Minneapolis — as well as exhibitions of the work that resulted. WPA publications occasionally featured children's artwork, such as a set of twenty linoleum-block prints — produced, in the tradition of Franz Cižek's pupils, by junior high school students in Milwaukee — that were selected by the

WPA's Milwaukee Printmakers in a 1938 competition among public schools. One of the twenty prints published was a lively, charged image of a musician and instruments by a young artist named Le Roy Prodoehl (no. 25).

In addition to brightening the everyday lives of schoolchildren with art, New Deal programs made a drastic impact on their public environments. The Federal Works Agency reported that by the end of 1941 about 37,500 schools and 1,000 libraries had been "built, enlarged, or reconditioned" by WPA workers.[10] In new, modern school structures (including 1,500 new nursery schools) and existing schools, WPA workers served hot lunches, fixed shoes, provided vaccinations, and served as traffic guards. WPA artists also designed, built, and repaired toys, which children could borrow using a system, as in the Soviet Union, similar to a public library's. Building and infrastructure projects, which resulted in 650,000 miles of roads and 78,000 bridges, improved access to these new and renovated spaces for both children and adults, who used them as community centers.

By 1936 the Federal Writer's Project employed more than six thousand writers from every state, creating books that were both educational tools and pleasant diversions from the hardship of the period. Books for children featured simple texts, frequent illustrations, and strong modern graphic design (sometimes all by the same person) in striking and accessible combinations. In order to foster patriotism and excitement for the wonders of modern American life, many of the books specifically addressed American history and culture, modern materials (aluminum, steel, plastics), citizenship, and morality. Helen Johnson's *Farm Book* (no. 26), which married stylized animal forms with inspiring pithy poems, is an exemplar of WPA aesthetics and ideology, addressed to the children struggling along with the rest of the country: "This is a team of percheron mares/Teams, you know, are pairs/Together they pull a load all day/And never get in each other's way."

Aidan O'Connor

BLACK & TAN SORIOTA   SOLOMON JUNEAU   LE ROY PRODOEHL

This is a team of percheron mares.
Teams, you know, are pairs.
Together they pull a load all day
And never get in each other's way.

IN EARLY-TWENTIETH-CENTURY BRITAIN the concept of child art put children and adolescents at the center of a debate that encompassed progressive art and so-called primitive art, the effects of industrialization, and the responsibilities of colonialism. With a narrative of rescue, progressive educators sought to free the British child and children under colonial rule from a highly controlled system of art education dominated by accurate copying, a system established in the previous century by the British government's department of science and art in order to improve public taste and the standards of industrial manufacture. The widely shared belief that the arts of Europe were spiritually exhausted encouraged this turn toward the child and toward cultures that Western domination had undermined.[1] Since the late nineteenth century, artists, designers, and thinkers such as William Morris and E. B. Havell, principal of the Government School of Art in Calcutta, had argued that colonialism had broken the artistic cultures of the Asian subcontinent, and by the 1920s this concern had expanded to include sub-Saharan Africa.[2] This essay looks briefly at art education for children in Britain and, in more detail, at a largely forgotten project to save African children from degraded European taste by restoring "that naturalness which no trained European can now hope to attain."[3]

Marion Richardson, a charismatic young teacher, mounted an early practical challenge to orthodox art instruction in British schools.[4] Richardson began her career in 1911 in a polluted mining and manufacturing area known as the Black Country just north of Birmingham. There, at Dudley Girls' High School, she discouraged any kind of copying and instead invited the children to sit, eyes closed, listening to "word pictures," Richardson's term for her vivid spoken descriptions of local and imaginary scenes, which became the source material from which her pupils drew and painted. Other techniques used by Richardson included "beauty hunts," in which the children sought subjects in Dudley's industrial landscape, and "mind pictures," visual reports of what they saw when their eyes were closed, which produced remarkable abstract images. Richardson also encouraged vigorous pattern-making exercises, which were subsequently developed into *Writing and Writing Patterns* (nos. 27, 28), a series of handwriting books.

The art critic Roger Fry was a keen supporter of Richardson and her methods; as early as 1909 he had suggested that children, if "left to themselves," never copy "but express, with a delightful freedom and sincerity, the mental images which make up their own imaginative lives."[5] In 1917, in the context of the Dudley work, he argued that to appreciate children's art it was necessary to have an understanding

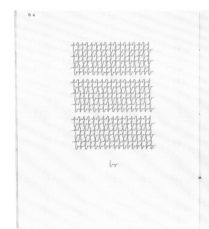

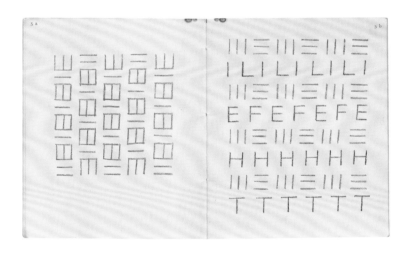

27 MARION RICHARDSON (British, 1892–1946)
"On Being Black," by Dr. James Aggrey (a founder of Achimota School, Gold Coast), from *Writing and Writing Patterns*, book 5 (overseas edition). 1951
8 3/8 x 6 11/16" (21.3 x 17 cm)
Published by University of London Press Ltd
Private collection

28 MARION RICHARDSON (British, 1892–1946)
Double-page spread from *Writing and Writing Patterns*, book 1. 1935
8 7/16 x 6 7/8 x 3/16" (21.5 x 17.4 x 0.4 cm)
Published by University of London Press Ltd
The Museum of Modern Art Library, New York

of Gothic and early Italian and Byzantine art, early Oriental art, and, finally, Aztec and African art.[6] In art by children Fry recognized a simplicity, directness, intensity, and freshness that bypassed the formulaic nature of most adult art, but he noted that both children and "native races" were "singularly at the mercy of outside influences," ready to "make bad copies of the vilest products of modern European industrialism."[7] This linking of the child artist to anti-industrialism and to the increasing appreciation of non-Western art was played out most tellingly in a handful of progressive schools in British West Africa.

In Britain by the 1920s progressive artists and art critics had come to recognize the importance of the material culture of sub-Saharan Africa. Fry led the way, with an essay written in 1920 that argued that African sculpture was "greater, I think, than anything we produced even in the Middle Ages."[8] In parallel with such thinking, colonial guilt and anxiety often took an aesthetic form, bemoaning the ways in which vernacular African taste was being undermined, from the influx of shoddy materials — colonial administrators regularly deplored the import of corrugated iron; cheap, industrially produced cloth; ugly shop signs; and kerosene cans into West Africa — to the way children were being taught.[9]

Art education for African children was debated in the pages of *Oversea Education*, a journal for colonial teachers published by the Colonial Office from 1929 until 1963.[10] In that journal in 1929 William Rothenstein, principal of the Royal College of Art, responded enthusiastically to an exhibition of art by trainee teachers and kindergarten children from Achimota School, Gold Coast, held at the Imperial Institute in London, describing their paintings as being "full of promise and redolent of West Africa."[11] Rothenstein noted with embarrassment that in most colonial schools in East and West Africa children, like their British counterparts, were set to "copying feeble outline maps — drawings they were not — of English candlesticks, chairs and wash-stand jugs; nowhere was any understanding shown of the beautiful shapes and swift rhythmical forms evolved by local genius."[12]

Achimota was an elite coeducational school, colonially funded, just outside Accra in what is present-day Ghana, that took in children from kindergarten age to those old enough for teacher training and preuniversity study. Between 1924 and 1929 George Alexander Stevens, Achimota's art master, put an end to copying and set his pupils to recording remembered everyday scenes in which "originality counted for more than knowledge."[13] He showed them lantern slides and photographs of works from Asia, Europe, and Africa, including impressive masks made in the Congo. His pupils' paintings shared the vivid quality of works by Richardson's pupils, but Stevens, attempting to create a new African tradition, sought to encourage links to "the older indigenous" art of West Africa (nos. 29, 30). The results, he believed, bore "less and less resemblance to second-rate European drawing."[14]

In the 1930s Kenneth Murray, another young modernist, was teaching art to boys between eight and eighteen years old at a boarding school at Omu-Aran, in present-day Kwara State in Nigeria.[15] Murray directly acknowledged and made use of Richardson's methods of fixing the image in the mind's eye and taking local scenes and activities as subject matter (no. 31). Like Stevens, he avoided imposing European conventions and did not teach linear or geometrical perspective, in order "to encourage the students to be sincerely themselves, hoping that thereby an African style will evolve which will have as great artistic value as the work of the past."[16] Also like Stevens, he showed his pupils selected images from world art, in particular African sculpture and masks, "to establish some standards of taste since so many illustrations and advertisements in English books and newspapers are inevitably seen."[17] Murray exhibited his pupils' work in London; one of them, Ben Enwonwu, went on to become Nigeria's first internationally acclaimed artist.

As teachers, Stevens and Murray wanted to encourage an art that was essentially African, untainted by commercial modernity yet inspired by a carefully introduced modernist canon. These ideas led to the *Syllabus for Tropical and Sub-Tropical Dependencies of 1936*, formulated by Stevens and the artist Richard Carline, and, in 1935, the publication of *Arts of West Africa*, a textbook intended for use in West African schools. The latter took the form of a photographic survey of West African masks, sculpture, musical instruments, and pots, drawn from British collections and artfully photographed, under the direction of the documentary filmmaker John Grierson, as still life tableaux. African art, condemned for more than a century by missionaries, was thus re-presented for African schoolchildren, purged of ritual significance. The goal was to counteract what Rothenstein described as "the evil influence of bad European models."[18] From today's perspective these

well-intentioned efforts to save the West African child and salvage indigenous culture appear shot through with Eurocentric values, an uncomfortable ideological position underlined by Stevens's hopeful prediction that "we shall obviously have our African Giottos and Raphaels and Michaelangelos sooner or later."[19]

Tanya Harrod

FROM THE Theresienstadt concentration camp in 1943, Friedl Dicker wrote, "The best allies against 'ready-made production,' against clichéd aesthetic conceptions, against becoming paralyzed in the stagnating adult world are artists and children."[1] As a versatile designer, progressive educator, and pioneering art therapist, Dicker was immersed in the world of children at the time of cataclysmic upheaval that led ultimately to her murder, with many of her pupils, at Auschwitz-Birkenau. When applying for a position, funded by Vienna authorities, to start a class for kindergarten teachers in 1931, she provided two letters of glowing recommendation. The first was from the charismatic Swiss-born Johannes Itten, with whom she had studied in Vienna during World War I and then followed to the Weimar Bauhaus, and the second came from that institution's first director, the architect Walter Gropius, who wrote, "[Miss Dicker] was distinguished by rare, unusual artistic gifts; her work constantly attracted attention. The multifaceted nature of her gifts and her unbelievable energy made her one of the best students so that already in her first year she began to teach the beginners. As the former director and founder of the Bauhaus, I follow with great interest the successful progress of Miss Dicker."[2] Her student teachers were encouraged to engage in spontaneous artistic activity through methods that drew not only on the *Vorkurs*, the preliminary course taught by Itten at the Bauhaus, but also her earlier experience as a pupil of Franz Cižek at the Kunstgewerbeschule in Vienna. What distinguished Dicker from her mentors was her fearless political activism; to prime her students' imaginations she was more likely to read them the *Communist Manifesto* than a fairy story.

Dicker, with her then-partner Franz Singer, had in 1930 designed a Montessori kindergarten, widely admired as a showpiece of Vienna's enlightened educational policy and a model of modernist design. At a time of little statutory provision in Europe for kindergarten education, the city was an enclave of experimental pedagogy, child psychology, and modern arts, championing reform methods that focused on the child's interests and developmental needs — it was, in fact, popularly known as Red Vienna. The left-wing authorities introduced a mandate for more urban schools, among a raft of other initiatives aimed at improving working-class lives in a period of escalating unemployment and economic privation. As might have been predicted of two Bauhaus-trained designers, the Dicker-Singer kindergarten was created in a modernist idiom defined by flexibility (a room could be transformed from canteen into dormitory or playroom) and spatial use of color, with classrooms equipped with simple geometric furniture and educational toys. This was one of the institutions that affirmed Paul and Marjorie Abbatt's commitment to modernist design and inspired them to set up their innovative toy enterprise in England following a visit in 1930 (see "Ernő Goldfinger and the Abbatts: From Toys to Urban Health," p. 111).[3]

Dicker was also making a series of iconoclastic anti-Fascist and anticapitalist posters for the Communist Party (nos. 32, 33), which responded to the rapidly deteriorating economic and political situation of 1932–33. By cutting and reassembling photographs and text into dense montages, she presented a view of the present and future positions of children in society, touching on themes of poverty, birth control, unemployment, hunger, slum dwelling, and Nazism. One of the posters was interspersed with the poetry of Bertolt Brecht: "This is how the world looks, my child, that you were born into. If you do not like this world, then you will have to change it."[4] In style, content, and quality these works are better compared with the political photomontages that John Heartfield was making in Berlin (no. 34) than with any art being produced in Austria. During a right-wing putsch in February 1934, the Montessori kindergarten was targeted and destroyed, and Dicker was briefly imprisoned for Communist activity before fleeing to Prague. The power of liberal education to alarm totalitarian regimes was evident in the simultaneous ban on Montessori schools in Fascist Italy.

In 1942, after working for the Czechoslovak underground resistance, Dicker was deported to Theresienstadt, a concentration camp northwest of Prague. She was assigned to L410, a barracks for young girls, where she encouraged children to create art using whatever materials were available, including coffee grounds, dirt, used paper, and cotton balls (no. 35). These classes, she declared, were meant "to free and broaden such sources of energy as creativity and independence, and to awaken the imagination, to strengthen the children's powers of observation and appreciation of reality."[5] Dicker had undergone psychoanalysis in Prague with Annie Reich, and at Theresienstadt she began a study of art as therapy for children, which she hoped to write up once the war was over. In 1943 she organized an exhibition in the basement of the children's home and a seminar for teachers, in which she talked about the distinctive characteristics visible in children's drawings at different ages and stages of psychological development.[6] (Such activities were tolerated by the Nazi authorities to support their presentation of the camp to the outside world as a model ghetto.) Following the deportation of her husband, Pavel Brandeis, from Theresienstadt in 1944, however, and believing him to have gone to his death (in fact, he survived), she volunteered for the next transport to Auschwitz-Birkenau. There she perished in the gas chambers with thirty-six of her young students.

Ripples of her influence were felt in the exhibition *Art Work by Children of Other Countries* (no. 36), at The Museum of Modern Art in 1948, which featured drawings by Jewish children who were released from Theresienstadt and sent by the United Nations to Windermere, England. There, in a studio run by Marie Paneth (another former pupil of Cižek), the children had drawn their memories of the concentration camp followed by "subjects from fantasy or observation, such as pleasant landscapes or formal patterns."[7] The MoMA exhibition also included artworks by twenty-five displaced children who had been in the United States for a year and a half. In a press preview, these children were photographed drawing for an hour with Paneth, in MoMA's War Veterans' Art Center (a facility established for such activities in 1944).[8]

Creative and Mental Growth, a major art-therapy text, had just been published in 1947; Viktor Lowenfeld, the author, was another of Cižek's protégés in Vienna and had studied psychoanalysis there before emigrating to the United States in 1938.[9] Lowenfeld's contribution, which influenced a wide audience of therapists, artists, and educators, was to elevate the early creative output of the child in this crucial developmental period: "The process of drawing, painting, or constructing is a complex one in which the child brings together diverse elements of his environment to make a new meaningful whole. In the process of selecting, interpreting and reforming these elements, he has given us more than a picture, he has given us part of himself."[10] The giving was a two-way process according to Edith Kramer, a former pupil of Dicker, who also established a career as an artist and art therapist in New York and who said of her mentor, "Nobody on earth could have given me what she did — an understanding of a thing's essence and the non-acceptance of lies and manneredness. She was one possessed, unbelievably temperamental, passionate — she either loved something or she hated it. And she couldn't endure hypocrisy at all!"[11]

Juliet Kinchin

34 JOHN HEARTFIELD (Helmut Herzfelde)
(German, 1891–1968)
Das Letzte Stück Brot (The last piece of bread),
campaign poster for Communist Party member
Ernst Thälmann. 1932
38 $^3/_{16}$ x 28 $^3/_8$" (97 x 72 cm)
Museum für Gestaltung Zürich, Plakatsammlung

35 RUTH GUTTMANNOVA
(Czechoslovak, 1930–1944)
Untitled collage created during internment at
the Theresienstadt concentration camp prior to
deportation to Auschwitz-Birkenau. c. 1942–44
Collage, 5 $^7/_8$ x 8 $^1/_4$" (15 x 21 cm)
Jewish Museum in Prague Photo Archive

36 Group of formerly displaced children at the
opening of the exhibition *Art Work by Children
of Other Countries*, The Museum of Modern Art,
New York, April 23–May 23, 1948
Gelatin silver print, 7 $^1/_2$ x 9 $^1/_2$" (19 x 24.1 cm)
Photograph by William Leftwich
Photographic Archive. The Museum of Modern Art
Archives, New York

WHEN THE Spanish Republican government was elected in 1931 it immediately embarked on a program of radical reforms to bring Spain into line with its European neighbors (no. 37). In this new society children assumed a special position, expressed, above all, by an extensive program of teacher training and school building that would accommodate all children between the ages of five and thirteen.[1] The government identified its goals as those promoted by the New School movement, which encouraged play and artistic expression rather than discipline and learning by rote (see "The New School," p. 99). The architect of this program was Lorenzo Luzuriaga, a professor of education at the Universidad de Madrid, who campaigned for free education as both a unifying and a liberating agent in modern society.[2] In his view, the new school should be "active, public and secular."[3] The program's most controversial aspect was the removal of the Roman Catholic Church from public education, a policy that became one of the issues around which the Nationalists launched their opposition to the Republic.

The Spanish Civil War, which ravaged the country from 1936 to 1939, was a struggle between two ideologies: a government attempting to establish a modern, secular state versus a right-wing faction, which included the army and wanted to restore the traditional privileges of the land-owning classes and the church. These more traditional sections of Spanish society met the government's new reforms with a mounting sense of outrage, and a 1936 revolt in Morocco, launched by a group of army generals, plunged the country into conflict and unleashed a torrent of nearly primeval violence. Many politicians felt that the outcome would determine the direction Europe would take in subsequent decades. Both the Republicans and the Nationalists depended on support from foreign governments and non-Spanish volunteers, and in order to recruit this support, as well as to maintain morale among demoralized civilians, both sides initiated vigorous propaganda campaigns.[4] The posters put up in Spanish cities attracted a good deal of attention, providing a powerful visual accompaniment to the war. George Orwell, the British journalist and volunteer on the Republican side, observed that "the revolutionary posters were everywhere, flaming from the walls in clean reds and blues that made the few remaining advertisements look like daubs of mud" (no. 38).[5]

This was an early example of total war, with the full force of mechanized weaponry turned on the civilian population. Women and children were often the principal victims of the indiscriminate bombing of cities by the Nationalists, and images of dead children and grief-stricken mothers featured prominently in Republican propaganda (no. 39).

37 *Ciutadà!* (Citizen!). c. 1933
19 ¹/₂ x 13 ³/₁₆" (49.5 x 33.5 cm)
Published by I. G. Seix & Barral Hermanos S.A., Barcelona
Museum für Gestaltung Zürich, Plakatsammlung

38 CAÑAVATE (nationality and dates unknown)
Evacuad Madrid (Evacuate Madrid). 1937
Lithograph, 39 1/2 x 28 1/4" (100.3 x 71.8 cm)
Printed by Unión Polígrafa, Madrid
The Museum of Modern Art, New York. Purchase

39 Attributed to AUGUSTO (Spanish, dates unknown)
¿Que fais-tu pour empêcher cela? (What are you
doing to prevent it?). 1937
Lithograph, 31 3/4 x 22" (80.6 x 55.9 cm)
Photograph by Robert Capa
Published by Ministerio de Propaganda, Spain
The Museum of Modern Art, New York. Purchase

40 EMILIANO ESPINOSA (Spanish, dates unknown)
Drawing of an air raid over a city, December 13, 1937
Pencil and crayon on paper, 9 3/8 x 13 3/8"
(23.8 x 34 cm)
Avery Architectural and Fine Arts Library, Columbia
University, New York

There were atrocities committed on both sides, but the bombing of the Basque town of Guernica by German and Nationalist forces on April 26, 1937, became the most notorious of many attacks on the defenseless civilian population, inspiring numerous posters, newspaper articles, films, and, most famously, Pablo Picasso's painting from that year, all of which were intended to stir the conscience of the outside world.

As civilians came under attack, schoolchildren were encouraged by their teachers to draw pictures of their experience of daily life to help them process the trauma (no. 40).[6] This practice was maintained even after the children were evacuated from the war zone to the relative safety of the Pyrenees and the south of France; drawing what they remembered of their former lives was thought to help them to come to terms with displacement and loss and gave them a sense of attachment to their families, although some of them would never be reunited. The Spanish Board of Education and outside relief agencies, such as the Carnegie Institute and the American Friends Service Committee, collected and exhibited the drawings in Spain and elsewhere in Europe and the United States in order to expose the plight of Spanish children and to raise funds for further aid and evacuation. These works provided outsiders with a particularly touching record of events, in a manner that posters and photographs could not approach; the writer Dorothy Parker, who visited Spain in October 1937, wrote of them, "When they first came to the colony, the children drew the things that were nearest and deepest to them — they drew planes and bursting bombs and houses in flames. You could see by the dreadful perfection of the detail how well they knew their subjects."[7] It was a foreign audience the Republican government wanted to reach, and in 1938 the exhibition *They Still Draw Pictures* traveled to Britain and the United States, with a catalogue featuring an essay by Aldous Huxley, the British novelist.

Beyond their propaganda value, the drawings reveal a fascination with the technology of war — with planes, tanks, bombs — that is not

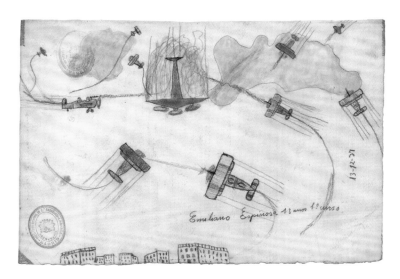

necessarily horrifying in and of itself but often treated in a playful, matter-of-fact style. Nevertheless, harnessing the power of art in a supportive milieu undoubtedly helped many of the children in a process of psychological organization and was one of the earliest uses of art therapy to help children caught in the trauma of wartime separation, displacement, and death.

Juliet Kinchin

41 FRED L. FOX (nationality and dates unknown)
Cover of the book *Keedle*, by Deirdre and William
Conselman, Jr. 1940
10 $^1/_4$ x 8 $^5/_8$" (26 x 22 cm)
Published by Hillman-Curl, New York
The Wolfsonian–Florida International University,
Miami Beach. Gift of Pamela K. Harer

ALTHOUGH THE PRODUCTION of war-themed products for children did not begin with World War II, the output of such items increased dramatically during it. Even as books and other paper and cardboard products came under wartime regulations and rationing, democratic nations and totalitarian regimes alike permitted publishers and manu-facturers to continue to produce illustrated books, comics, board games, and other materials as long as they had patriotic themes. Children's book authors, illustrators, and publishing houses did their part, putting out items aimed at enlisting even the youngest citizens in the war effort. These publications employed time-tested techniques to reach juvenile readers: stories about animals, both real and imaginary; illustrations of smiling children dressed in military uniforms, to make war seem appealing; and instructive works that taught the ABCs of war or offered ways for children to help on the home front, by planting vic-tory gardens, exchanging coins for victory stamps, and participating in scrap drives. Wartime coloring books, postcards, paper puppets, and puzzles glorified national leaders and the heroism of the soldiers or vilified enemy leaders, combatants, and populations. Board games for the very young reinforced war messages through images, while those intended for older children trained future soldiers in combat tactics.

In some materials the physical traits of enemy leaders were exaggerated to make them appear ugly and evil or ridiculous and impo-tent, such as on the cover of *Keedle* (no. 41), a children's book published in New York in 1940. The image is a parody of the Nazi armband, with the bright red band made a muted orange and the bold black swastika omitted, so that the white sphere in the center appears empty and hol-low but for the inclusion of a thin line drawing of the German dictator. The caricature of young Adolf Hitler — with inky hair, abbreviated mustache, and angry eyes — would have been instantly identifiable to parents; the addition of a disembodied, elongated arm with fork-like fingers raised in the Fascist salute reduced the obnoxious man-child to an overeager class bully that young schoolchildren would readily recognize. Written before Hitler's army crushed and routed French and British forces on the Western Front, the book (naively, in hindsight) suggested that this bully could best be handled by calling his bluff and responding to his calls for attention with dismissive and derisive laughter.

The abecedary evolved out of early hornbooks and battledores, and in the early nineteenth century it was the most popular way to teach children their ABCs and at the same time inculcate moral precepts and codes of behavior. During both world wars the format was employed to promote patriotism, demonize the enemy, and introduce young children to the vocabulary of war. *Mon alphabet* (My alphabet) (no. 42), illustrated by F. Touzet and published in Lyon, France, with the approval of the Vichy government, featured modern illustrations intended to rally children behind Maréchal Pétain and impress on them the Fascist alignment of the collaborationist government. The book includes chill-ing lessons, such as "Punish the traitors!" and calls on the children of France to be ready to take up arms in the country's defense.

Anthropomorphized animals make frequent appearances in the children's literature published during World War II, with ravenous wolves, furtive foxes, insidious snakes, bloodthirsty bats, gluttonous hogs, and carrion-consuming vultures wearing the uniforms of a nation's enemies. By contrast, the forces of good are often represented by

42 F. TOUZET (nationality and dates unknown)
Double-page spread from the book *Mon alphabet*
(My alphabet). 1940
8 5/8 x 5 7/8" (22 x 15 cm)
Published by Éditions Centres d'Information
et de Renseignements, Paris
Printed by Impressions Alfa, Lyon
The Wolfsonian–Florida International University,
Miami Beach. The Mitchell Wolfson, Jr. Collection

43 JOOP GERLACH (Dutch, dates unknown)
Double-page spread from *Pietje Pluimstaart*
(Little Peter Bushytail), by Henk Niesen. 1946
10 5/8 x 7 1/2" (27 x 19 cm)
Published by W. Blok, Amsterdam
The Wolfsonian–Florida International University,
Miami Beach. Gift of Pamela K. Harer

44 JOSEPH AVRACH (British, dates unknown)
Cover of the book *The Lion and the Vulture*,
by Paul Tabori. 1944
10 1/4 x 8 1/4" (26 x 21 cm)
Published by Peter Lunn, Ltd, London
The Wolfsonian–Florida International University,
Miami Beach. Gift of Pamela K. Harer

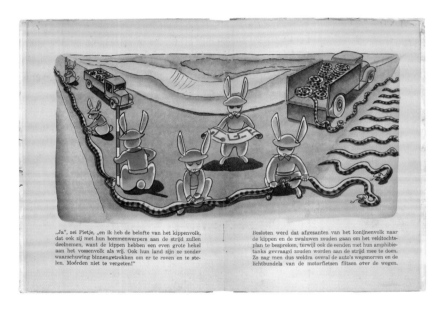

45 ARTISTS & WRITERS GUILD, INC.
Cover of the book *The Gremlins*, by Roald Dahl. 1943
11 x 9" (28 x 23 cm)
A Walt Disney Production published by Random
House, New York
The Wolfsonian–Florida International University,
Miami Beach. Gift of Pamela K. Harer

46 MUNRO LEAF (American, 1905–1976)
Double-page spread from *A War-Time Handbook
for Young Americans*. 1942
10 ¼ x 7 ⅞" (26 x 20 cm)
Published by Frederick A. Stokes Company,
Philadelphia
The Wolfsonian–Florida International University,
Miami Beach. Gift of Pamela K. Harer

47 Cover of the book *Declaration of Greater
East Asian Cooperation*. c. 1943
10 ¼ x 7" (26 x 18 cm)
Published by Kodansha Company, Tokyo
The Wolfsonian–Florida International University,
Miami Beach. Gift of Pamela K. Harer

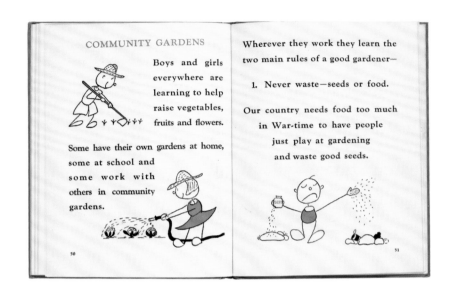

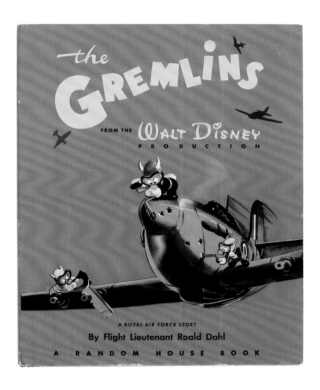

48 Gioco delle 3 oche (Game of the 3 geese). c. 1944
12 1/2 x 22 1/2" (31.8 x 57.2 cm)
The Wolfsonian–Florida International University,
Miami Beach. The Mitchell Wolfson, Jr. Collection

cute, domesticated, and productive creatures, or by animals with symbolic nationalist associations. Cuddly but cunning rabbits are the protagonists of several children's books published toward the end of the war, including the famous French comic book *La Bête est morte!* (The beast is dead!) (1944) and a lesser-known Dutch work *Pietje Pluim-staart* (Little Peter Bushytail) (no. 43). Since the courageous lion has graced the royal coat of arms of England since the time of Richard I, called Coeur de Lion or Lionheart, in the twelfth century, it is not surprising that the dust jacket of *The Lion and the Vulture* (no. 44), illustrated by Joseph Avrach, shows a band of herbivores looking to the King of the Jungle for leadership. This was one of several children's books published by Peter Lunn in London, intended to shore up the strength and stability of the British monarchy and empire during wartime.

When the United States entered the war, some of America's best-known children's book authors and illustrators lent their talents to the war effort. Theodor Seuss Geisel, better known as Dr. Seuss, employed his imaginative cartoon characters in anti-Axis editorials and animated propaganda shorts for the U.S. military.[1] Walt Disney Productions drafted Donald Duck and featured him in an animated anti-Nazi film; the cover of the sheet music for the film's title song, "Der Fuehrer's Face," pictures him pelting Hitler with tomatoes.[2] Disney also collaborated with Flight Lieutenant Roald Dahl on a film project that was ultimately never realized but resulted in the publication of Dahl's first children's book, *The Gremlins* (no. 45). The mischievous creatures in Dahl's story are displaced from their forest dwellings by a British aircraft factory and take revenge by sabotaging Royal Air Force planes. When a pilot convinces them to join the fight against Hitler, they begin to repair Allied aircraft and sabotage Nazi planes.[3]

Early in his career Munro Leaf recognized the need to tailor "truths worth telling" to "the young in terms that were understandable to them," and in his books he used simple language and illustrations to promote good citizenship and encourage children's participation in the war effort.[4] Just before the outbreak of the Spanish Civil War, Leaf wrote *The Story of Ferdinand* (1936), with illustrations by his friend Robert Lawson, a tale about a gentle Spanish bull who prefers sniffing

flowers to bullfighting. The pacifist message of this children's book so incensed right-wing groups that it was banned and burned in Fascist countries. Among liberals and anti-Fascists, however, it was warmly received during the period of the Popular Front, became an international best seller, and was adapted into an animated Disney film that won an Academy Award in 1938. In the years leading up to and during World War II, Leaf wrote numerous children's books, including *Fair Play* (1939), *My Book to Help America* (1942), and *A War-Time Handbook for Young Americans* (no. 46).

The Japanese military government encouraged and produced illustrated children's books, paper fans, wooden toys, and other items for children that glorified the war. *How to Make a Consolation Gift for Soldiers* (1943) provided children with ideas and instructions for making paper gifts to keep up the morale of their fathers fighting on the front.[5] The simple text and illustrations of the *Declaration of Greater East Asian Cooperation* (no. 47) made it clear to young readers that the nation was fighting to liberate the Asian peoples of the world from domination by Western imperialists, a message reinforced by the book's cover, with two unarmed Japanese boys in military uniforms leading a parade of smiling Southeast Asian children in civilian dress.

In both Allied and Axis countries, toy manufacturers produced board games, puzzles, and toys intended to make war appear fun. Children in Italy could play Gioco delle 3 oche (Game of the 3 geese) (no. 48), an allegorical game depicting the enemy as silly geese ready for slaughter. Although there were still some fanatically devout Italian Fascist illustrators making propaganda for Benito Mussolini's government in exile in Salò, this particular game is thought to have been designed by the members of the Staffel and Wehrmacht, the branches of the German army that pulled the strings of Mussolini's puppet regime. Players landing on squares containing Semitic symbols or unflattering caricatures of Allied leaders and Italian defectors were penalized; those landing on squares depicting the banners, weaponry, and other symbols of Axis nations advanced toward victory.

Francis Luca

49 FRANTIŠEK SÁDEK (Czechoslovak, 1913–1998) and HERMÍNA TÝRLOVÁ (Czechoslovak, 1900–1993)
Animation still from *Vzpoura hraček* (Revolt of the toys). 1947
35 mm (black-and-white, sound). 13:50 minutes
Krátky Film Praha, Prague

AN UNPRECEDENTED NUMBER of children were killed and orphaned across Europe and Asia during World War II, and many others endured rationing, blackouts, gas-mask drills, displacement, and internment. Children were destabilized and even devastated by the war's factional conflict and violence, in ways enumerated in professional reports such as "Effect of War upon the Minds of Children," which described children suffering night terrors and rapid heart rates, becoming negative and evasive, and turning to truancy, theft, and sexual delinquency.[1] In response, designers and artists applied their talents to helping children process this traumatic period, often comforting themselves and other adults at the same time. One such example is British artist Ronald Searle's depictions of the spindly, delinquent young girls at the fictional boarding school St. Trinian's. These postwar cartoons, which were developed into a popular series of books and films, followed the wicked ways of the girls and even the destruction of the school by an atomic bomb; they were informed by Searle's experience in a Japanese POW camp, during which time he continued to draw.

A large crop of books and animations produced in the mid- to late 1940s, featuring bold contemporary aesthetics and techniques, spoke directly to children recently surrounded by darkness and now heirs to a new world order. In Czechoslovakia the Cultural Section for Children (Osvětové Oddělení), a special division of the new State Films agency, carefully studied the influence of films on young children and deemed puppet films (with a prominent "emotional side") especially well adapted to their mentality.[2] The short film *Vzpoura hraček* (Revolt of the toys) (no. 49), directed and animated in 1945 by the Czechoslovak artist Hermína Týrlová with František Sádek, was a popular example of a work made for the psychological benefit of children: a timely tale of comeuppance in which a Nazi officer is roundly vanquished by a shop full of wooden toys that defend themselves and their territory when he tries to destroy them. The simple, robust toys are childlike in appearance, and, being by definition objects controlled by children, they empowered young viewers with their victory. The detailed animation of so many small toys, in combination with a live actor and explosive effects, made the film appealing to children everywhere it was distributed, in Central and Western Europe, Scandinavia, and the United States. Týrlová, who had worked in theater and then experimented with animation in commercials in the 1920s, was a pioneer in postwar Czechoslovak animation and continued making films for children into the 1970s.

Pippi Longstocking and the Moomins, two modern book series whose first installments were published in 1945, both by authors from Nordic countries, have an appeal that has lasted beyond their wartime roots, into the present day. Pippi Långstrump (no. 50) was created by Astrid Lindgren, a Swedish writer whose daughter dreamed up Pippi's fanciful name in 1941, prompting Lindgren to invent stories about her through the war years. Over the course of three early books and numerous short stories, films, and television specials, an unconventional heroine's story unfolds: nine years old, with supernatural strength, vibrant spirit, and trademark upturned pigtails, Pippi lives alone (her mother dead, her father lost at sea) and seeks adventures with her pet monkey and a horse. Her irrepressible, eternally young character is evocative of Peter Pan, and the philosophy of her stories has been compared to Socrates.[3] Illustrator Ingrid Vang Nyman, the young Danish artist and single mother who first gave Pippi visual presence, believed that children's books should benefit from the same artistic quality as work for adults. She applied her knowledge of color and cutting-edge printing technology to bring this bright, modern character to life.

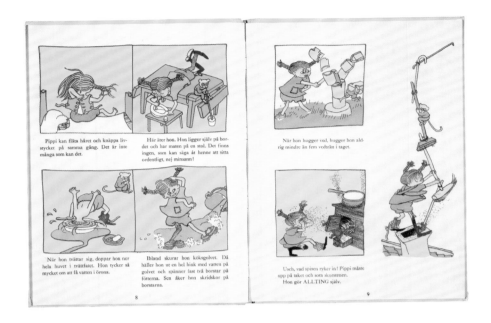

50 INGRID VANG NYMAN (Danish, 1916–1959)
Double-page spread from *Känner du Pippi Långstrump?* (Do you know Pippi Longstocking?), by Astrid Lindgren. 1947
Published by Rabén & Sjögren, Stockholm
Cotsen Children's Library, Princeton University Library

51 TOVE JANSSON (Finnish, 1914–2001)
Original illustration for *Kometjakten* (*Comet in Moominland*). 1946
Ink on paper, $6^5/_{16}$ x $5^5/_8$" (16 x 14.3 cm)
Tampere Art Museum Moominvalley, Finland

52 Young boy at Barnbyn Skå, a home for emotionally troubled children. 1949
Photograph by Mark Kauffman
Getty Images

53 Horse-shape child's seat by Louise Nevelson, 5th prize in *The Arts in Therapy*, The Museum of Modern Art, New York, February 1–March 7, 1943 Gelatin silver print, 7 ¹/₂ x 9 ¹/₂" (19 x 24.1 cm) Photograph by Sochi Sunami The Museum of Modern Art Archives, New York. Department of Circulating Exhibitions Records

In contrast to Pippi's humorous antics and autonomy, the Moomins face real darkness in their fantasy world. Moomintroll, Moominmamma, and Moominpappa are trolls rendered rotund (like hippopotamuses) and disarming by the Finnish writer, painter, and political cartoonist Tove Jansson, who studied at the Konstfack in Stockholm and the École des Beaux-Arts in Paris and claimed that her proclivity for drawing was due to her own happy childhood. The Moomins, surrounded in the forest of Moominvalley by a cast of unique cohorts (Snork Maiden, Too-Ticky, Little My, Groke, Sniff, Snufkin), have all the trappings of pleasant fairy-tale life, but their stories contain danger and desolation that reflect the wartime context in which they were conceived.[4] Jansson produced the first book in the series, *The Moomins and the Great Flood* in 1945, and the story of Moominmamma and Moomintroll's search for Moominpappa in a dark forest is likely to have resonated with children displaced or otherwise separated from their parents. In the following book, *Comet in Moominland* (1946) (no. 51), the valley is threatened (though spared in the end) by a hurtling comet, a metaphorical stand-in for a nuclear weapon. In a richly illustrated world that reflected the psychological depth of her characters, Jansson intertwined indications of doom with warm relationships and positive messages about tolerance and freedom, all of which unspooled through more than ten books plus various adaptations and a comic-strip version for adults. In the decade following the war, Jansson also applied her talents to designing murals, including several for schools and a children's hospital in Helsinki.

In addition to books and animation, psychologists, educators, and other professionals turned to art therapy to divert children from the horrors of war and help them process trauma. The concept was not new, but acceptance of the practice grew over the postwar years, a period in which family therapy also became more common. The idea that art could reveal and improve the true mental states of children was at the center of experimental programs such as at Barnbyn Skå, a therapeutic community and home for emotionally disturbed children outside of Stockholm. Here children drew and painted freely on the facility walls with the express support of the home's director, Dr. Gustav Jonsson (no. 52).

The Museum of Modern Art was also involved in the art-therapy movement during the war, although primarily focused on works of art and design by and for disabled and recovering members of the armed forces. James Thrall Soby, director of the Museum's Armed Services Program, had called for all American artists and designers to contribute to the war effort by producing "attractive and useful articles" to be used as models for patients (including children) to reproduce, explaining, "The remedial work involved in creating well-designed objects contributes not only to physical recovery but also to the patient's mental rehabilitation."[5] The result, a 1943 *Arts in Therapy* competition, was followed by an exhibition that displayed paintings, sculptures, and drawings as well as weaving, woodworking, paper construction, metalwork, and pottery. This exhibition, designed by prominent *Bauhausler* Herbert Bayer and organized by Soby's program and the Committee on Art in American Education, also featured artworks by children, including crayon drawings from patients at the New York State Psychiatric Institute and Hospital; toys and objects designed for children, including a child's seat by sculptor Louise Nevelson (no. 53) and a cloth book designed by Juliet Kepes and Marli Ehrman; and creative projects that summoned the children within adults.[6] "Alexander Calder," a press release exclaimed, "has created two dozen or more gay and fantastic toys made in the simplest fashion of cigar boxes, paper match boxes, scraps of tin, leather, old piano wire, rags, yarn, thread and bits of wood.... A soldier or sailor would have to be very much disabled indeed not to laugh at first sight and then demand that the wastebasket be emptied on his bed to furnish him with similar materials for comic creations of his own."[7]

Aidan O'Connor

INTRODUCTION

An appeal to the authorities — The artist, essential ally of the child, is there to lessen the conflict. If childhood is a journey let us see to it the child does not travel by night.
—Aldo van Eyck, 1962[1]

IN AN ATMOSPHERE of optimism immediately following World War II, children became a primary target of international aid agencies, of planners of urban and social policy, and of manufacturers making the transition from armaments to peacetime production. For millions of displaced, starving, and orphaned children, life in Europe and the Asia Pacific after 1945 was particularly perilous, but massive children's health, welfare, and school-building programs captured a spirit of hopeful postwar reconstruction (no. 1). Poland and Japan, for example, were traumatized nation-states that required fundamental reconfiguration, but also laboratories in which postwar idealism and experimental ideas about the education, social welfare, and safety of children took form.

Newly established international organizations like UNICEF, SOS Children's Villages, and the World Council of Early Childhood Education (Organisation Mondiale pour l'Éducation Préscolaire), highlighted the plight and human-rights struggles of children, and across the ideological spectrum children were seen as key to visions of constructing better, more egalitarian worlds. At the same time, however, the treatment of children rapidly became a crucial sphere of Cold War ideological contest. During the baby boom years of the late 1940s and the 1950s, idealized child-centered images of community and family life intensified on both sides of the East-West divide.

Schools, a potent symbol of both liberation and day-to-day normality, were to provide a space for what was natural, simple, and healthy to flourish. As old European empires crumbled, a gradual shift to greater acceptance of otherness and difference was manifest in school architecture and textbooks. Architects, artists, and educators collaborated to enhance the fabric of school buildings. There was also an expansion of creative arts in many schools' curricula, and learning resources.

Soaring toy sales furthered economic development but also triggered debates about a field of design apparently riddled with militarism, pernicious nationalism, and negative racial or gender stereotyping. International groups of concerned child psychologists, manufacturers, educators, and designers joined forces to promote "good toys" that were well-designed and nonviolent. In the ruins of many European cities, similarly interdisciplinary groups of professionals worked with children to reclaim bombed-out areas through therapeutic play.

In the aftermath of brutality and devastation, it seems natural that many designers sought to recover a lost innocence embodied in the spontaneity and directness of children's art, and to emulate the constructive, creative impulse of children's play. Charles and Ray Eames in California, Aldo van Eyck and CoBrA artists in Amsterdam, and members of the Independent Group in London — all epitomized this preoccupation with the child and its worldview. For Van Eyck, the search for the very nature of architecture was to be found in children, because only they still had an unmediated view of the world that allowed them to identify people's essential problems and needs, while the Eameses led the way in letting "the fun out of the bag" through their films, toys, and furniture for children.[2] For all of these designers, direct observation of children stimulated approaches that were characterized by a new interdisciplinarity and visual eclecticism.

Juliet Kinchin

1 *Sota sorti, rauha rakentaa. SKDL turvaa siirtoväen elämän*
(War destroys, peace builds. SKDL protects evacuees),
poster for the Suomen Kansan Demokraattinen Liitto
(SKDL; Finnish People's Democratic League), Helsinki. 1947
23 13/16 x 16 3/4" (60.5 x 42.5 cm)
Museum für Gestaltung Zürich, Plakatsammlung

"CHILDREN ASKING QUESTIONS" — and they had some tough ones for their elders in 1949 — was the title of a controversial mural painted by twenty-eight-year-old Karel Appel in the cafeteria of the Amsterdam City Hall. Though the artist was a founding member of CoBrA, an international avant-garde group that drew inspiration from children's drawings and the idea of play as a creative and cultural force,[1] there was outrage at Appel's use of a violently expressionist and childlike style, undoubtedly tinged with discomfort at his evocation of hungry children in a place where the city's political elite sat down to eat. (Some sixteen thousand Dutch had died of starvation in the winter of 1944, mostly children and the elderly.) Nevertheless, the CoBrA artists' fascination with children was indicative of a more general cultural role reversal between generations that would gain momentum in the following decades. As innocent victims of World War II, children became the focus of collective, often guilt-ridden, outpourings of concern, with many artists and designers struggling to give them a voice and

visibility in a world run by adults. An American electoral poster from 1946 by Ben Shahn (sponsored by the Political Action Committee of the Congress of Industrial Organizations), in which the phrase "We want Peace" appears alongside an emaciated boy (no. 2), seems designed to shame adults into exercising their democratic rights. The rough handling of pigment in the poster's image emphasizes the boy's neglected appearance, while the oblique viewpoint that positions the onlooker as an adult reinforces his vulnerability.

In 1946 the United Nations established UNICEF (no. 3), an international emergency fund for coordinated action on behalf of children in countries devastated by the war. David Seymour, a member of the recently formed Magnum Photos agency, documented UNICEF's work in a book of photographs, *The Children of Europe* (1949). The preface took the form of a "Letter to a Grown Up," which began: "I would like to speak a little about myself, but mainly about the 13,000,000 abandoned children in Europe who had their first experience of life in an atmosphere of death and destruction, and who passed their first years in underground shelters, bombed streets, ghettoes set on fire, refugee trains and concentration camps.... You must help us make up for lost time."[2] Agencies like UNICEF supported and created vital international networks that brought architects and designers into contact with specialists in education, child psychology, childcare, and medical research. The most pressing needs were for the construction of hospitals, schools, and orphanages, and for effective public education about nutrition and health.

At a time of chronic austerity in Finland, sufficient international funds were raised for the completion of Helsinki's majestic new children's hospital, Lastenlinna (Children's castle) (no. 4), in 1948. Architect Elsi Borg had taken over the project's design from her brother Kaarlo Borg after his death in 1939, but construction was stalled by the war.[3] The hospital, with sweeping views over the sea, was Finland's most memorable public building of the late 1940s. Aided by Otto Flodin and Olavi Sortta, Borg combined a functionalist approach to spatial planning and technical detailing (including a swimming pool for the relief of infantile paralysis and glass-walled isolation wards) with a decorative scheme on the facade of the tower consisting of bas-reliefs, patterned stucco, and small statues that drew on Finnish vernacular sources and mythology. Inside, elegantly modern furniture, colorful textiles, and lighting were all designed or selected by Borg to create a homey, noninstitutional feel. Also in the late 1940s, funds for two Norwegian children's hospitals, in Bergen and Oslo, were presented by Swedish donors to

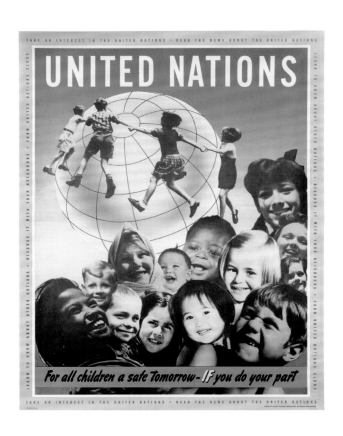

2 BEN SHAHN
(American, born Lithuania. 1898–1969)
We Want Peace. Register, Vote. 1946
Lithograph, 41 1/4 x 27" (104.8 x 68.6 cm)
The Museum of Modern Art, New York. Gift of
S. S. Spivack

3 *United Nations: For All Children a Safe
Tomorrow – IF You Do Your Part*, poster for the
United Nations Department of Public Information,
Visual Information Section. 1947
Lithograph, 27 15/16 x 22 1/16" (71 x 56 cm)
The Museum of Modern Art, New York. Purchase

4 ELSI BORG (Finnish, 1893–1958)
Lastenlinna Children's Hospital, Helsinki. 1939–48
Designed in collaboration with Otto Flodin and
Olavi Sortta; sculptures and reliefs by Sakari Tohka;
decorative stuccowork by Yrjö Kyllönen
Museum of Finnish Architecture, Helsinki

5 HERBERT MATTER
(American, born Switzerland. 1907–1984)
*One of Them Had Polio, Skilled Teamwork
Brought Recovery.* 1949–50
Offset lithograph, 45 11/16 x 28 7/8" (116 x 73.3 cm)
The Museum of Modern Art, New York. Gift of
the National Foundation for Infantile Paralysis

6 JAN LE WITT (British, born Poland. 1907–1991)
Cover of the book *The Vegetabull*. 1956
11 x 8 1/2" (28 x 21.5 cm)
Published by Collins, London
Private collection

7 HANS FISCHLI (Swiss, 1909–1989)
Stairwell of Pestalozzi Children's Village, Trogen,
Switzerland. 1945–49
Photograph by Theo Schäublin
Nachlassarchiv SIK-ISEA Zürich

8 ALDO VAN EYCK (Dutch, 1918–1999)
Aerial view of Amsterdam Municipal Orphanage.
1955–60
The Museum of Modern Art, New York. Department
of Architecture and Design Study Center

9 Interior of Children's House, Kibbutz Givat
Brenner. c. 1950
Photograph by Hanan Bahir
Courtesy of Yuval Yasky

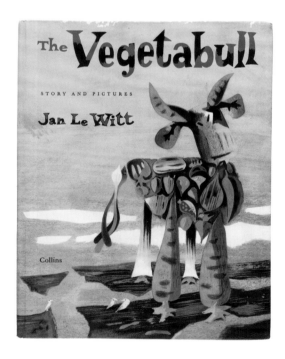

the Norwegian government. The buildings were to be designed by
Swedish architect Gustaf Birch-Lindgren, a specialist in this area of
design.[4] The Bergen hospital, opened in 1950, was in a pure modernist
style and situated above a lake with a garden planned by the architect.
Like Lastenlinna, it reflected recent innovations in medical science
and building technology, and accommodations for mothers of the
child patients.

The fight against polio, a terrifying disease that before 1955
crippled thousands of once active, healthy children, was the theme
of a poster competition initiated by The Museum of Modern Art in
1949, cosponsored with the National Foundation for Infantile Paralysis.
Twenty-three invited artists were asked to come up with poster designs
and slogans to raise awareness of this disease and the new treatments
becoming available. Herbert Matter made full use of a modern graphic
idiom in his winning entry, *One of Them Had Polio, Skilled Teamwork
Brought Recovery* (no. 5), showing figures of a running girl and boy
that epitomized how medical advances had allowed afflicted children
a newfound sense of freedom.[5] Graphic design was also deployed in the
struggle for better nutrition. Jan Le Witt's children's book *The Vegetabull*
(no. 6), for example, composed as a backstory to his 1943 wartime poster
for the British Ministry of Information on the same theme, was both
an entertaining fairy-tale and designed to make eating vegetables fun.

Children's villages for orphans sprang up everywhere in war-devastated countries throughout Europe. Some were makeshift and run by the children themselves around networks of thieving and prostitution,[6] but others had a strong architectural formulation and philosophical intent. In 1946 the Pestalozzi Children's Village in Trogen, Switzerland (no. 7), welcomed orphans from Austria, Britain, Finland, France, Germany, Greece, Hungary, Italy, and Poland. The initiative for this particular community was led by philosopher Walter Corti, who recruited the services of Marie Meierhofer (a pediatrician and child psychologist), Elizabeth Rotten (a progressive educator), and Bauhaus-trained architect Hans Fischli. The village followed Swiss pedagogue Johann Heinrich Pestalozzi's (1746–1827) concept of education based around domestic life and the family circle. The cohabitation of children from previously warring nations was fundamental to a framework of tolerance and intercultural education established by Corti at the outset. To emphasize this idea, Fischli designed a group of relatively small timber houses on a child-friendly scale, loosely arranged around a central square, moderating his otherwise functionalist style with regional influences from the surrounding area. Volunteers from various countries helped to construct the houses and the furnishings, also designed by Fischli.

Aldo van Eyck's Amsterdam Orphanage (no. 8) is seen by many to be that architect's masterpiece — a new type of configuration that had a great influence on the developing theories and architecture of urban renewal. He approached the design as a large house for a fluctuating population of around 125 children of various ages. Situated diagonally on its site, the orphanage was organized around a sequence of nonhierarchical, interlocking spaces with a connecting roof made of domes, and containing little "streets" and "squares" — intermediary spaces where the children could meet and mix.[7] Van Eyck described the importance of such in-between spaces in easing the transition between the reality outside and that inside, and helping "to mitigate the anxiety that abrupt transition causes, especially in these children. Leaving home and going home are often difficult matters.... The job of the planner is to provide a built homecoming for all, to sustain feeling of belonging.... I tried to articulate the transition by means of defined in-between places

which induce simultaneous awareness of what is significant on either side."[8] The interiors were full of thoughtful details — a space for a kettle in the infants' area, well protected from tiny hands; circular "dips" in the concrete to collect water for play; the use of antique tiles, mirrors, colored glass, and paint to delineate and decorate space.

In the new state of Israel, proclaimed on May 14, 1948, the architecture of kibbutzim — self-contained communities with children at their core — was also used to actively shape egalitarian relationships among war orphans and immigrants from many parts of the world. Richard Kauffmann, one of several Bauhaus-trained architects who had shaped fundamental models of kibbutz planning in the 1920s, described children as "the first concern of every kibbutz, the whole community striving to provide the best possible conditions for them."[9] From their establishment in the early twentieth century until the 1970s, most kibbutzim had a system whereby the children would sleep in communal infants' homes (beit tinokot) followed by children's homes (beit yeladim), instead of in their parents' apartments, until the age of eighteen (no. 9).[10] The theory was that children would become socialized from a very early age, and that trained nurses and teachers could supplement the care provided by parents, making it possible for mothers to start a phased return to work within six to twelve weeks of giving birth instead of spending many hours a day on child care. The merits of this approach, however, were increasingly disputed, and many kibbutzim began to abandon the idea of "collective sleeping" in the 1970s and '80s.

Juliet Kinchin

THOUGH THE ATOMIC BOMBS that were dropped on Hiroshima and Nagasaki (code names "Little Boy" and "Fat Man") in August 1945 marked perhaps the most dramatic conclusion to any major war in history, Japan had already sustained months of conventional bombing of cities and civilian populations. The survivors were faced with both the Allied occupation and a process of reconstruction that involved the prohibition of many earlier aspects of Japanese life. It was illegal to show the Japanese flag and whole subject areas were expunged from films, books, and comics. For several years, the Japanese were forbidden by the Allied powers even to see images of the war and its cataclysmic ending that had killed more than two hundred thousand and maimed countless others (no. 10). It was only in the 1950s, after Japan was once again declared a sovereign state, that these events could be confronted in collective, popular culture. This process was explored in a 1951 book by Arata Osada titled *Children of Hiroshima*, and in the film it inspired, directed by Kaneto Shindō, released the following year (no. 11). Both works focus on the trauma of the bombs and their devastating effects through the experiences of children — for many, the only truly innocent victims of the destruction. As children came to occupy a key position in Japanese public life, schools and children's institutions began to be perceived as the building blocks of the new society. International funds were used for a range of cultural and welfare facilities, including the Hiroshima children's library and park, situated on former military land, designed by Kenzo Tange in 1953 (no. 12). Children were seen in public life more often than before the war, observing the roles of family piety and remembrance that provided a sense of continuity with Japan's historic past while also symbolizing the country's move toward becoming a modern, Westernized state.

Though the institutions and democratic system of the United States certainly provided a general blueprint, the process of rebuilding Japanese society was an improvised affair fraught with contradictions and hardship. Nevertheless, this time has also been described as a period of "unusually creative vitality" (nos. 13, 14).[1] A key aim was to rebuild Japanese industry and to move it away from the wartime economy that had shaped the infrastructure of the previous decade. One policy of the U.S.-led reconstruction was to allocate to Japan the low-profit but labor-intensive manufacturing tasks that would stimulate industrial expansion but not threaten well-established Western companies and markets. Tin toys were a perfect example.

Even amid the chaos of the early occupation, Japanese metal-workers were adapting discarded tin cans for a variety of everyday goods such as kitchen utensils and toys. With a little financial support, industrial conglomerates like Bandai and Marusan moved this up to full-scale factory production of toy cars, boats, and figures for a worldwide market. *Buriki* (tin plate), the traditional process of pressed and printed metal, was employed to replicate the most modern examples of the automotive industry, celebrating the massive expansion of American consumerism. The bulbous forms, chrome details, and streamlined tail fins of Fords (no. 15, left), Cadillacs, and Chevrolets were soon being manufactured in miniature at factories in Tokyo that supplied the toy shops of the Western world. European models were also produced, but the extravagant bodywork and new models unveiled by American manufacturers every year gave the Japanese factories a readily expanding product range.

A Japanese car joined the ranks of the iconic vehicles reproduced as toys when, in 1958, Bandai produced a tinplate version of the Subaru 360 (no. 15, right), the first Japanese-manufactured car to go in to full-scale production for both the domestic and foreign markets. Although small, the car was a significant improvement on the three-wheelers and microcars that had been adapted from wartime airplane technology. The success of the Subaru 360 was heralded by its reproduction as a toy, but it prefigured a much greater development in the world economy. By starting with simple technologies and low-grade products, the Japanese turned Western industrial management practice on its head. Within a couple of decades, Japanese manufacturers would dominate the world car market, and the old makes of Europe and the United States, with all their claims for style and prestige, would be struggling to keep afloat.

If Japan sustained the most extensive destruction in the Far Eastern theater of war, Poland could be regarded as its counterpart in Europe. Almost twenty percent of the Polish population had been killed between 1939 and 1945, and Polish cities were devastated (no. 16).[2] After the armistice, there was a widespread sense among the survivors that the primary aim should be to rebuild, but also to recapture the life and culture that had been cut off in September 1939. Many leading figures from the prewar period returned to the newly recreated state and set about picking up the threads of their lives and work. Designers Jan Kurzątkowski and Władysław Wincze, for example, revived the Ład collective workshop in Warsaw, which in the 1920s had pioneered a uniquely Polish form of modern craft and design rooted in vernacular materials and traditions.[3] Kurzatkowski was noted for his paper sculpture: experimenting with texture, malleability, and shadow play, he created

10 KEN DOMON (Japanese, 1909–1990)
Blind Boy. c. 1955
Gelatin silver print, 11 x 14 ¼" (27.9 x 36.2 cm)
The Museum of Modern Art, New York. Gift of
Nihon Keizai Shimbun

11 JAN LENICA (Polish, 1928–2001)
Dzieci Hiroszimy (Children of Hiroshima),
Polish-language poster for the 1952 Japanese
film directed by Kaneto Shindō. 1955
Silkscreen, 31 ½ x 23 ⅝" (80 x 60 cm)
The Museum of Modern Art, New York.
Architecture and Design Purchase Fund

12 KENZO TANGE (Japanese, 1913–2005)
Hiroshima Children's Library, Tokyo. 1953
Photograph by Chuji Hirayama
Tange Associates, Tokyo

13 HIROSHI OHCHI (Japanese, 1908–1974)
Poster advertising children's schoolbooks. 1954
Silkscreen, 28 3/8 x 20 1/8" (72.1 x 51.1 cm)
The Museum of Modern Art, New York. Gift of
Jack Banning

14 HIROSHI OHCHI (Japanese, 1908–1974)
Poster advertising children's shoes. 1954
Silkscreen, 29 1/8 x 20 3/4" (74 x 52.7 cm)
The Museum of Modern Art, New York. Gift of
the artist

15 (left) Ford convertible toy car and original
box. c. 1956
Tinplate and various materials, car:
3 7/8 x 5 1/8 x 13 1/4" (9.8 x 13 x 33.7 cm)
Manufactured by Marusan Shoten Ltd,
Tokyo (est. 1947)
Bruce Sterling Collection, New York

15 (right) Subaru 360 toy car and original
box. c. 1963
Tinplate, car: 3 3/8 x 3 3/8 x 7 7/8" (8.6 x 8.6 x 20 cm)
Manufactured by Bandai, Tokyo (est. 1950)
Bruce Sterling Collection, New York

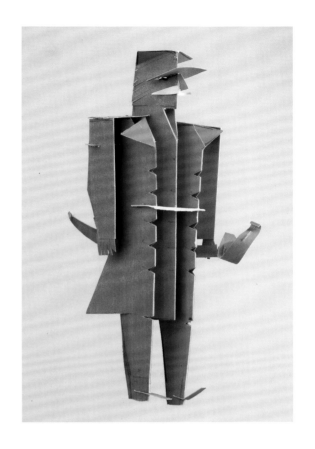

16 DAVID SEYMOUR (American, 1911–1956)
The Blackboard, Poland (Tereza), 1948, as
reproduced in *Homeless Children: Report of
the Proceedings of the Conference of Directors
of Children's Communities*, 1950
The Museum of Modern Art Library, New York

17 JAN KURZĄTKOWSKI (Polish, 1899–1975)
Paper soldier. 1946–49
Folded card, 7 $^7/_8$ x 3 $^1/_8$ x $^{13}/_{16}$" (20 x 8 x 2 cm)
National Museum, Warsaw

18 WŁADYSŁAW WINCZE (Polish, 1905–1992)
and Olgierd Szlekys (Polish, 1908–1980)
Fawn chair. c. 1942 (manufactured 1946–70)
Wood, 26 x 13 x 17 $^{11}/_{16}$" (66 x 33 x 45 cm)
Manufactured by Ład Artists' Cooperative
(est. 1926), Warsaw
National Museum, Warsaw

MIĘDZYNARODOWY DZIEŃ DZIECKA

Towarzystwo Przyjaciół Dzieci

19 ZENON JANUSZEWSKI (Polish, 1929–1983)
Międzynarodowy Dzień Dziecka (International
children's day). c. 1960
Lithograph, 39 3/8 x 25 9/16" (100 x 64.9 cm)
The Museum of Modern Art, New York. Architecture
and Design Purchase Fund

complex figurines for both adults and children out of this modest material (no. 17). The simplicity and affordability of these toys fulfilled the popular Communist slogan "Beauty for all" that seemed to sum up the optimism of the period. Given the severe depopulation, it is small wonder that children and play came to have a special importance for this fragile new country.

Both Kurzątkowski and Wincze were also engaged in furniture design. One of their first projects was to put Wincze's Fawn chair for children (no. 18) back into production for the postwar market. Designed in 1942, during the occupation, it reflected the earlier, prewar virtues of Ład in its use of native woods and modern updating of vernacular forms. The solid plank construction and economical use of materials suited a country suffering from severe shortages and limited technological resources. Playful yet practical, its allusion to the traditional motif of the deer served as a symbol of nature and freedom. The Fawn chair continued in production until the mid-1950s and was celebrated as an example of continuity throughout a period of political instability.

Following the Communist takeover of Poland, as in other Stalinist regimes in Central and Eastern Europe, cultural activities in Poland were placed under the control of government agencies to ensure that party policy was observed. Moscow enforced strict control over all aspects of private and public life. However, within these limitations the Communist Party placed considerable emphasis on activities and resources for children. This was obvious from official propaganda, from the significant funds devoted to schools and other children's services, and, above all, from the support of children's organizations to inculcate a sense of civic responsibility and collective identity. As graphic designer Andrzej Dudzinski has remarked, "Stalin had quite a decent

reputation among the youngsters.... Our parents were quaking with fear while we were having a great time. There were parades and rallies, we sang songs, and watched films. For an eight-year-old child, this was a fantastic, colorful world."[4] May Day and International Children's Day festivities throughout the Soviet bloc were among the most extravagant showpieces of the Communist calendar. International Children's Day, which from 1952 was celebrated in Poland on June 1, was marked by specially commissioned posters (no. 19) and festivities in parks, schools, and children's clubs. Parents would congratulate their children and often give them small gifts. In 1968 the Polish magazine *Kurier Polski* introduced The Order of the Smile, an award given by children to adults who had shown them exceptional love and care, which in 1979 was recognized by the United Nations as part of the International Year of the Child.

What was missing from this world were the consumer goods that increasingly dominated the Cold War competition to establish industrial superiority, and ideological debates about the merits of capitalism versus a command economy. Factory-made toys were in short supply in Poland, and most families relied upon homemade toys and entertainment. Though created in response to extreme hardship, the wooden trucks, papier-mâché puppets, and handmade dolls from this time are now recalled extremely fondly. Many Poles look back on this period of deprivation, when they had to improvise with limited resources, as one of great imaginative stimulus. This could be put down to "*ostalgie*" (nostalgia for the pre-1989 Communist era), but, interestingly, these basic wooden toys and hand-painted dolls also conformed more closely to modern ideals of creative play than the mass-produced toys from East Germany that began to enter Poland and other Eastern bloc countries by the mid-1950s, largely sweeping away this period of domestic innovation.

Juliet Kinchin

IN A RECENT INTERVIEW, Polish designer Tomasz Jastrun recalled his childhood spent among bombed-out houses in Warsaw following World War II: "We lived in the ruins of a lost world, a lost civilization. A new world was emerging. It was dangerous and strange, but it was ours."[1] The exuberant reappearance of children in public urban space after the wartime experience of confinement or evacuation was marked in films, photography, and painting with images of children's anarchic, spontaneous, and unregulated play.[2] Ben Shahn's 1945 gouache drawing *Liberation* (no. 20) depicts three girls, left to their own devices in a desolate landscape, who swing precariously around a pole. Meanwhile in Berlin, Friedrich Seidenstücker captured the *Aufstieg der Begabten* (Rise of the gifted) — the title of his 1950 photograph of boys clambering over and balancing on the facade of a former health insurance building (no. 21). The boys' provocative occupation of a prewar monument signaled an alternative conception of the city, one that challenged conventional architectural codes and manifestations of authority and proposed new forms of order. Children's appropriation of urban space in the aftermath of war made visible the existence of a new attitude — at once disruptive and challenging but also cathartic and humanizing — that would reconfigure the shattered cityscapes of Europe.

Inspired by a visit to Carl Theodor Sørensen's experimental "junk" playground in Emdrup, Copenhagen, in 1946, Lady Allen of Hurtwood proposed the designation of certain British bomb sites as adventure playgrounds in which children could channel their playful energy in therapeutic and constructive ways.[3] As a landscape architect, pacifist, and children's welfare advocate, Lady Allen felt these spaces, by helping children to process and reinterpret the rubble, had the potential to repair the physical and psychological damage caused by war. Following the designation of the first two such playgrounds, located in the London districts of Camberwell and Morden, these urban experiments received extensive press coverage, and were heralded as a means of addressing the growing problem of juvenile delinquency. An image from a newspaper taken around 1950, for example, shows children working to convert a derelict bomb site into Lollard Adventure Playground (no. 22), another early example. The project, strategically situated near the Houses of Parliament, was supported by the National Playing Fields Association and the local community. It was also symbolic as a venture that recouped the ruins of a bombed-out school through play, prior to the site's redevelopment in 1960 with a new school building.

Around 1950, photographer Nigel Henderson showed a similar concern with the activities of children in the severely bomb-damaged

East End of London, documenting their play as they intuitively explored the dilapidated surroundings (no. 23). He had moved to the area of Bethnal Green in 1945 with his anthropologist wife, Judith Stephen, who was conducting a study of working-class patterns of living. The couple became fascinated by children's ability to make unexpected connections between the contingent aspects of their surroundings, and to humanize their environment through new patterns of association. The architects Alison and Peter Smithson were directly inspired by Henderson's photographs, seeing in them "a perceptive recognition of the actuality around his house in Bethnal Green.... The 'as found' [aesthetic] was a new way of seeing the ordinary, an openness as to how prosaic 'things' could re-energise our inventive activity."[4]

The Smithsons were critical of the top-down view of urban planning embraced by the Congrès Internationaux d'Architecture Moderne (CIAM), epitomized by Le Corbusier's Ville Radieuse plan of 1933, which had envisaged a functional, zoned city, characterized by widely spaced apartment blocks and landscaped public places (see "To the Mountains and the Sea," p. 114); instead they were searching for new architectural equivalents to the nonhierarchical forms of children's

20 BEN SHAHN
(American, born Lithuania. 1898–1969)
Liberation. 1945
Gouache on board, 29 3/4 x 40" (75.6 x 101.4 cm)
The Museum of Modern Art, New York. James Thrall Soby Bequest

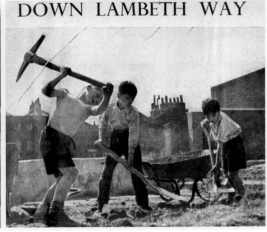

association observed by Henderson. Together with Henderson, the Smithsons were involved in the Independent Group, a radical organization of young artists, architects, filmmakers, and writers, and in 1953 they collaborated on an influential visual statement of the Smithsons' new approach to urban planning, titled "Urban Re-identification," which was presented at the ninth CIAM gathering. Laid out as a grid, their exhibit featured Henderson's photos, representing the Smithsons' guiding principle of "human association," which informed their mapping of the interconnected layers of urban experience in architectural form, from "House" to "Street," and "District" to "City." Children at play — seen as a connecting force with the potential to create new "clusters" and forms of association — pointed the way to a new architecture and urban design: an alternative to the prevailing modernist orthodoxy of demarcated functions that, in the Smithsons' view, threatened to create sterile cities devoid of community spirit.

In Amsterdam, Aldo van Eyck had also been looking at found environments and at the relationship between the child and the city. He was in the process of building hundreds of playgrounds that he considered an essential part of children's development and sense of place (no. 24). Working deliberately with derelict "in-between" and already existing spaces, Van Eyck defined areas for children's play without closing them off from the surrounding community (no. 25). Uniting around ideas of growth, mobility, and cluster planning of cities, younger members of CIAM, including Van Eyck and the Smithsons, joined forces as Team 10 following a meeting at Dorn, the Netherlands, in 1954. On this occasion, Van Eyck presented his own version of the Smithsons' exhibit (also using photographs of children at play), the first panel of which announced the problem of "Lost Identity": "A city without the child's particular movement is a paradox. The child discovers its identity against all the odds."[5]

On both sides of the Cold War divide, attempts were made to engage the young in imagining future cities and to prepare them for adult participation in urban planning, building, and administration. A number of construction toys and educational books and programs helped to foster children's social skills, environmental awareness, and appreciation of modern architecture. Toys, such as Tinkertoy's Curtain Wall Builder (no. 26), were updated to reflect postwar construction techniques and modern architectural forms. Taking a more anthropological view of urbanism was Friedrich Böer's popular book *Drei Jungen erforschen eine Stadt* (Three boys explore a city) (no. 27), which was first published in 1933. By the time revised editions appeared in 1946 and 1954, Berlin, the model of the city in the original book, lay in ruins. Böer triggered children's imaginative engagement with the physical landscape of the city through an innovative combination of text, photomontage, drawings, and architectural plans. The style was similar to the kind of diary the author had kept in his own childhood, in which he compiled his personal observations, press clippings, and photographs. Olga Adams, one of the best-known kindergarten teachers in the United States, took children's appreciation of how cities worked a step further by involving her classes in the process of urban planning. At the Laboratory School in Chicago, she initiated a classroom project called Our City (no. 28). Through extensive discussion with the children about how they interacted with and understood the city, followed by group decision-making, the pupils imagined a model town and then went on to develop their ideas into a cardboard community that they governed themselves.

A collective action of a different kind took place in Czechoslovakia in 1949. For two days in May, the city of Brno was entirely run by children, who took the place of their elders in every aspect of daily life, including directing traffic (no. 29), working in factories, schools, and offices, cleaning the city, writing the newspapers, and appearing on television broadcasts. The event was designed to foster civic awareness, aesthetic appreciation of the urban environment, and a sense of responsibility about how to manage local resources, but also "to develop artistic talents among the young" as part of a larger

21 FRIEDRICH SEIDENSTÜCKER
(German, 1882–1966)
Aufstieg der Begabten (Rise of the gifted),
children climbing on the facade of the former
AOK administration building on Rungerstrasse,
Berlin. 1950
Gelatin silver print, 22 $^{13}/_{16}$ x 17 $^{15}/_{16}$" (58 x 45.6 cm)
Bildagentur für Kunst, Kultur und Geschichte

22 Lollard Adventure Playground, Borough
of Lambeth, London. c. 1950
Lambeth Archives Department, London

23 NIGEL HENDERSON (British, 1917–1985)
Untitled, from Chisenhale Road Series. 1951
Part of Alison and Peter Smithson's "Urban
Re-identification" grille, presented at the ninth
gathering of the Congrès Internationaux
d'Architecture Moderne (CIAM), 1953
Gelatin silver print, 6 $^1/_4$ x 7 $^3/_4$" (15.9 x 19.7 cm)
Maharam, New York

24 ALDO VAN EYCK (Dutch, 1918–1999)
Drawing of sandpits, somersault frames,
climbing frames, play tables, and climbing
mountains, designed by Aldo van Eyck, issued for
construction by the Site Preparation Division of the
Department of Public Works (scale 1:200). 1960
Ink on paper, 11 $^3/_4$ x 23 $^3/_8$" (29.8 x 59.4 cm)
Aldo van Eyck Archive, Loenen aan de Vecht,
the Netherlands

25 ALDO VAN EYCK (Dutch, 1918–1999)
Dijkstraat Playground, Amsterdam. 1954
Amsterdam City Archives

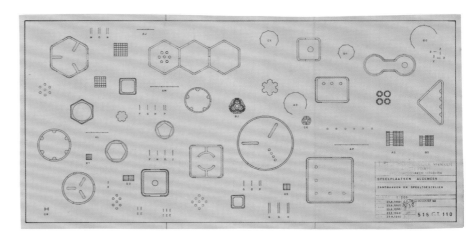

community project — The Competition of Creative Youth — to which a special issue of the art review *Blok* was devoted.[6]

In the 1950s and '60s, children would find their urban liberty ever more constrained by the proliferation of motorized vehicles and traffic codes (no. 30). "Increasingly motor traffic has impeded the orderly development of our towns, and as a result play areas for children have become dangerously limited," commented Arvid Bengtsson in his study *Environmental Planning for Children's Play*. He added, "With ever-increasing motor traffic the street has ceased to be a playground, although it still attracts children in spite of its dangers."[7] Speaking at an international symposium on play in the 1960s, Lady Allen was critical of the postwar redevelopment of cities. "In towns the gardens are fast disappearing, streams are hidden in the sewers, hills and mounds are leveled out, and good earth is buried under concrete and the trees are not for climbing."[8] As far as she was concerned, the lack of public space allocated to children, boring playgrounds, and the overbearing presence of cars were indications of adults' lack of respect for children's freedom and basic human rights.

Juliet Kinchin

26 Curtain Wall Builder. c. 1959
Manufactured by Toy Tinkers, A. G. Spalding
& Bros., Evanston, Illinois
The Museum of Modern Art, New York. Purchase

27 FRIEDRICH BÖER (German, 1904–1987)
Cover of the book *Drei Jungen erforschen eine
Stadt: Eine kleine Stadtkunde mit vielen Fotos und
farbigen Bildmontagen* (Three boys explore a city:
A small city with many photographs and color
montages). 1946
Drawings by Werner Bürger and Erich Krantz
8 7/16 x 6 11/16" (21.5 x 17 cm)
Published by Herbert Stuffer Verlag, Baden-Baden
The Museum of Modern Art Library, New York

28 FRANKIE FARUZZA (American, dates unknown)
Cover of the book *Children and the City*, by Olga
Adams. 1952
8 1/4 x 11" (21 x 28 cm)
Sponsored by the South Side Planning Board,
Michael Reese Hospital Planning Staff,
Metropolitan Housing and Planning Council,
Laboratory School of University of Chicago, Illinois
Institute of Technology, and American Society
of Planning Officials
Published for the sponsors by R. R. Isaacs, Chicago
The Museum of Modern Art Library, New York

29 Girl directing traffic in Brno, Czechoslovakia, 1949, as reproduced in *Blok* 3, no. 8 (1949)

30 WERNER JOHN (Swiss, born 1941)
Kinder Verkehrs Garten (Children's traffic garden), poster advertising a children's traffic school. 1959
Lithograph, 51 x 36" (129.5 x 91.4 cm)
Printed by Allgemeine Gewerbeschule, Basel
The Museum of Modern Art, New York.
Architecture and Design Purchase Fund

NEW SCHOOLS built after World War II were created in response to postwar conditions of physical destruction, a booming population that dramatically increased the need for new school seats, and pedagogical ideals that considered the child's own experience in the learning process. As the everyday environment for school-aged children, the primary, or elementary, school was an important site for nourishing values of the individual, the community, and the state. Postwar schools were indebted to well-publicized, low-rise models developed for reformist pedagogies before the war (see "The New School," p. 99, and "'A Setting for Childlife': The New School in the United States," p. 105), but they normalized this scheme in new institutions across Europe and North and South America in the 1950s and '60s. In plan, design, interior decoration, and furnishings, such schools gave material form to an ideal vision of the future.

The wartime devastation in Europe, rising birthrates, and a shortage of materials made the problem of building new schools quickly an opportunity for unique collaborations and invention. In Britain, experimental infant schools showed how prefabricated parts and an educator's input could enhance the child's experience. Architects combined steel frames erected on a grid plan with large plate-glass windows, making the new schools bright, flexible, and expandable. In 1950 émigré architect Ernő Goldfinger produced an experimental cast-concrete frame with brick and glass walls for two London County Council schools (no. 31). Wartime bombing had disproportionately affected London, where, at the conflict's end, more than 1,300 schools were damaged or destroyed. Goldfinger's design was economical, and as his model indicates, required a single crane to erect the precast frame, which could be accomplished in only twenty-four days.

Scrutiny of the technical aspects of construction and a growing acceptance of the psychological effects of space also informed postwar schools. In addition to an emphasis on building economically with steel frames and glass walls, architects and engineers examined lighting, airflow, and color to determine what was best for learning. Architect William W. Caudill of the Texas Experimental Engineering Station, at Texas A&M University, studied the entire schoolhouse environment, from structure, lighting, airflow, and layout of the classrooms to the design of the walls, blackboard, and storage. In 1950 he wrote a research publication titled "Take a Good Look at Your Schools" (no. 32), intended for a wide audience, including community members, local government officials, and school planners and administrators. Caudill advocated for new designs to suit a changing curriculum that de-emphasized formality and memorization and encouraged a greater variety of learning methods. In contrast to the forbidding multistory schoolhouses of the past, he argued, the new postwar one- or two-story schools should provide a cheery homelike atmosphere for the youngest pupils, and include flexible spaces for large classes and small-group work alike.

An enduring population boom and the development of new suburban towns made housing and schooling urgent international issues. From the early 1940s and throughout the postwar period, The Museum of Modern Art showcased modern schoolhouse architecture and argued that "a good neighborhood has an elementary school."[1] The integration of schooling near housing also concerned Le Corbusier, whose Unité d'habitation in Marseille (1947–52), a vertical community in cast concrete that housed 1,600 people, 900 of whom were children, included a school and children's play areas on the roof (no. 33), designed by his collaborator Blanche Lemco van Ginkel. The school, for ages two to seven, encompassed a bright, open space with pivoting walls, child-sized tubular steel furniture, and a wall of vitrines for the display of small objects. The curriculum included painting and drawing, and play in the pool, protected garden areas, climbing rocks, and a gym on the expansive roof terrace. At Chandigarh, the new capital of Punjab after the partition of India, Le Corbusier created the capital complex and the city plan, and his cousin Pierre Jeanneret designed furniture, housing, and single-story nursery schools (following a new compulsory education law) that were located in park areas for play and outdoor study (no. 34).

School planning was a local concern in the United States, but in other countries it was highly centralized, although many designs were sensitive to local context. In Mexico, Swiss architect Hannes Meyer led the Instituto del Urbanismo y Planificación between 1942 and 1949, making schools a priority for regional development. The newly established Comité Administrador del Programa Federal de Construcción de

31 ERNŐ GOLDFINGER
(British, born Hungary. 1902–1987)
Model demonstrating the assembly of a prefabri-
cated concrete construction system for Westville
Road Primary School and Brandlehow Road
Infants School, Hammersmith, London. 1950
Approx. 7 $^{1}/_{16}$ x 27 $^{15}/_{16}$ x 22 $^{13}/_{16}$" (18 x 71 x 58 cm)
RIBA Library Drawings & Archives Collection, London

32 ANNABEL BERTRAND (American, 1915–2007)
and EMMETT TRANT (American, born 1925)
Cover of the booklet "Take a Good Look
at Your Schools," by William W. Caudill. 1950
8 $^{1}/_{2}$ x 11" (21.6 x 27.9 cm)
Published by A&M Press, College Station, Texas
The Museum of Modern Art, New York. Department
of Architecture and Design Study Center

33 LE CORBUSIER (French, born Switzerland.
1887–1965) and BLANCHE LEMCO VAN GINKEL
(Canadian, born England 1923)
Rooftop kindergarten, Unité d'habitation,
Marseille. 1947–52
Photograph by Lucien Hervé
The Museum of Modern Art, New York. Department
of Architecture and Design Study Center

34 PIERRE JEANNERET (Swiss, 1896–1967)
Chandigarh kindergarten, as reproduced in
*Chandigarh 1956: Le Corbusier, Pierre Jeanneret,
Jane B. Drew, E. Maxwell Fry. Fotografien von Ernst
Scheidegger*, by Stanislaus von Moos (Zurich:
Scheidegger & Spiess, 2010). 1953–56
Photograph by Ernst Scheidegger

35 Front and back cover of the magazine
Construyamos escuelas (Let us build schools), no. 1
(August 1947), published by the Comité Adminis-
trador del Programa Federal de Construcción de
Escuelas (CAPFCE), Mexico City
Two-color print, 11 ³/₄ x 8 ³/₄" (29.8 x 22.4 cm)
gta Archives, ETH Zürich. Bequest of Hannes Meyer

36 AFFONSO EDUARDO REIDY
(Brazilian, born France. 1909–1964)
Primary School and Gymnasium, Pedregulho,
Rio de Janeiro. 1948–50
Photograph by Rollie McKenna
The Museum of Modern Art, New York. Department
of Architecture and Design Study Center

37 ARNE JACOBSEN (Danish, 1902–1971)
View of a classroom in the Munkegårds School,
north of Copenhagen. c. 1952–56
Photograph by Strüwing
The Museum of Modern Art, New York. Department
of Architecture and Design Study Center

38 ARNE JACOBSEN (Danish, 1902–1971)
Aerial perspective drawing of the Munkegårds
School, north of Copenhagen, from the
southwest. c. 1950
Pencil and watercolor on handmade paper,
31 1/8 x 22 1/2" (79 x 57.2 cm)
Danish National Art Library, Copenhagen

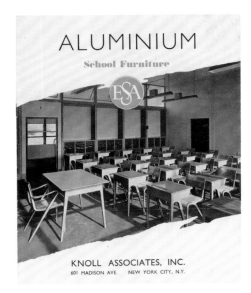

Escuelas (CAPFCE) sponsored the construction of small, low-cost rural schools that would express a strong regional architectural identity (no. 35). Architect Enrique Del Moral designed five schools between 1944 and 1946 for his home state of Guanajuato, including a primary school in Casacurán built of local brick and tile, and a row of rustic tree-trunk columns supporting the deep overhang.

In many postwar schools there was an effort to please children with friendly spaces and bright decoration, and as such art was often a deliberate addition. The facade of Affonso Eduardo Reidy's primary school gymnasium in Rio de Janeiro (no. 36), for example, was covered with Candido Portinari's mural of painted tiles showing children jumping and resting. By including murals, colored glass panes, stone relief panels, and sculptural playgrounds, architects and designers claimed children's attention and embellished the quotidian environment of learning.

The belief that children were more at ease in intimate spaces designed for the child's body affected the plan and decoration of schools, and resulted in numerous low-rise school plans with access to small gardens adjacent to the classroom. Danish architect and designer Arne Jacobsen's Munkegårds School (no. 37), in Søborg, north of Copenhagen, embodied this ideal. The plan for the school included individual classrooms with large plate-glass windows, set around a central double-height auditorium and against a bank of specialized classrooms. Although the school was large (designed for a thousand students from ages seven to fifteen), it retained a sense of intimacy. The plan for the twenty-four one-story classrooms was laid out on a grid with parallel corridors, making each classroom a self-contained unit complete with its own anteroom for informal group work. Two classrooms shared small paved

courts, which Jacobsen landscaped with different flagstone patterns and plant species (no. 38). The low-rise profile gave priority to accessibility, neighborly proximity, and access to the outdoors. Ample lighting was also an important postwar concern. In addition to the glass window-walls that let in plentiful natural light, Jacobsen incorporated diffused clerestory fenestration and incandescent fixtures of his own design that were nearly flush with the ceiling. He also chose copies of ancient and modern sculpture that were placed in or near the patios.

The design of school furniture also enhanced the postwar school environment. For Munkegårds, Jacobsen designed three sizes of furniture, including a plywood desk on a tubular steel frame with a hook for a satchel and a green Formica writing surface, along with laminated beech chairs that were lightweight and could be moved according to the classroom's needs. Portability was one of the key concerns for postwar schoolroom furniture. British designer James Leonard developed designs for chairs and desks for the Educational Supply Association, which Knoll Associates imported to the United States in 1949 (no. 39). Leonard's chairs, which could be easily moved, stacked, and stored, combined a lightweight metal frame manufactured from pressure die-cast aluminum alloy with smooth, curved laminated birch seats. The desks came in three sizes: a small stacking kindergarten table, a junior version that accommodated two, and a single-seat design for older students. Jean Prouvé's 1946 desk for two pupils from ages eight to fourteen, made of laminated steel with an oak writing surface, was stationary but durable and space-saving (no. 40).

Amy F. Ogata

39 Cover of the Knoll Associates catalog showing aluminum school furniture designed by James Leonard
Distributed by Knoll Associates, New York. c. 1950
10 x 8" (25.4 x 20.3 cm)
The Museum of Modern Art, New York. Department of Architecture and Design Study Center

40 JEAN PROUVÉ (French, 1901–1984)
School desk. 1946
Enameled steel and oak, $28^{1}/_{2}$ x 45 x 34"
(72.4 x 114.3 x 86.4 cm)
Manufactured by Ateliers Jean Prouvé, Nancy
The Museum of Modern Art, New York. Dorothy Cullman Purchase Fund

THE TOY, long understood as an important element of child training and education, is surely one of childhood's most romantic objects. In Europe, the United States, and the Soviet bloc after World War II, a host of "good toys" that promised to stimulate imagination, develop the mind, and exercise the body offered a therapeutic, nonviolent image of children's play. These objects enhanced a sentimental notion of the vulnerable child in need of guidance. Like the international organizations UNICEF and the World Council of Early Childhood Education (Organisation Mondiale pour L'Éducation Préscolaire), both founded after the war to protect and promote children's well-being, postwar educators and psychologists claimed that the opportunity for play was one of the most solemn rights of childhood around the world.[1]

"Goodness" in postwar playthings implied wholesome objects of simple design made from materials that carried a whiff of tradition. Indeed, many such toys derived from designs of the prewar era, such as those manufactured by the British firm Paul & Marjorie Abbatt Ltd starting in the 1930s (see "Ernő Goldfinger and the Abbatts: From Toys to Urban Health," p. 111). The goodness of the good toy was tied to both an educational vision and a sense of quality design and manufacture. Swiss sculptor and toy maker Antonio Vitali drew on the rural tradition of handmade wooden toys for his small animals (no. 41), pull toys, and cars, initially produced for his own children and eventually for sale in larger stores, such as Heimatwerk, the Swiss national crafts shop. Vitali's belief in the importance of tactile engagement led him to carve forms that molded to the child's hand and, as a result, became bound to a child's own imaginary world. Eschewing facial features, doors and windows on vehicles, or painted decoration, he believed, enabled the child more fully to make the object his or her own. Kurt Naef, also Swiss, similarly venerated carpentry traditions. The colorful, wooden interlocking blocks of his signature Naef-Spiel encouraged the child to experiment with an infinite variety of forms and structures.

Like its European counterparts, the American toy manufacturer Creative Playthings also sold sturdy, traditional toys, many of which reflected progressive nursery school pedagogy. Its directors, Frank Caplan and Bernard Barenholz, were both former teachers,

die neue sammlung münchen

Umwelt des Kindes

1. März bis 29. April 1956

41 Cover of the exhibition catalogue *Umwelt des Kindes* (Children's environments). 1956
Toys and photograph by Antonio Vitali
8¼ x 5⅞" (21 x 14.9 cm)
Published by Die Neue Sammlung–Staatliches Museum für angewandte Kunst, Munich
The Museum of Modern Art, New York. Department of Architecture and Design Study Center

and Creative Playthings' toys gained a reputation for good design as well as educational value. In 1953 the company commissioned Vitali to design a series of wooden toys called Playforms, adapting his hand-carved objects for mass production while retaining their visual abstraction and haptic appeal. In the mid-1960s, Creative Playthings, which was based in Princeton, New Jersey, and operated a factory in Herndon, Pennsylvania, was sold to the Columbia Broadcasting Corporation. The company expanded its range of objects and manufactured more experimental forms, including an abstract plywood rocking horse design with a blue handle (no. 42) in the early 1970s. It also imported numerous European designs into the United States, and in addition to its mail-order business opened shops in New York and in other major American cities. Caplan and his wife, Theresa, eventually left the business to become, like Paul and Marjorie Abbatt before them, child research experts.

In the Soviet bloc countries, toys were part of a politically useful state-sponsored consumer culture. Goodness in Communist toys was, as elsewhere, linked to pedagogical value and sophisticated design,

42 GLORIA CARANICA (American, born 1931)
Child's rocker. c. 1970
Plywood and painted wood, 16 x 11 3/4 x 25 3/4"
(40.6 x 29.8 x 65.4 cm)
Manufactured by Creative Playthings, Princeton,
New Jersey (est. 1949)
The Museum of Modern Art, New York. Gift of
John C. Waddell

43 HANS BROCKHAGE (German, 1925–2009)
and ERWIN ANDRÄ (German, born 1921)
Schaukelwagen (Rocking car). 1950
Beech frame and birch plywood seat,
15 3/4 x 39 3/8 x 14 15/16" (40 x 100 x 38 cm)
The Museum of Modern Art, New York. Architecture
and Design Purchase Fund

44 VIKTOR FIXL
(Czechoslovak, born Austria. 1914–1986)
Toy Car with Women's Brigade. 1958
Painted wood, 4 5/16 x 3 9/16 x 9 7/16" (11 x 9 x 24 cm)
Museum of Decorative Arts, Prague

45 VIKTOR FIXL
(Czechoslovak, born Austria. 1914–1986)
Toy Bricklayer. c. 1954
Painted wood, 5 1/2 x 11 13/16" (14 x 30 cm)
Museum of Decorative Arts, Prague

46 Nicke, dachshund pull toy. c. 1960
Painted wood and string, 7 1/2 x 7 x 4 3/4"
(19.1 x 17.8 x 12.1 cm)
Manufactured by Brio, Stockholm (est. 1908)
Collection of Margot Weller, New York

47 KAY BOJESEN (Danish, 1886–1958)
Monkey. 1955
Teak and limba wood, 23 5/8 x 18 1/2 x 15 9/16"
(60 x 47 x 39.5 cm)
Kay Bojensen Denmark

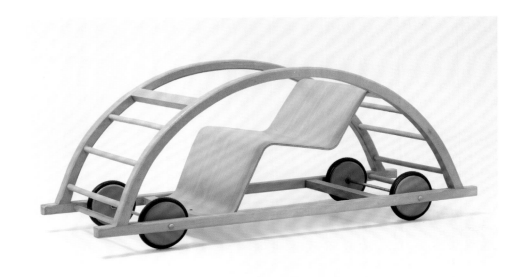

but also to enhancing party doctrine. Hans Brockhage came from East Germany's Erzgebirge region, which is well known for its wooden toy-making, and had trained as a woodworker before he studied under the Dutch designer Mart Stam at the Art Academy in Dresden. In 1950, as a student, he developed his Schaukelwagen (Rocking car) with Erwin Andrä (no. 43). A lightweight, flexible plywood seat is suspended between rails that form a streamlined racing car on bright red wheels; flipped over, it becomes a rocking chair. The Schaukelwagen belongs to an experimental period of East German design that valued the child as the radiant future citizen. Czechoslovak toys manufactured under Communist rule reflected vernacular wooden animals and spool-like dolls, but these models too were updated to suit a political narrative. Václav Kubát's Toy Car with Women's Brigade, a small car with eight peg-shaped figures (no. 44), was shown along with Viktor Fixl's Toy Bricklayer (no. 45) as part of a toy town in the Czechoslovak pavilion at the Brussels World's Fair in 1958. These objects taught real-world lessons of hard work and cooperation, and with the state championing "good toys" for their ideological suitability as much as their forms and intellectual stimulation, toy designers such as Fixl were valorized as important culture-makers and given prestigious posts at arts academies.

Scandinavian playthings have long embodied the notion of the good toy. Modern versions of Swedish, Finnish, and Danish objects made of wood from the region's abundant forests were created according to the craft traditions that these countries consciously aimed to preserve. Such toys were also part of a vigorous concern for education and child welfare. In the 1930s, Swedish social reformer Alva Myrdal championed what she called "real toys" — those that were educational and age appropriate — over faddish and expensive amusements.[2] The Swedish firm Brio, which developed from a maker of wooden baskets and handles, had by the mid-twentieth century become one of the largest manufacturers of brightly painted wooden cars, trains, and animals (no. 46). Danish designer Kay Bojesen's teak monkeys (no. 47) were publicized in both parenting magazines and postwar design periodicals. Along with the stylish furniture that was exported internationally in the

postwar era, wooden toys furthered a reputation for Scandinavian design and quality. In some cases, toys were also furniture. Kristian Vedel's 1957 design for a steam-bent plywood toy had removable slats that could transform the curved shell into a child's chair, table, tunnel, or doll's cradle (no. 48). Similarly, Nanna Ditzel's smooth Trissen stools (no. 49) came in three sizes and were at once small-scale furniture and playthings. If these objects expressed the desire for a child to be free to build or modify his or her environment, their higher price tags also suggested that children's play was a serious and worthwhile investment.

Not all good toys were wooden. Lego, the Danish construction toy, derives its name from *leg godt*, or "good play." Originally designed in wood in the early 1940s, the bricks achieved worldwide fame in the 1960s as a hard injection-molded plastic form that snapped together, losing none of the positive associations of solitary, edifying amusement (see p. 20, no. 13). Likewise, the Slinky (no. 50), a metal spring that seemed to move by itself as its weight shifted, was an entertaining novelty, but also asked the child to ponder principles of gravity (and received a *Parents* magazine commendation).

The determination of quality or value in toys is highly subjective and contentious. Like The Museum of Modern Art's postwar Good Design program, the German Working Committee on Good Toys began designating quality in design and manufacture in 1954, affixing a round orange Spiel Gut (good play) sticker on approved toys that echoed MoMA's own Good Design tag.[3] The discourse of the good toy, which stressed timelessness and individual discovery, promised the opportunity for an innocent child to imperceptibly acquire a range of positive qualities through play.

Amy F. Ogata

48 KRISTIAN VEDEL (Danish, 1923–2003)
Play stool as seen in promotional brochure. 1957
Halftone relief and letterpress, open: 3³/₄ x 22¹/₄"
(9.5 x 56.5 cm)
The Museum of Modern Art, New York. Department
of Architecture and Design Study Center

49 NANNA DITZEL (Danish, 1923–2005)
Children on Trissen stools. 1963
Photograph by Michael Rougier
Getty Images

50 BETTY JAMES (American, 1918–2008)
and RICHARD JAMES (American, 1914–1975)
Slinky. 1945
Steel, compressed: 2³/₈ x 2⁷/₈" (6 x 7.3 cm)
Manufactured by James Spring & Wire Company,
Frazer, Pennsylvania
The Museum of Modern Art, New York. Gift of
the manufacturer

51 MARCEL BREUER
(American, born Hungary. 1902–1981)
Installation view of the exhibition *The House in the Museum Garden*, The Museum of Modern Art, New York, April 12–October 30, 1949
Gelatin silver print, 7 ¾ x 9 ½" (19.7 x 24.1 cm)
Photograph by Ezra Stoller
The Museum of Modern Art Archives, New York. Photographic Archive

THE MID-CENTURY MODERN PLAYROOM was envisioned as a site of free expression and discovery. After World War II, the word "playroom" was used to describe a variety of play places, from the family dwelling to school areas. As a space for children in the domestic environment, the playroom was an extension of the idea of the nursery as it had emerged over the nineteenth century. If, however, the nursery, which separated children from their parents but not from governesses, nannies, and nurses, had elite associations, then the modern playroom embodied the child-centered culture of middle-class postwar America. Experts Jean Piaget, Arnold Gesell, and Benjamin Spock argued that time alone playing with toys was essential for promoting autonomy and stimulating motor development. Architects and designers, building on these theories, produced widely publicized model playrooms for children. These spaces imagined an ideal child, an innocent, creative being who was the designer's alter ego. Whether designed to stimulate the senses, build a fragile identity, or simply to amuse, the playroom was assembled to nurture the desirable qualities that would shape the child into an adult.

In 1949 Marcel Breuer built a model house, specifically designed for modern families, for display in the garden of The Museum of Modern Art. A key element was the large playroom located at the back of the house, with a window into the kitchen and direct access to the outdoors (no. 51). The open space implied freedom, and the room's amusements, which were lent from Creative Playthings and New Design, included large building blocks that could be rearranged as a desk or seating, a wooden train set, a carpentry set, and a loom. The House in the Museum Garden, as it was called, received nearly one hundred thousand visitors in six months, and a survey revealed that the playroom was among the most popular aspects of the exhibit. Although the three-bedroom house was supposed to reflect a "typical" American family, it was criticized by many for its lavishness.[1] The following year, MoMA erected another house, by Gregory Ain, which although far less expensive, also featured a playroom separated from the children's shared bedroom with a retractable partition.

Postwar child development experts contended that room for play should be part of a child's everyday space. Throughout the period, *Parents* magazine regularly featured a section called "Room to Grow in," recommending that children would feel a greater sense of emotional security and aesthetic appreciation in spaces devised with their interests and personalities in mind. American mid-century playrooms were tied to a discourse of "correct" decoration, to cultivate taste, and a strong belief in the educational potential of the child's first surroundings. To this end, the artist-designers György and Juliet Kepes created a room for their five-year-old daughter in their Cambridge, Massachusetts, house in 1949 (no. 52). Designed to develop both her muscles and her senses, the Kepes room included a bed with a large piece of driftwood and plywood cutouts for climbing (no. 53), a table that could be raised, a wire mobile, a large clock of cork balls, a peg board wall on which to create compositions, and a ceiling mapped with moons and stars. In addition, Juliet Kepes, who designed children's books, painted a mural of animals (no. 54), silkscreened curtains with playful monkeys, and made a shaggy rug featuring the body of a lion. The Kepeses claimed, "The first years are a time of concentrated learning and development. They should also be a time of wonder and delight...the room should contain materials with which to color, mold, and make things...structures to climb...light, air, warmth, and quiet."[2]

52, 53 JULIET KEPES (American, born England. 1919–1999) and GYÖRGY KEPES (American, born Hungary. 1906–2001)
Playroom in Kepes House, Cambridge, Massachusetts, 1949
Photograph by Ralph Morse
Getty Images

54 JULIET KEPES
(American, born England. 1919–1999)
Preparatory drawing for playroom mural in Kepes House, Cambridge, Massachusetts. c. 1949
Color wash on thick paper, 20 x 26" (50.8 x 66 cm)
From the collections of Imre Kepes and Juliet Kepes Stone, Pelham and Cambridge, Massachusetts

55 BRUCE ALONZO GOFF
(American, 1904–1982)
*Gene and Nancy Bavinger House: Interior View
Showing Stairs and Suspended Child's Spaces.*
1950–51
Graphite and colored pencil on paper,
23 1/4 x 21 3/16" (59 x 53.8 cm)
Delineator: Herb Greene (Greenberg)
The Art Institute of Chicago. Gift of Shin'enKan, Inc

One of the most unconventional playrooms of the postwar era was a suspended circular platform with only netting for walls (no. 55). The Bavinger House play space, one of five stepped, carpet-covered, saucers hung from metal rods, was open to the unusual living space in Bruce's Goff's 1950–55 design for the Bavinger family outside Norman, Oklahoma. Eugene and Nancy Bavinger, who were both artists, sought a dwelling that would defy the boxy conventions of postwar housing. The logarithmic spiral-shaped plan enclosed the open living area, which had no interior walls and thus no regular rooms. The house's rocky walls, hand-built of red sandstone, ironstone, and blue glass cullet, rose organically from the site near a shallow ravine and stream. A large interior pond and lush plantings took up much of the ground floor. Instead of ordinary bedrooms, the Bavinger children had a sleeping area near the top of the house and a play space one level down, above the built-in dining table. The house became so renowned that the family offered tours and, like the Kepes playroom, it was covered in *Life* magazine. The experimental openness of the dwelling, which Goff's design highlights, made the entire house, with its suspended roof, saucers, and continuous skylight, seem enchanted and futuristic. Indeed, the Bavingers claimed their youngest son would "grow up a true 20th Century space child."[3]

Furnishing the child's playroom was equally important in the discourse of raising future citizens. Although prewar designers, such as Gilbert Rohde, had created suites of furniture for children's rooms, the postwar market offered new possibilities for play. One of Charles and Ray Eames's earliest designs was a 1945 series of children's furniture molded from a single piece of plywood; the chair, stool, and table were diminutive in scale and dyed in saturated hues of red, blue, yellow, black, and magenta. Like other modernist bentwood designs, the pair's children's furniture exemplified efficient modern technology and rational production, yet the heart-shape motif on the chair back (no. 56) also signified innocence and sweetness. And, since plywood was lightweight, a child could rearrange the furniture, making it another plaything in the playroom.

The Eameses' interest in children's goods extended to many different kinds of objects for the playroom. In addition to paper building toys, such as the House of Cards, The Toy (no. 57), and The Little Toy, the firm produced a rack for hanging things from colorful wooden balls (no. 58). Their collaborator Alexander Girard, who created textile designs for Herman Miller, established his own shop in New York in 1961. Called Textiles and Objects, the store sold Girard's fabrics and

whimsical, screenprinted pillows and hangings, and a selection of Marilyn Neuhart's stuffed and embroidered dolls, along with folk toys.

The agency of the child was one of the motifs of the modern playroom. Richard Neagle's child's clothes tree, called The Bamboozler (no. 59), was designed to encourage children to hang up their things. The architect and designer Henry P. Glass, who emigrated to the United States from Vienna in 1939, created a line of children's furniture that was, like the Eameses' designs, colorful and lightweight, but that relied on a pivoting action that children could manipulate without the help of adults. The 1952 Swingline series, produced by the Fleetwood Furniture Company of Grand Haven, Michigan, included a wardrobe, table, toy chest (no. 60), easel, bookcase, and other pieces. Instead of conventional doors, the Swingline toy chest had compartments that pivoted open for ease of access.

Amy F. Ogata

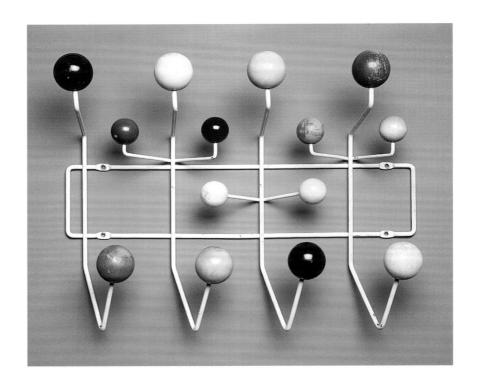

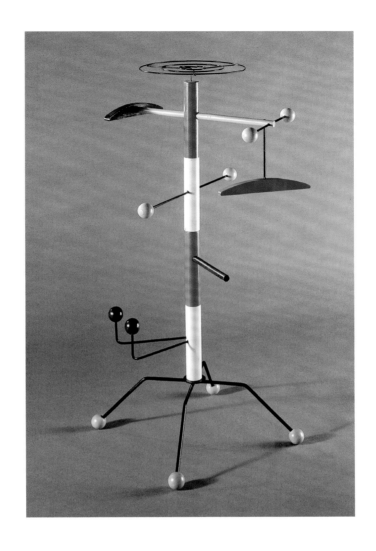

56 RAY EAMES (American, 1912–1988) and
CHARLES EAMES (American, 1907–1978)
Child's chair. c. 1944
Stained molded plywood, 14 1/2 x 14 1/2 x 11"
(36.8 x 36.8 x 27.9 cm)
Manufactured by Evans Products Co.,
Molded Plywood Division, Venice, California
The Museum of Modern Art, New York. Gift of
Herman Miller Furniture Co.

57 RAY EAMES (American, 1912–1988) and
CHARLES EAMES (American, 1907–1978)
The Toy. c. 1950
Photograph by Charles Eames
Manufactured by Tigrett Enterprises, Jackson,
Tennessee
The Museum of Modern Art, New York. Department
of Architecture and Design Study Center

58 RAY EAMES (American, 1912–1988) and
CHARLES EAMES (American, 1907–1978)
Hang-It-All coat rack. 1953
Enameled metal and painted wood, 16 x 19 3/4 x 6 1/4"
(40.6 x 50.2 x 15.9 cm)
Manufactured by Tigrett Enterprises Playhouse
Division, Jackson, Tennessee
Brooklyn Museum, H. Randolph Lever Fund

59 RICHARD NEAGLE (American, born 1922)
The Bamboozler child's clothes tree. c. 1953
Wood and metal, 44 1/8 x 18 1/4 x 20 1/4"
(112.1 x 46.4 x 51.4 cm)
Brooklyn Museum, Alfred T. and Caroline S.
Zoebisch Fund

60 HENRY P. GLASS
(American, born Austria. 1911–2003)
Nursery Line toy chest, from Swingline Juvenile
Furniture. c. 1952
Colored pencil, pastel, and graphite on tracing
paper, 13 x 13 7/8" (33 x 35.3 cm)
The Art Institute of Chicago. Gift of Henry P. Glass

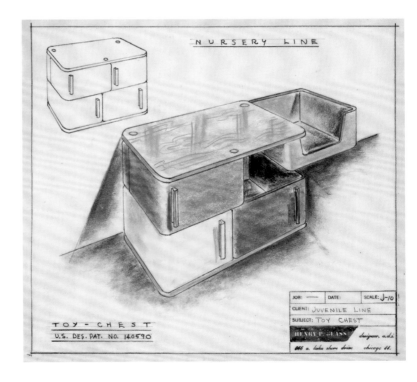

VICTOR D'AMICO, the leader of The Museum of Modern Art's Education Department from its origins in 1937 through his retirement in 1970, built a unique, child-focused legacy within the history of the Museum as well as the larger world of art education.[1] "Furnishing popular instruction" was one of the Museum's founding principles, and D'Amico was extraordinarily active and innovative in extending this instruction to children. Influenced by the experience-based pedagogy of John Dewey, D'Amico created his own laboratory-style approach to vitalize children's connection to modern art and design in their everyday lives.[2]

D'Amico came to MoMA to direct the new Education Project, as it was called at the time, which launched with the opening of the Young People's Gallery, an off-site experiment dedicated to making the Museum's collections more accessible to schoolchildren. The gallery moved to the Museum building in 1939 as a permanent classroom and display space on the third floor, and MoMA's initiatives for children soon grew in number and impact. "Last year," a 1941 Bulletin cited, "students made more than 10,000 visits to the Museum; 25,000 students saw its Rotating Exhibitions in the schools; at least 100 teachers used its resources."[3] School groups were even invited to curate and design their own exhibitions in the Young People's Gallery.

D'Amico devised special projects that also allowed young students to participate in formal Museum exhibitions. For architecture and design shows, this often meant engagement with models. As part of the landmark exhibition *Modern Architecture: International Exhibition* (1932), for example, children were invited to arrange the geometric block units

of an interactive model; in *Machine Art: Modern Interiors* (1940), they could experiment with various arrangements of miniature furniture and wall sections.

D'Amico believed that children were all born with creative talents, but that these talents required nurturing by sensitive teachers. (Accordingly, MoMA offered free art classes for public school teachers.) A variety of children's programs promoted learning through art-making, rather than structured lessons, in order to develop "each individual's sensitivity to the fundamentals of art and thus to increase his creative power."[4] The goal was to discourage imitation in favor of helping children discover their own methods of seeing and self-expression. A number of exhibitions held at the Museum reinforced the importance of such endeavors, including *Understanding the Child through Art* (1944); *Developing Creativeness in Children* (1955); *Art of the Young Child* (1955–56); and *Art Education for Every Child* (1960). These high-profile shows foregrounded D'Amico's passionate beliefs — in *Developing Creativeness in Children*, photo panels of children being taught to make art by copying were juxtaposed with those of marching Hitler youth — as well as the ascendant role of education at the Museum. *Art Education for Every Child*, for example, was prominently installed within a large geodesic dome constructed in the Museum's sculpture garden.

In addition to early art practice, D'Amico was concerned with children's understanding of design through everyday objects. He believed that toys were especially formative both to children's artistic spirit and to their development of taste. "Toys have an important place in the creative growth of the child," he explained. "They are his first possessions and the objects of profound interest and affection. Through them he is introduced to the elements of design, texture, pattern, form, color and rhythms as they become the tools of his activity and his imagination."[5] In 1953 D'Amico organized the exhibition *Premium Toys Designed for Industry* (no. 61), in which he highlighted what he saw as exemplary designs of the most common and inexpensive type of toy — "premiums" acquired as giveaways or exchanged for box tops. The eighty toys featured — puzzles, mobiles, cardboard rockets — were created by two designers: A. F. Arnold and Joseph Zalewski, both fathers of young children at the time.

D'Amico recognized the potential role of parents as teachers of art and design principles. His groundbreaking thirteen-week television series *Through the Enchanted Gate* (1952–53), which aired on NBC, projected MoMA's progressive, child-centered, and process-based approach to art education into living rooms across the country. Echoing the modernist doctrine of the Museum's ambitious Good Design program

(1950–55), which has been criticized as elitist, D'Amico used the shows to offer "taste" guidance, in one episode using a cat-shaped cookie jar in a message to parents not to expose children to so-called false design in the home. Following the success of the show, he wrote the MoMA publication *Art for the Family* (with teachers Frances Wilson and Moreen Maser) in 1954. The book was based on the conviction that "all people have creative ability and that anyone at any age can enjoy and develop his aptitudes in art."[6] It was promoted as the first book of its kind designed to enhance the creative interests of parents and children together, as a family unit.

The most famous and long-running of D'Amico's programs was MoMA's annual Children's Festival of Modern Art (later called the Children's Holiday Fair, Children's Holiday Circus, and Children's Holiday Carnival), which ran from 1942 to 1969 (no. 62). D'Amico designed the spaces, furnishings, and games for these highly publicized events. There were generally two galleries: one for inspiration and the other for participation. Other than trained teachers, adults were not allowed to enter. Children accessed the galleries through an "enchanted gate" made of metal wire shaped to form the silhouettes of a typical four- and twelve-year-old (representing the age limits for entrance). Children first spent thirty minutes in the inspiration area, a darkened, cool, and quiet atmosphere intended to enhance creativity, with toys and art games "lighted to look like jewels" and music such as *The Nutcracker* and *Swan Lake* playing in the background.[7] Then they spent an hour in the adjacent workshop—light and open, with adjustable easels, turntables, and countless art materials.

The festival program was so successful that D'Amico was able to launch a mobile version—the Children's Art Carnival. Each carnival was constructed on-site in locations from Harlem to Barcelona, Milan, Hong Kong, and New Delhi. In 1958, 34 crates loaded with motivational toys, 104 gallons of paint, almost 600 brushes, paper, pipe cleaners, colored tissue, cardboard, straws, burlap, and yarn were shipped to Brussels for the Children's Creative Center operated by MoMA in the American Pavilion at the World's Fair.[8] In 1969 D'Amico conceived his final (unrealized) dream for the program, the Children's Art Caravan—a mobile vehicle that could make a circuit of New York City public schools.

Another lively mid-century manifestation of MoMA's involvement in design for children was the Play Sculpture project (1953–54), which sought to motivate more imaginative and stimulating design for modern public playgrounds.[9] Through a national competition, for which D'Amico was a juror, eleven prizewinning creations by young designers, painters, and sculptors were selected for display, at full scale or as models, at the Museum through the summer of 1954. The top three designs—Fantastic Village (by Virginia Dortch Dorazio), Stalagmite Cave (by Robert J. Gargiule), and Tunnel Maze (by Sidney Gordin)—were subsequently manufactured by the toy company Creative Playthings' newly established Play Sculptures division. The judges considered Tunnel Maze (no. 63) the most successful in regard to play value, safety, and ease of supervision. Children could run, jump, slide, crawl, and find "shelter nooks" around the "hilly field" of bridge-shaped units installed in a staggered pattern for the exhibition. In this simple design there were both beauty and versatility: "Small movable toys… may be rolled down the outside slopes by younger children or driven through the tunnels where alternating patches of light and shade make interesting patterns. Older children may play ball games over or around the bridged or use them for group singing or story telling."[10]

Aidan O'Connor

61 Installation view of the exhibition *Premium Toys Designed for Industry*, The Museum of Modern Art, New York, October 13–December 27, 1953
Gelatin silver print, 7 x 9 1/2" (17.8 x 24.1 cm)
Photograph by Soichi Sunami
The Museum of Modern Art Archives, New York. Photographic Archive

62 Participants at the Children's Holiday Carnival, The Museum of Modern Art, New York, December 10, 1956–January 13, 1957
Gelatin silver print, 7 1/4 x 9 1/2" (18.4 x 24.1 cm)
Photograph by Soichi Sunami
The Museum of Modern Art Archives, New York. Photographic Archive

63 Sidney Gordin's Tunnel Maze, The Museum of Modern Art Play Sculpture Competition, The Museum of Modern Art, New York, June 30–August 22, 1954
Photograph by Todd Webb
The Museum of Modern Art, New York. Department of Architecture and Design Study Center

INTRODUCTION

THE CHILD and consumer culture — social constructions that embody the sacred and the profane — have exerted power over each other (as well as adults) for more than a century. After World War II, innovation and mass production, the hallmarks of modern design, fueled a proliferation of goods for children, contributing to intensified market research and advertising aimed at children all over the world, as well as concerns about children being exploited by corporations and media (no. 1). This chapter maps significant points of intersection between children and the commercial realm in relation to modern design, focusing on the period from the 1960s to 2000, a broad span of time held together by the prevailing concept of the child consumer as an individual agent, cognizant and autonomous.

Daniel Cook, a professor of childhood studies and founder of the Consumer Studies Research Network, has explained that the construct of the child as a little consumer replaced previous models used to represent the child in the context of the marketplace (the developing being, the tabula rasa, the novelty seeker) as market researchers have increasingly studied children and developed new tactics to elicit their preferences.[1] By 1969 child researcher and marketing professor James U. McNeal defined the child market (and its power) as children between the ages of five and thirteen who "make purchases of goods and services for personal use and satisfaction...in order for a group to be termed a market, it must be sizable, it must have desire and must have the ability to buy."[2]

McNeal was writing about the United States, which, being relatively less damaged by the war than Europe, had a more significant baby-boom generation and the economic stability to support a surge of new child-focused product designs, media, and companies. Some ventures exploded in popularity, such as Barbie, or became global empires, such as Disney and McDonald's. The spirit of abundance that characterized the new children's goods gave rise to inventive environments for their promotion and sale, such as Ladislav Sutnar's conceptual Park of Pleasures (1952) and Studio Works' multimedia store for Creative Playthings (1969).

During the Cold War, children in the United States and the Soviet bloc, as well as in Western Europe and Japan, participated in that power struggle via space-themed toys, playgrounds, accessories, animations, and furnishings. Here, savvy modern designers and manufacturers produced new forms that happily combined the child's power of imagination with the adult concept of children as the future. An intensive focus on the present, by contrast, was the defining trait of designers who shaped new children's products inspired by the youth-minded principles of Pop art and by consumer culture itself. These rebellious figures (in Italy, France, Germany, Britain, Sweden, and Czechoslovakia, for example) experimented successfully with new materials (especially plastics) and manufacturing techniques.

Throughout the decades covered in this chapter, the status and quality of life of children — and their relationship with design and commercial goods — varied widely depending on where they lived and their families' economic position. But in general the shifting power dynamics between young and old and between the child and the marketplace have been inextricable from the process and products of design. In the electronic and digital realms of gaming and communication, children often have a better command of innovative design, being "digital natives," with parents and teachers who are mostly "digital immigrants," struggling to catch up.[3] Children process the images and text of material culture and mass media in their own ways, sometimes in active subversion of intended meanings and purposes, as in contemporary Japan, where a deep fascination with youth is interpreted by young girls shaping their identities through fashion, accessories, and creative products.

In recent decades children have been identified as agents who not only wield more purchasing power themselves but also exert more (or even inordinate) influence on adult decisions about consumer products, primarily through what is still known as "pester power."[4] "The marketplace wants kids, needs kids, and they're flattered by the invitation and happy to oblige," consumption expert and consultant Paco Underhill observed at the close of the century. Speaking rhetorically to children in a chapter dedicated to them, he proclaimed, "You no longer need to stay clear of the global marketplace just because you're three-and-a-half feet tall, have no income to speak of and are not permitted to cross the street without Mom. You're an economic force, now and in the future, and that's what counts."[5]

Aidan O'Connor

1 STILETTO STUDIOS (Germany, est. 1981)
Short Rest chair. 1989
Plastic powder-coated steel and plastic,
22 1/4 x 15 3/4 x 20 1/16" (56.5 x 40 x 51 cm)
Vitra Design Museum, Weil am Rhein, Germany

imaginations of children and adults. People of all ages and on both sides of the Cold War were buoyed by childlike wonder and optimism, even as the space race engendered fear of the prospects of outer space and the threat of nuclear war. In a complex translation of these awesome unknowns, adult space-age material culture (especially in the United States) was generally limited to novelty items, such as Hoover's satellite-shaped Constellation Vacuum, and a parade of decorative motifs featuring starbursts, atoms, and planetary forms.[2] Design for children, on the other hand, was often more inventive, producing stylish (and implicitly ideological) toys, environments, films, and television programs that furnished fantasy worlds for children in whose real worlds the distinctions between possible and impossible, science fact and fiction, were increasingly blurred.

The ongoing space race was a time of mounting ambitions and anxieties for adults, but for children all over the world it was a time of great imaginative play in which they could act out their own aerospace adventures in new designed environments. Junior astronauts and cosmonauts commanded scaled-down rockets and satellites, the most striking of which were abstract sculptural departures from the conventional forms, such as artist Zdeněk Němeček's interpretation of Sputnik's aluminum sphere as an elegant concrete play sculpture encased in multicolored ceramic with climbing tube and slide (no. 2), originally installed in Stromovka Park in Prague. In the United States scores of skeletal rocket climbers (no. 3) were installed in public parks through the 1960s, shifting the very nature of popular imaginative play. "'Bang, bang, you're dead!' is giving way to 'Blast Off!'" observed *Life* magazine in 1963. "This space-age switch from the TV-style fast-draw to the countdown is encouraged no end by the latest in playground equipment. The new gear, some of it as colorful as modern art, is as different from the old-fashioned slide, seesaw and teeth-busting swing as Telstar is from a Conestoga wagon."[3]

Rockets, both simple and complex, were a popular form for toys as well as playgrounds. In 1968 the British company Polypops developed three flat-packed spacecraft toys designed by Roger Limbrick — Lunartrack, Space Station, and Space Rocket (no. 4).[4] The Space Rocket, just large enough to accommodate one child passenger, had an exterior coated in foil and an interior intricately printed with dials and circuits. The Hungarian toy Holdrakéta (no. 5) was even more sophisticated; this mechanical tin rocket traveled horizontally across the floor until it met an obstacle, at which point it righted itself and let down a ramp, revealing a cosmonaut inside, ready for the child to launch.

IN 1954 the German-American rocket scientist and aerospace engineer Werner von Braun posed with Walt Disney for a press photograph. At the time Braun, who had worked for the Nazis before coming to the United States and working for NASA, was collaborating with Disney on educational television films about space exploration, and the two men, presenting a model rocket and futuristic passenger aircraft, beam in this photograph like children with new toys.[1]

In the early space age — a period of powerful technological, political, and cultural transformation that began with the Soviet Union's launch of the satellite Sputnik in 1957 and peaked with the United States' first manned moon landing, by Apollo 11 in 1969 — the seemingly limitless possibilities of design collapsed the distance between the

2 ZDENĚK NĚMEČEK (Czechoslovak, 1931–1991)
Sputnik play sculpture. c. 1959
Photograph by Petr Karsulin
Dolce Vita Magazine, Prague

3 Rocket jungle gym, originally installed in a
playground at Coney Island, New York. c. 1958
Painted metal, 11' 3" x 24 1/4" x 6' 7 1/2"
(342.9 x 87 x 201.9 cm)
Space Age Museum/Kleeman Family Collection,
Litchfield, Connecticut

4 ROGER LIMBRICK (British, born 1933)
Space Station and Space Rocket cardboard toys. 1968
Fluted cardboard, with silver foil and flexographic
print design, rocket: 59 x 38" (150 x 96 cm)
Manufactured by Polypops Products Ltd, London
Photograph by Timothy Quallington
Design Council/University of Brighton Design Archives

5 Holdrakéta and original box. c. 1960
Tin, box: 24 x 6" (61 x 15.2 cm)
Manufactured by Lemezaru Gyar, Budapest (est. 1950)
Collection of Joan Wadleigh Curran, Philadelphia

6 OLDŘICH LIPSKÝ (Czechoslovak, 1924–1986)
"Children in the Museum of the Twentieth
Century," still from the film *Muž z prvního století*
(Man from the first century). 1961
35 mm (black-and-white, sound). 92 minutes
Národní Filmovy Archiv, Prague

7 JIŘÍ TRNKA (Czechoslovak, 1912–1969)
Animation still from the film *Kybernetická Babička*
(Cybernetic grandma). 1962
35 mm (color, sound). 28:12 minutes
Krátky Film Praha, Prague

8 Space Helmet with Radar Goggles and
original display insert and box. 1953
Helmet: 7 x 8 x 7" (17.8 x 20.3 x 17.8 cm),
box: 9^1/$_2$ x 8^1/$_4$ x 8^1/$_4$" (24.1 x 21 x 21 cm)
Manufactured by Banner Plastics Corp.,
Paterson, New Jersey
Space Age Museum/Kleeman Family Collection,
Litchfield, Connecticut

9 Action Planet Robot and original box. c. 1958
Tin and plastic, 8^1/$_2$ x 4^1/$_2$" (21.6 x 11.4 cm)
Manufactured by Yoshiya (KO), Kobe
Space Age Museum/Kleeman Family Collection,
Litchfield, Connecticut

10 Boys in a Glasgow back court show off their
Christmas presents, which include astronaut suits
and Space Hoppers. 1970
Published in *The Scotsman*
Photograph by Gordon Rule
Licensor SCRAN, Glasgow

11 Capsela 700 construction set. 1978
Plastic, box: 3 x 20 x 15" (7.6 x 50.8 x 38.1 cm)
Manufactured by Play-Jour, Inc., New York (originally
manufactured by Mitsubishi Pencil Co., Tokyo)
The Museum of Modern Art, New York. Gift of
the manufacturer

The adult politics and projections of the future embodied in space-age toys and other designs were articulated with added dimension in children's films. In Czechoslovakia advanced animation and filmmaking produced outstanding works of entertainment for children in this period; in two examples, both from the early 1960s, space themes both telegraph and question government-sponsored visions of a Communist-utopian future. Oldřich Lipský's *Muž z prvního století* (Man from the first century) was the first Czechoslovak film set entirely in the future. In a memorable scene (no. 6) children are shown marching in obedient formation behind a robot guide through a rocket-packed Museum of the Twentieth Century. By contrast, a surreal stop-motion film by the renowned animation designer Jiří Trnka questions the outcome of unfettered advancement. The compellingly titled *Kybernetická Babička* (Cybernetic grandma) (no. 7), follows a young girl as she explores a strange future world of automated buildings, conveyor belts, and plastic sky cars. Tension mounts in a mysterious chamber where a robotic armchair attempts to substitute for the girl's grandmother, bewildering her until her human relative reappears. (It is interesting to note that the word "robot" entered the English language via the Czech word *robota*, for "forced labor," in Karel Čapek's play *RUR* [1921].)[5]

In addition to the glamorous vehicles and voyages of space travel, space-age play also explored the fantasy of inhabiting other worlds. Modern graphics and materials were applied to mass-produced toys and board games to engage children whose heroes were popular media protagonists such as Dan Dare, Pilot of the Future, from the comic strip (1950) in Britain; Robot Emil, from the television show (1960) in Czechoslovakia; and The Jetsons, from the animated television show (1962) in the United States. In the United States and the Soviet Union the marketplace was flooded with metal and plastic spacecraft toys, radar guns, and other cosmic accessories (no. 8). Space themes and premiums were skillfully incorporated in product merchandising, such as the moon-rocket kit accompanying an "out of this world breakfast" of Cheerios and V-8 in 1960.[6] Japan, meanwhile, excelled in the design and manufacture of tin windup robot toys (no. 9). Robots

had for decades been both a hopeful and anxious representation of the power of machines and were often depicted in popular media as aids to space exploration and as threatening alien beings. In toy form they were particularly dynamic, exciting objects, with children bringing their multifarious powers under control.

The new frontier of outer space was sufficiently vast and mysterious to allow designers and toy manufacturers near-complete freedom of imagination and creation. One rather enigmatic but popular product was Mettoy's Space Hopper (1969). These bright orange vinyl bouncing balls, two feet in diameter, with kangaroolike faces and handles that resembled horns, are said to have been inspired by children bouncing on fishing buoys in Norway.[7] A photograph (no. 10) taken behind Glasgow tenement housing in December 1970, showing two young boys with astronaut suits, helmets, and Space Hoppers — new Christmas presents that must have cost their parents a relative bundle — captures their bleak environs but also suggests escape, freedom, and hope, principles that were at the core of design for children in this period.

Christmas season during the space age brought flurries of publicity for new science-related toys and games, some emphasizing their educational potential. "Santa will have to be 'in orbit' this year," advised the *Science News-Letter* in 1959, "if he is going to stuff the stockings of space-age children.... Today's children are surprisingly knowledgeable about the latest electronic marvel, moonshot, or chance of stumbling on the secret crossover between life and non-life."[8] Shirley Moore, the article's author, recommended hundreds of toys that encouraged a child's interest in space and scientific discovery and suggested that these gifts were "quite likely to result in the sprouting of thousands of brand new scientists under the nation's Christmas trees this year."[9] This idea carried serious weight in a period marked by intense international competition in science and technology, and educational kits became increasingly popular at home and in schools. Capsela (no. 11), a modular toy for building experiments, originally designed and manufactured in Japan in 1975, was advertised as "the construction set of tomorrow."[10] With it, children could combine plastic capsules with electric motors, gears, propellers, wheels, and pumps to create real and imaginary vehicles, many of which resembled instruments appropriate for lunar deployment. The designer and educator Victor Papanek distinguished Capsela from a sea of questionable contemporary toys in his 1971 manifesto (see "Design for the Real World," p. 226).

Aidan O'Connor

12 Walt Disney with original aerial-view painting of Disneyland, produced for ABC Television, October 1954
Painting by Peter Ellenshaw (British, 1913–2007)
Walt Disney Imagineering, Glendale, California

DISNEYLAND, Walt Disney's enchanted and lucrative world, opened in July 1955. It was originally intended as a kiddieland, an amusement area adjacent to the Burbank television studios, but when it became clear that the studio lot was too small, Disney moved quickly in 1953 to purchase a 160-acre plot, carved out of orange and walnut groves in Anaheim, California, for what would become one of the most significant statements of twentieth-century American popular culture (no. 12). Unlike earlier carnivals, seaside boardwalks, or state fair and world's fair midways, Disneyland was designed as a wholesome middle-class family experience, and the baby boom, which began in 1945 and ended around 1964, provided both a television and film audience for Walt Disney productions and a steady stream of visitors for Disneyland.

Disneyland was conceived as a physical extension of Walt Disney's cinematic and television projects but quickly became a spectacle that dwarfed them both. Following the model of world's fairs of the 1930s, Disney planned a miniature city, with a nostalgic Main Street based on his boyhood hometown of Marceline, Missouri, that linked four distinct areas mixing notions of past and future in what he called his "magic kingdom." The park was partially financed by ABC, the station that aired Disney's Sunday-evening television program, also called *Disneyland*, which, along with Disney's animated films and children's variety show, *The Mickey Mouse Club*, provided the park's key themes of innocence, exploration, and adventure and an essential opportunity to sell the experience on the air.

Disney, working with experienced Hollywood animators, set designers, engineers, and architects (whom he called "imagineers"), contrasted a sentimental image of nineteenth-century America with the foreign and futuristic. Main Street was erected at a reduced scale to make it appear toylike and to complement the park's miniaturized railroad.[1] The carefully appointed, perennially fresh Victorian store-fronts were designed in the nostalgic image of the small town and for the pedestrian shoppers rather than the automobile. If Main Street and New Orleans Square (added in 1966) were the urban centers, Frontierland was the antithesis, a mythical American West based on Disney's sensationally popular mid-1950s television program *Davy Crockett, King of the Wild Frontier*. Sleeping Beauty Castle, the gateway to Fantasyland and the centerpiece of the park, was placed on the axis with Main Street, making it a focal point for visitors from the moment they entered the park. Based on Neuschwanstein, a nineteenth-century royal retreat in Schwangau, Germany, the castle reversed the diminutive scale of Main Street, with the forced perspective of ascending turrets and towers exaggerating its size and height (no. 13). Fantasyland brought to life Snow White, Peter Pan, Cinderella, and Alice in Wonderland, in rides such as the Mad Hatter's Tea Party. Adventureland, inspired by Disney's True-Life Adventures series of nature documentaries, simulated exotic exploration via a steamboat Jungle Cruise, a Polynesian Tiki Room, and the fanciful dwelling of the marooned Swiss Family Robinson. Tomorrowland, a Cold War utopia that evoked the outer space that

both the United States and the Soviet Union were still racing to conquer in the mid-1950s, seemed equally fantastic. In its earliest form Tomorrowland's exhibits, such as Monsanto's Home of the Future and GM's Carousel of Progress, relied on corporate sponsors who placed their products and industries in proximity to images of the future. Autotopia, a car race, embellished the experience of traveling by car to Disneyland, and on the (real) Santa Ana Freeway, connecting Los Angeles to Orange County, extra lanes were added in anticipation of Disneyland traffic.

Disneyland presented itself as timeless and magical, but the technology and research behind the park were highly sophisticated. Early on, Disney hired the Stanford Research Institute to study traffic flow and consumer satisfaction and to identify a location for the site. The Disneyland monorail was a new technology and the first in the United States when it launched in 1959. Disney's Audio-Animatronic technology, which allowed figures and other parts of the exhibits to move pneumatically along with recorded sound, animated the Tiki Room (1963), It's a Small World (1966), and the Bear Jamboree (1971). It's a Small World was originally part of the Pepsi and UNICEF pavilion at the New York World's Fair in 1964–65. In it, continuously loaded boats carried visitors efficiently on a cruise that provided the spectacle of hundreds of childlike dolls moving and singing the same song in different languages. The dolls, which Disney carefully supervised, all had identically shaped faces but were clothed to represent different countries and set against abstracted and stereotyped images of those lands (no. 14).

Disneyland's popularity was apparent from its chaotic opening day, and attendance rose from one million visitors in the first year to ten million in 1970. In 1959 Disney began planning another park, to be erected south of Orlando, Florida, to attract visitors from the East Coast. Walt Disney World, a sprawling thirty-thousand-acre park, was more than 180 times larger than Disneyland; because it required a longer stay to see all of its attractions and because Disney envisioned a more unified experience, two resort hotels opened along with the park in the autumn of 1971. The park's main lands were larger and more spread out over the site, which later included the Experimental Prototype Community of Tomorrow, or EPCOT. Although Disney conceived of EPCOT as a working radial city that the children of the future might inhabit, the version that was eventually built and which opened in 1982 was not a city but an international and futuristic theme park within Spaceship Earth, a geodesic dome containing the exhibits. Disney's enterprise grew into an empire, with parks in Paris, Tokyo, and Hong Kong;

a cruise line; and a private island. Critics have charged that Disney's sentimental vision of American culture and history, which Disneyland embodies, masks its aggressive marketing and has changed how we understand American childhood.[2]

Amy F. Ogata

WRITING IN 1963 for *Design Quarterly*, the journal of the Walker Art Center, Minneapolis, artist-designer Anna Campbell Bliss observed several problems endemic to conventional design for children:

> Children's furniture through the ages has generally reflected the stylistic manner of the period rather than an understanding of the child. Despite our extensive research and preoccupation with the problems of childhood, we continue to design miniature versions of adult styles. Furniture for the early years shows little attention to function or to the changing patterns of contemporary living.[1]

These issues were effectively confronted in the rebellious design movement, emergent at the time of Bliss's article, inspired by the principles of Pop art. Designers in Britain, Germany, France, Sweden, Czechoslovakia (featured in this section), and Italy (in the following section) created innovative products shaped by the interests of Pop artists and the Independent Group, their precursors: youth and mass culture, transience and ephemerality, consumerism and expendability. Successful Pop designs for adults, such as the inflatable Blow chair (1967) or the Sacco beanbag chair (1968), reinterpreted functional objects to suit more flexible, casual, and nomadic lifestyles, using new industrial materials and techniques. The same influences and factors were applied with exuberance to new designs specifically for children, which rejected the idiom of miniaturizing existing adult products and created surprising new forms with vibrant colors and character.

One of the most famous, affordable, and disposable children's chairs from this period was made out of cardboard. Spotty (no. 15), designed by Peter Murdoch in 1963, while he was a student at the Royal College of Art in London, is a single-sheet cardboard chair made surprisingly robust by its sophisticated folded form. It was inexpensive to produce and distribute (since it could be flat-packed) and could be easily constructed (thanks to its prescored lines) and washed (thanks to its polyethylene coating). The strength and success of this chair led the *New York Times* to reconsider the potential of paper furniture:

15 PETER MURDOCH (British, born 1940)
Spotty chair. 1963
Cardboard and polyethylene, 20 1/2 x 21 5/8 x 13 3/4"
(52 x 55 x 35 cm)
Les Arts Décoratifs, Paris

"The pundits who had predicted an era of disposable furniture some years ago may not be quite so kookie as they sounded."[2] Paper was also turned into clothing, in a contemporary craze extended to young girls by designers such as Joseph Love, who created dresses made of Kaycel, a fabric made of cellulose and nylon.

Another fruitful material for innovative furniture was polyester, often reinforced with fiberglass. In West Germany in the early and mid-1960s the designers Walter Papst (whose work was featured in Bliss's article) and Günter Beltzig (who worked with his brothers under the name of Brüder Beltzig until 1976) produced light and colorful polyester-and-fiberglass children's furniture, playground equipment, and toys such as a rocking horse. Soon after, Marc Berthier, described by *Design* magazine as one of the best young designers in France, created the first polyester-and-fiberglass furniture series to be made in that country, with a line called Ozoo.[3] In collaboration with the Société Ozoo ("maker of high class touring caravans") Berthier produced a complete set, including dining and bedroom furniture for adults as well as a play desk for children (no. 16), which featured a hiding space

16 MARC BERTHIER (French, born 1935)
Ozoo 700 desk. 1967
Polyester and fiberglass, 20 $\frac{1}{16}$ x 28 $\frac{1}{8}$ x 31 $\frac{3}{16}$"
(51 x 71.5 x 79.2 cm)
Manufactured by Roche-Bobois International,
Paris (est. 1950)
Les Arts Décoratifs, Paris

17 LUIGI COLANI (German, born 1928)
Zocker chair. 1972
Polyethylene, 22 $\frac{7}{16}$ x 19 $\frac{11}{16}$ x 12 $\frac{5}{8}$" (57 x 50 x 32 cm)
Manufactured by Top-System Burkhard Lübke,
Gütersloh, Germany
Les Arts Décoratifs, Paris

18 STEPHAN GIP (Swedish, born 1936)
Inflatable furniture shown on the cover of
Form magazine (no. 9). 1967
Photograph by Carl-Johan Rönn
Manufactured by Hagaplast, Sweden
Svensk Form, Stockholm

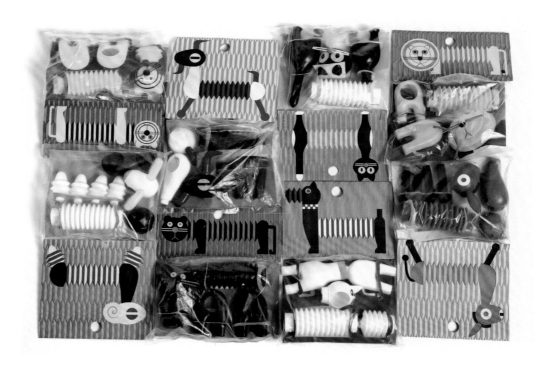

19 LIBUŠE NIKLOVÁ (Czechoslovak, 1934–1981)
Train dispatcher, Barbórka, chimney sweeper,
nurse, doctor, motorcyclist, lion tamer, and
cosmonaut. 1964; Hanka. 1958–59
Blown PVC, each: approx. 7 x 3" (17.8 x 7.6 cm)
Manufactured by Gumotex, Břeclav, Czechoslovakia
(est. 1950)
Petr Nikl, Prague and New York

20 LIBUŠE NIKLOVÁ (Czechoslovak, 1934–1981)
Sound-producing animals in their original
packaging. 1963–65
Hand-painted polyethylene, paper, PVC, each:
approx. 13 3/4 x 8 11/16 x 7 1/2" (35 x 22 x 19 cm)
Manufactured by Fatra, Napajedla, Czechoslovakia
(est. 1935)
Archive Fatra, Napajedla, Czech Republic

Inflatables were a distinctly Pop type of furniture, embodying both impermanence and fun. The Swedish architect Stephan Gip, known primarily for his children's designs in wood, including a modular furniture-and-toy system called Fun on Wheels (1959) and a frequently copied trayless high chair (1962), created in 1967 a line of vinyl plastic furniture for adults and children that could be inflated with a vacuum cleaner (no. 18).[4] The colorful pieces were produced in Sweden and distributed in Britain by Conran and Company. In the late 1960s Gip explored the possibility of inflatables as a tool for socially responsible design, such as an inflatable nursery, approximately one thousand feet square, that would quickly and cheaply provide space for childcare and education as populations increased. Gip presented this idea at the Moderna Museet in Stockholm in October 1968, the same month that artist Palle Nielsen took over the museum with his radical children's exhibition *The Model* (see "Dismantling the Museum," p. 222).

Libuše Niklová was a Czechoslovak designer fluent in various Pop materials, whose children's toys have recently been internationally rediscovered.[5] Niklová studied plastic molding, a new industrial field that flourished after World War II. She began her career as a toy designer at Gumotex, in Břeclav, where she experimented with squeaky animal toys in molded rubber (1956–58) before creating, for a 1964 competition, a series of blown PVC figures representing various professions (no. 19). At Fatra, a major plastics producer in Napajedla, she designed a successful series of polyethylene animals distinguished by their accordion-shaped torsos, the most common and beloved of which was a cat. These toys came disassembled in packaging that Niklová also designed, with striking two-dimensional graphic representations of the accordion feature (no. 20). Niklová's most lively toys were her inflatables: stylized figures that included children of different races and cultures, an airplane, an astronaut, a clown, and—her favorite theme—animals. She further developed this series with what she called "indoor sitting toys" (1969–76), a group of play-furniture structures in large-eyed and disarming animal forms, including a buffalo, elephant, and giraffe (no. 21). In a country famous for its wooden toys, Niklová fully embraced plastic, especially for children. "Development cannot be held back," she declared in 1971. "In the future products from plastic will surround man just like the air, and they will become commonplace. Increasingly, natural materials will be a luxury and the object of admiration. The future, however, belongs to plastic."[6]

Aidan O'Connor

created between the integrated seating and work surfaces. The desk, which was lightweight, stackable, and offered in six colors, was selected for use in several French schools, including a kindergarten in Crétail.

Other types of plastics produced enduring examples of children's furniture, including Alexander Begge's Casalino Jr. chair (1970), made of ABS, and Luigi Colani's polyethylene Zocker chair (no. 17). Colani, who was born in Berlin and studied in Paris, is known for his quirky, biomorphic forms, in this case produced by rotational molding. The Zocker was specifically designed to support young sitters working and playing in numerous positions, including reverse straddling. Because of its material it can be used indoors or out, is scratch- and shock-resistant, and can float. It has safe, rounded edges and a stable base and is, surprisingly, stackable. Colani was inspired to adapt this chair into an adult version, the Sitzgerät Colani (Colani sitting machine).

OF ALL THE COUNTRIES left defeated by World War II, it was Italy that most self-consciously reinvented itself in terms of modern design and style as part of its political realignment and economic regeneration after the war. The major Italian designers were quick to relaunch their classic design magazines, including *Domus* and *Casabella*, which had been discontinued during the war, and to establish a new ethos that rejected their Fascist heritage; the Milan Triennale exhibitions displayed the new style in domestic goods, car design, textiles, and ceramics to an international audience. In this postwar spirit of optimism and rebirth, throughout the 1950s and '60s, design for children figured prominently in the exhibitions, magazines, and products that emerged from Milan and Turin. Highlights of the 1954 Triennale, for example, were the Fantastic Village, by Virginia Dortch Dorazio, and the playful spiral Children's Labyrinth, designed by the architectural firm BBPR and decorated with a mural by Saul Steinberg, who had fled Milan in 1941 following the introduction of anti-Jewish racial laws.[1]

As early as 1960 Marco Zanuso and Richard Sapper turned to polyethylene and polypropylene, materials that were suddenly cheaper because their patents were due to expire and that were solid, sufficiently thick, easy to clean, and lightweight. Their stackable plastic child's chair, Model No. 4,999 (1964), was the first piece of furniture manufactured by Kartell, a firm founded in 1949 by the chemical engineer Giulio Castelli to make use of new polymers. Sistema Scuola (1979), a Kartell product for children designed by Centrokappa, the company's in-house design studio, was similarly modular, with bench, table, and divider elements added to the chairs. An advertisement from around 1980 (no. 22) captures the playfulness of the system, which is assembled like a construction game.

Chica (also called Junior) (no. 23) was designed in 1971 by Jonathan De Pas, Donato D'Urbino, Giorgio DeCurso, and Paolo Lomazzi, a group of architects from Milan. It, too, was a modular system of plastic components that could be fitted together in a variety of ways to create seats, tables, and play structures. The elements, made in four bright colors, were light enough for older children to play with and reconfigure, in a product that exemplified the fun, flexible spirit of Italian postwar design. The prototypes featured in 1972 in the exhibition *Italy: The New Domestic Landscape*, at The Museum of Modern Art, demonstrated the concept of "contestatory" design: objects with the potential to create environments that were "flexible in function and [permitting] multiple modes of use and arrangement."[2] The exhibition, organized by Emilio Ambasz, confirmed that Italian design outpaced other countries in aesthetic, conceptual, and technological innovation.

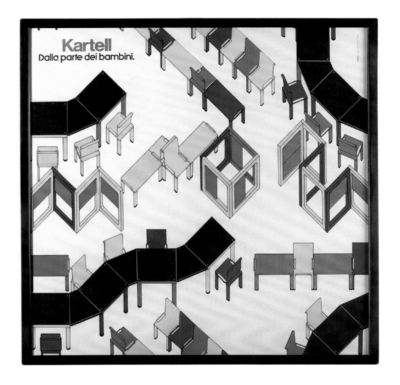

22 CENTROKAPPA DESIGN AND COMMUNICATION (Italian, est. 1972)
Advertisement for Kartell's children's furniture.
c. 1980
28 7/16 x 28 7/16 x 13/16" (72.3 x 72.3 x 2 cm)
Published by Kartell SpA, Milan (est. 1949)
Collection of Maurizio Marzadori, Bologna

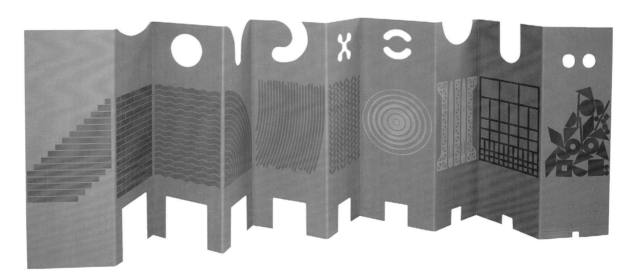

23 JONATHAN DE PAS (Italian, 1932–1991),
DONATO D'URBINO (Italian, born 1935),
GIORGIO DECURSO (Italian, born 1927),
and PAOLO LOMAZZI (Italian, born 1936)
Chica modular children's chairs. 1971
ABS plastic, assembled: 19 1/4 x 13 x 13"
(48.9 x 33 x 33 cm)
Manufactured by BBB Bonacina, Spilimbergo
The Museum of Modern Art, New York. Gift of
the designers

24 ENZO MARI (Italian, born 1932)
Pesci (Fish), jigsaw puzzle composed of sixteen
aquatic animals. 1974
Nontoxic expandable resin, 1 9/16 x 9 7/16 x 14 3/16"
(4 x 24 x 36 cm)
Manufactured by Danese Srl, Milan (est. 1955)
The Museum of Modern Art, New York. Gift of
the manufacturer

25 ENZO MARI (Italian, born 1932)
Il posto dei giochi (A place for games). 1961
Corrugated pressboard, open: 35 7/16" x 10' 2 1/16"
(90 x 310 cm)
Courtesy of Corraini Edizioni, Mantua

Danese, another forward-thinking manufacturer of small objects and artworks for the home, was established in Milan in 1957 by Jacqueline Vodoz and Bruno Danese. The company worked with designers such as Enzo Mari to produce (among other things) educational and creative toys and games that would appeal to both children and their parents. Mari's Animali (Animals) and Pesci (Fish) (no. 24) were puzzles of sixteen pieces each, both in the tradition of wholesome "good toy" design (see "Good Toys," p. 171). His Posto dei giochi (Place for games) (no. 25) took the child's play environment into consideration: a cardboard screen of ten panels, each with different cutout shapes and colored graphics (abstract representations of a brick wall, a shining sun, the waves of the sea), that could be arranged in numerous ways to create a safe space for young imaginations to flourish.

Bruno Munari, a designer who collaborated with Danese and whose work was featured in *Italy: The New Domestic Landscape*, rooted his approach in the desire to understand and expand the worldview of children. He is well known as a designer of children's books that were among the most innovative of the period, going further than any of his contemporaries in exploring the complementary nature of books as both stimulants to the imagination and objects to be handled. He was as fascinated by materials as by contents, so that books such as *Nella notte buia* (*In the Dark of the Night*) (1956) and *Un libro illegible* (*The Unreadable Book*) (1953) incorporate different types of paper and tipped-in effects that are a constant surprise. He also invited readers to experience books in a way inspired by (and fascinating to) children, a naive and illogical approach entirely unlike conventional, passive reading; some of his books have to be followed in counterintuitive sequences, sometimes back to front or upside down, and others require readers to move the book around and manipulate it, thus physically participating in the story. In *Nella nebbia di Milano* (1968), published in English as *The Circus in the Mist* (no. 26), translucent pages create new combinations of images as they are turned, building a narrative based on visual progression with minimal text. Such effects are now part of mainstream children's publishing, but their origins lie in an approach to design that Munari developed in the 1930s, and many of his books and related toys are still in production. In 1960 he published an alphabet book and a letter-composition toy, *ABC con fantasia* (*ABC with Imagination*) (no. 27), with twenty-six brightly colored, nontoxic plastic pieces, in linear and curved shapes that can be combined to make capital letters; both have been reissued in several editions and are still available.

Munari's most remarkable children's product was on a much larger scale: a modular bed, storage, and play environment called Abitacolo (no. 28), made of powder-coated steel and reminiscent of warehouse storage systems or high-tech industrial equipment. The Italian word *abitacolo* refers to a cockpit, suggesting a sophisticated combination of fantasy and practicality that differentiates the design from the mainstream tendency to identify children's furniture by applying childish motifs and crude colors. In an unusual move nonetheless typical of this unusual designer, Munari wrote a poem emphasizing the product's practical and elemental qualities (see p. 198).

Juliet Kinchin

26 BRUNO MUNARI (Italian, 1907–1998)
Double-page spread from the book *The Circus in the Mist*, translation of *Nella nebbia di Milano*. 1969
8⁷/₁₆ x 8⁹/₁₆" (21.5 x 21.7 cm)
The Museum of Modern Art Library, New York

27 BRUNO MUNARI (Italian, 1907–1998)
ABC con fantasia (*ABC with Imagination*). 1960
Plastic and cardboard, box: 6 3/4 x 6 3/4" (17.1 x 17.1 cm)
Manufactured by Danese Srl, Milan (est. 1955)
The Museum of Modern Art, New York. Gift of
Elaine Lustig Cohen

28 BRUNO MUNARI (Italian, 1907–1998)
Abitacolo (Cockpit) play environment. 1971
Coated steel, 6' 8 11/16" x 7' 9 11/16" x 32 5/16"
(205 x 238 x 82 cm)
Manufactured by Robots, Milan
Collection of Maurizio Marzadori, Bologna

Abitacolo

Two meters high
It's made of steel with an epoxy skin
It's a structure reduced to the essentials
A space delimited and yet open
Adaptable to one or two people
It can even hold twenty
Although this is not recommended because
of the difficulty of moving
It weighs fifty-one kilos
It's two meters wide by eighty centimeters
It's a large object that casts no shadow
It's an inhabitable module
It's a habitat
It contains all personal things
It's a container of microcosms
It's a placenta of plastic-coated steel
A place to meditate
And at the same time
A place for listening to music that you like
A place to read and study
A place to receive visitors
A place to sleep
A lair, light and transparent
Or closed
A space hidden in the midst of people
A real space
your presence renders furnishings superfluous
Dust doesn't know where to settle
It's the minimum but gives the maximum
Numbered but unlimited
Habitat is the environment
Adaptable to the personality of the inhabitant
At every moment transformable

Bruno Munari, *Codice ovvio* (1971)[3]

IN THE 1950S AND '60S, as the United States and Europe moved beyond postwar recovery and regeneration efforts, designers became increasingly involved in the creation of new children's products and toys as well as new environments for their promotion and sale. Especially in the United States, where youth-oriented consumer culture was strengthened by a national affluence unparalleled in history or in any other country, innovative environmental design for retail purposes explored possibilities beyond the models long used by department stores (which had been charming their youngest visitors with playrooms, parades, premiums, and pageants since the early twentieth century) and more recently by shopping malls (which appeared in the mid-1950s).[1] Two particularly fantastical designs, from either end of this period, intended to enhance the experiential component of public consumption for children are the Park of Pleasures (nos. 29, 30), an unrealized project from 1952, and the Creative Playthings store (no. 31) at 1 East Fifty-third Street in New York, from 1969.

The Park of Pleasures, designed by the multitalented Czechoslovak émigré Ladislav Sutnar (see "Manufacturing the Artistic Toy," p. 84), was a novel concept for an outdoor commercial center with day-care facilities, designed to be located off any generic American highway and first presented in Sutnar's 1952 book *Design for Point of Sale*. Sutnar developed this "dream world for children" through drawings and a detailed

model with wire maquettes and landscape elements made of actual plant material, both presenting large, theatrical scenery elements and billboards in the shapes of castles, ice-cream cones, a boat, a milk bottle, an egg, and a fanciful lady chicken.[2] The scheme was devised with two objectives: "to bring to more effective use the efforts of many different outdoor advertisers of standard brand-name products by concentrating them in one attractive and easily accessible place" and "to create an area that will be a source of pleasure to children and, through them, also to reach their parents."[3] By manipulating scale and color as well as dramatic lighting effects to produce elements of surprise, Sutnar hoped to create a playful environment that would both delight children and encourage their parents to buy "products of use and appeal" for them.[4] Unusual for a shopping center, though not surprising given the general inclination at the time for making positive efforts toward child development, he insisted that the Park of Pleasures should be held to the highest possible standards, selling "only such brand-name products as would be beneficial to the child's health and well-being."[5]

Creative Playthings, founded by Frank Caplan as a small toy shop in Greenwich Village before becoming one of the foremost manufacturers

29 LADISLAV SUTNAR (American, born Bohemia [now Czech Republic]. 1897–1976)
Park of Pleasures. 1952
Museum of Decorative Arts, Prague

30 LADISLAV SUTNAR (American, born Bohemia [now Czech Republic]. 1897–1976)
Figurine for Park of Pleasures. 1951
Wire and paper, 16 1/2 x 10 1/2 x 1" (41.9 x 26.7 x 2.5 cm)
Cooper-Hewitt, National Design Museum, Smithsonian Institution

31 STUDIO WORKS (USA, est. 1969),
KEITH GODARD (British, born 1942),
CRAIG HODGETTS (American, born 1937),
ROBERT MANGURIAN (American, born 1944),
and LESTER WALKER (American, born 1939)
Creative Playthings store, 1 East 53rd Street, New York. 1969
Photograph by Michael Evans
The New York Times/Redux

of postwar "good toys" (see "Good Toys," p. 177), opened its new interactive store in 1969 to enthusiastic reviews. "There are buttons to push, knobs to whirl, toys to test," buzzed the *New York Times*, "and a host of electronic babysitters to keep the children occupied while the adults shop at leisure."[6] The store was designed by the architects of Studio Works and was intended to engage both children and adults through multisensory and multimedia elements. Outside, the letters CP, rendered on an aluminum-and-neon sign, glowed warmly to complement, as architect Lester Walker has explained, the materiality of the company's famous wooden toys.[7] Inside, bright yellow floors, walls, and ceilings energized the dense installation of toys, which were grouped in themes, such as "ponder play," identified by suspended signs. The most vibrant area of the store was the high-tech playroom in the back, where a child-sized geodesic-dome climber was surrounded by large screens showing continuous and surreal slide-show projections, a cinematic counterpart to Sutnar's theatricality. The audiovisual components were created by Broadway lighting designer Jules Fisher and electronic-music composer Morton Subotnick, who in the 1990s went on to be a pioneer in creative musical tools for children on CD-ROMs and the Internet.

Aidan O'Connor

SINCE THE 1960S the rise of the purchasing power of children, and the concomitant increase in marketing aimed at them, have helped to fuel new designs for mass-market products that celebrate modern living. Toys such as Barbie and Playmobil have fostered aspirations for modern adult lifestyles, and companies such as Magis and Ikea have surrounded children with modern furnishings while they are still young. These and other products, shaped by the preferences of both children and their adult proxies, have continued to promote notions of modern not only as a form of design but as its promise.

The first Barbie doll, designed by Ruth Handler and inspired by Germany's Lilli doll, was launched at the New York Toy Fair in 1959. Barbie shifted the convention of the fashion doll, which had been marketed to women since the eighteenth century, to appeal to young girls. Over the years, in various iterations, she fluctuated in age from sixteen to thirty but has always boasted a hypermature figure.[1] Barbie may not be considered a model of modern womanhood (she was completely stiff until given a bendable waist and knees in the mid-1960s), but her clothing and accessories have kept in step with the times, and the I Can Be... series, launched in 2001, has expanded her professional possibilities to computer engineer, race-car driver, and, most recently, architect. Barbie's first Dream House (no. 32), from 1962, strikingly modern in appearance compared with her subsequent and current dwellings, was a cardboard studio apartment that when folded and closed could be carried, using a handle on top, like a suitcase. With no kitchen in sight and contemporary paper furnishings (including a hi-fi, television, and hip, minimalist furniture) for the child to assemble, it provided Barbie with a youthful, modern environment to support an independent lifestyle. Nearly forty years later, artist Laurie Simmons and architect Peter Wheelwright created the Kaleidoscope House (no. 33), a contemporary counterpart to the Dream House, to offer a different and more playful representation of domesticity than what they found to be available for their own children. This miniature tribute to contemporary design was interactive from all sides, featuring sliding transparent color walls, which changed in hue and value as they overlapped, and doll-size furniture designed by Karim Rashid, Ron Arad, and Michael Graves. Unlike the Dream House, the $250 toy (sold at MoMA stores, among other outlets) did not sell well, and the manufacturer, Bozart, eventually folded.

Playmobil figures (no. 34), which have been an international success since they were introduced in 1975, were designed by Hans Beck, a model-airplane enthusiast who apprenticed as a cabinetmaker before becoming a toy developer at the German company Geobra. The company had experience manufacturing toy hoops and large plastic toys, but when the early-1970s oil crisis made plastic manufacture more expensive, Beck turned to something new. With Horst Brandstätter, the company's owner, Beck pursued the concept of small, movable figures that could be paired with various accessories. The core unit of Playmobil, akin to the Lego building brick or Erector Set beam, is the 2¾-inch figure, which Beck scaled to fit in a child's hand and enlivened with a simple face like a child's drawing. Like Lego, Playmobil toys have explored the realms of fantasy and nostalgia (with structures such as a

32 Barbie's Dream House. 1962
Offset lithography on cardboard, 13³/₄ x 26 x 33"
(34.9 x 66 x 83.8 cm)
Manufactured by Mattel, Inc., Los Angeles (est. 1945)
The Museum of Modern Art, New York. Purchase

33 LAURIE SIMMONS (American, born 1949) and
PETER WHEELWRIGHT (American, born 1949)
Prototype for Kaleidoscope House and Pool
Pavilion. 2000
Polystyrene and acrylic, overall: 23³/₄ x 53 x 31¹/₄"

(60.3 x 134.6 x 79.4 cm)
Manufactured by Bozart Toys Inc.,
Philadelphia (est. 1996)
The Museum of Modern Art, New York.
Gift of the artists

magic castle and Victorian house), all the while maintaining the modern roots of the system: simple forms and modularity. The toys have also introduced children to modern environments and occupations, such as in various versions of a hospital set.

Among the designers who have demonstrated a commitment to modern furnishings for children, sometimes as a complement to their own playful, even rebellious personas, Gaetano Pesce and Philippe Starck are two who have taken different approaches to the issue of scale in production and consumption. Pesce's Crosby chair (no. 35), from 1998, named for the location of his New York workshop, is a bright and colorful design that is also two-faced: the eerie smile suggested by the holes pierced in its back is balanced by the subtler and expressionless profile formed by its seat. The chair was made with industrial synthetic material but treated like a craft piece: only about forty were produced, and the colors and details are unique to each one. By contrast, in 2002 Starck collaborated with Target, the Minneapolis-based discount retailer with more than 1,500 stores across the United States, to produce the Starck Reality line. More than one-third of the distinctive, everyday items were products for babies and children, including a training toilet, dishes and tableware, a stylized fluorescent yellow push-car, and three pop-up playhouses. Starck was among the first high-profile designers engaged by Target to enhance the company's "Design for All" identity, and the first to apply the motto to products for children.

Magis, an Italian domestic-design company that works with well-known designers in creating more expensive objects for mass production, launched a collection for two- to six-year-olds in 2004. Eugenio Perazza, the company's owner, has explained that Me Too was named for "the voice of children demanding, insisting to have their own objects, their own furniture that correspond to their own world." For this line Magis rejected scaled-down adult furnishings and instead sought, in consultation with a developmental psychologist, new forms from designers who were "able to think with the mind of a child."[2] One successful result has been Puppy (no. 36), an abstracted plastic

bubble-dog created by Finnish designer Eero Aarnio. Puppy is a lovable sculpture/toy/seat that retains the fanciful flexibility of the designer's Pony, which he created in 1973, originally for adults.

Ikea, another prominent design-conscious company, has made the modernizing of children's environments an affordable possibility across the world. The company, founded by Ingvar Kamprad in Sweden in 1943, when he was seventeen years old, has long espoused egalitarian domestic values, and its promotional imagery has often featured happy families in comfortable surroundings with slogans such as "Home is the most important place in the world." Since the 1960s Ikea has extended the Swedish design principle *vackrare vardagsvara*, or beautiful things for everyday use, to children's design, to produce such memorable objects as Karin Mobring's beech-and-plywood Anna table and reversible chairs (1963), Knut and Marian Hagberg's bright and adjustable Puzzel stools (1986), Allan Östgaard and Morten Kjelstrup's cartoonish Mammut series (1993), and Thomas Eriksson's charming chartreuse sofa, whose two levels put parent and child eye to eye (1995). Children's Ikea, launched in 1997, was a comprehensive initiative conceived by Kamprad to be the company's "most important project in modern times."[3] New designers, most of them parents, were recruited to devise six hundred new products, and all of Ikea's stores were revamped, at a cost of more than $25 million, to incorporate playrooms for young visitors, called Småland, after the Swedish province where Kamprad grew up and as a play on *små*, or "small."[4] Children's products continue to be among the company's most recognizable, including the PS Lömsk swivel chair (no. 37), by Monika Mulder, a graduate of Design Academy Eindhoven. It is a popular and playful piece from a series designed to enhance motor skills, social development, and creativity. With the chair's hood pulled down, a child can enjoy being hidden from the world — an appealing illusion for such heavily scrutinized agents of the global marketplace.

Aidan O'Connor

34 School and playground Playmobil toys. 1970s–80s
Manufactured by Geobra Brandstätter & Co. KG,
Zirndorf, Germany
Plastic, dimensions variable
Collection of Mia Curran, New York

35 GAETANO PESCE (Italian, born 1939)
Crosby chair. 1998
Metal rod with molded and poured polyurethane
resin, 20 x 15 ^{3}/$_4$ x 13 ^{1}/$_2$" (50.8 x 40 x 34.3 cm)
Manufactured by Fish Design, New York
Mondo Cane, New York

36 EERO AARNIO (Finnish, born 1932)
Puppy, from the Me Too collection. 2005
Polyethylene, largest: 31 ^{11}/$_{16}$ x 40 ^{3}/$_8$ x 24 ^{3}/$_{16}$"
(80.5 x 102.5 x 61.5 cm)
Manufactured by Magis SpA, Torre di Mosto, Italy
Magis, Torre di Mosto, Italy

37 MONIKA MULDER (Dutch, born 1972)
Ikea PS Lömsk swivel chair. 2003
Polypropylene and polyester, 29 ^{1}/$_2$ x 23 ^{1}/$_4$ x 24 ^{3}/$_8$"
(74.9 x 59.1 x 61.9 cm)
Manufactured by Ikea of Sweden (est. 1943)
Ikea, Älmhult

WHEN RAY KROC BOUGHT the national franchise rights for the McDonald brothers' Self-Service Restaurants in 1954, he already envisioned children as a potentially lucrative market. Since then McDonald's has built its monumental success, with more than thirty-three thousand restaurants in more than one hundred countries, on enticing children to eat and play. McDonald's sells quickly prepared food at a low price. But with the creation of an elaborate scheme to market it to children — with commercials, signature characters including Ronald McDonald, the McDonaldland fantasy landscape, birthday parties, indoor and outdoor playgrounds, videos, game websites, licensed goods, and, especially, the toys that come with Happy Meals — the McDonald's Corporation has become a fixture of childhood around the world.[1]

The prize included in every Happy Meal, a selection of McDonald's foods in a red, square cardboard box with golden arch-shaped handles designed to resemble the loops of a bow, makes McDonald's one of the nation's largest distributors of children's toys (no. 38). The Happy Meal, introduced nationally in 1979, is aimed at children between three and nine years old, and the toys, which are made for McDonald's, are often small action figures or snap-together plastic characters, frequently promotional tie-ins with current children's movies. Kroc did not receive a concession from his friend Walt Disney when Disneyland opened in 1955, but in the mid-1990s McDonald's and the Walt Disney Corporation signed a ten-year agreement to jointly promote Disney films through character licensing and toy giveaways. In addition to Disney toys, Happy Meals have also included Hot Wheels, Barbie, the Smurfs, Pokémon, Lego, and Transformers toys; in 1997 the inclusion of a Teenie Beanie Baby increased Happy Meal sales from an average of ten million to one hundred million in a week.[2] The premiums have also included books, crayons, and educational CD-ROM games.

Even before the Happy Meal, McDonald's embraced children's entertainment as a retail strategy. Indeed, Kroc claimed he was really in show business, not the restaurant business.[3] The character Ronald McDonald, a redheaded clown in a yellow suit and large red shoes, was based on the popular live children's show *Bozo's Circus* and first appeared in 1966 in television commercials and at franchises, played by Willard Scott, a former Bozo clown.

In 1971 Ronald acquired a supporting cast of friends, including Mayor McCheese, a bumbling politician; Officer Big Mac, a stern figure who keeps law and order in McDonaldland; Grimace, a purple monster in constant need of a milk shake; the Hamburglar, a masked and caped villain; Captain Crook, who craves Filet-O-Fish sandwiches; and the

French Fry Goblins (later French Fry Guys and French Fry Kids). Based on the imaginary adventure landscapes of Disneyland and the children's television program *H.R. Pufnstuf*, McDonaldland, as depicted in television commercials, was a pastoral world free from adults, populated with verdant burger patches, french-fry gardens, and large apple-pie trees. The McDonaldland characters launched a host of merchandise, including cloth Ronald McDonald and Hamburglar dolls, which were sold for one dollar in the restaurants, and items such as decals, plastic cups, watches, and record albums that were offered as a premium with the purchase of meals. In 1974 McDonald's licensed its image to Playskool, one of the largest preschool toy companies, to make a play restaurant with signature brown roof and roadside sign, merry-go-round, patio table, and a hamburger patch (no. 39), in which workers with peaked hats and customers in small cars could be animated by children. The box touted that kids could "spend hours doing one of their favorite things — going to McDonald's."

McDonaldland also spawned playgrounds designed for various franchises by Los Angeles set maker Don Ament, with equipment based on the McDonaldland characters, such as a Captain Crook spiral slide and Officer Big Mac jail. The first playground debuted at the Illinois State Fair in 1972 (no. 40), and the same year a large McDonaldland Park opened in Chula Vista, California, attracting nearly ten thousand people during its two-day grand opening. In the late 1980s and through the 1990s the McDonaldland character playgrounds were gradually replaced with indoor play spaces with climbing tubes and ball pits.

McDonald's continues to court children's attentions with programs of report card rewards, teachers' nights, school bus advertising, and nutrition workshops.[4] A series of animated cartoon videos, *The Wacky Adventures of Ronald McDonald*, released between 1998 and 2003, was designed for a younger set. And there is McDonalds's play food, cash register, and drive-through kitchen for preschool children, whose consumer preferences are still forming.

Amy F. Ogata

38 McDonald's Happy Meal transformers. 1987–90
Plastic, each: approx. 2 x 2" (5.1 x 5.1 cm)
Manufactured by McDonald's Co., San Bernardino,
California (est. 1955)
Collection of Margot Weller, New York

39 McDonald's toy, from Playskool's Familiar Places
series. 1974
Plastic, mat: 24 x 24" (61 x 61 cm)
Manufactured by Playskool Inc., Chicago (est. 1928)
The Museum of Modern Art, New York. Purchase

40 Page from the McDonaldland Setmakers
promotional packet showing McDonaldland Teeter
Totter, statue of Ronald McDonald, Evil Grimace
Bounce & Bend, and Big Mac Climber. c. 1972
Published by McDonald's Co., San Bernardino,
California (est. 1955)
Collection of Jason Liebig, New York

PEE-WEE'S PLAYHOUSE, the children's television show broadcast on CBS from 1986 to 1991, was modern and spectacular in every way. This quirky and ambitious Saturday-morning program was the only one of its time to incorporate live action with animation and puppetry. In the first season 150 artists and technicians worked to achieve the unique set, characters, and effects.[1] Thoughtful design planning went into the creation of the titular environment, described in the opening theme as "wacky," "nutty," and "cuckoo," and the effort did not go unnoticed: the show, which won twenty-two Emmy awards, was celebrated by critics and the popular press for its design elements (art direction, set design, costume design, graphics, and title design) as well as its original writing, music, and performances.

Pee-wee (no. 41) was a man-child character originally developed by Paul Reubens for a live theatrical show for adults that was broadcast on HBO in 1981. The film *Pee-wee's Big Adventure* (1985), Tim Burton's directorial debut, caught the attention of both television executives and younger viewers, and the character was adapted for a children's television program. Unlike most shows at the time, which relied on a strictly dichotomous view of gender preferences (*Care Bears* for girls, *He-Man* for boys), *Pee-wee's Playhouse* was designed to appeal to all children. Reubens intended it to be educational, entertaining, and artistic. "I'm just trying to illustrate that it's okay to be different," he explained. "Not that it's good, not that it's bad, but that it's all right. Tell kids to have a good time...be creative...question things."[2]

Each episode mixed positive moral lessons with zany antics. Young viewers, rather than being patronized with formulaic plots and characters, were expected to keep up with the frenetic pace of the show, which cut between main plot events and dilemmas, visits from outside characters, stop-motion animation and Claymation segments (many of them designed by animation virtuosos Nick Park and Prudence Fenton), sequences using chroma key and stock footage, running gags (such as "scream real loud" for the secret word of the day), clips of bizarre 1930s cartoons, and direct addresses by Pee-wee and other human characters.[3] Pee-wee often brought incongruous excitement to crafts projects based on the simplest materials — at least twice with raw potatoes — supplemented by creativity and imagination.

The show's dense and lively format was complemented by flat, high-key lighting and the set itself (no. 42), which was primarily the work of production designer Gary Panter (creator of the comic series *Jimbo* in the late 1970s and the children's playroom at Philippe Starck's Paramount Hotel in 1990) with Wayne White and Ric Heitzman. The playhouse, like the narrative structure it housed, is best characterized as pastiche: juxtaposed against a backdrop of countless patterned wall coverings were an Ionic column and a barber's pole, a tiki-style statue and a replica of the Venus de Milo, portraits of George Washington and Judy Garland, a plastic flamingo and Jambi the Genie's bejeweled box, a Conestoga wagon bunk bed and the show's trademark sawtooth door in metallic red Naugahyde. With a prevailing aesthetic shaped by a surreal 1980s interpretation of a 1950s American diner or bowling alley, the visual concoction was eclectic and complex, providing rich material for analysis in media scholarship as well as in popular magazines. In 1987 *Rolling Stone* described the playhouse as "the collision of *The Cabinet of Dr. Caligari* with a raspberry-and-lime Jell-O mold constructed by Disney technicians recovering from Taiwan flu."[4] Among the scores of cultural references that contributed to the show's quintessentially postmodern feel were heaps of toys representing five decades of design for children. This evident nod to consumerism (in a show necessarily punctuated by commercials aimed at children) was complicated by Pee-wee's regular and emphatic rejection of his nemesis, a door-to-door salesman.

In the *Playhouse* a cast of regular characters was created from everyday objects, each unique and anthropomorphized: Mr. Window, a googly-eyed announcer; Chairy, an affectionate armchair; Conky, a robot made of stereo equipment; Globey, a worldly globe with a French accent; Clocky, a punctual wall clock; and Magic Screen, a proto-iPad on wheels. In addition to this core team, everything in this fantasy world — from the floorboards to the futuristic video-phone, the fish in the fish tank, the ants in the ant farm, the food in the refrigerator, the flowers in the flowerbed, and the family of dinosaurs in the mouse hole — was alive and active.

Set, characters, animation: these design elements not only enraptured young viewers and energized the show but also contributed to a profoundly child-centric agenda that may have been lost on adults put off by its trappings. The show's most appealing segments, as media scholar Henry Jenkins III has explained, dealt with "the disruption of domestic space, the undermining of adult authority or the violation of basic cultural categories: the 'crazy fridge' scenes where fruits and vegetables dance and perform acrobatics while making a shambles of Pee-wee's icebox...the robot who keeps bumping into the furniture...and the enormous foil ball that threatens to overwhelm everything in its path. Pee-wee invites us to enter an anarchic realm where desire and disorder are indistinguishable and where infantile urges are given free rein."[5]

Aidan O'Connor

41 *Pee-wee's Playhouse* c. 1989
Photograph by Bruce W. Talamon
Herman World

42 *Pee-wee's Playhouse* interior c. 1987
Herman World

43 Atari 2600. 1977
Various materials, 3 $^1/_2$ x 13 $^1/_2$ x 9"
(8.9 x 34.3 x 22.9 cm)
Manufactured by Atari Inc., Sunnyvale, California
(est. 1972)
Mike Gibbons, New York

44 Nintendo Game Boy. 1989
Various materials, 5 $^{13}/_{16}$ x 3 $^1/_2$ x 1 $^5/_{16}$"
(14.8 x 9 x 3.3 cm)
Manufactured by Nintendo Co., Kyoto (est. 1889)
Image courtesy of Nintendo

45 KEITA TAKAHASHI (Japanese, born 1975)
Main visual for the video game Katamari
Damacy. 2004
Distributed by Namco Ltd, Tokyo (est. 1955)
Courtesy of Namco Bandai Games America, Inc.,
San Jose

THE ATARI 2600 (no. 43), also known as the Atari Video Computer System (VCS), released in 1977, was the most successful of the early home-gaming consoles that brought the arcade into the home.[1] Atari popularized what would become the dominant form of home gaming: a device that allowed the play of different games via changeable cartridges. Up until this point most home-gaming consoles had a single game built into it, such as Pong, Tennis, or other versions of the back-and-forth two-player game, such as handball or hockey. Although Atari's was not the first cartridge-based gaming system, it was the first to provide both original games, such as Combat, and versions of arcade favorites, such as Pac-Man and Space Invaders. Almost one thousand games were eventually programmed for the Atari system, from dog fighting to dental care, and the name itself became synonymous in the early 1980s with home video games. But this flexibility, as well as the console's affordable price, was not the result of complex technology and sophisticated coding but of simplicity: the console was compatible with a number of input devices (joystick, paddles, keyboards), and because its technology was rudimentary at the time of its release, developers were able to adapt it to a wide range of games.[2]

Nintendo's Game Boy system (no. 44), released in 1989, was a hybrid of innovation and familiarity. The Game Boy combined the

portable video game, which had been available since the 1970s, with interchangeable game cartridges for an already loyal fan base.[3] The Game Boy used the now-familiar controls (A and B buttons, "select" and "start" buttons, directional pad) from the Nintendo Entertainment System (NES) home console, ensuring that it could be played immediately by anyone who had experience with the NES, as well as allowing companies that had already developed game titles for the NES to easily translate them into software for the Game Boy. The Game Boy's battery life clinched its success; because the unit had no backlighting and ran a monochrome LCD screen — not considered cutting-edge by any means and actually outdated by the time the system was released — which displayed only four-color grayscale eight-bit graphics, it was extremely economical in terms of energy usage, requiring four AA batteries for ten to thirty hours of game play.[4]

The Game Boy was marketed to an older audience of serious gamers, with advertisements showing adults playing while on the go. But the device also exploded in popularity with people who were unfamiliar with NES or gaming entirely, thanks to the game cartridge that it came with: Tetris, an abstract puzzle game created by Russian computer programmer Alexei Pajitonov, that had an appeal transcending age, gender, and skill. Many people bought the device just to play Tetris,

and despite the unit's lack of cutting-edge technology, Nintendo sold tens of millions of Game Boys, making it to date the most successful gaming system of all time.

Katamari Damacy (no. 45), a game designed by Keita Takahashi for the Playstation 2 console, was released in 2004. The game's premise is simple, if unconventional: the player takes on the role of an extraterrestrial prince sent to earth by the King of the Cosmos to gather balls of anything and everything, which will be turned into new stars that populate the cosmos. The game's controls are simple and controlled by a joystick, while the graphics are psychedelically rich and stimulating. The narrative, characters, and details are unique, but the player's tasks are not complex, and are in fact limited to rolling clumps of debris — starting with erasers and bits of sushi and moving to cows and houses — into progressively larger spheres, until whole mountains and cities are adhering themselves to the ball. As such, the game plays with the idea of scale, allowing the player to interact in a creative, surreal way with ordinary objects and built environments, and renders fantastical the objects of everyday life.

The paradox of simple technology and popularity has been true in the realm of digital playmates as well. The more complex (and expensive) robots designed in the 1980s and '90s were of limited appeal, whereas a very basic character with emotional appeal was wildly successful. The Japanese word *aibo*, which means "pal," is also an acronym of sorts for Artificial Intelligence Robot (no. 46), an electronic pet released by Sony in 1999. It had the ability to react to its environment and learn: it was trainable, responded to touch, and was programmed to simulate the behavior of a living animal (sit, stay, come) and perform certain tasks, such as appointment reminders and e-mail notification. Although at two thousand dollars it was an inexpensive platform for

artificial intelligence, it was still very expensive for a toy and was thus geared toward adults rather than children. Aibo's much more primitive ancestors, popular in the early 1980s, were the Omnibot range of robots for children (no. 47), designed by Tomy, a Japanese toy company. Programmable by cassette tape and controlled by remote, the Omnibot could move and speak, but rather than presenting any real help, it merely suggested a futuristic life modified by robots. (Its utility was limited to clawlike fingers that could grasp items and a tray for transporting drinks.)

By contrast, Tamagotchi (no. 48), the ubiquitous portable pet of the 1990s, was neither expensive nor technologically sophisticated, nor did it promise a future populated by robotic assistants. Designed by Akihiro Yokoi and Aki Maita, it was a tiny, inexpensive keychain with a rudimentary eight-bit black-and-white LCD screen, in which lived a character that, rather than providing help, demanded attention. Here, the experience of caring for another being was more compelling than what the relatively simple technology could do; in other words, the feeling outweighed the appearance.[5] No one, it seemed, was immune to its appeal, from teenagers to businesspeople; the Tamagotchi, developed for children, really reversed what a toy can be, from a thing exclusively for children to a companion for whoever wants to care for it.

Kate Carmody

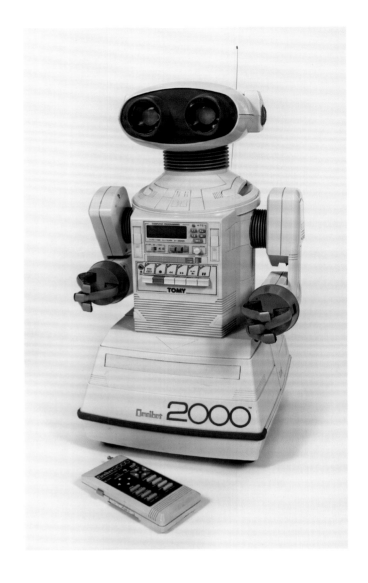

46 HAJIME SORAYAMA (Japanese, born 1947)
Aibo Entertainment Robot (ERS-110). 1999
Various materials, 10 $\frac{1}{2}$ x 6 x 16 $\frac{1}{4}$"
(26.7 x 15.2 x 41.3 cm)
Manufactured by Sony Corporation, Creative
Center, Tokyo (est. 1961)
The Museum of Modern Art, New York. Gift of
the manufacturer

47 Omnibot 2000, remote-controlled robot. c. 1985
Various materials, 24 x 15 x 14" (61 x 38.1 x 35.6 cm)
Manufactured by Tomy (formerly Tomiyama),
Katsushika, Tokyo
Space Age Museum/Kleeman Family Collection,
Litchfield, Connecticut

48 AKIHIRO YOKOI (Japanese, born 1955) and
AKI MAITA (Japanese, born 1967)
Tamagotchi. 1996
Various materials, 4 $\frac{3}{4}$ x 1 $\frac{9}{16}$ x $\frac{1}{2}$" (12.1 x 4 x 1.3 cm)
Manufactured by Bandai, Tokyo (est. 1950)
The Museum of Modern Art, New York. Purchase

49 Assorted Japanese teen fashion magazines. 2011
The Museum of Modern Art, New York. Purchase

IN THE 1990S many teenagers in Japan began to dress according to the codes of various subcultures, often influenced by Western design. This has been understood by cultural scholars to be a kind of postponement of adulthood, an extension of childhood in part the result of the financial, political, and social uncertainty in Japan in the second half of the twentieth century, particularly since the bursting of the country's economic bubble at the end of the 1980s.[1] Sociologist Yuniya Kawamura has posited that in this unstable climate, middle- and high-school-aged girls created and continue to create a sense of belonging through design and style. "It is under these changing social and economic conditions," she wrote, "that Japanese street fashion and subcultures have become increasingly creative and innovative. They go against the grain of normative ideas about how one should dress in the public sphere or assume a persona."[2] With the disappearance of the old authoritarian state, the young adults who adopt the character of the child, according to curator Bruce Grenville, are turned into "complex protagonists, active agents of change who undermine and reveal the biases of an adult world that has betrayed them."[3] Japanese young adults, particularly girls, have come to embrace desexualizing and infantilizing

fashions, often derived from archetypal children's clothing and accessories, which are spread via youth magazines (no. 49). Manga and anime, which were largely read and watched by children in the postwar period, have similarly evolved in recent decades and now include sophisticated and adult subjects. Central to both of these phenomena is the widespread culture of *kawaii*, which loosely translates to "cuteness"; in addition, although both manga and anime are uniquely Japanese genres, they have been thoroughly influenced by Western culture.[4]

The look of the characters in *kodomomuke*, a type of manga originating in postwar Japan and made extremely popular by the work of Osamu Tezuka, was in part inspired by Disney animation and American comic books, which appeared in Japan during the Allied Occupation.[5] Tezuka's characters, including Astro Boy (no. 50) and Kimba the White Lion (1965), have the wide, round eyes now considered typical for anime and manga.[6] In both series, boy heroes are outraged by adult corruption and fight its injustice; this was a major theme of *shōnen*, or manga and anime produced specifically for boys beginning in the 1960s.[7]

Manga, which by the 1980s was being read by both adults and children, became the source of endless character-driven merchandise

50 OSAMU TEZUKA (Japanese, 1928–1989)
Astro Boy manga (no. 11), 2011 reprint of 1955 original
6 x 4" (15.2 x 10.2 cm)
Published by Kodansha Comics, Tokyo
The Museum of Modern Art, New York. Purchase

51 TAKASHI MURAKAMI (Japanese, born 1962)
N-CHA!. 1999
Screenprint, sheet: $18^7/_8$ x $26^3/_8$" (48 x 67 cm)
Published by Tomio Koyama, Tokyo
Printed by Chiaki Kayama and Tsuyoshi Hirai, Tokyo
Edition: 50
The Museum of Modern Art, New York. Katsko
Suzuki Memorial Fund

52 MARIKO MORI (Japanese, born 1967)
Star Doll (for *Parkett* no. 54). 1998
Mixed mediums, $10^1/_4$ x $3^1/_8$ x $1^9/_{16}$" (26 x 8 x 4 cm)
Published by Parkett Publishers, Zurich
Fabricated by Marmitte, Tokyo
Edition: 99
The Museum of Modern Art, New York. Linda Barth
Goldstein Fund

53 H. NAOTO (Japanese, born 1977)
Goth Lolita ensemble with matching angry doll. 2008
Lace, satin, tulle, chiffon, metal, and plastic
The Museum at the Fashion Institute of
Technology, New York. Museum purchase

that permeated all aspects of Japanese culture. Paintings, sculptures, and toys by the artist Takashi Murakami (no. 51), as well as his collaborations with high-end fashion companies such as Louis Vuitton, draw on a youthful aesthetic of mass-produced manga combined with fantasy and luxury.[8] His own characters are rendered in a manga-inflected style that he characterizes as "superflat," a visual language that combines the "art history and pop-cultural production of Japan...which emphasizes the surface and the experience of seeing."[9]

Shōjo, *shōnen*'s counterpart for girls, estimated to be read by more than three-quarters of teenage girls in Japan, is largely associated with romantic fantasy stories told in a visual style that features graceful, tall, and thin characters.[10] Naoko Takeuchi's *Sailor Moon*, another manga series that later became popular as an anime television series, features strong female characters, a group of teenage girls who fight evil throughout the solar system. They all wear naval-style school uniforms, an important Japanese cultural symbol and part of a long and controversial history. Based on late-nineteenth-century European dress designed for young girls, this look has also acquired connotations of rebellion and sexuality, thanks to the military-style uniforms worn by Japanese gangs and the frequent appearance of the schoolgirl uniform in Japanese pornography.[11] By the 1990s many schools had switched to a more modern uniform, with pleated skirt and blazer, to avoid this fetishistic association. This style, too, as curator Valerie Steele has pointed out, has since been subject to similar mutations of meaning, as in Mariko Mori's *Birth of Star*, in which the artist becomes a "pop idol with android eyes," in a short, plaid, uniform-style skirt (no. 52).[12] Mori may have been influenced by Kogal, a 1990s style, popularized by teenage girls who congregate in the Shibuya district of Tokyo, of school uniforms with skirts considerably shortened and paired with loose kneesocks, a childish yet sexualized look that contrasts accessories such as stuffed animals with exposed underwear. The subversion

of embracing the school uniform as a form of rebellion is particularly inflammatory in Japan, a society with a long and complex history of uniformed dress.[13]

The Lolita style, one of the more well known and elaborate of the subversive Japanese fashion subcultures, is also characterized by cuteness but shuns the erotic overtones of Kogal. It generally involves extremely childlike and feminine garments, with pinafores, ruffles, and bows, loosely based on nineteenth-century French dolls, Lewis Carroll's *Alice's Adventures in Wonderland* (1865), and Victorian mourning dress. Despite the style's nominal reference to Vladimir Nabokov's 1955 novel, girls who adopt the Lolita style do not necessarily identify with the heightened sexuality these personas may broadcast to others; the name is simply another Western influence taken out of context and transformed by Japanese youth until it takes on an entirely new meaning, in this case with a complex vocabulary and sub-subcultural iterations that include gothic (no. 53) and punk Lolita and embrace the creepy along with the cute. The prolonging of childhood, as one Lolita noted, can be liberating as well as fun. "Lolitas wear a girl's Victorian dress, and a girl is not a woman . . . she is a child, and a child is free of any responsibility, and she can do whatever she wants to. She can play and have fun."[14]

Kate Carmody

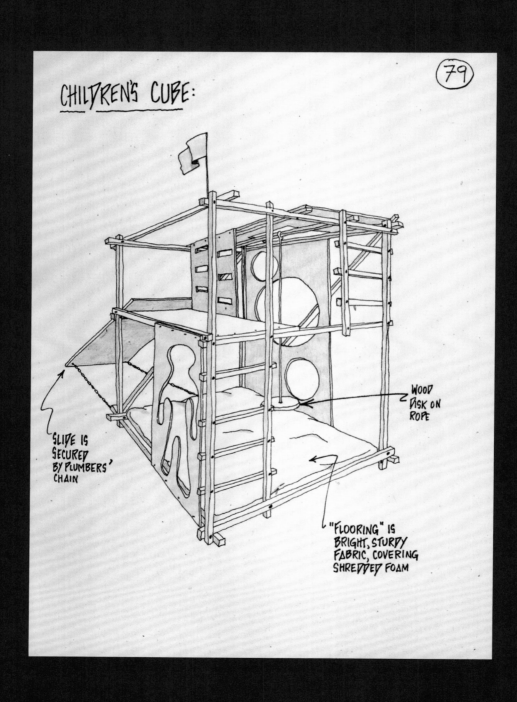

INTRODUCTION

IN THE LAST HALF-CENTURY, complex and often contradictory ideas about the place of children in the modern world have been articulated through passionate public discourse among educators, parents, and politicians, as well as through design. Shifting sociocultural currents — from the antiyouth sentiment summed up in "Wondering if Children Are Necessary," a 1979 article in *Time* magazine, to the emergence of the so-called global or universal child in the 1980s and '90s — have produced divergent new objects and environments for children. These changing forces, abstract but directly felt by children, are made manifest in design; this chapter focuses on design for children developed concurrently with the works featured in the previous chapter but heralding a more pronounced ethical, progressive, or idealistic philosophy. The designs presented here attempt to communicate to children that they deserve a better world and that this world might be possible.

Starting in the 1960s, students and professional designers broke with established conventions and challenged institutional, authoritarian, and commercial structures. Alternative living environments, such as communes and cohousing spaces, responded to the idea of a community's collective responsibility for children; exhibitions such as Palle Nielsen's *The Model*, at the Moderna Museet in Stockholm in 1968, destabilized the authority of the museum and formal definitions of art by encouraging children's free and chaotic play in a serious institutional setting; and designer-activists, such as Ken Isaacs and Victor Papanek, advocated an ethical and sustainable design culture with pragmatic and anticonformist projects that included no-frills educational toys and do-it-yourself plywood environments and cardboard furniture. Papanek, along with dedicated designers around the world,

also started a movement to produce and promote inclusive, therapeutic, and assistive design for children with disabilities and other challenges. Meanwhile, new educational television shows such as *Blue Peter*, in Britain (1959–present), and *Sesame Street* (1969–present) and *Free to Be… You and Me* (1974), in the United States, transformed children's programming (and viewing) with messages that encouraged creative growth, individuality, and self-expression. And an international playground revolution reshaped public play spaces into active, stimulating, and beautiful community cornerstones — a transformation that continues today.

Nelson Mandela said in 1995, "There can be no keener revelation of a society's soul than the way in which it treats its children."[1] In a recent *New York Times* article, "The Kids Are Not All Right," Joel Bakan used this statement to underscore the severity of what he and many others see as childhood "in crisis," characterized by relentless advertising and commercialization, childhood obesity, withdrawal into electronic media, increasing use of psychotropic medication, and exposure to toxic chemicals.[2] All over the world children continue to suffer from violence, exploitation, and devastating injustice. Reparative efforts — driven by governments and aid organizations and fortified by events such as the Convention on the Rights of the Child (1989), the World Summit for Children (1990), and Growing by Design, the International Design Conference in Aspen (1990) — rely on innovative design to give form to a more equitable world. The problems that children face in the twenty-first century are both new and a century old; the progressive design solutions shown here offer inspiring ways to physically build a better future.

Aidan O'Connor

See page 229

1 JAMES HENNESSEY (nationality and dates unknown) and
VICTOR PAPANEK (American, born Austria. 1927–1998)
Children's Cube, as illustrated in the book *Nomadic Furniture*. 1973
10 7/8 x 8 1/2" (27.6 x 21.6 cm)
The Museum of Modern Art Library, New York

2 ART WORKERS' COALITION (AWC)
(USA, est. 1969)
Q. And Babies? A. And Babies, poster combining
Ronald L. Haeberle's photograph of the My Lai
Massacre with quote from a CBS News interview
with US soldier Paul Meadlo. 1970
Offset lithograph, 25 x 38" (63.5 x 96.5 cm)
The Museum of Modern Art, New York. Gift of
the Benefit for Attica Defense Fund

THE SCHOOL-REFORM MOVEMENT of the 1960s and early '70s, like the civil rights and other social-justice movements of the era, sought equitable access to resources and rejected the conditions in which a generation of children had been raised (nos. 2, 3). Publications such as the *Whole Earth Catalog*, first published in 1968, and Ivan Illich's *Deschooling Society*, published in 1971, capture some of the breadth of the movement's conversation about schools and the rights of children. Both Illich and Stewart Brand, the founding editor of the *Whole Earth Catalog*, proposed the development of networks to provide access to tools and information for learning and rethinking learning spaces.

The *Whole Earth Catalog* was produced for a young generation of social and cultural activists, and its pages and supplements became a community-in-print for participants to read and respond to the "conjuring and living of new forms" (no. 4).[1] Brand conceived the catalog as a new type of information service, one that would promote self-education. The audience for this service that Brand had in mind was made up of his friends who were attempting to live on communes or self-sustaining homesteads throughout the United States and Canada, and in 1968 he created Access Mobile, which would provide them with information about new tools, building and land-use designs, and general philosophical texts. Access Mobile was literally the first manifestation of the *Whole Earth Catalog*: a truck packed with books that Brand and Lois Jennings drove to communes in New Mexico and

Colorado in the summer of 1968. They traveled with samples of books that Brand had assembled in "a mimeographed 6-page 'partial preliminary booklist' of what I'd gathered so far (Tantra Art, Cybernetics, The Indian Tipi, Recreational Equipment, about 120 items)" and "did a stunning $200 of business."[2]

The idea was that the *Whole Earth Catalog* would accompany the late-1960s and early-1970s counterculture into these new communal living experiments and back-to-the-land settlements around North America, where tens of thousands of young people had gone to escape contemporary culture, in a heady haze of experimental drugs, anarchic politics, rock 'n' roll, and holistic consciousness (nos. 5–7).[3] These young adults, in places such as Drop City and Libre, in Colorado, and Hog Farm, in New Mexico, rejected their parents' world and the materialism and militarization of American culture in which they were raised. In these and other new spaces (nos. 8, 9), young people attempted to create new kinds of families and other communal groups.

Brand felt that in order to foster self-reliance and sustain the initial energy of the back-to-the land movement, these experiments needed greater access to information. The *Whole Earth Catalog* proposed an extremely broad view of the self-education necessary for this project, spanning a near-comical gamut of subjects — John Cage, airplane building, emergency medical care, knot tying, architectural design, cooking, filmmaking, computer design, art instruction, bookmaking,

librarianship, government services, education theory, puppetry, and so on—all covered under section headings that announced the working categories: "Understanding Whole Systems," "Shelter and Land Use," "Industry and Craft," "Communications," "Community," "Nomadics," and "Learning."

The "Learning" section, with its active and evolving account of new and available publications, games, and toys, all documented in extensive reviews, influenced a generation of young educators, school reformers, and parents. It promoted publications about new types of schools and learning environments, the rights of children, and critiques of the existing educational system. Some of the featured titles were *Teaching as a Subversive Activity* (1969), by Neil Postman and Charles Weingartner; *Escape from Childhood* (1974), *How Children Fail* (1964), and *How Children Learn* (1967), by John Holt; *The Open Classroom* (1969), by Herbert R. Kohl; *The Lives of Children* (1969), by George Dennison; and *How to Change the Schools* (1970), by Ellen Lurie; as well as the magazines *This Magazine Is about Schools* (1966–present) (p. 231, no. 30), based in Toronto, and *Big Rock Candy Mountain* (1970–71). *Big Rock Candy Mountain* was an extension of the *Whole Earth Catalog*, with its issues produced in the same style and format, but its focus was children's education; it included regular contributions by Holt, who had been a middle school teacher for several years and, through his firsthand accounts of classroom experience, became one of the leading voices against

3 LISA LAW (American, born 1943)
Bring the Troops Home. Anti–Vietnam War March, San Francisco, April 15, 1967
Gelatin silver print, 14 x 11" (35.6 x 27.9 cm)
Courtesy of the artist

4 Page from the magazine *Big Rock Candy Mountain: Resources for Our Education*. 1971
14 1/2 x 10 1/2 x 11/16" (36.8 x 26.7 x 1.8 cm)
Edited by Samuel Yanes and Cia Holdorf
Published by Delacorte Press, New York
The Museum of Modern Art Library, New York

5 JOHN PHILLIP LAW (American, 1937–2008)
Tom, Lisa, and Pilar Law at Hog Farm Commune Camp, El Valle, New Mexico. 1970
Gelatin silver print, 11 x 14" (27.9 x 35.6 cm)
Courtesy of Lisa Law

6 LISA LAW (American, born 1943)
The Road Hog at the El Rito 4th of July Parade, New Mexico. 1968
Chromogenic color print, 11 x 14" (27.9 x 35.6 cm)
Courtesy of the artist

7 LISA LAW (American, born 1943)
George Robinson with Kids Michael Reich & Chris Robinson, Inside a Tipi at New Buffalo Commune, Arroyo Hondo, New Mexico. 1968
Gelatin silver print, 11 x 14" (27.9 x 35.6 cm)
Courtesy of the artist

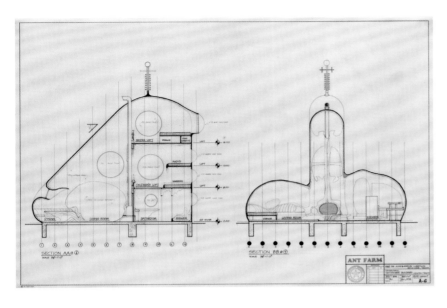

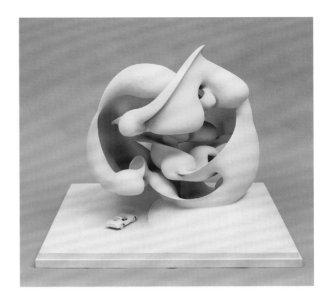

compulsory schooling and for the developing homeschool movement in the United States. His books, along with Paul Goodman's *Growing Up Absurd* (1964), were early attempts to describe how and why the classroom had ceased to be a place of learning.

    Deschooling Society, which was listed in the "Learning" section of the 1974 edition of the *Whole Earth Catalog*, took shape at the Centro Intercultural de Documentación (CIDOC), in Guernavaca, Mexico, an institute, founded by Illich, that was a destination for young intellectuals and activists in the 1960s and early '70s. CIDOC was officially a language institute, teaching Spanish to the many young people arriving to do development work in Latin America, but under Illich's guidance it also became an international gathering place for a cast of notable thinkers and activists concerned with school reform and other areas of public education.

    In 1970 at CIDOC, Illich presented a series of lectures that would become the main chapters of *Deschooling Society*. He called into question three basic assumptions: that children belong in school, that they learn in school, and that they can be taught only in school. The philosophy of deschooling asserted that learning flourished outside conventional spaces for instruction, and it advocated a shift from dependence on teaching to an ethic of facilitating access to things, information, and games conducive to learning. Throughout *Deschooling Society*, Illich sought to distinguish schooling from learning and also proposed new kinds of learning environments. He was convinced that the resources for education were plentiful, but schools and related institutions typically rendered these resources inaccessible or scarce, especially for the poor. Among his prescriptive changes for education systems were new community-education networks that would be developed through grassroots organizing and the pragmatic use of computers and other information technology. "Technology," he wrote, "is available to develop either independence and learning or bureaucracy and teaching."[4] Illich proposed the use of existing communication technology to form learning webs: new education networks that would facilitate the sharing of learning materials; skills exchange among community members via social networks; and peer matching, to bring together parents and older children seeking the benefits of self-directed learning.

    Illich's critique found an attentive audience among educators, reformers, and counterculture activists who wanted to redesign the education system in the United States through developing new types of schools and learning centers, and for them *Deschooling Society* became a defining work. Even though there were those who disagreed with the extent of the critique, a large international audience was inspired by his appeal for free access to educational tools and new community-based networks for learning and the exchange of skills.

David Senior

10 VANDKUNSTEN (Denmark, est. 1970)
Future residents of Tinggården, Herfølge,
Denmark, taking part in the democratic process
of planning. c. 1973
Photograph by Jens Thomas Arnfred
Vandkunsten Architects, Copenhagen

11 VANDKUNSTEN (Denmark, est. 1970)
Model of Tinggården, Herfølge, Denmark,
designed for a housing competition. c. 1971
Photograph by Jens Thomas Arnfred
Vandkunsten Architects, Copenhagen

IN 1967 Danish journalist Bodil Graae published "Every Child Should Have a Hundred Parents," a newspaper article that took its title from a statement attributed to the radical socialist designer Poul Henningsen.[1] Taking as its premise the idea that children might be "the most persecuted creatures in Denmark (after dogs)," Graae's dark but playful manifesto assumed different voices, from a child whose favorite play areas are forbidden or destroyed ("It's really irritating that there are so few grown-ups who were once children") to sociologist Erik Høgh ("If you don't have a good relationship with your neighbors, the road is almost straight to neuroses and worse").[2] Inspired by the communality of the Israeli kibbutz model, Graae lamented the deterioration in Northern Europe of space for children's free play, and she challenged the conventional disciplinary treatment of children based on arbitrary restrictions: "What if [children] were welcome to go in and out of the houses, apartments, and homes around us? What if they were accepted among the flowers and as climbers of fences? What if they had the feeling of belonging?"[3] Her sentiments reflected a longing for the shared experience of the tightly knit rural and working-class communities whose

bonds were disintegrating owing to the postwar glorification of the nuclear family and its single-family dwelling.

Jan Gudmand-Høyer, an architect and the leading figure in the emergent Danish cohousing movement, was concurrently exploring concerns similar to Graae's. In 1964 he returned to Denmark from graduate school at Harvard (where he studied informal American utopian communities such as Drop City in Colorado) and, with a group of friends, purchased a site on the outskirts of Copenhagen to explore the possibility of a living environment that would be more supportive of families and social well-being — a hybrid of the commune and the single-family house. Although sanctioned by city officials, the project was rejected by neighbors, and Gudmand-Høyer ended up selling the site. But just a few years later, when he published the article "The Missing Link between Utopia and the Dated One-Family House," he received inquiries from more than one hundred interested families. That article is now seen as a founding manifesto of the international cohousing movement, which continues to be influential in Sweden, the Netherlands, the United States, Canada, Australia, and beyond.[4] The Danish model of collaborative living in communal facilities, a socioarchitectural phenomenon pioneered by Gudmand-Høyer and the architectural firm Vandkunsten, has been characterized by the active participation of residents in the design process (no. 10) as well as in the everyday management of the settlements that result. It has offered a compelling alternative to isolated living patterns for individuals and families, and in this respect it continues a tradition of utopian living schemes, from the turn-of-the-century Garden City movement in Britain and artists' colonies across Europe to the 1930s Swedish Kollektivhus (collective house) model and Peter and Alison Smithson's postwar Cluster City concept.

Vandkunsten has produced many examples of successful cohousing. The firm, established in 1970 by Svend Algren, Jens Thomas Arnfred, Michael Sten Johnsen, and Steffen Kragh, continues to thrive

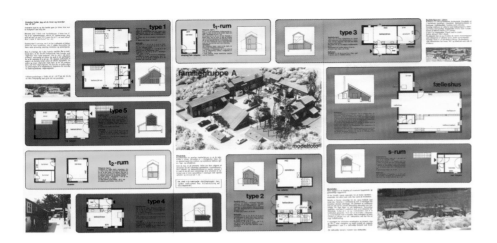

12 VANDKUNSTEN (Denmark, est. 1970)
Brochure for Tinggården, Herfølge,
Denmark. 1977
11¹³/₁₆ × 17¹¹/₁₆" (30 × 45 cm)
Vandkunsten Architects, Copenhagen

13 VANDKUNSTEN (Denmark, est. 1970)
View of interior street at Jystrup Savværk,
outside Copenhagen. 1984
Photograph by Finn Christoffersen, foto C
Vandkunsten Architects, Copenhagen

today, with more than half of its projects focused on low-cost social housing. In 1971 the firm won a competition (no. 11) organized by the Danish Ministry of Housing, which turned out to be a breakthrough commission and resulted in Tinggården, a cohousing settlement completed in 1978 in Herfølge, a suburb of the town of Køge, to the southwest of Copenhagen. To engage locals in the planning of the new intentional community, the Vandkunsten architects organized a *boligaktion circus* (housing-action circus) in Herfølge's main square, with their youthful spirit and age-inclusive design philosophy declared by colorful, hand-painted signs: "BOLIGER BOLIGER BOLIGER" (Housing housing housing) and "Det drejer sig om os alle sammen, gamle, børn, unge, voksne, syge og raske" (It concerns us all, elderly, children, adolescents, adults, sick and healthy).

Tinggården has been recognized as the decisive break with Denmark's postwar modernism (embodied by the architecture of

Arne Jacobsen) and a prototype of the country's *tæt-lav* (dense and low) building style, used as an alternative to high-rise modernist housing blocks.[5] Its private dwellings are arranged in six family groups, each with twelve to seventeen apartments of four different types (no. 12). Communal space makes up ten percent of the entire settlement, and the living experiment is carried out here through shared duties (childcare being paramount among them), community meetings, and an organic kind of socializing. Thousands of visitors — architects, engineers, students, environmentalists — have come to Tinggården since its completion.

An even stronger example of the core principles of cohousing (and Vandkunsten's most radical project) is the still-active Jystrup Savværk (1983–84), a settlement on the site of a rural sawmill outside Copenhagen. Where earlier cohousing designs still incorporated detached elements, Jystrup pushes the ideology to its physical limits with all of its spaces completely integrated. The settlement is L-shaped, with interior glass-covered hallways forming streets (no. 13) that unite its twenty-one apartments. The streets are an extension of the private dwellings where residents store toys, winter clothing, and plants; a safe and light-filled play area for children (and adults), in sight of private kitchens and shared facilities; and a pathway to the heart of the settlement, where there are game areas, a communal kitchen, a fireplace, and a library. Modest but robust mixed materials — cement, brick, wood, and corrugated metal — create a hearty industrial structure for an environment that nevertheless radiates *hygge*, the coziness that is fundamental to Danish culture. In this willing community of original and eager new residents — the model is especially attractive to young professional couples with children and single-parent families — continuous generations of children seem to be achieving Graae's vision: flowing in and out, belonging, engaging with other families.[6] At twelve they begin to participate in shared chores, and eventually they become adults — who were once children.

Aidan O'Connor

THE ANTI-INSTITUTIONAL SENTIMENT of the 1960s and '70s swept through museums, exposing them to charges of elitism, conservatism, even authoritarianism by the public as well as by artists engaged in art activism.[1] As institutions rarely perceived as child-friendly, museums were ripe for dismantling by children. Three important events took place in this period, in Sweden, Germany, and Denmark, which challenged traditional relationships among museums, their contents, and their visitors, all designed with the underlying stimulus of children's play.

The first activist experiment was *Modellen: En modell för ett kvalitativt samhälle*, or *The Model: A Model for a Qualitative Society* (no. 14). Organized in 1968 by the Danish artist Palle Nielsen at the

Moderna Museet, Stockholm, *The Model* took the form of an adventure playground installed in a museum. The exhibition catalogue explained its groundbreaking (and cheeky) premise: "*There is no exhibition*. It is only an exhibition because the children are playing in an art museum. It is only an exhibition for those who are not playing. That's why we call it a model."[2] After dropping out of the Royal Danish Art Academy in the late 1960s, Nielsen had worked with local artists, architects, activists, and residents to surreptitiously build playgrounds in under-privileged parts of Copenhagen and its immediate suburbs.[3] It was similar work that brought him in 1968, at the request of the group Aktion Samtal (Action dialogue), to Stockholm, where he turned his attention from neglected courtyards and alleys to the classic white cube of the museum gallery. After a period of fund-raising, *The Model* was built with the assistance of students, designers, and anti–Vietnam War activists. Support was provided by the Ministry of Education, the Swedish Building Research Institute, the Stockholm Council for Children's Welfare, and the newspaper *Dagens Nyheter*.[4]

For three weeks in October, *The Model* took over the museum's primary exhibition space. The installation was dense, chaotic, and exuberant. An extensive wooden structure — part jungle gym, part tree house, part construction scaffolding — provided various heights from which to jump into a pit full of foam blocks below. There were ramps and slides, rope swings, water chutes, tools and building materials, and endless art supplies. An assortment of period costumes was donated by the Royal Theater, and Nielsen provided masks of political figures, one hundred each of Charles de Gaulle, Mao Tse-tung, and Lyndon B. Johnson. Completely unfettered, children played, built, and painted the walls in a chaotic tangle of raw energy, complete with loudspeakers pumping music from turntables operated by the children themselves. Few adults dared enter this creative anarchy; most of them, a mix of parents, artists, and psychologists, watched the action from a distance through live video feed, on screens in the museum's theater.

Although frightening to some parents and more conservative adults, *The Model* was an overwhelmingly popular experiment. In three weeks there were thirty-five thousand visitors, twenty thousand of them children, who entered free of charge. Swedish Minister of Education Olof Palme was captured in a photograph — shoeless, flinging himself into the foam pit — on a visit with his own sons.[5] In order to include children of every social class, the museum encouraged kindergartens and schools not in the habit of arranging museum trips to book visits. It was the children, in the end, who were the agents and power source of Nielsen's design. "*The Model*," writer and curator Lars Bang Larsen has explained, "was concerned with the meaning of the social and subjective change that the playing child generates within the machinery of society. As such, the event was nothing short of a mass utopia of art activism."[6]

A few years later, in Frankfurt, a group of design students from the Hochschule für Gestaltung (University of art and design) Offenbach erected *Kinderplanet* (no. 15), another liberated play environment. Linette Schönegge, Regina Henze, and Karin Günther-Thoma, with their professors Thomas Bayrle and Wolfgang Schmidt, chose for their site the Frankfurt fairgrounds' main exhibition venue. More than one thousand children came each day to the three-week July event, where they participated in open-ended art workshops (on silkscreen and papier-mâché, among others), free play, games, and music and theater events. Teaching assistants were available if needed, but the creativity of the children ran the show, with no restrictions or prohibitive rules. A review of the event noted the energetic activity of children at work and play throughout the site — hammering, gluing, painting, and sewing.[7]

A similar event took place in 1978, just before UNESCO's International Year of the Child, at the Louisiana Museum of Modern Art in Humlebæk, Denmark, outside of Copenhagen. Organized by curator Kjeld Kjeldsen, *Børn er et folk* (Children are a people) advanced the progressive perspective that children were not only full-fledged human beings but also members of a group with its own cultural significance.[8] One hundred and sixty thousand parents and children visited this sprawling exhibition, which included installations by various artists, from the sculptural (a Volkswagen Beetle encased in grass) to the environmental (huge inflated tubes and balls that took over the museum's garden space) (no. 16). Like the other exhibitions, *Børn er et folk* was meant to be polemical as well as playful, encouraging critical debate about "the situation of children in society," with a series of conferences on the subject taking place during the exhibition's run.[9]

Other exhibitions inspired by children's play, and in some cases inspired directly by these three examples, have since been organized.[10] But these early and influential archetypes remain stirring reminders that museums can be — if not fully radicalized — sympathetic to revolutionary spirits beyond their walls and, at least temporarily, dismantled by avant-garde artists and willing children.

Aidan O'Connor

THE REGGIO EMILIA APPROACH to early-childhood education is widely regarded as one of the most influential pedagogical philosophies of the postwar era. Named for the town in Italy, located in the Emilia-Romagna region, where it first emerged and continues to be practiced, this set of principles for learning encourages independent and creative thinking, collective interaction, and visually stimulating spaces and activities. In contrast to other early-childhood education systems, the Reggio Emilia approach places special emphasis on the collaboration among teachers, children, and parents, which is understood as a co-construction of knowledge, as well as the meticulous documentation of the classroom activities, the role of the learning environment, and the use of visual arts.

Shortly after the end of World War II and Italy's Fascist dictatorship, a group of teachers and parents from Reggio Emilia created a new school for children with the primary objective of raising better citizens of the world.[1] This educational impulse and progressive philosophy, which were influenced by the international women's movement (no. 17), were also characteristic of the region's history of activism, emphasis on community participation, and belief in education as a foundation of civil society.

Children were no longer regarded, as they had been in the schooling systems of prewar Europe, as weak human beings who needed to be taught through a unified regimen of lessons; instead they were treated as individuals with "native potentiality with extraordinary richness, strength, and creativity" and the right to independence and their own thoughts.[2] With its constructivist stance — a theory of learning that argues for obtaining knowledge via experience rather than transmittal

by teachers — the Reggio Emilia approach recognized that children learn in myriad ways, given their varied interests and individual strengths, termed by Loris Malaguzzi, one of the movement's leading thinkers, "the hundred languages of children."[3] Thus the method of teaching would be modified to the particular situation of each child, requiring, in turn, a substantial degree of adaptability among the *pedagogisti* (instructors who develop the curriculum) and *atelieristi* (instructors who facilitate activities). Since the first school's founding, the Reggio Emilia approach has been adapted, interpreted, and implemented around the world. Reggio Children, an organization founded by Malaguzzi, has created a formal network of thirty-two partners, including schools and organizations in Europe, the United States, and Latin America.

The learning environment is of paramount importance in a Reggio Emilia school, so much so that it is considered a third teacher. A typical Reggio school is characterized by its transparency, with large windows allowing plenty of sunlight. Plants in the classrooms and a garden outside promote a close relationship with nature. In the center of the school there usually is a piazza, a central space where children congregate at various times of the day to eat, socialize, and interact, with a variety of child-scaled structures that can function as areas for reading, play, or rest; the experience of interacting in the piazza allows children to develop a sense of public identity (no. 18).[4] The goal is to construct a place where knowledge and culture are jointly constructed, a laboratory of innovation in the political, civil, and cultural spheres as well as in educational research. In the words of Malaguzzi, the original school sought to "give a human, dignified, and civil meaning to existence, to be able to make choices with clarity of mind and purpose, and to yearn for the future of mankind."[5]

Children take the lead in deciding their activities, which can last a few hours or continue for days or weeks, and the Reggio educators adjust their curriculum accordingly. The *atelieristi* spend a significant amount of time arranging materials in painstaking order, in shelves and other areas of the classroom, creating a space of rich visual and sensorial diversity (no. 19). And the documentation of the learning process is critical, with records and visuals of the child's daily activities compiled and placed in a designated location in the classroom, within the reach of the child, who has an active role in the process. Thus the child is brought together with teachers and parents in a communal dialogue of learning.

Pablo Helguera

17 Women at a UDI (Italian Women's Union) demonstration after World War II, Reggio Emilia, Italy. c. 1950
UDI (Italian Women's Union) Archive, Reggio Emilia, Italy

18 Mirror triangle, piazza in the Diana Municipal Preschool, Reggio Emilia, Italy. 1983
Preschools and Infant-Toddler Centres, Istituzione of the Municipality of Reggio Emilia, and Reggio Children, Italy

19 Atelier in the Diana Municipal Preschool, Reggio Emilia, Italy. 2010
Preschools and Infant-Toddler Centres, Istituzione of the Municipality of Reggio Emilia, and Reggio Children, Italy

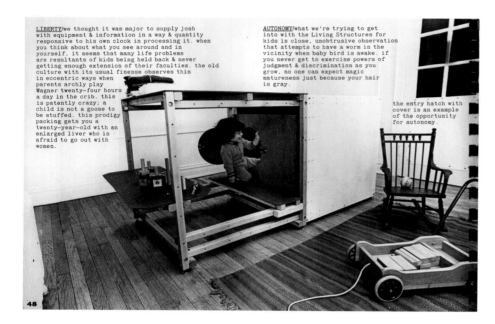

LIBERTY/we thought it was major to supply josh with equipment & information in a way & quantity responsive to his own clock in processing it. when you think about what you see around and in yourself, it seems that many life problems are resultants of kids being held back & never getting enough extension of their faculties. the old culture with its usual finesse observes this in eccentric ways when parents archly play Wagner twenty-four hours a day in the crib. this is patently crazy; a child is not a goose to be stuffed. this prodigy packing gets you a twenty-year-old with an enlarged liver who is afraid to go out with women.

AUTONOMY/what we're trying to get into with the Living Structures for kids is close, unobtrusive observation that attempts to have a worm in the vicinity when baby bird is awake. if you never get to exercise powers of judgment & discrimination as you grow, no one can expect magic matureness just because your hair is gray.

the entry hatch with cover is an example of the opportunity for autonomy.

48

20 KEN ISAACS (American, dates unknown) and CAROLE ISAACS (American, dates unknown) Josh Henry Living Structure, page from the book *How to Build Your Own Living Structures*, by Ken Isaacs. 1974
Published by Harmony Books, New York
Public Collectors, Gift of the Library of Radiant Optimism for Let's Re-Make the World

VICTOR PAPANEK, the Vienna-born designer and educator, was one of the most influential advocates of socially and ecologically responsible design.[1] He spent about ten years writing *Design for the Real World* (1971), a provocative manifesto that outraged many colleagues with its biting indictment of industrial design ("There are professions more harmful...but only a few") and accusations that designers were negligent and entangled with corporate bottom lines, artificial obsolescence, and copyright bureaucracy.[2] The book was so polemical that it was published in Sweden (as *Miljön och Miljonerna* [The environment and the millions] in 1970) before any publisher in the United States would accept it. Papanek encouraged designers to pursue more meaningful responses to universal needs and neglected audiences, with a particular emphasis on children: the book contains more than one hundred references to children, with example after example of areas for thoughtful development, including experimental cube-based childcare centers, better childproof containers for medicines and household cleaners, and safer playgrounds and school buses. He also described innovative projects for children that he and his students had already developed: a sensory-stimulation wall, the developmental and therapeutic Fingermajig toy, and a cloth book for infants made with various textures, intended to be produced by blind adults.[3]

Confounded by products like My Puppy Puddles ("a toy whose sole purpose is to make a dog go to the bathroom") and Dynamite Shack ("a toy that teaches youngsters how to blow up buildings"), Papanek favored toys, both old and new, that promoted open-ended play: Lincoln Logs, Legos, Capsela construction kits.[4] But most toys, he lamented, even if well conceived, taught dangerous lessons. "[They are] made of cheap plastic, and stain, break, or wear out quickly," he wrote. "Playing with them the child cannot help but to assimilate certain values: things are badly made, quality is unimportant, garish colors and cutesy decorations are the norm, and when things wear out they are to be pitched and replacements arrive miraculously."[5] Papanek's concerns and fundamental ideology radiate a radical pragmatism that was shared by an international network of designers who were experimenting with design for children, an ideal outlet for playful, flexible, recyclable forms that could be produced by willing amateurs.

One of these contemporaries was Ken Isaacs, an American designer who had directed the design department at Cranbrook Academy of Art in the late 1950s and appeared on the cover of *Life* in September 1962 as a leader of the "Take-Over Generation." Like Papanek, Isaacs was an advocate for the ethical, do-it-yourself design culture that emerged in the 1960s and '70s.[6] In 1974, the year he published the manual *How to Build Your Own Living Structures*, Isaacs, his wife, Carole, and their son, Joshua Henry, occupied a microhouse they had built in the woods of Illinois. The book offered plans for flexible, ecological structures built from matrix systems of modules made of

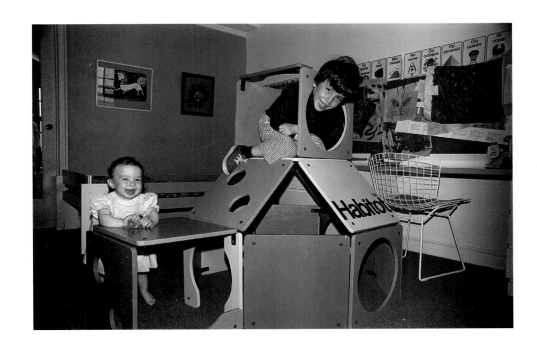

21 RICHARD DATTNER
(American, born Poland 1937)
Habitot play system. 1974
Plywood and stainless steel, 44 1/2 x 44"
(113 x 111.8 cm)
Photograph by Richard Dattner
Courtesy of the designer

22 KEITH GODARD (British, born 1942),
CRAIG HODGETTS (American, born 1937),
and ROBERT MANGURIAN (American, born 1944)
Brochure for Punch-out furniture. 1973
Lithograph, open: 7 1/2 x 29 3/4" (19.1 x 75.6 cm)
The Museum of Modern Art, New York. Gift of
the designers

23 Victor Papanek at Helsinki Design Lab
in Suomenlinna, Finland. 1968
Photograph by Kristian Runeberg
SDO – Sitra Archive

24 MARIMEKKO (Finland, est. 1951)
Lautturi child's overalls. 1966
Textile in Noppa pattern, designed by
Vuokko Eskolin-Nurmesniemi (1953)
Cotton and plastic buttons, 23⁵/₈" (60 cm) tall
Design Museum Finland, Helsinki

25 MARIMEKKO (Finland, est. 1951)
Möhköfantti toy. 1979
Textile in Linjarattaat pattern, designed by
Vuokko Eskolin-Nurmesniemi (1959)
Cotton, stuffing, and wooden wheels, toy:
9⁷/₁₆ x 11¹³/₁₆" (24 x 30 cm); sheet: 29¹⁵/₁₆ x 36¹/₄"
(76 x 92 cm)
Design Museum Finland, Helsinki

wooden frames, plywood, and simple hardware. Several examples of his and Carole's living structures — hybrids of furniture and architecture — were inspired by and intended for Joshua Henry, whose arrival (which Isaacs described as a "benign explosion," beyond "supercool") both rocked and reinforced the couple's simplified lifestyle.[7] As first-time parents inhabiting a small apartment in Chicago, they encountered new challenges, such as a brush with conventional consumerism:

> One day I found myself in a suburban department store hallucinating Carole asking the lady if she could buy a crib. This immediately induced hyperventilation in my system... she calmly said that the kid's head was going to be flat on top (or if we were lucky, slightly geodesic) unless he got a bigger place to sleep...so we got the nifty crib & it hung there for quite a while like the albatross.[8]

This "monstrous negative act" was all the motivation Isaacs needed to create, based on a design by Carole, a more suitable environment for their son, the Josh Henry Living Structure (no. 20).[9] This matrix was made up of two thirty-six-inch cubes — one for activity, with a table and sliding bench, and the other for "relaxation and renewal," with a sleeping surface that could be adjusted to six different heights,

a chalkboard face, and a porthole hatch. The entire system could grow with Joshua, include a playmate or overnight guest, and even host his parents for dinner.[10]

Another proponent of do-it-yourself expertise was Mario Dal Fabbro, the author of *How to Make Children's Furniture and Play Equipment* (1963), who came to the United States in 1948 from Italy, where he had worked in his family furniture shop near Venice. Richard Dattner, designer of the first adventure playgrounds in New York's Central Park (see "The Playground Revolution," p. 242), was inspired by his own children to create modular play structures, including the Habitot (no. 21), a plywood play system that he produced between the time of design (in 1972) and widespread manufacture (in 1976–77) of his cuboctahedron PlayCubes, which were low-cost outdoor versions of the same concept. Sympathetic parents not blessed with design or construction skills could still participate in the DIY movement with kits such as Punch-out cardboard furniture (no. 22), which was distributed by the progressive Design Research shop in Cambridge, Massachusetts. The Punchout line was designed by Craig Hodgetts, Keith Godard, and Robert Mangurian, the architects who designed the Creative Playthings store in New York in 1969 (see "Retail Fantasies," p. 199). Hodgetts playfully introduced the product to a popular audience on the television show *What's My Line?*.[11]

At the Helsinki Design Lab (HDL) in 1968, 150 like-minded luminaries mixed with Papanek, as well as his colleague and friend R. Buckminster Fuller. (This was the same year that Fuller published *Operation Manual for Spaceship Earth*, an imaginative summons on behalf of the planet, for its maintenance and care of its limited resources.)

26 JAMES HENNESSEY (nationality and
dates unknown) and VICTOR PAPANEK
(American, born Austria. 1927–1998)
Cover of the book *Nomadic Furniture.* 1973
10⁷/₈ x 8¹/₂" (27.6 x 21.6 cm)
Published by Pantheon Books, New York
The Museum of Modern Art Library, New York

27 EDDIE COLEMAN
(nationality and dates unknown)
Design for disposable car seat, page from the
book *Nomadic Furniture*, by James Hennessey
and Victor Papanek. 1973
10⁷/₈ x 8¹/₂" (27.6 x 21.6 cm)
Published by Pantheon Books, New York
The Museum of Modern Art Library, New York

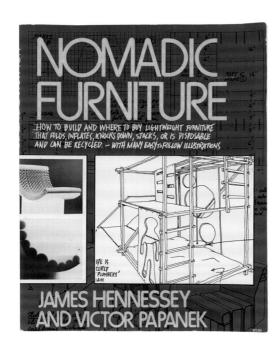

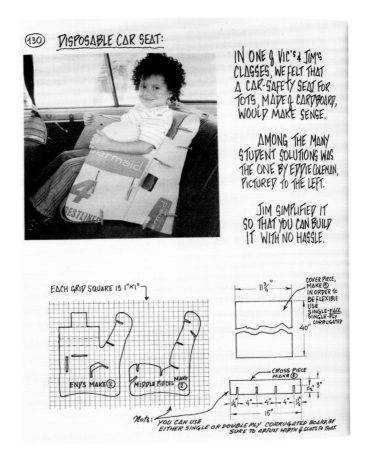

This global summit was organized by a group of engineers, designers, and architects to address "the changing role of design" and "the emerging needs of a new world," in sessions that discussed necessities, innovation, design methods, and education, all with a humanitarian and ecological bent.[12] Papanek was a key speaker at the opening and closing sessions, and he also led a workshop that resulted in a six-and-a-half foot collapsible, portable, and low-cost cubic play-and-exercise environment for children with cerebral palsy (no. 23). The project was rapid-prototyped over the course of thirty hours at HDL, based on interviews with children and parents and visits to clinics, playgrounds, and homes that had taken place before the event.

Elements of this environment, dubbed the CP-I, appear to have been covered with distinctive Marimekko textiles; the connection is likely given the attendance of Armi Ratia, the founder of the Finnish textile and fashion house. Marimekko had historical links both to children and to the movement to create thoughtful, ecologically sound products. Since its establishment in 1951 it has produced bold geometric prints that, when applied to durable, comfortable, unisex clothing for children (no. 24), build on the principles of the dress-reform movement at the turn of the century. In 1958 the company opened a children's clothing store in Helsinki called Muksula, which can be loosely translated as "a place for kids."[13] Starting in the late 1950s, Marimekko also produced and sold plans for simple, abstract animal dolls that parents and children could make themselves, using leftover fabric scraps and wooden spools as wheels (no. 25).[14]

What Marimekko rejected — and what Papanek most detested in design for children — was the spirit of conformity that was tacitly encouraged by designers and manufacturers. Papanek saw this quality as pervasive and reinforced by adult and institutional pressures, especially in the school environment. "The mysterious quality called 'creative imagination' seems to exist in all people," he wrote, "but is severely diminished by the time an individual reaches the age of six."[15] In opposition he published (with James Hennessey) *Nomadic Furniture* (no. 26), a handbook of inventive designs for adults and children that encouraged home-built works over "sleazy or dangerous" manufactured products.[16] On the cover is Papanek's own design for a children's play cube (p. 214, no. 1), a larger cousin to Josh Henry's minidwelling, for active play. Inside the book, a more jarring student project is illustrated (no. 27): "In one of Vic's & Jim's classes, we felt that a car-safety seat for tots, made of cardboard, would make sense."[17] Clearly, like the rest of the real world, ethical design was not without humor, or missteps.

Aidan O'Connor

To expect a "turned on" child of the electric age to respond to the old education modes is rather like expecting an eagle to swim. It's simply not within his environment, and therefore incomprehensible.
    —Marshall McLuhan, 1969[1]

The telephone: speech without walls.
The phonograph: music hall without walls.
The photograph: museum without walls.
The electric light: space without walls.
The movie, radio, and TV: classroom without walls.
    —Marshall McLuhan, 1964[2]

IN THE MIDDLE OF THE CENTURY the Canadian educator and media historian Marshall McLuhan began writing about the new mass media — changing forms of communication that included television, print, film, and radio — and one of his frequent topics was the radically new information environments for children that it created. For McLuhan, these environments constituted a new culture with new languages, "their grammars yet unknown."[3] Children were immersed in this culture and identified with its messages, but schools were structured without relation to it, remaining tethered solely to the media language of the book. It was clear to McLuhan that the previous methods of instruction

were out of step with the TV child (nos. 28, 29). He suggested that the nineteenth-century classroom had been equipped with materials that exceeded the information available outside it, but that in the postwar twentieth century the circumstances were reversed (no. 30).

From this perspective, McLuhan disputed the efficacy of the traditional subjects of study and proposed that educators must enlarge their curriculum to address the expanding media world. He argued that children were fully fluent in the languages of media — in most cases much more so than their elders — but there was no instruction to help them parse its structure, as he pointed out, with the anthropologist Edmund Carpenter, in 1956:

> In the schoolroom officialdom suppresses all their natural experience; children of technological man are divorced from their culture, they cease to respond with untaught delight to the poetry of trains, ships, planes, and to the beauty of machine products. They are not permitted to approach the traditional heritage of mankind through the door of technological awareness; this only possible door for them is slammed in their faces.[4]

As part of their research, McLuhan and Carpenter ran, starting in 1953, the Seminar on Culture and Communication at the University of Toronto, a groundbreaking effort to consider media as a subject of study, in particular to discern the specific grammars of its new languages. In effect, McLuhan felt, popular culture — "press-mags-film-TV-radio" — had created a "classroom without walls," and educators must try to address and understand this new territory.[5]

The publication of *Understanding Media* in 1964 launched McLuhan as the "the oracle of the electric age" for an international audience.[6] His ideas were a matter of public conversation and his book essential reading for the North American counterculture; his analysis of media culture provided a critical vocabulary for a generation of young adults who had been politically galvanized by seeing the era's violent events

28 WILLIAM WEGMAN (American, born 1943)
RCA. c. 1976
Gelatin silver print with applied color,
13³/₄ x 10¹¹/₁₆" (34.9 x 27.1 cm)
The Museum of Modern Art, New York.
Gift of the Peter Norton Family Foundation

29 Still from "Jazz Numbers," *Sesame Street*. 1969
Animation by Jeffery Hale, Imagination, Inc.
Courtesy of Sesame Workshop

30 Cover of the magazine *This Magazine Is about Schools*, Fall/Winter 1971
8 $\frac{11}{16}$ x 5 $\frac{15}{16}$ x $\frac{7}{16}$" (22.1 x 15.1 x 1.1 cm)
Published by Everdale Place, Toronto
The Museum of Modern Art Library, New York

31 Cover of the magazine "Video & Kids: Radical Software/Changing Channels," special issue of *Radical Software*, Summer 1974
Edited by Peter Haratonik and Kit Laybourne of the Center for Understanding Media
Published by Gordon and Breach, New York
12 x 9" (30.5 x 22.9 cm)
The Museum of Modern Art Library, New York

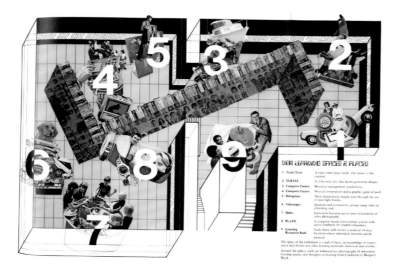

32 Design for the exhibition *New Learning Spaces and Places*, Walker Art Center, Minneapolis, January 27–March 10, 1974, double-page foldout from *Design Quarterly* (nos. 90/91), double issue devoted to the exhibition. 1974
11 $^{13}/_{16}$ x 8 $^{1}/_{2}$" (30 x 21.6 cm)
The Museum of Modern Art Library, New York

on television: the assassination of John F. Kennedy, the state suppression of the American civil rights movement, the shooting of four college students by the Ohio National Guard at Kent State University, and the Vietnam War.[7] In response to McLuhan's ideas, the young men and women of the counterculture actively developed new tools to compete with conventional media outlets, with results such as the *Whole Earth Catalog* (see "Deschooling Society," p. 216), a network of new tools for cultural change.

Another tool that emerged in the late 1960s and early 1970s, with the release of the Sony portable video system (or Portapak), was video, with its utopian promise of a people's media movement. The system provided relative ease of movement, allowing for a mobile practice in streets, in communities, and in schools, and it generated a sensation among practitioners. Early adopters considered the video camera a tool for social change that allowed communities to see themselves represented in local broadcast initiatives — a way of taking control of the media.

Among the young artists and activists using new video tools, Raindance, an alternative video group in New York, espoused McLuhan's key ideas and put them into action with the agenda of creating alternatives to mainstream television. In 1970 the group began publishing the magazine *Radical Software*, which brought together a diverse group of video artists and activists under the motto "You are the information"; the magazine contained essays about the new information economy, with sections about equipment and centers where people could exchange the skills and tools necessary for making video and broadcast content. The last issue, in 1974, edited by Kit Laybourne and Peter Haratonik, was devoted to the theme "Video & Kids" (no. 31) and took a close look at projects that placed mass media tools in the hands of children. The educators behind these projects united the guerilla-television movement with McLuhan's ideas about the outmoded nature of the traditional classroom, in activities meant to limit the contrast between the media environments provided by the classroom and the general culture. These activities were also part of a progressive trend toward new learning spaces: open classroom environments where children were allowed the space to discover and manipulate the tools on their own (no. 32).

The "Video & Kids" issue of *Radical Software* was produced with the support of the Center for Understanding Media, a nonprofit educational organization in New York, where Laybourne and Haratonik worked at the time. John Culkin, an early advocate of media studies in public education, had brought McLuhan to Fordham University to teach in 1964 and founded the center in 1969. In accordance with McLuhan's ideas, Culkin advocated an inclusive media education, giving children the means to analyze what they were seeing on television, an idea about media literacy that directly connects to Carpenter and McLuhan's earlier research.[8]

The main activity of the Center for Understanding Media was finding ways to try out their ideas in actual classrooms. *Doing the Media*, a publication produced by the center in 1972, provided documentation of activities that took place during an intensive eighteen-month residency by the center's staff at an elementary school in Mamaroneck, New York, a project funded by the Ford Foundation. In the introduction, Culkin set out the center's goals: "The mandate for schools seems simple enough.... We must acknowledge the existence and influence of this new media culture and enable the child to master its codes and to control its impact."[9] The activities included workshops on photography, film, video, animation, and theater that were theoretically and practically based on Culkin's analysis of media culture; *Doing the Media* spelled out the curriculum with lists of resources and supplies accompanying each section and included responses from the participating teachers about the effectiveness of the different workshops and classes. This was one effort in the movement toward media literacy and the wider use of educational tools that used media, a movement that was itself a residual effect of those new tools, along with the general climate of education reform. Video, cable-access broadcasts, and other experimental media were tools of the moment; McLuhan's classroom without walls was the subject these educators had in mind.

David Senior

THE EFFORT to accommodate children in the physical world of adults, to give them equal footing, in a way characterizes all design for children as inclusive, with results that can be poignant as well as practical. Peter Opsvik designed the adjustable Tripp Trapp chair (1972) after watching his son, Thor — too big for a high chair but too small for an adult chair — struggle for a place at the family dining table; as part of the design process he produced oversize versions of the Tripp Trapp and a standard table and chair (no. 33) to help his team empathize with an average three-year-old child. More than seven million Tripp Trapp chairs have since been sold.

The term "inclusive" also refers to a moral imperative that took hold in the design world in the 1970s and '80s, to consider the perspectives of previously marginalized groups. In the subsequent shift, designers began to think carefully about people whose needs were not always met by conventional environments and objects, including people with disabilities. Since then, many talented designers have expanded the broad field of inclusive design (also called "universal design") and, more specifically, therapeutic design (to treat or alleviate specific conditions) and assistive design (to enhance abilities and independence) for people

with audiovisual, motor, and developmental disabilities.[1] In some cases, such as Smart Design's Good Grips series of kitchen tools for OXO (originally conceived in 1989 to make kitchen tasks easier for arthritic hands), the results of this pursuit have been beneficial to mainstream users as well as being commercially pragmatic. Inclusive design has proved to be a uniquely thoughtful, demanding, and often quite personal realm of the profession, all the more so when it focuses on children.

The disability-rights movement began in the 1960s, in the wake of the civil rights and women's liberation movements, by agitating against discrimination and for public accommodation.[2] In the same era there was a surge in products and facilities for rehabilitative and assistive technology, both of them dependent on good design. Legislation began to have an impact on architecture and design, including, in the United States, the Architectural Barriers Act (1968), the Education for All Handicapped Children Act (1975), and the Americans with Disabilities Act, or ADA (1990).[3] As medical and therapeutic treatments improved, expanding the capabilities and extending the life spans of people with illnesses and disabilities, designers thought of ways to prevent them from being segregated or stigmatized.

Two exhibitions, one at each end of the 1980s, were important showcases for this growing field. In *Design and Disability*, organized in 1981 at the Design Centre in London, a section dedicated to children with disabilities featured toys, mobility aids, and clothing (no. 34). One of the highlights was the Rocking Spinning Toy (c. 1981), designed by

33 PETER OPSVIK (Norwegian, born 1939)
"Maxi" set including Tripp Trapp chair. 1972
Lacquered beech wood, 61 x 36 1/4 x 39 1/4"
(154.9 x 92.1 x 99.7 cm)
Photograph of Lars Hjelle and Kjell Heggdal
by Dag Lausund
Stokke

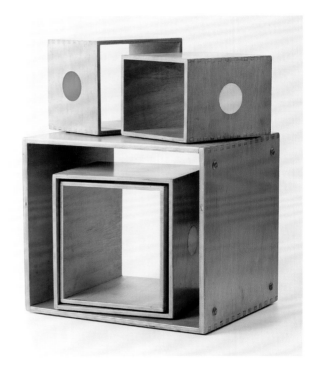

Rosemary Martin, a toy that multiple children could use, thus counteracting the isolated play Martin witnessed while visiting children in hospitals. At The Museum of Modern Art, New York, Cara McCarty organized *Designs for Independent Living* in 1988, featuring recent mass-produced products primarily for older adults and those with physical disabilities but also including therapeutic play mats and brightly colored support systems for children with motor disabilities. McCarty aligned her selection of objects with the classic principles of modernism, explaining, "In the hands of sensitive designers, these products have been enhanced by an aesthetic value not usually associated with adaptive technology. Beauty is found in their economy of design, and the purity of form is determined by their function."[4] Half of the forty-five works presented were Scandinavian, with Sweden strongly represented by Ergonomi Design, a pioneer of inclusive design, founded by Sven-Eric Juhlin and Maria Benktzon, among others (no. 35). Since 1969

the firm has specialized in progressive user-oriented design and demonstrated a commitment to equality as well as quality of life, design principles for which the Nordic countries are still known.

Teresa Kruszewska and Renate Müller are two prolific woman designers who specialized in coordinated series of objects and complete environments that provide the developmental and healing benefits unique to play. Kruszewska began working with children in the 1950s, helping her sister and brother-in-law run a rehabilitation hospital in Jastrzębie-Zdrój, Poland. She experimented with making playful furniture

before her abilities were first tested, she said, in 1959, by a commission to furnish the Krakow Prokocim Hospital.[5] A decade later, after studying ergonomics and new technologies at the Rhode Island School of Design and in Finland, she returned to Poland and, in 1974–75, revived some of her ideas from Prokocim in furnishings and toys for the Children's Health Center in Warsaw, including wheeled screens, abacuses, pin boards, blocks, and a "growing chair" system not unlike the Tripp Trapp. For this scheme Kruszewska also developed Furnitoys (no. 36), a set of neutral developmental tools based on her observations and contact with pediatricians and child psychologists. These nesting box forms, with their circles of brightly colored plexiglass, encouraged children to participate in the creation of their own spaces, enhancing feelings of independence, control, and privacy.[6]

Born and raised in Sonneberg, an East German manufacturing center known as Spielzeugstadt (toy town), Müller grew up in an environment infused with the material culture of childhood.[7] Her grandfather and father ran the toy company H. Josef Leven, which had been established in 1912, and Müller began representing it at trade fairs when she was fourteen years old. She started training in toy design in 1964 and soon launched a career in design for children with special needs.[8] Using a limited material vocabulary of jute, leather, and wood, she created high-quality therapeutic toys and environments for active play, in handmade designs that are simple, combining robust forms (ideal for strength, balance, and motor exercises) with refined tactile qualities, bright colors, and straps or handles to encourage physical engagement. Her early series of burlap beasts, marketed as "coarse but cute," made their debut in Leipzig in 1967 and were produced by the family business, which was acquired by the state and became the VEB Therapeutisches Spielzeug (Centralized distribution facility for therapeutic toys).[9] Müller worked closely with rehabilitation professionals to balance her rigorous quality standards with the economic limitations of East German industry. She founded her own workshop in 1978 and headed the Kindumwelt (child environment) department of the Verband Bildender Künstler

der DDR (Association of visual artists of the GDR). In the 1980s, with her beasts already popular in kindergartens and hospitals throughout the region, Müller turned to larger objects and environments such as suspended puppet theaters and outdoor playgrounds for children with physical disabilities. Her unique modular indoor playground (no. 37) features stick-puppet characters that can be used to secure loose cushions into endless arrangements of playful structures.[10]

The tactile significance of Müller's creations is a critical part of therapeutic design function. Since her groundbreaking work, designers have sought to expand the possibilities of therapeutic play through sensory stimulation, which is important for early cognitive development and used in the treatment of certain disabilities and neurological disorders.[11] Graphic designer Katsumi Komagata understands these correlations well, and in his exquisite children's books he activates both the visual and tactile senses. In projects that adopt Bruno Munari's conception of books as objects, Komagata has explored different approaches to binding and reading, which has led him to create a series of books for partially sighted and blind children. In *Plis et plans* (Folds and planes) (no. 38), thick pages with brightly colored shapes and Braille text are unexpectedly transformed as the child folds and unfolds them.

Inspired by the Dutch therapy *snoezelen* (from *snuffelen* [to seek out] and *doezelen* [to relax]) from the 1970s, designer Twan Verdonck created the Boezels (no. 39) in 2001, a series of seventeen soft toys, each a kind of artificial pet that, by emphasizing physical contact, both encourages sensory exploration and reduces anxiety; the Boezels are suitable for all children, as well as for adults with developmental

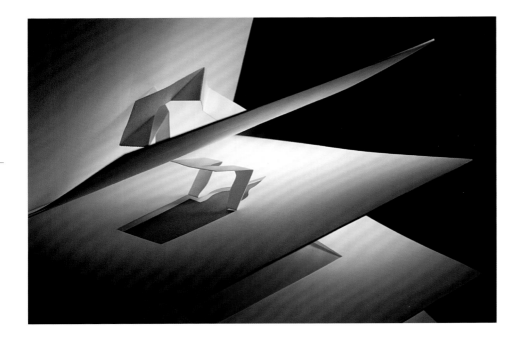

38 KATSUMI KOMAGATA (Japanese, born 1953)
View of the book *Plis et plans* (Folds and planes).
2000
11 $^{13}/_{16}$ x 8 $^{11}/_{16}$" (30 x 22 cm)
Published by Les Doigts Qui Rêvent, Talant, France;
Les Trois Ourses, Paris; and One Stroke, Tokyo
Courtesy of the artist

39 TWAN VERDONCK (Dutch, born 1979) and
NEO HUMAN TOYS (The Netherlands, est. 2003)
Tummy (warm belly monkey), from the Boezels
collection. 2001
Fake fur, cotton, and cherry pits, 23 $^5/_8$ x 18 $^7/_8$ x 8 $^5/_8$"
(60 x 48 x 22 cm)
Manufactured by De Wisselstroom
The Museum of Modern Art, New York. Dorothy
Cullman Purchase Fund

disabilities. Verdonck incorporated unique sense-specific characteristics in the toys, using heating pads, mirrors, sound, scent, and durable textiles with different tactile properties, and the shapes are abstract, leaving freedom for imaginative interpretation and narrative. The first Boezels were developed and produced with the input of patients in a workshop at a mental health–care facility in Hapert, the Netherlands.

Recent developments in inclusive, therapeutic, and assistive design suggest that designers are increasingly considering the agency and emotions of children. Ergonomi Design (for Pfizer) has created a genotropin injection pen (1991–96), for children with growth-hormone deficiencies, that is easier for children to hold and hides the needle in a chamber that can be personalized with decorative plates and pendants.[12] The emotional and physical benefits of play are brought to the fore in a concept by the young designer Mariana Uchoa for a radical prosthetic, the Toobers & Zots Interactive Arm (2009), made of colorful foam pieces in infinite combinations, which she designed as a student in the School of Visual Arts' Prosthetics Project.[13] It is also noteworthy that major multidisciplinary design firms have entered this field; Frog Design, a global firm famous for its innovations in consumer electronics, created Tango! (c. 2006), an assistive-communication device for children with hearing or speech impairments, for the company Blink Twice, founded by the father of a boy with cerebral palsy.[14] New firms with unprecedented specializations are emerging and excelling, such as Krabat, a small Norwegian company that focuses on innovative pediatric technical aids; their active chair, Jockey, was recently acquired by MoMA.[15] Designers who consider the whole child — and reject simply making miniature versions of adult products or rendering them decoratively juvenile — continue to contribute objects and environments that extend the ability of design to improve and transform everyday life.

Aidan O'Connor

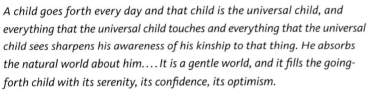

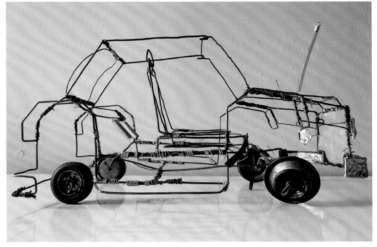

A child goes forth every day and that child is the universal child, and everything that the universal child touches and everything that the universal child sees sharpens his awareness of his kinship to that thing. He absorbs the natural world about him....It is a gentle world, and it fills the going-forth child with its serenity, its confidence, its optimism.

— Charles Stubblefield, 1965[1]

THE MODERN WORLD has not been gentle to all children. It has been and continues to be fraught with inequity and drastic disparities in security and quality of life; many children are hungry or sick, some labor in deplorable conditions, some are victims of violence and abuse and exploitation (no. 40). In times of armed conflict they become casualties, witness atrocities, and — as coerced combatants — commit them. Some of these dark realities originated long before the beginning of the twentieth century, and others are the result of more recent political and sociocultural shifts and may be linked to developments in modern design. The AK-47, for example, an assault rifle designed in the Soviet Union at the end of World War II and since then the weapon of choice for child soldiers, is simple and light enough to be wielded, stripped, and reassembled by children as young as eight years old. In impoverished

areas children become designers themselves, producing their own toys from the detritus of modern industry (no. 41).

In the past three decades the emergence of a so-called global civil society and the increasing influence of transnational aid organizations have shaped the idea of the "universal child," signifying children across the globe linked in kinship to all other humans and the natural world (as expressed in Stubblefield's verse) as well as possessing universal inalienable rights: basic human rights shared with adults, although more precious because children generally cannot protest their abrogation or fight for their reinstatement.[2] The Declaration of the Rights of the Child, adopted by the General Assembly of the United Nations in 1959, codified these rights and was celebrated twenty years later with UNESCO's International Year of the Child, a year's worth of events and observances that drew attention to children's rights and made them a prominent topic in global discourse.[3] Animator and director Eugene Fedorenko's short film *Every Child/Chaque Enfant* (1979), Canada's contribution to a longer film celebrating the Year of the Child, illustrated the declaration's third principle (of ten) — every child's right to a name and nationality — and won an Academy Award that year.[4] The Year of the Child highlighted the activities of international, national,

40 ÉVA KÉMENY (Hungarian, 1929–2011) and LÁSZLÓ SÓS (Hungarian, born 1922) *Fido patée pour chats.* 1982 Gelatin silver print, 29 3/8 x 39 3/8" (74.6 x 100 cm) The Museum of Modern Art, New York. Gift of the designers

41 TSHEPO, RALLY, and MAWISA, children of the Makuleke Village, South Africa, with SHARING TO LEARN (USA, est. 2010) Wire car. 2010 Metal wire and various materials found at a dumping site in Makuleke Village, 7 x 13 x 7" (17.8 x 33 x 17.8 cm) Courtesy of Sharing to Learn

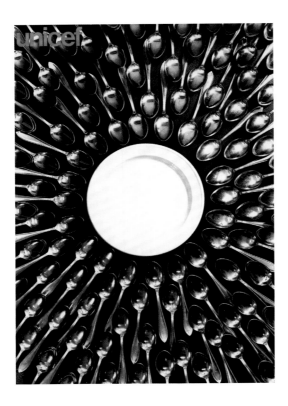

43 *Bad Water Kills More Kids Than War,*
UNICEF advertisement. 2008
Photograph by Henrik Halvarsson after an idea
by Johan Jäger at Jung von Matt, Stockholm
Courtesy of UNICEF Sweden, Stockholm

45 *Year of the Child, Child Labor Throughout
the World,* workers in a brick factory in
Bogotá, advertisement for the United Colors
of Benetton. 1979
11 $^{13}/_{16}$ x 16 $^{9}/_{16}$" (30 x 42 cm)
Photograph by Jean-Pierre Laffont
United Colors of Benetton, New York

42 JUKKA VEISTOLA (Finnish, born 1946)
UNICEF poster. 1969
Offset lithograph, 39 $^{1}/_{2}$ x 27 $^{1}/_{2}$" (100.3 x 69.9 cm)
The Museum of Modern Art, New York. Gift of
the designer

44 PAUL RAND (American, 1914–1996)
Poster for SOS Children's Village. 1996
33 $^{1}/_{16}$ x 23 $^{5}/_{8}$" (84 x 60 cm)
Museum für Gestaltung Zürich, Plakatsammlung

46 School-in-a-Box. 1994
Various materials, box: 9 5/8 x 31 1/8 x 23 1/4"
(24.5 x 79 x 59 cm)
Distributed by UNICEF United Nations
Children's Fund (est. 1946)
Courtesy of U.S. Fund for UNICEF

47 Bracelet of Life, Middle Upper Arm
Circumference (MUAC) measuring device. 1994
Polypropylene, 12 3/4 x 3/4" (32.4 x 1.9 cm)
Distributed by Doctors Without Borders
(Médecins Sans Frontières) (est. 1971)
Manufactured by Trapinex Sérigraphie-Offset, France
The Museum of Modern Art, New York. Gift of Doctors
Without Borders/Médecins Sans Frontières (MSF)

and local nongovernmental organizations, as well as of UNICEF, the program's coordinator, and the work of these groups culminated ten years later, in 1989, in the Convention on the Rights of the Child.

The convention, a landmark human-rights treaty, created guiding principles for state and local governments as well as for UNICEF and other international aid organizations, and it has been ratified by every member of the United Nations except for the United States and Somalia.[5] Drawing on various legal and cultural systems, it established a set of nonnegotiable standards for children's health care, education, and legal, civil, and social services. It was the first enforceable international treaty to set forth a full range of human rights for children (the 1959 declaration was nonbinding), from the right to survival and protection from harmful influences, abuse, and exploitation to full development and participation in family, cultural, and social life.[6] Advocates, including Marian Wright Edelman of the Children's Defense Fund, have reminded us that these liberties require constant watch and activism everywhere, including in prosperous nations like the United States.[7]

To advocate for and further the rights and well-being of the universal child, designers have applied their talents to powerful graphics and functional products in service of the fund-raising, research, and field activities of aid organizations. Good graphic design can send powerful messages with minimal text, as do UNICEF's photographic campaigns promoting nutrition and clean water, designed by Jukka Veistola (no. 42), who won first prize in a 1969 UNICEF poster competition in Paris, and Jung von Matt (no. 43), a firm that did pro bono work for UNICEF's office in Sweden. Paul Rand's depiction of a child balancing on a textual tightrope (no. 44) — playful but precarious — was designed to promote SOS Children's Village, an international charity for orphaned and abandoned children. The poster, which incorporates an intriguing detail of *Children's Games* (1560), by Pieter Bruegel the Elder, is thought to be Rand's last work before his death.[8]

Promotional graphics often blur the boundary between aid and commercialism, with designers drawing on the conventions of one to enhance the impact of the other. Designers Éva Kémeny (a Holocaust survivor) and László Sós (her husband) juxtaposed deprivation and comfort by integrating, in a photocollage meant to raise awareness of extreme child hunger, images of starving children (standard in aid campaigns)

with a healthy girl and her pampered pet (more suggestive of cat-food advertising) (no. 40). Conversely, Benetton, the Italian clothing company, used images from current events — the AIDS epidemic, racial conflict, political violence and exile — to create obliquely promotional graphics for commercial goods. The controversy over these radical advertisements reached a peak in the 1980s and '90s, during the tenure of creative director Oliviero Toscani, but an early example depicting child laborers in Colombia was created for the International Year of the Child (no. 45). Such fearless (as well as productless and captionless) designs achieved an effective if uncomfortable balance between cultivating social awareness through "shock of reality" advertising (as the campaign was named in the early 1990s) and profiting from real human suffering.

In disaster situations and conflicts involving children, both objects and their systems of distribution must perform quickly and efficiently. Aid organizations such as UNICEF and Doctors Without Borders rely on

48 NICHOLAS NEGROPONTE (American, born 1943), REBECCA ALLEN (American, born 1953), MARY LOU JEPSEN (American, born 1965), MARK FOSTER (American, born 1960), MICHAIL BLETSAS (Greek, born 1967), and V. MICHAEL BOVE (American, born 1960) of ONE LAPTOP PER CHILD (USA, est. 2005); YVES BÉHAR (Swiss, born 1967) and BRET RECOR (American, born 1974) of FUSEPROJECT (USA, est. 1999); JACQUES GAGNÉ (Canadian, born 1959) of GECKO DESIGN (USA, est. 1996); COLIN BULTHAUP (American, born 1976) of SQUID LABS (USA, est. 2004); JOHN HUTCHINSON (South African, born 1952) of FREEPLAY ENERGY PLC. (England, est. 1996); and QUANTA, Taiwan (China, est. 1988)
XO Laptop from the One Laptop per Child project. 2005–ongoing
PC/ABS plastic, rubber, and other materials, 9 1/2 x 9 x 1 1/8" (24.2 x 22.8 x 3 cm)
Manufactured by Quanta, Taiwan (est. 1988)
The Museum of Modern Art, New York. Gift of Yves Béhar/fuseproject

the logic and methodical structure of design thinking in the development of new tools for responding to pressing needs in the field. UNICEF's School-in-a-Box (no. 46), part of the Inspired Gifts series of products and kits, whose proceeds support nutrition, vaccination, and education for children in need, is a compact metal case containing the materials to set up a makeshift school for eighty students: writing materials, teaching clock, tape measure, scissors, plastic blocks for counting, and exercise books. The box itself is robust enough for shipment and lockable for safe storage, and the inside of the lid can be coated with chalkboard paint (which is provided). Thanks to designs like this, education continues to play a part in emergency response, gathering children in safe spaces and fostering positive development and a comforting sense of normalcy.

Another valuable design for children is the Bracelet of Life (no. 47), first implemented in 1998 during a devastating famine in Sudan and available on the Doctors Without Borders website for printing.[9] The bracelet allows emergency volunteers to quickly assess the level of malnourishment in children under five years old by fitting the plastic band around a child's upper arm. Appropriate treatment for malnourished children, in the form of ready-to-use therapeutic food packets (such as Plumpy'nut, a peanut butter–like paste), are themselves the products of thoughtful design: the packets are sealed against contamination, come in individual servings to prevent unhygienic sharing, and require no additional water or heating.[10]

Design is also used in projects intended to give children more equal footing with their universal peers and assist in local and regional development, such as recent initiatives that have focused on bridging the digital divide.[11] The XO Laptop (no. 48) was an inexpensive computer, conceived in 2005 by One Laptop per Child (a nonprofit organization started at the MIT Media Lab), with the design studio fuseproject, that has been distributed by governments and nongovernmental organizations to schools throughout the developing world. The laptop was specifically adapted to the needs and habits of children without looking like a toy: it was the size of a textbook and lighter than a lunch box, with soft edges, a handle, and a rubber keyboard; it was recyclable, drop-proof, splash-proof, and dust-proof; it could be manually recharged; and its wireless antennae resembled playful rabbit ears.[12] More than seven hundred thousand XO Laptops, many equipped with the innovative and child-friendly interface Sugar (which was designed in 2006–07 with the design firms Pentagram and Red Hat), have been distributed in Argentina, Brazil, Cambodia, China, Ethiopia, Libya,

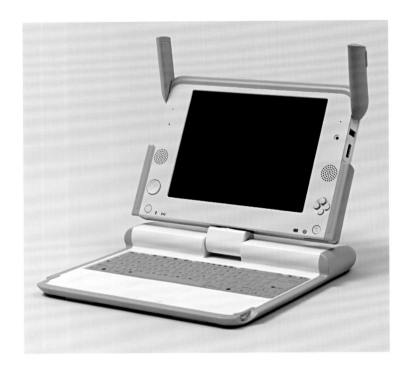

Mexico, Mongolia, Nigeria, Pakistan, Paraguay, Peru, Romania, Rwanda, Thailand, and Uruguay. A newer model, XOXO, was developed with feedback from children and released in 2010.

A program called Hole-in-the-Wall uses a different approach, one based on collaboration, to provide interactive learning stations for children in urban slums and rural locations in India, Bhutan, Cambodia, and, recently, in parts of Africa (nos. 49, 50). The project originated with an experiment conducted by Sugata Mitra, a scientist and education researcher, who in 1999 knocked a hole in the wall that separated his office building from a slum in the Kalkaji neighborhood of New Delhi and inserted a desktop PC with a touch pad and high-speed Internet connection. Amazed by the active response and quick browsing abilities of children with little or no experience with computers or even television, Mitra extended the experiment to rural areas and reported that children, unstructured and unsupervised in self-organized groups, rapidly and steadily acquired computer skills and Internet basics (as well as simple English). Through interviews, expanded testing, and statistical analysis, Mitra eventually concluded that with this kind of computer access, six- to thirteen-year-old children can teach themselves, and that with a single computer over the course of three months, more than three hundred children can become computer literate: proficient with basic

navigating functions, browsing, playing games, chatting and e-mail, downloading music, and playing with educational software.[13] Hole-in-the-Wall Education Limited was established to support this departure from conventional computer-based learning in the classroom, and in addition to providing computers, the organization has designed rugged and tamperproof learning stations that protect mass-market PCs in various extreme weather conditions. The stations are remotely monitored and regularly maintained, with fault-tolerance systems to keep software running and protective covers for the hardware. There are now six hundred such stations through which Mitra's pedagogical approach, Minimally Invasive Education, is stimulating further investigation into new alternatives to primary-education models and reinforcing the ability of children to assist and benefit from their peers, both immediate and universal.

Aidan O'Connor

51 SAUL BASS (American, 1920–1996)
Longwood Development – Recreational Park
Design. c. 1961
Saul Bass papers, Margaret Herrick Library,
Academy of Motion Picture Arts and Sciences

BY THE EARLY 1960S two major developments in playground design had shattered conventional ideas about environments for play and had revealed as outmoded and inadequate the standard kit of parts — swings, slides, seesaws. The first was the radical junk or adventure playground pioneered by Carl Theodor Sørensen in Copenhagen in 1943, during the German occupation, an idea that spread throughout Scandinavia and into the Netherlands and Britain in the 1950s and '60s. Images circulated in the press of children sawing, hammering, digging, and zip-lining in bomb sites and desolate lots, establishing that playgrounds could be dynamic, rough (with, its advocates have maintained, only an illusion of danger), and educational.[1] The second development was play sculpture, which posited, as *Architectural Review* explained, a "new relationship between art and citizen."[2] Abstract, often freestanding structures satisfied the notion that modern design could make playgrounds beautiful while providing new and artistic forms for imaginative recreation; the movement generated photogenic results (such as the colorful Ägget [The egg], by Danish artist Egon Møller-Nielsen, in Stockholm) that were celebrated in highbrow periodicals, and it peaked with the Play Sculpture project at The Museum of Modern Art in 1953–54 (see "'Developing Creativeness in Children': Victor D'Amico at MoMA," p. 180).[3]

In the 1960s, however, critics turned on the idea of play sculpture, calling it static, slick, and more suited to adult sensibilities than children's,

and it also became clear that the adventure-playground concept was not always practicable beyond its war-damaged places of origin.[4] Over the last several decades, new play environments have combined features of these models, in designs fueled by modern ideas about the agency of children, engagement with nature, and potential social impact. As a result, the playground revolution (a term originating in the 1960s) has been an ongoing transformation of design thinking and practice, and in spite of hindrances, failures, and criticism, it has produced innovative playgrounds around the world.

Its early years were defined by attention to play environments in poor urban areas, in the interest of creating socially responsible design and curbing juvenile delinquency. This objective activated educators, philanthropists, parents, and politicians as well as designers from various backgrounds. The graphic designer Saul Bass, best known for his film titles and corporate logos, imagined uplifting play environments for children in low-income housing projects; one such design, although never realized, was conceived for a development called Longwood, with landscaping and sculptural elements creating different activity zones (no. 51). In 1964 MoMA (led by Victor D'Amico and Arthur Drexler, director of the Department of Architecture and Design), along with the Citizens' Committee for Children and the Park Association of New York City, commissioned architect Charles Forberg to design a playground (no. 52) at the Cypress Hills Houses in the East New York

52 CHARLES FORBERG & ASSOCIATES
(USA, est. 1948)
Playground model for Cypress Hills Houses,
Brooklyn. 1964
5 x 19 ¹/₂ x 21 ³/₄" (12.7 x 49.5 x 55.2 cm)
The Museum of Modern Art, New York. Gift of
the architect

53 COLIN GREENLY (British, born 1928)
Design for Wishbone House, winning design
from the Corcoran Gallery School of Art's
National Playground Sculpture Competition, 1967,
as reproduced in *Art in America*, vol. 55 (no. 6),
November–December 1967
Photograph by Victor Amato
The Museum of Modern Art, New York. Department
of Architecture and Design Study Center

section of Brooklyn, a high-rise development housing more than 1,400 families.[5] Forberg's circular environment for young children, seventy-two feet in diameter, was dominated by a forest of seven-foot-tall vertical concrete slabs, to encourage running and hiding while providing shade and shelter. The space was illuminated by one large, elevated spherical lamp in the center, emphasizing the site's sculptural qualities. The playground was admired by critics when it opened in 1967, but there were serious safety concerns, primarily regarding parental sight lines, and the site was eventually renovated with standard equipment.[6]

A more successful sculptural project emerged in 1964 from the Corcoran Gallery School of Art's National Playground Sculpture Competition, supported by the National Endowment for the Arts. Artist Colin Greenly's winning design, Wishbone House (no. 53), was a six-foot-high precast concrete A-shaped frame that encouraged both active climbing and quiet play in the shaded bench area within. For this project Greenly considered, as he explained, "playground, sculpture, climb on, climb in, sit on, shade essential, minimum upkeep, maximum shape, minimum cost, reproducibility."[7] He objected to the placement of the original cast in a wealthy section of Washington, D.C., and Lady Bird Johnson arranged for a second installation in an underserved neighborhood. Others followed, and multiple Wishbone Houses still exist today, including at the Potomac School in McLean, Virginia.[8]

Although he had long been invested in revolutionizing play-grounds, Japanese-American sculptor Isamu Noguchi declined to participate in the Corcoran competition. His unique and fantastical proposals for playscapes of molded earthworks and abstract structures for New York City (Play Mountain [1933], United Nations Playground [1952], Riverside Park Playground [1960–61]) had been thwarted for decades by Robert Moses, the city's parks commissioner, who believed them too different, dramatic, and expensive.[9] In 1964, after a particu-larly bitter legal struggle over the Riverside project, a collaboration with architect Louis I. Kahn, Noguchi despaired, but he hopefully predicted, "I do not doubt that the cause will now bloom."[10]

Landscape architect M. Paul Friedberg and architect Richard Dattner, friendly rivals who were directly inspired by Noguchi's designs and by adventure playgrounds, became leading figures of the playground revolution. Aided by the new parks commissioner, Thomas Hoving, they established New York as the movement's epicenter. Hoving's appoint-ment in 1965 took place the same year that Lady Allen of Hurtwood, an advocate of adventure playgrounds, visited New York, Boston, Philadelphia, Baltimore, and Washington, D.C., and criticized the

average American playground as "an administrator's heaven and a child's hell." "I think it's better," she opined, "to risk a broken leg than a broken spirit."[11]

Both Friedberg and Dattner were advocates of experiential, active play encouraged by diverse component structures or zones and manipulable materials such as sand and water. Complexity and continu-ous challenges, they agreed, were the key to enriching the learning experience inherent in play. Both published manifestos on this subject: Dattner's Design for Play, in 1969, and Friedberg's Play and Interplay, in 1970. In 1965 Friedberg designed and executed (in only ten months) a public playground for the Jacob Riis Houses, a development with eight thousand residents on the Lower East Side. The project, funded by the Astor Foundation, was a compound environment, also used for theatrical performances by adults, with an exciting topography of mounds, pyramids, metal arches, and a tree house, with elements of sand, water, stone, and wood. For his temporary, movable playgrounds — easy to dismantle and reassemble elsewhere — Friedberg successfully experimented with low-cost, prefabricated, and modular parts, and he stimulated communities with his vest-pocket playgrounds and parks on modest quarter-acre sites in dense neighborhoods.

Dattner experimented with new kinds of playgrounds, such as the short-lived Check-a-Child in Union Square in 1967 and accessible playgrounds for children with physical disabilities. He designed six playgrounds in Central Park, including the Adventure Playground (no. 54), at Sixty-seventh Street and Central Park West, in 1967, and the Egyptian-themed Ancient Playground north of the Metropolitan Museum of Art.[12] The Adventure Playground was covered with sand, which Dattner appreciated for activating the surface as well as for keeping adults at bay, and featured climbing pyramids, a splashing pool, an

55 LINA BO BARDI (Brazilian, born Italy. 1914–1992)
Preliminary study for play sculptures for the
Belvedere Museum of Art Trianon, São Paulo. 1968
Collage, ink, and watercolor on paper, 22 ¹/₈ x 30 ¹/₈"
(56.2 x 76.5 cm)
MASP, Museu de Arte de São Paulo Assis
Chateaubriand

56 HUGO KÜKELHAUS (German, 1900–1984)
Designs for a bicycle-powered *Wasserstrudel*
(Whirlpool) for Expo 67, Montreal. 1967
Colored pencil on paper, 23 ¹/₁₆ x 17 ¹/₈" (58.5 x 43.5 cm)
Stadt Soest, Stadtarchiv, Nachlass Hugo Kükelhaus

amphitheater, a hill-in-a-hill, a tree pit, a volcano, tunnels, and slides. With private funding, Dattner was able to introduce and maintain unconventional features such as adult play facilitators and loose elements (planks, blocks, slotted boards, bamboo sticks, sacks, paper, and paint) for building and creative experimentation.[13] Friedberg's and Dattner's playground designs were taken up so quickly that by the early 1970s the *New York Times* was remarking that "the New Left of playground designers has practically become Establishment."[14]

Innovative playground designs with progressive social agendas were hardly exclusive to New York or the United States in this period. In 1968 modernist architect Lina Bo Bardi envisioned a large playscape that would cover the public square behind the Museu de Arte de São Paulo, which she had designed (no. 55).[15] The playscape — a vast, open area juxtaposing the glass and concrete museum facade with a colorful animal merry-go-round, ribbonlike slides, a cluster of climbing tubes, and a giant reflective globe — was an exercise drawn just before the museum opened.[16] It would have complimented her whimsical design inside the museum, where freestanding plexiglass panels allowed viewers to choose their own paths through painting installations. But her utopian vision for an inclusive play-centered public oasis was never realized; instead it became a favored location for displays of authority by Brazil's military regime (in power until 1985) and now is commonly occupied by drug addicts and the homeless.

In Germany, Hugo Kükelhaus was less concerned about carving out public urban space than he was with using play to put children in touch with the wonders of the natural world. Kükelhaus, a master carpenter who studied sociology, philosophy, mathematics, and physiology in Heidelberg, began designing for children in the 1930s, with a series of simple but "all-meaning," or *Allbedeut*, wooden toys for infants, inspired by watching his own young children play with clothespins. In the mid-1960s, after creating a *Naturkundliche* (nature trail) for the schools of Dortmund, Germany, Kükelhaus designed forty sculptural play-work stations to compose an "experience field for the senses" that illuminated principles of nature (gravity and balance, sound and hearing, color and sight).[17] A selection of these stations made their international debut in the German pavilion at Expo 67, in Montreal, where visitors of all ages could engage, for example, with a bicycle-powered *Wasserstrudel* (whirlpool) (no. 56).

The Israeli *chatzar grutaot*, or junkyard playground (no. 57), another educational playground intended to engage the senses and body, originated with Malka Haas, in her design for Sde Eliyahu,

a kibbutz in the Jordan Valley. Haas, a teacher, has studied children's creativity since the 1950s. At Sde Eliyahu she developed a network of kindergarten junkyard playgrounds, each for approximately twenty children to use throughout the day. These playgrounds, in outdoor yards that are seen as extensions of the classroom, have become a critical part of the early-childhood programs (*gan hayeladim*) of many kibbutzim. Here, young children build and play with pipes, old pieces of fabric, large wooden spools, metal drums, and machinery parts — materials that have belonged to adults but are given new meaning through the innate creativity of children.

A similar perspective on "junk" informed a rural play landscape planned for a hillside outside the Hungarian town of Zalaegerszeg, although never realized. The project, an alternative to regimented Soviet Pioneer camps, was devised in conjunction with the 1979 Zalaegerszeg Space and Form Symposium and conceived as a miniature universe, with elements of earth, fire, and water to encourage discovery and growth. One of its main features was to be an excavation area of sandpits with submerged objects for children to unearth like archaeologists, including giant nonsensical machines that were carved from wood by the performance artist and sculptor Imre Bukta (no. 58) and other relics

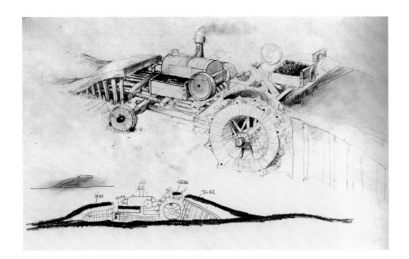

of an imaginary industrial society. Bukta and his immediate circle were a group of dissident (although not all anti-Communist) artists known as the Nomadic Generation, including architect Imre Makovekz. Inspired by the educational philosophy of Rudolf Steiner, Makovekz pioneered the new organic architecture in Hungary, with its politically inflected natural and vernacular characteristics.[18]

The spirit of the Zalaegerszeg project was unwittingly reincarnated in 2008 at Geopark (no. 59), a public play area in the city of Stavanger, Norway's oil capital, created in partnership with the Norwegian Petroleum Museum, that is an outstanding tribute to both play and ethics. Architects Siv Helene Stangeland and Reinhard Kropf (of the firm Helen + Hard) initiated and built this experimental project, which transforms redundant material from the petroleum industry into objects of play. The park takes its form from the topography of a vast underwater natural gas and oil field in the North Sea, called Troll, and is itself a 1:500 scale model of it. Bright orange buoys, salvaged pipelines, and recycled drilling platforms form bike ramps and interactive play spaces for running, climbing, and jumping, delineated on one side by a wall for graffiti. By conducting workshops with different community groups, Helen + Hard was able to incorporate the opinions of young people in the park's design, in accordance with the idea that sustainable practices depend not only on materials and building methods but also on fostering a supportive network of industry representatives and regular citizens, children included.

Playgrounds remain touchstones and rallying points for the well-being of children in the modern world; they are still a critical part of the discourse among designers, parents, educators, and politicians — fiercely debated and widely scrutinized (David Rockwell's Imagination Playground, which opened in Lower Manhattan in 2010 and revives the adventure playground's loose parts and adult facilitators, is a particularly high-profile example).[19] As values and concerns have shifted — changing ideas about accessibility, safety and liability, environmental regulations, and demographic needs — many of the designs of the playground revolution have been compromised or completely demolished, and play advocates decry the homogenous equipment that has taken their place.[20] Activists are working to enrich play landscapes

beyond their current post-and-platform conventions, stir up parents and teachers, and combat indifference and risk aversion. Their work draws on and moves forward the pleas and passions of their twentieth-century predecessors, while the playground endures as a thorny but rich area for future innovation.[21]

Aidan O'Connor

58 IMRE BUKTA (Hungarian, born 1952)
Design for an adventure playground in Zalaegerszeg, Hungary, as reproduced in folio of project proposals published in conjunction with the Space and Form Symposium, organized by Ifjúsági Forum (Youth forum). 1979
Private collection, New York

59 HELEN + HARD AS (Norway, est. 1996)
(Siv Helene Stangeland [Norwegian, born 1966] and Reinhard Kropf [Austrian, born 1967])
Geopark, Stavanger, Norway. 2011
Photograph by Emile Ashley
Courtesy of the architects

HIDE AND SEEK: REMAPPING MODERN DESIGN AND CHILDHOOD

1 This lyrical monologue was written by Steve Reinke, a Canadian artist and writer born in 1963, as part of his fictionalized, autobiographical video omnibus *The Hundred Videos* (1996). The work is in the collection of The Museum of Modern Art, New York.
2 Philippe Ariès, *L'Enfant et la vie familiale sous l'Ancien Régime* (Paris: Plon, 1960). Published in English as *Centuries of Childhood: A Social History of Family Life*, trans. Robert Baldick (New York: Vintage, 1962), p. 125. Ariès tackled the uncritical Romantic conceptualization of children and childhood as determined in nature and set the direction of the socially inflected perspectives on childhood that have followed into the present day. See Hugh Cunningham, *The Invention of Childhood* (London: BBC, 2007).
3 Ellen Key, *Barnets århundrade* (Stockholm: Albert Bonniers Förlag, 1900). Published in English as *The Century of the Child*, trans. Marie Franzos (New York: G. P. Putnam, 1909). The book appeared in some thirteen other languages, including Japanese. By 1926 the German version had been printed in thirty-six editions.
4 "Murdering the Soul in Schools," a chapter of *The Century of the Child*, was originally published as an article in the journal *Verdandi* in 1891 and was followed by Key's elaboration of these ideas in *Bildning: Några synpunkter* (Stockholm: Albert Bonniers Förlag, 1897).
5 Originally published in Swedish as "Skönhet för Alla," a pamphlet with a cover designed by Carl Larsson. Published in English as "Beauty for All," in Lucy Creagh, Helena Kåberg, and Barbara Miller Lane, eds., *Modern Swedish Design: Three Founding Texts*, trans. Anne-Charlotte Harvey (New York: The Museum of Modern Art, 2008), pp. 32–57. See also Key, "Popular Education with Special Consideration for the Development of Aesthetic Sense," 1906, and Thorbjörn Lengborn's review of her writing, "Ellen Key (1849–1926)," in *Prospects: The Quarterly Review of Comparative Education* 23, nos. 3/4 (1993): 2–4.
6 *Ett Hem* (Stockholm: Albert Bonniers Förlag, 1899). The book includes a series of twenty-four watercolors that explore the house room by room, accompanied by text that weaves the scenes into an ideal image of happy family life. The German selection of the watercolors, published as *Das Haus in der Sonne* (The house in the sun) in 1909, sold forty thousand copies in three months. Since 1968 many versions, with new texts for children, have been published in Sweden, Denmark, Norway, Finland, the Netherlands, Germany, the United States, England, and Canada.
7 *The Century of the Child* included statistical materials about child labor in various European countries. The National Child Labor Committee was established in 1904, with headquarters in New York. Lewis Hine, who was hired in 1908, had studied sociology at The University of Chicago, Columbia University, and New York

University. Alfred H. Barr, Jr., the founding director of The Museum of Modern Art, was also on the committee.
8 "If the twentieth century deserves the label of the 'century of the child,' as it was christened by Ellen Key…then it must also be seen as the century of the child-consumer." Daniel Thomas Cook, "The Other 'Child Study': Figuring Children as Consumers in Market Research, 1910s–1990s," *Sociological Quarterly* 41, no. 3 (Summer 2000): 501.
9 George Boas, *The Cult of Childhood*, Studies of the Warburg Institute, no. 29, (London, Warburg Institute, 1966).
10 Jane Clark Chermayeff, "Monday Morning Introduction," June 18, 1990, 40th International Design Conference in Aspen, June 17–22, 1990, unpublished typescript.
11 Robert Krulwich, quoted in Chermayeff, "Growing by Design: The 1990 International Design Conference in Aspen; A Notebook," *Children's Environments Quarterly* 8, nos. 3/4 (1991): 89.
12 The work of Mike Kelley is one such example. See Anne Pontégnie, ed., *Mike Kelley: Educational Complex Onwards, 1995–2008* (Zurich: JRP/Ringier, 2009); and *Childish Things* (Edinburgh: Fruitmarket Gallery, 2010), a catalogue of an exhibition of art from the 1980s and '90s organized by David Hopkins. For cultural studies in this vein, see Shirley R. Steinberg and Joe L. Kincheloe, eds., *Kinderculture: The Corporate Construction of Childhood* (London: Open University Press, 1997); Willem Koops and Michael Zuckermann, eds., *Beyond the Century of the Child: Cultural History and Developmental Psychology* (Philadelphia: University of Pennsylvania Press, 2003); Neil Postman, *The Disappearance of Childhood* (1982; New York: Vintage Books, 1994); and Anne Higonnet, *Picture of Innocence: The History and Crisis of Ideal Childhood* (London: Thames & Hudson, 1998).
13 The existing literature has been dominated by three kinds of studies: monographic books that focus on one artist or designer (on Jessie M. King, Alvar Aalto, Antonio Vitali, Libuše Niklová, Bruno Munari) or on particular types of design (toys, furniture, books, kindergartens, playgrounds etc); studies of child-centered design within specific centers, countries, or periods; or studies in related disciplines such as material culture, anthropology, pedagogy, and psychology.
14 See Yvonne Brentjens, *Piet Zwart, 1885–1977. Vormingenieur* (Zwolle, the Netherlands: Waanders Drukkers, 2008).
15 Cecilia de Torres has begun to explore this rich topic in several catalogues and articles, such as "Torres-García's Toys: Deconstructing the Object," in José Librero Stals and Carlos Pérez, *Toys of the Avant-Garde* (Málaga: Museo Picasso Málaga, 2010), pp. 264–99.
16 See Beverley Gordon, "Women's Domestic Body: The Conceptual Conflation of Women and Interiors in the Industrial Age," *Winterthur Portfolio* 31, no. 4 (1996): 281–301; Penny Sparke, *As Long as It's Pink: The Sexual Politics of Taste* (London:

Pandora, 1995); and Pat Kirkham, ed., *The Gendered Object* (Manchester, U.K.: Manchester University Press, 1996).
17 For an analysis of gendered language in design criticism, see Naomi Schor, *Reading in Detail: Aesthetics and the Feminine* (New York: Routledge, 2006. See also Juliet Kinchin, "Interiors: Nineteenth-Century Essays on the 'Masculine' and 'Feminine' Room," in Kirkham, ed., *The Gendered Object*, pp. 12–18.
18 Douglas Newton's statement about children as a "savage tribe" is often quoted but hard to pin down to an original source. See, for example, Iona and Peter Opie, *The Lore and Language of Schoolchildren* (Oxford: Clarendon Press, 1959), p. 2.
19 This is the theme of Boas's *The Cult of Childhood* (see note 9) and has been most fully explored in Jonathan Fineberg's exhibition and catalogue *The Innocent Eye: Children's Art and the Modern Artist* (Princeton: Princeton University Press, 1997) and collection of essays, *Discovering Child Art: Essays on Childhood, Primitivism and Modernism* (Princeton: Princeton University Press, 1998).
20 Bruce Brooks Pfeiffer, *Treasures of Taliesin: Seventy-six Unbuilt Designs* (Carbondale: Southern Illinois University Press, 1985), plate 18. On the Rosenwald schools, see Mary Hoffschwelle, "Children and the Rosenwald Schools of the American South," in Marta Gutman and Ning de Coninck-Smith, eds., *Designing Modern Childhoods: History, Space, and the Material Culture of Children* (New Brunswick, N.J.: Rutgers University Press, 2008), pp. 213–32.
21 See Ezra Shales, "Toying With Design," *Journal of Design History* 22, no. 1 (2009): 3–26; and Anthony Burton, "Design History and the History of Toys: Defining a Discipline for the Bethnal Green Museum of Childhood," *Journal of Design History* 20, no. 1 (1997): 1–21.
22 The Alfred H. Barr, Jr., Papers in the MoMA Archives also indicate his involvement with the Children's Aid Society, the National Child Labor Committee, the Citizens' Committee for Children of New York City, the Association for the Mentally Ill Children in Manhattan, the Child Welfare League of America, and the League for Emotionally Disturbed Children.
23 See René d'Harnoncourt, *The Hole in the Wall* (New York: Alfred A. Knopf, 1931). D'Harnoncourt illustrated two children's books written by his friend Elizabeth Morrow, one of which, *The Painted Pig* (New York: Alfred A. Knopf, 1930), was inspired by his collection of Mexican toys.
24 Rudolf Steiner, "Practical Training in Thought," lecture, Karlsruhe, Germany, January 18, 1909, trans. Henry Monges and Gilbert Church, Rudolf Steiner Archive, wn.rsarchive.org/Lectures/19090118p01 .html.
25 Theo van Doesburg, "Le Planisme de Torres-García," 1929, quoted in Jorge Castillo et al., *The Antagonistic Link: Joaquín Torres-García–Theo van Doesburg*, trans. Donald Gardner (Amsterdam: Institute of Contemporary Art, 1991), pp. 68–69.
26 Marcel Breuer, quoted in Gyula Ernyey, ed., *Marcel Breuer: Principles and Results*,

trans. Balázs Sinkovits (Pécs, Hungary: Pannónia, 2010), p. 106.
27 "Rubik's Cube 25 Years On: Crazy Toys, Crazy Times," *The Independent*, August 16, 2007, www.independent.co.uk/news/science/rubiks-cube-25-years-on-crazy-toys-crazy-times-461768.html.
28 Walter Determann's utopian site plan of 1920 for a Bauhaus-Siedlung in Weimar included a Vorbereitungsschule für Kinder (Preparatory school for children), which was never built. The Cranbrook Educational Community was brought to fruition, including the Cranbrook School for Boys (1925–28), Brookside School Cranbrook (1925–29), and Kingswood School, for girls (1925–31).
29 Anni Albers, quoted in Gillian Naylor, *The Bauhaus Reassessed: Sources and Design Theory* (New York: E. P. Dutton, 1985), p. 109.
30 Thomas Pynchon. *Gravity's Rainbow* (1973; New York: Penguin, 1995), p. 419.
31 Svetlana Boym, *The Future of Nostalgia* (New York: Basic Books, 2001), pp. 345–46.
32 Krulwich, quoted in Chermayeff, "Growing by Design," p. 89.
33 Sarah Kember, *Virtual Anxiety: Photography, New Technologies and Subjectivity* (Manchester, U.K.: Manchester University Press, 1998), pp. 63–78.
34 See Steinberg and Kincheloe, eds., *Kinderculture*.
35 Key, *The Century of the Child*, p. 74.
36 See Postman, *The Disappearance of Childhood*; and Douglas Kellner, "Beavis and Butt-Head: No Future for Postmodern Youth," in Steinberg and Kincheloe, eds., *Kinderculture*, p. 98.
37 Trung Le, "Teaching Kids Design Thinking, So They Can Solve the World's Biggest Problems," Co.Design, March 16, 2011, www.fastcodesign.com/1663416/teaching-kids-design-thinking-so-they-can-solve-the-worlds-biggest-problems. Sir Ken Robinson has a similar take on the need for teaching lateral design thinking; see "Changing Paradigms," RSA Edge Lecture, London, June 16, 2008, www.thersa.org/events/video/archive/sir-ken-robinson.
38 "What is the Play Ethic?," The Play Ethic website, www.theplayethic.com/what-is-the-play-ethic.html. Pat Kane has expanded on this theme in *The Play Ethic: A Manifesto for a Different Way of Living* (London: Macmillan, 2004).

NEW CENTURY, NEW CHILD, NEW ART

Introduction

1 Friedrich Nietzsche, *Also Sprach Zarathustra: Ein Buch für Alle und Keinen*, 1883. Published in English as *Thus Spoke Zarathustra: A Book for All and None*, trans. Walter Kaufmann (New York: Modern Library, 1995), p. 26.
2 G. Stanley Hall frequently referred to a correspondence between childhood stages and evolutionary history as "recapitulation," a theme explored, for example, in his book *Adolescence: Its Psychology and Its Relations to Physiology, Anthropology,*

Sociology, Sex, Crime and Religion, 2 vols (New York: Appleton, 1904).
3 Hall, with some of his pupils, *Aspects of Child Life and Education*, ed. Theodate L. Smith (Boston: Ginn, 1907), p. ix.

The Kindergarten Movement: Building Blocks of Modern Design
1 Friedrich Froebel, *Die Menschenerziehung* (Keilhau, Germany: Verlag der allgemeinen deutschen Erziehungsanstalt, 1826). Published in English as *The Education of Man*, trans. Josephine Jarvis (New York: A. Lovell, 1885), p. 30.
2 Arthur Heygate Mackmurdo, "Autobiographical notes for Elinor Pugh," 1936, p. 2, unpublished manuscript, The William Morris Gallery, Walthamstow, U.K.
3 James Liberty Tadd, *New Methods in Education: Art, Real Manual Training, Nature Study* (New York: Orange Judd, 1899), pp. 9–10.
4 See, for example, Norman Brosterman, *Inventing Kindergarten* (New York: Harry N. Abrams, 1997); and Jonathan Fineberg, ed., *Discovering Child Art: Essays on Childhood, Primitivism and Modernism* (Princeton: Princeton University Press, 1998).

Glasgow: Children in the City Beautiful
1 Thomas Carlyle, quoted in James Pagan, *Sketches of the History of Glasgow* (Glasgow: Stuart, 1847), p. 105.
2 Hamish Davidson, "Interesting Sidelights on Mackintosh and His Work," manuscript dated May 8, 1968, for the *Glasgow Herald*, The Hunterian, University of Glasgow. The Mackintoshes' nephew, born in 1900 to the designers Frances Macdonald and Herbert MacNair, was named Sylvan, another example of the perceived connection between children and trees.
3 Toward the end of his career Charles Rennie Mackintosh designed a toy catalog for his major patron, W. J. Bassett-Lowke, a committed modernist and the force behind the toy-train market in Britain.
4 For a list of drawings, archival sources, and publications relating to Scotland Street Public School, see the University of Glasgow's online catalogue, *Mackintosh Architecture: Context, Making and Meaning*, www.mackintosh-architecture.gla.ac.uk/catalogue.
5 "Glasgow School Board: New South-Side School," *Glasgow Herald*, April 14, 1906, p. 5.
6 Mackintosh, "Seemliness," 1902, in *Charles Rennie Mackintosh: The Architectural Papers*, ed. Pamela Robertson (Oxford: White Cockade Publishing, 1990), p. 222.
7 Frank Lloyd Wright, quoted in Nikolaus Pevsner, *Pioneers of Modern Design: From William Morris to Walter Gropius* (1936; Harmondsworth, U.K.: Penguin Books, 1960), p. 214.

Chicago: Progressive Era Laboratory
1 Frank Lloyd Wright, "In the Cause of Architecture: VI. The Meaning of Materials—Glass," *Architectural Record* 64 (July 1928): 200. Quoted in Mark Dudek, *Schools and Kindergartens: A Design Manual* (Basel: Birkhäuser, 2007), p. 12.
2 Wright, *Frank Lloyd Wright: An Autobiography* (1932; Petaluma, Calif.: Pomegranate Communications, 2005), pp. 13–14.
3 Ada Louise Huxtable has noted that Wright had a somewhat distant relationship with his children and was acutely aware of his lack of paternal instincts. Huxtable, *Frank Lloyd Wright* (New York: Viking, 2004), pp. 104–05.
4 The original "Kindergarten Chats" were published over fifty-two issues of *Interstate Architect & Builder*, from February 16, 1901, through February 8, 1902.
5 Louis Sullivan, "Kindergarten Chats," reprinted in *Kindergarten Chats and Other Writings* (New York: Dover, 2012), p. 100.
6 This 1901–03 project is known as Hillside Home School II; Wright designed the original Hillside Home School, a Shingle-style predecessor, in 1887, the year he moved to Chicago. It was the first building he designed and completed on his own.
7 The residents and leader of Hull House also pushed for change at the national level, lobbying for women's suffrage and new child-labor laws. They helped pass the Juvenile Court Act in 1899, which ended the jailing of children under twelve. Hull House resident Julia Lathrop was appointed by President William Howard Taft to head the Children's Bureau (in the Federal Department of Labor) when it was first created, in 1912.
8 Jane Addams, *Twenty Years at Hull House* (New York: Macmillan, 1912), p. 106.
9 Ibid.
10 John Dewey, "My Pedagogic Creed," *School Journal* 54 (January 1897): 77–80. Reprinted in *The Collected Works of John Dewey: The Early Works*, vol. 5., ed. Jo Ann Boydston (Carbondale: Southern Illinois University Press, 1972), p. 93.
11 The Massachusetts Emergency and Hygiene Association opened sand gardens for Boston children in the late 1880s. Soon thereafter, small playgrounds were introduced by social workers in New York and Philadelphia. The movement picked up steam in the mid 1890s, with additional playgrounds in these cities as well as in Baltimore, Pittsburgh, Providence, Milwaukee, and San Francisco, usually sponsored by women's groups to keep children from playing in the streets.
12 Sadie American, "The Movement for Small Playgrounds," *American Journal of Sociology* 4 (1898): 309.
13 Jacob Riis's *How the Other Half Lives: Studies among the Tenements of New York* had been published by Charles Scribner's Sons in 1890.
14 Henry S. Curtis, "The Playground Survey," *American Journal of Sociology* 19 (May 1914): 799.
15 "President Says Get Playgrounds," *New York Times*, February 21, 1907.
16 Graham Romeyn Taylor, "How They Played at Chicago," *Charities and the Commons* 18, no. 18 (August 3, 1907): 471.
17 Ibid., p. 474.
18 Walter Wood, *The Playground Movement in America and Its Relation to Public Education* (London: HMSO, 1913), p. 19.
19 Ibid., p. 21.

Comics and Early Animation
1 The film's title card reads, "Winsor McCay, the Famous Cartoonist of the N.Y. Herald and His Moving Comics."

Rome: Modern Arts, Crafts, and Education
1 The Socialist Party in Italy was founded in 1892, and the related movement of *socialismo umanitario* was particularly strong in central and northern Italy, among artists, educators, philosophers, and politicians.
2 Associazione Culturale Arte Educatrice Museum Onlus, Rome, www.arteeducatrice.it/storia_nascita.htm.
3 Maria Montessori, *Il metodo della pedagogia scientifica applicato all'educazione infantile nelle case dei bambini*, 2nd rev. ed. (1909; Rome: E. Loescher, 1913), p. 51.
4 Ibid.
5 Montessori, *Il metodo della pedagogia scientifica applicato all'educazione infantile nelle case dei bambini* (Città di Castello, Italy: Lapi, 1909). The book was translated into more than twenty languages in subsequent years; the first edition in the United States was *The Montessori Method: Scientific Pedagogy as Applied to Child Education in the Children's Houses with Additions and Revisions by the Author* (New York: Stokes, 1912).
6 Alessandro Marcucci, quoted in Frank Martin Snowden, *The Conquest of Malaria: Italy, 1900–1962* (New Haven: Yale University Press, 2006), p. 81.

Living in Utopia: Children in the Gödöllő Arts and Crafts Colony
1 For a fuller discussion of such colonies, see Michael Jacobs, *The Good and Simple Life: Artist Colonies in Europe and America* (Oxford: Phaidon, 1985).
2 Aladár Körösfői Kriesch, "Művészi program," *Magyar Iparművészet* 12, no. 1 (1909): 1.

Vienna: Drawing Out the Child Within
1 Sigmund Freud's youngest daughter, Anna, went on to develop his ideas to include the psychoanalytic treatment of children themselves.
2 Franz Cižek, quoted in Francesca Wilson, *The Child as Artist: Some Conversations with Professor Cižek* (London: Save the Children Fund, 1920), p. 6.
3 See G. Bast et al., *Wiener Kinetismus: Eine bewegte Moderne* (Vienna: Springer, 2011).
4 Gustav Klimt, opening speech for 1908 *Kunstschau*, printed in the introduction to *Katalog der Kunstschau Wien 1908* (Vienna, 1908). Quoted in Peter Vergo, *Art in Vienna, 1898–1918* (London: Phaidon, 1975), p. 180.
5 Oskar Kokoschka, "...eine Bericht in Wort und Bild über meinen damaligen Seelenzustand," in *Mein Leben* (Munich: Bruckmann, c. 1971), p. 52. Translation by the author.
6 Richard Muther, "Die Kunstschau," *Die Zeit* (Vienna), June 6, 1908.
7 Fritz Wärndorfer, letter to Carl Otto Czeschka, Vienna, March 4, 1908, private collection, Hamburg. Translation by the author.
8 "Studio Talk," *The Studio* 44 (1908): 312.
9 Amelia Levetus, "Modern Viennese Toys," *The Studio* 38 (1906): 278.
10 On the contribution of Erika Klien, Marianne Ullmann, and Elisabeth Karlinsky to Viennese Kinetism, see Ulrike Matzer, "*Die drei Stars der Klasse: Klien–Ullmann–Karlinsky*," in Monika Platzer and Ursula Storch, eds., *Kinetismus Wien entdeckt die Avantgarde* (Ostfildern, Germany: Hatje Cantz, 2006), pp. 60–87. On Friedl Dicker, see "'This Is How the World Looks, My Child': Friedl Dicker in Vienna and Auschwitz," p. 138. Margareta Hamerschlag-Berger wrote an autobiographical account of her emigration to London and work with children and teenagers during and after World War II. Hamerschlag-Berger, *Journey into a Fog* (New York: Sheed and Ward, 1956). Emmy Zweybrück-Prochaska ran her own art school for children in Vienna and went on to publish and edit numerous books and magazine articles on crafts for children in Vienna and the United States, to which she emigrated in 1939.

AVANT-GARDE PLAYTIME

Introduction
1 Otto van Tussenbroek, *Speelgoed, Marionetten, Maskers en Schimmenspelen* (Rotterdam: W. L. & J. Brusse, 1925), p. 4. Cited in Petra Timmer, "The Dutch Avant-Garde and the Child," in Carlos Pérez, ed., *Infancia y arte moderno* (Valencia: IVAM Centre Julio González, 1998), p. 372.
2 Paul Scheerbart, quoted by Bruno Taut in a letter to the Crystal Chain, January 1, 1920, in Iain Boyd Whyte, ed. and trans., *The Crystal Chain Letters: Architectural Fantasies by Bruno Taut and His Circle* (Cambridge, Mass.: MIT Press, 1985), p. 34. The original letter is in the Akademie der Künste, Berlin.
3 "Innocent eye" is a phrase first used by British art critic John Ruskin in 1850, and the title of a landmark publication and exhibition, *The Innocent Eye: Children's Art and the Modern Artist*, organized by Jonathan Fineberg (Princeton: Princeton University Press, 1997).
4 Wyndham Lewis, quoted in Charles Harrison, *English Art and Modernism, 1900–1939* (New Haven: Yale University Press, 1994), p. 190.
5 Ellen Key, *The Century of the Child*, trans. Marie Franzos (New York and London: G. P. Putnam, 1909), p. 109. Key's book was originally published in two volumes under the Swedish title *Barnets århundrade* (Stockholm: Albert Bonniers Förlag, 1900).

The Crystal Chain and Architectural Play
1 Bruno Taut (using the pen name "Glas"), letter initiating the Crystal Chain correspondence, November 24, 1919, in Iain Boyd Whyte, ed. and trans., *The Crystal Chain Letters: Architectural Fantasies by Bruno Taut and His Circle* (Cambridge, Mass.: MIT Press, 1985), p. 19. The group was also sometimes known as the Glass Chain. The complete correspondence has been translated and edited by Whyte in his excellent volume.
2 Taut, letter to the Crystal Chain, December 26, 1919, in ibid., p. 25. The original letter is in the Akademie der Künste, Berlin.
3 Hans Scharoun, letter to the Crystal Chain, n.d., in ibid., p. 45.
4 Wenzel Hablik, letter to the Crystal Chain, n.d., in ibid., p. 28. The original letter is in the Hablik Collection, Itzehoe, Germany.
5 Little is known about Blanche Mahlberg, cited as the inventor of the blocks in the patent register, other than that she was married to Paul Mahlberg, a Berlin architect, poster designer, and member of the Deutscher Werkbund, and that she did a translation of H. G. Wells's *The Open Conspiracy: Blue Prints for a World Revolution* (1928) into German.
6 Taut, letter to the Crystal Chain, April 15, 1920, in Whyte, ed. and trans., *The Crystal Chain Letters*, p. 84.
7 Paul Scheerbart, quoted in Dennis Sharp, *Modern Architecture and Expressionism* (New York: George Braziller, 1966), p. 87. He was attracted to Berlin University by the lectures of Professor Weiss, under whom he studied mineralogy, geology, and crystallography.
8 Friedrich Froebel, *Autobiography of Friedrich Froebel* (Syracuse, N.Y.: C. W. Bardeen, 1889). Cited in Norman Brosterman, *Inventing Kindergarten* (New York: Harry N. Abrams, 1997), p. 29.
9 Wassili Luckhardt, letter to the Crystal Chain, n.d., in Whyte, ed. and trans., *The Crystal Chain Letters*, p. 31.

Performing the Modern: Swiss Puppets
1 Charles Baudelaire, "Morale du joujou" (1853), in *Œuvres complètes*, vol. 1 (Paris: Gallimard, 1975), p. 583.
2 The theater was founded at the initiative of Alfred Altherr, the director of the School and Museum of Arts and Crafts in Zurich and chair of the Swiss Werkbund.
3 See Gabrielle Buffet-Picabia, "Matières plastiques," *XXe siècle*, no. 2 (1938): 31–35.

Italy: The Unruly Child
1 Giacomo Balla and Fortunato Depero, from the Futurist manifesto *Riconstruzione futurista dell'universo* (March 11, 1915). Cited in Luigi Cavadini, "The Avant-Garde and Toys in Italy," in *Toys of the Avant-Garde* (Málaga: Museo Picasso Málaga, 2010), p. 183.
2 All furniture elements created by Balla were unique pieces and were not conceived for reproduction.
3 Maria Montessori, *L'autoeducazione* (Rome, 1916; Milan: Garzanti, 1970), p. 17.
4 *Corriere dei piccoli* ceased publication in 1995.
5 The book *Cuore* by Edmondo De Amicis, published in 1886, a heartrending story of

a good child, was essential reading for two generations of very young children in Italy.
6 Rubino designed his children's rooms to be reproduced in small series. Gio Ponti also created a line of furnishings, La Domus Nova, for Rinascente during this same period.

De Stijl, Children, and Constructivist Play
1 In 1906, for example, a design reform association, Kunst aan het Volk (Art for the people), organized an exhibition titled *Kind en Kunst* (Children and art) at Amsterdam's Stedelijk Museum, showing an international range of children's books and toys. For a fuller discussion, see Petra Timmer, "The Dutch Avant-Garde and the Child," in Carlos Pérez, ed., *Infancia y arte moderno* (Valencia: IVAM Centre Julio González, 1998), pp. 372–76.
2 For more detail on this furniture, see Marijke Kiiper and Ida van Zijl, eds., *Gerrit Th. Rietveld: The Complete Works* (Utrecht: Centraal Museum, 1992).
3 Truus Schröder, interview by Lenneke Büller and Frank den Oudsten, 1982. First published in *Lotus International*, no. 60 (1988): 41. Cited in Alice T. Friedman, *Women and the Making of the Modern House: A Social and Architectural History* (New Haven: Yale University Press, 2007), p. 76.
4 See Martin Filler, "A Living Landmark," *House and Garden* (September 1984): 82–88.
5 Published in 1925 by Aposs Verlag, Schwitters's publisher in Hanover.
6 *The Montessori Method* was translated into Dutch in 1916, and the following year Maria Montessori lectured in Amsterdam and the Netherlands Montessori Association was established. In 1920 Montessori gave a series of lectures at the University of Amsterdam, and by the mid-1930s more than two hundred Montessori schools had been established in the Netherlands, including the open-air school in Amsterdam designed by Jan Duiker and the kindergarten in Wassenaar furnished by Piet Zwart (see "The New School," p. 99). In 1935 the headquarters of the Association Montessori Internationale moved permanently to Amsterdam.
7 Otto van Tussenbroek, article in *De Groene Amsterdammer*, June 23, 1928. Cited in Timmer, "The Dutch Avant-Garde and the Child," p. 372.
8 The column appeared in a magazine called *De Mosroene*. The book, titled *Wat Moeder kleine Kitty vertelde* (Amsterdam: Metz, 1923), appeared simultaneously in English (*What Mother Told Little Kitty*) and French (*Les Contes de maman à la petite Kitty*). See Petra Timmer, *Metz & Co.: De Creatieve Jaren* (Rotterdam: 010, 1995), pp. 62–66.

Bauhaus Play and Pedagogy
1 Johannes Itten, letter to Viennese artist Anna Hollering, December 15, 1919. Cited in Rolf Bothe, Peter Hahn, and Hans Christoph von Tavel, eds., *Das frühe Bauhaus und Johannes Itten* (Ostfildern-Ruit, Germany: Hatje Cantz, 1994), p. 451. Translation by Art in Translation. The text appeared almost verbatim in Itten's diary, which is in the Kunstmuseum, Bern.
2 For a recent example, see Barry Bergdoll and Leah Dickerman, eds., *Bauhaus 1919–1933: Workshops of Modernity* (New York: The Museum of Modern Art, 2009).
3 The exhibition, *Bauhaus 1919–1928*, concentrated almost exclusively on the last five years of Gropius's directorship of the school, between 1923 and 1928.
4 See Mark Dudek, *Kindergarten Architecture: Space for the Imagination* (London and New York: Spon Press, 2000), p. 34.
5 Itten, letter to Matthias Hauer, Weimar, November 5, 1919, in Willy Rotzler, ed., *Johannes Itten: Werke und Schriften* (Zurich: Orelli Füssli Verlag, 1978), p. 68. Cited in Éva Forgács, *The Bauhaus Idea and Bauhaus Politics* (New York: Oxford University Press, 1995), p. 55.
6 Mazdaznan, a branch of Zoroastrianism that Itten himself advocated, was one of the more extraordinary and problematic cults. See Paul Citroën, "Mazdaznan at the Bauhaus," in Eckhard Neumann, ed., *Bauhaus and Bauhaus People*, trans. Eva Richter and Alba Lorman (New York: Van Nostrand Reinhold, 1993), pp. 46–52.
7 Lou Scheper, quoted in Frank Whitford, ed., *The Bauhaus: Masters and Students by Themselves* (London: Conran Octopus, 1992), p. 94.
8 Oskar Schlemmer, quoted in Hans Wingler, *The Bauhaus: Weimar, Dessau, Berlin, Chicago* (Cambridge, Mass.: MIT Press, 1969), p. 65.
9 Subsequent editions were published under the revised title *Pioneers of Modern Design*. The 2005 edition by Yale University Press includes a historiographical introduction by Richard Weston. Susie Harries's recent biography *Nikolaus Pevsner: The Life* (London: Chatto & Windus, 2011) refers to the purchase of the Haus am Horn furniture and contextualizes the significance of Pevsner as a preeminent historian of modern design.

"Colorful, Specific, Concrete": Soviet Children's Books
1 El Lissitzky, quoted in Carlos Pérez, "The Child at the Heart of the Modern Utopia," in José Lebrero Stals and Carlos Pérez, eds., *Toys of the Avant-Garde* (Málaga: Museo Picasso Málaga, 2010), p. 65.
2 Translation by Susan Cook Summer. For Summer's full translation and a thorough discussion of *Samozveri*, see Susan Cook Summer and Gail Harrison Roman, "Autoanimals (Samozveri)," in *Art Journal* 41, no. 3 (Autumn 1981): 242–47.
3 According to Summer and Roman, it is thought that Rodchenko wanted to produce the images as actual pop-ups. He would use pop-up images in other works, including a 1935 issue of the journal *USSR in Construction* (no. 12).
4 Vladimir Lebedev, quoted in "Vladimir Lebedev," in Albert Lemmens and Serge Stommels, eds., *Russian Artists and the Children's Book, 1890–1992* (Nijmegen, the Netherlands: L. S., 2009), p. 344.

Manufacturing the Artistic Toy: Joaquín Torres-García and Ladislav Sutnar
1 Ladislav Sutnar, "Bauhaus from a Neighbour," reproduced in Iva Knobloch, *Mental Vitamins* (Prague: Museum of Decorative Arts, 2011), p. 44.
2 Joaquín Torres-García, "La recuperación del objecto, Lecciones sobre plástica," *Revista de la Facultad de humanidades y* ciencias (1952): 9. Cited in Cecilia Buzio de Torres, "Joaquín Torres-García: Art and Teaching," in Carlos Pérez, ed., *Infancia y arte moderno* (Valencia: IVAM Centre Julio González, 1998), pp. 354–58.
3 There is a copy of this advertisement, which dates from the late 1920s, in the collection of The Art Institute of Chicago.
4 From Sutnar's notes, archive of Ladislav Sutnar in the Museum of Decorative Arts, Prague. Cited in Iva Knobloch, "Mental Vitamins for the Future," in José Lebrero Stals and Carlos Pérez, eds., *Toys of the Avant-Garde* (Málaga: Museo Picasso Málaga, 2010), p. 219.
5 Ladislav Sutnar, *Visual Design in Action: Principles, Purposes* (New York: Hastings House, 1961), entry 22/b.

LIGHT, AIR, HEALTH

Introduction
1 Samuel A. Challman, "Some Observations as to the Character of Legislation Affecting Schoolhouse Construction," *The American School Board Journal* 62, no. 1 (January 1921): 41.
2 Dr. Benzion Liber, *The Child and the Home: Essays on the Rational Bringing-up of Children*, 3rd ed. (New York: Vanguard Press, 1927), p. 166.

The Healthy Body
1 Ellen Key, *The Century of the Child*, trans. Marie Franzos (New York and London: G. P. Putnam, 1909), p. 1. Key's book was originally published in two volumes under the Swedish title *Barnets århundrade* (Stockholm: Albert Bonniers Förlag, 1900).
2 Ibid., p. 5.
3 James Liberty Tadd, *New Methods in Education: Art, Real Manual Training, Nature Study* (New York: Judd, 1899), p. 48.
4 Rudolf Steiner, "A Lecture on Eurythmy," August 26, 1923.
5 Teacher training for women in physical education was offered at the Loheland Colony in Germany, established in 1919 by Louise Langgaard and Hedwig von Rohden.
6 Advertising copy on reverse of the flyer.
7 Jan Duiker, "Hoe is het met onze kleeding?" (What about our clothes?), *De 8 en Opbouw* (1932): 166. English translation reprinted in E. Jelles and C. Alberts, "Duiker 1890–1935," special issue of *Forum* 22 (January 1972; reprinted 1976): 136.
8 Aimé Dupuy and Marguerite Brunot, "Enfants à travers le monde," in *Le Visage de l'enfance* (Paris: Horizons de France, 1937), pp. 301–02. Translation by the author.
9 See, for example, M. Angles, "L'Éducation des enfants fragiles, malades, infirmes," pp. 199–215, and Marc Augier, "L'Enfant en plein air," pp. 133–96, in ibid.

At Home with Modernism
1 John Gloag, *Simple Schemes for Decoration* (London: Duckworth, 1922), p. 125.
2 Ibid., p. 129.
3 Ibid., p. 126.
4 As early as 1876 progressive architect-designer and critic E. W. Godwin had noted, "My chairs are light enough for a child to carry and strong enough for a child to clamber on." See "My house 'in' London. Chapter III," *Architect*, July 29, 1876, p. 59.
5 Dr. Benzion Liber, *The Child and the Home: Essays on the Rational Bringing-up of Children*, 3rd ed. (New York: Vanguard Press, 1927), pp. 23–24. Julia Grant discusses the medicalization of mothering in the interwar period in *Raising Baby by the Book: The Education of American Mothers* (New Haven: Yale University Press, 1998).
6 See, for example, Dorothy Canfield Fisher and Sidonie Matsner Gruenberg, *Our Children: A Handbook for Parents*, Child Study Association of America (New York: Viking Press, 1932).
7 Henri Clouzot, "Chambres d'enfants," *L'Illustration* (Paris), no. 4760 (May 26, 1934): 150. Translation by the author.
8 Le Corbusier, *Towards a New Architecture*, trans. F. Etchells (London: John Rodker, 1927), p. 115. Originally published as *Vers une architecture* (Paris: G. Cres & C., 1924).
9 Watson wrote, "Give me a dozen healthy infants, well-formed, and my own specified world to bring them up in and I'll guarantee to take any one at random and train him to become any type of specialist I might select—doctor, lawyer, artist—regardless of his talents, penchants, tendencies, abilities, vocations and race of his ancestors," though clinical psychologists note that the claim is generally taken out of context. Watson, *Behaviorism*, rev. ed. (Chicago: University of Chicago Press, 1930), p. 82.
10 John Littlejohns and A. Needham, *Training of Taste in the Arts and Crafts. With an Account of Investigations on Children's Preferences by A. Needham* (London: Sir Isaac Pitman, 1933), p. 6.
11 Ibid., p. 77.
12 See Allan Carlson, *The Swedish Experiment in Family Politics: The Myrdals and the Interwar Population Crisis* (New Brunswick, N.J.: Transaction Publishers, 1990), p. 61. The first such housing unit was built in 1935 at John Ericssonsgatan 6 in Stockholm. Markelius lived there himself for many years.

The New School
1 Stefan Zweig, *The World of Yesterday*, trans. Anthea Bell (London: Pushkin Press, 2009). First published in German as *Die Welt von Gestern* (Stockholm: Bermann-Fischer, 1942), p. 57.
2 Fritz Wichert, "Die neue Baukunst als Erzieher" (The new building art as educator), *Das Neue Frankfurt*, nos. 11/12 (1928): 233. Translation by Susan Henderson.
3 Beatrice Ensor, "A New World in the Making," lecture at the 1937 meeting of the New Education Fellowship in Melbourne, Australia, cited in K. S. Cunningham, ed., *Education for Complete Living* (Melbourne: Australian Council for Educational Research, 1938), p. 97.
4 This talented illustrator and picture book author, the niece of Sigmund Freud, was also noted for adopting a man's name and wearing men's clothing. After the failure of her husband's publishing venture and his suicide in 1929, she took her own life in 1930. Her books remained popular but many copies were destroyed during Hitler's regime.
5 Peter Meyer, quoted in Hochbaudepartement der Stadt Zürich, *Schulhausbau. Der Stand der Dinge/School Buildings: The State of Affairs* (German and English edition) (Basel: Birkhauser, 2004), p. 82.
6 Jan Duiker, "Een gezonde school voor het gezonde kind" (A healthy school for a healthy child), *De 8 en Opbouw* (1932): 88–92. Cited in Paul Overy, *Light, Air, and Openness: Modern Architecture Between the Wars* (London: Thames & Hudson, 2007), p. 129.
7 Maria Montessori, *Spontaneous Activity in Education*, trans. Florence Simmonds (New York: Frederick A. Stokes, 1917), p. 144.
8 Like Duiker's open-air school in Amsterdam, this still operates as a school.
9 See Kaj Gottlob, "Skolen ved Sundet," *Arkitekten* 40, nos. 11/12 (1938): 173–88; and Ning de Coninck-Smith, "A Danish Open-Air School by Kaj Gottlob (1935–1938)," in Anne-Marie Châtelet, Dominique Lerch, Jean-Noël Luc, *L'École de plein air: Une Expérience pédagogique et architecturale dans l'Europe du XXe siècle/Open-Air Schools: An Educational and Architectural Venture in Twentieth-Century Europe* (Paris: Éditions Recherches, 2003), pp. 346–53.

"A Setting for Childlife": The New School in the United States
1 In 1944 Elizabeth Mock organized a follow-up to this exhibition, *Built in USA: 1932–1944*, which surveyed the best American architecture since Philip Johnson's exhibition. Both Corona Avenue School (Bell, California) and Crow Island School (Winnetka, Illinois)—the case studies of this essay—were featured in this exhibition.
2 MoMA press release, "School Buildings in New International Style of Architecture in Modern Architectural Exhibit," February 26, 1932. The Museum of Modern Art Archives, New York.
3 MoMA press release, "Modern Style in School Architecture Attracts Educators," February 27, 1932. The Museum of Modern Art Archives, New York.
4 Lescaze arrived from Switzerland in 1920. Neutra arrived from Germany in 1923. Before settling in California, Neutra worked in New York and Chicago. When he first arrived in Chicago in March 1924 he stayed at Jane Addams's Hull House and taught children's art classes to earn his keep. See Thomas S. Hines, *Richard Neutra and the Search for Modern Architecture* (New York: Rizzoli, 2005), pp. 48–49.

5 Ibid., p. 164.
6 Nicholas Olsberg, "Open World: California Architects and the Modern Home," in Wendy Kaplan, ed., *California Design, 1930–1965: Living in a Modern Way* (Cambridge, Mass.: MIT Press, 2011), p. 117.
7 Kellee Frith and Denise Whitehouse, "Designing Learning Spaces That Work: A Case for the Importance of History," *History of Education Review* 38, no. 2 (2009): 99.
8 Hines, *Richard Neutra and the Search for Modern Architecture*, p. 181.
9 Washburne had come to his position from California in 1919. He was originally from Chicago, where his mother had connections to John Dewey and another local progressive education heavyweight, Francis Parker.
10 Grant Pick, "A School Fit for Children," *Chicago Reader*, February 28, 1991, http://www.chicagoreader.com/chicago/a-school-fit-for-children/Content?oid=877158.
11 Carleton Wolsey Washburne and Sidney P. Marland Jr., *Winnetka: The History and Significance of an Educational Experiment* (Englewood Cliffs, N.J.: Prentice-Hall, 1963), p. 139.
12 This scheme immediately preceded Saarinen and Eames' collaboration for the prizewinning furniture featured in MoMA's 1940–41 competition/exhibition *Organic Design in Home Furnishings*.
13 Pick, "A School Fit for Children," http://www.chicagoreader.com/chicago/a-school-fit-for-children/Content?oid=877158.
14 Washburne et al., "Crow Island School, Winnetka, Ill.," *Architectural Forum*, no. 75 (August 1941): 16.
15 Ibid.

Grete Lihotzky: From Vienna to Ankara
1 See, for example, her autobiographical account, Margarete Schütte-Lihotzky, *Warum ich Architektin wurde* (Salzburg: Residenz, c. 2004), and unpublished manuscript, *Das Kinderhaus in der Flachbausiedlung* (Vienna: University of Applied Arts, 1929).
2 See Susan Henderson, "'New Buildings Create New People': The Pavilion Schools of Weimar Frankfurt as a Model of Pedagogical Reform," *Design Issues* 13, no. 1 (Spring 1997): 27–38.
3 Day Care Center for Children, Rinnbockstrasse, Vienna.
4 See Sibel Bozdogan, *Modernism and Nation Building: Turkish Architectural Culture in the Early Republic* (Washington, D.C.: University of Washington Press, 2001).

Ernő Goldfinger and the Abbatts: From Toys to Urban Health
1 Goldfinger was secretary of the French chapter of CIAM in 1933. His design possibly influenced Le Corbusier's famed Unité d'Habitation in Marseille (1946). See James Dunnet, *AA Files*, no. 27 (1994): 102.
2 The couple met at an annual meeting of the Order in 1926. The Affirmation of the Order of Woodcraft Chivalry reads: "To respond to the call of the world of nature, seeking from it simplicity, good sense and fortitude. To pursue bravely and gaily the adventure of life, cherishing whatever it holds of beauty, wonder and romance, endeavouring to carry the chivalrous spirit into daily life." Order of Woodcraft Chivalry, at http://www.orderofwoodcraftchivalry.org.uk/. Accessed December 11, 2011.
3 Paul Abbatt, "The Child's World: Psychology in Toys and Games," *Design for To-day*, December 1933, p. 291.
4 His 1906 trial introduction of free school meals in a deprived area of Bradford had demonstrated a direct link between children's diet and educational performance. City of Bradford Education Committee Report by the Medical Superintendent, Ralph H. Crowley M.D., M.R.C.P., in

conjunction with the Superintendent of Domestic Subjects, Marian E. Cuff, on a Course of Meals given to Necessitous Children from April to July, 1907 (The National Archives, London).
5 In 1933 Franz Singer redesigned their new showroom at Midford Place, Tottenham Court Road, London (Goldfinger and F. R. S. Yorke redesigned the adjacent factory, offices, and stockroom). Milan Morgenstern and Helena Löw-Beer lived with the Abbatts when they first arrived in Britain.
6 Paul Abbatt, "The Child," draft script, 1937 (The Abbatt Archive, Victoria and Albert Museum of Childhood, London, ABBA 3/2/3).
7 Goldfinger was an air-raid warden but also on the Evacuation Committee of the Association of Architects, Surveyors and Technical Assistants. For more on the massive expansion of day and residential childcare during World War II, see Denise Riley, "War in the Nursery," *Feminist Review*, no. 2 (1979): 82–108.
8 Paul Abbatt, "The Child" draft script, 1937 (The Abbatt Archive, Victoria and Albert Museum of Childhood, London, ABBA 3/2/3).

To the Mountains and the Sea
1 The proceedings of international congresses on health and sanitation, manuals for government medical officers, and the establishment of university degrees in public health all contributed to the growing body of data about public health and the transmission of diseases.
2 Josep Lluís Sert, *Can Our Cities Survive? An ABC of Urban Problems, Their Analysis, Their Solutions. Based on the Proposals Formulated by the C. I. A. M., International Congresses for Modern Architecture* (Cambridge, Mass.: Harvard University Press, 1942).
3 When Meyer was dismissed from the Bauhaus on account of his outspoken communism in 1930, he led a group of architectural students to Moscow. From 1942–49 he directed the Instituto del Urbanismo y Planificación in Mexico City, and oversaw Mexico's postwar school-building program.
4 Hannes Meyer, quoted in Claude Schnaidt, *Hannes Meyer, Bauten, Projekte und Schriften* (London: Tiranti, 1965), p. 79. Translation by D. Q. Stephenson.
5 "Education requires a natural, social environment which to Pestalozzi was the *family circle*, or something which approximates it in the school. The home atmosphere creates a direct feeling for reality. It is an immediate, close environment, and enforces particular immediate relations adapted to future situations....Pestalozzi gathered twenty vagabonds and made a household of them." "Report of Dr John Dewey's Recent Lecture on Rousseau, Pestalozzi, Froebel and Montessori," *Kindergarten-Primary Magazine* 26, no. 7 (March 1914): 186.
6 Mario Labó and Attilio Podestà, "L'architeturra dell colonie marine italiane," *Casabella costruzioni*, no. 167 (November 1941). English translation reproduced in Stefano de Martino and Alex Wall, *Cities of Childhood: Italian Colonies of the 1930s* (London: Architectural Association, 1988), p. 78.
7 Photographers Dan Dubowitz and Patrick Duerden have recorded this dilapidation in their book *Fascismo Abbandonato* (Stockport: Dewi Lewis Publishing, 2010).

Urban Health: Two Centers
1 Innes H. Pearse and Lucy M. Crocker, *The Peckham Experiment: A Study in the Living Structure of Society* (London: Allen and Unwin, 1943).
2 Williamson, quoted in David Goodway, "Anarchism and the Welfare State: The Peckham Health Centre," May 2007,

History and Policy, http://www.historyandpolicy.org/papers/policy-paper-55.html.
3 Cited in Owen Hatherley, *Militant Modernism* (Ropley, UK: Zero Books, 2009), p. 10.
4 Churchill thought it to be "exaggerated and distorted propaganda," particularly for its implications of social neglect by the interwar government. See Catherine Moriarty, "Abram Games: An Essay on His Work and Its Context," in Naomi Games, Catherine Moriarty, and June Rose, *Abram Games, Graphic Designer: Maximum Meaning, Minimum Means* (Aldershot: Lund Humphries, 2003), pp. 65–68.

CHILDREN AND THE BODY POLITIC

Introduction
1 *Reichspost*, October 13, 1923. Quoted in Hans Bisanz, "Franz Cizek—Kunstpädagogik für das 'Jahrhundert des Kindes,'" in *Franz Cižek, Pionier der Kunsterziehung (1863–1946)* (Vienna: Kunsthistorisches Museum der Stadt Wien, 1985), p. 14. Translation by the author.

Pioneering the Revolution: Children in Soviet Russia
1 Leon Trotsky, "The Struggle for Cultured Speech," *Pravda*, May 15, 1923. Reprinted in Trotsky, *Problems of Everyday Life and Other Writings on Culture and Science* (New York: Monad Press, 1973), p. 53.
2 Tricia Starks, *The Body Soviet: Propaganda, Hygiene, and the Revolutionary State* (Madison: University of Wisconsin Press, 2008), p. 12.
3 Vitaly Zhemchuzhny, "Russland und Fotografie," in Edward Weston, ed., *Internationale Ausstellung des Deutschen Werkbundes Film und Foto* (Stuttgart: Deutscher Werkbund, 1929), p. 15. Cited in Margarita Tupitsyn, ed., *El Lissitzky: Beyond the Abstract Cabinet; Photography, Design, Collaboration* (New Haven: Yale University Press, 1999), p. 55.
4 El Lissitzky, *Russia: An Architecture for World Revolution*, trans. Eric Dluhosch (1930; Cambridge, Mass.: MIT Press, 1984), p. 57.
5 VOKS, *The School in the USSR* (Moscow: Soviet Union Society for Cultural Relations with Foreign Countries, 1933), p. 62.
6 R. R. Tomlinson, "Crafts for Children," special issue, *The Studio* (London), Winter 1935, pp. 62–63.

Who Has the Youth, Has the Future: The German Youth Movement
1 The German Youth, the junior branch of the Hitler Youth, was for boys from ten to fourteen years old.
2 See Walter Lacqueur, *Young Germany: A History of the German Youth Movement* (New York: Transaction Publishers, 1962); and Hermann Giesecke, *Vom Wandervögel bis zur Hitlerjugend* (Munich: Juventa-Verlag, 1981). Derek Linton's recent revisionist history, however, downplays the significance of the Wandervögel. Linton, *'Who Has the Youth, Has the Future': The Campaign to Save Young Workers in Imperial Germany* (Cambridge: Cambridge University Press, 1991).
3 Leslie Paul, *The Republic of Children: A Handbook for Teachers of Working-Class Children* (London: G. Allen and Unwin, 1938), p. 25.
4 Friedrich Froebel, quoted in ibid., title page.
5 The Social Democratic Party, a center-left party during the Weimar Republic, was abolished by Adolf Hitler in 1933. The Austrian and German Red Falcons drew inspiration from the Czechoslovak Sokol movement (*sokol* meaning "falcon") (see "The Healthy Body," p. 90).
6 Andreas Gayk, ed., *Die rote Kinderrepublik* (Berlin: Arbeiterjugend Verlag, 1930), title

page. Translation by the author. The book's graphic design was by Niels Brodersen and Richard Grune.
7 Kenny Cupers, "Making Camp: Landscape and Community in the Interwar German Youth Movements," unpublished paper presented at the conference "Making a New World? Re-forming/designing Modern Communities in Interwar Europe," Katholieke Universiteit Leuven, Flanders, June 2006.

Italy: Colonial Adventurers
1 Tracy H. Koon, *Believe, Obey, Fight: Political Socialization of Youth in Fascist Italy, 1922–1943* (Chapel Hill: University of North Carolina Press, 1985), pp. 90–91.
2 Philip V. Cannistraro, ed., *Historical Dictionary of Fascist Italy* (Westport, Conn.: Greenwood Press, 1982), p. 569.
3 Koon, *Believe, Obey, Fight*, p. 149.
4 Ibid., pp. 96–98.
5 Translation by the author.
6 Antonio Rubino edited and contributed to the publication from 1926 to 1929, when he was dismissed for political reasons. Katia Pizzi, "'L'intuizione del fantastico': Antonio Rubino, Futurist Manqué," *Modern Language Review* 94, no. 2 (April 1999): 396.
7 Mario Lupano and Alessandra Vaccari, *Fashion at the Time of Fascism: Italian Modernist Lifestyle, 1922–1943* (Bologna: Damiani, 2009), p. 200.
8 Giulia Barrera, "Dangerous Liaisons: Colonial Concubinage in Eritrea, 1890–1941," working paper for Program of African Studies, Northwestern University, Evanston, Ill., c. 1996, www.northwestern.edu/african-studies/docs/working-papers/wp1barrera.pdf.
9 Patrizia Palumbo, ed., *A Place in the Sun: Africa in Italian Colonial Culture from Post-Unification to the Present* (Berkeley: University of California Press, 2003), pp. 229–34; and Angelo Del Boca, *Gli Italiani in Africa Orientale*, vol. 2, *La conquista dell'impero* (Roma: Laterza, 1979), p. 459.

The Japanese Military Child
1 See John Dower, "Japan's Beautiful Modern War," in Jacqueline Atkins, ed., *Wearing Propaganda: Textiles on the Home Front in Japan, Britain, and the United States, 1931–1945* (New Haven: Yale University Press, in association with Bard Graduate Center for Studies in the Decorative Arts, Design, and Culture, New York, 2007), pp. 93–113.

A New Deal for Youth
1 Eleanor Roosevelt, quoted in "Blind Voting Hit by Mrs. Roosevelt—Concerned Over Youth," *New York Times*, May 8, 1934.
2 Robert Cohen, "How the Depression Affected Children," New Deal Network (Institute for Learning Technologies, Columbia University), newdeal.feri.org/eleanor/er2a.htm.
3 Franklin Delano Roosevelt, inaugural address, March 4, 1933. Reprinted in Davis W. Houck, *FDR and Fear Itself: The First Inaugural Address* (College Station: Texas A&M University Press, 2002), pp. 3–8.
4 A *New York Times* report on contemporary murals, "the newest architectural fashion," noted the influence of Mexican muralists, especially Diego Rivera, as well as the frequent appearance of child imagery. "Arts of democracy," public works for the enjoyment of the masses, were given new status: "Architectural art and industrial art are now the only two roads that will lead painting and sculpture out of the garret." Anita Brenner, "America Creates American Murals," *New York Times*, April 10, 1938.
5 Ibid.
6 Lucienne Bloch, who was born in Switzerland and studied at the École des Beaux-Arts in Paris, was an apprentice and friend of Rivera and Frida Kahlo and designed dozens of murals around

the United States while also working as a photojournalist and illustrating children's books.
7 "WPA Art Brightens New Women's Jail," *New York Times*, September 25, 1935.
8 Bloch, "Women's House of Detention Mural," Greenwich Village History, aphdigital.org/GVH/items/show/403.
9 "Women's House of Detention Protects the First Offenders—New York's Model Prison," *New York Times*, March 8, 1931.
10 United States Federal Works Agency, *Second Annual Report* (Washington, D.C.: U.S. Government Printing Office, 1941), p. 189.

"Sincerely Themselves": Child Art in Britain and Colonial West Africa
1 See Colin Rhodes, *Primitivism and Modern Art* (London: Thames & Hudson, 1994); and Richard Carline, *Draw They Must: A History of the Teaching and Examining of Art* (London: Edward Arnold, 1968), p. 177.
2 William Morris, "The Art of the People," 1879, in *The Collected Works of William Morris*, vol. 22, *Hopes and Fears for Art: Lectures on Art and Industry*, reprint ed. (New York: Russell and Russell, 1966), p. 36. On E. B. Havell, see Carline, *Draw They Must*, p. 174.
3 K[enneth] C. Murray, "The Condition of Arts and Crafts in West Africa, Part 1," *Oversea Education* 4, no. 4 (July 1933): 174.
4 On Marion Richardson's methods, see Richardson, *Art and the Child* (London: University of London Press, 1948); Peter Smith, "Another Vision of Progressiveness: Marion Richardson's Triumph and Tragedy," *Art Education* 37, no. 3 (Spring 1996): 170–83; and Stuart Macdonald, *The History and Philosophy of Art Education* (London: University of London Press, 1970), pp. 320–54.
5 Roger Fry, "An Essay in Aesthetics," 1909, in *Vision and Design* (London: Chatto and Windus, 1928), p. 20.
6 Fry, "Children's Drawings," *Burlington Magazine*, June 1917, p. 225. See also Richard Schiff, "From Primitivist Phylogeny to Formalist Ontogeny," in Jonathan Fineberg, ed., *Discovering Child Art: Essays on Childhood, Primitivism and Modernism* (Princeton: Princeton University Press, 1998), pp. 157–200.
7 Fry, "Children's Drawings," p. 226. The same point was made by Richardson in a speech to the Royal Society of Arts in 1937, item 3,047, no. 2, Marion Richardson Archive, Institute of Art and Design Archives, Birmingham City University.
8 Fry, "Negro Sculpture," 1920, in *Vision and Design*, p. 100.
9 See A. W. Pickard-Cambridge, "The Place of Achimota in West African Education," *Journal of the Royal African Society* 39, no. 155 (April 1940): 149–50.
10 Murray, "The Condition of Arts and Crafts in West Africa, Part 1," pp. 173–81; Murray, "The Condition of Arts and Crafts in West Africa, Part 2," *Oversea Education* 5, no. 1 (October 1933): 1–9. On *Oversea Education*, see Clive Whitehead, "'Oversea Education' and British Colonial Education, 1929–63," *History of Education* 32, no. 5 (September 2003): 561–75.
11 William Rothenstein, "The Development of Indigenous Art," *Oversea Education* 1, no. 1 (October 1929): 5. The show that inspired Rothenstein's article was *Exhibition of Drawing by Modern Gold Coast African Artists*, at the Imperial Institute, London, in 1929.
12 Ibid.
13 G[eorge] A[lexander] Stevens, "The Aesthetic Education of the Negro," *Oversea Education* 1, no. 3 (April 1930): 89.
14 Stevens, "The Educational Significance of Indigenous African Art," in Michael Sadler, ed., *Arts of West Africa (Excluding Music)* (London: Humphrey Milford, 1935), p. 17.
15 For an account of the school, see J. D. Clarke, *Omu: An African Experiment in Education* (London: Longmans, 1937). On Murray's subsequent career, see Frank Willett, "Kenneth Murray: Through the Eyes of His Friends," *African Arts* 6, no. 4 (Summer 1973).
16 Murray, introduction to *Nigerian Wood-Carvings, Terracottas and Water-Colours* (London: Zwemmer Gallery, 1937), p. 2.
17 Ibid.
18 Rothenstein, introduction to Sadler, ed., *Arts of West Africa*, p. x.
19 Stevens, "The Aesthetic Education of the Negro," p. 91.

"This Is How the World Looks, My Child": Friedl Dicker in Vienna and Auschwitz
1 Friedl Dicker, quoted in Elena Makarova, *Friedl Dicker-Brandeis: Vienna 1898–Auschwitz 1944* (Los Angeles: Tallfellow/Every Picture Press, 2001), p. 40.
2 Walter Gropius, letter of reference, April 19, 1931, Bauhaus-Archiv, Darmstadt, Germany.
3 When Franz Singer fled Vienna for London in 1934, the Abbatts supported him with a small commission.
4 See Angelika Romauch, "Friedl Dicker: Marxistische Fotomontagen 1932/33, Das Verfahren der Montage als sozialkritische Methode," MPhil thesis, Studienrichtung Kunstgeschichte, Geistes- und Kulturwissenschaftliche Fakultät der Universität Wien, 2003. Translation by the author. Romauch was unable to locate a source in Bertolt Brecht's published work for this poem and surmises the text is Dicker's.
5 Dicker, quoted in Makarova, *Friedl Dicker-Brandeis*, p. 31.
6 A manuscript of her lecture "Children's Drawings" survives in the Jewish Museum in Prague.
7 MoMA press release, "Concentration Camp Children's Art from Europe to be Compared with Work of D.P. Children in America," April 16, 1948. The Museum of Modern Art Archives, New York.
8 Ibid. The War Veterans' Art Center opened as an experiment in a small space on West Fifty-sixth Street. The program proved successful, and an expanded center opened in October 1944 around the corner from the Museum, on the second floor of 681 Fifth Avenue. Until 1948 the center provided therapeutic and prevocational art programs for thousands of veterans, helping them readjust to civilian life.
9 Viktor Lowenfeld had previously been involved with *The Arts in Therapy* at The Museum of Modern Art; he loaned artworks made by patients at the Vienna Institute for the Blind.
10 Lowenfeld, *Creative and Mental Growth: A Textbook on Art Education* (1947; New York: Macmillan, 1964), p. 1. Quoted in Maxine Borowsky Junge, *The Modern History of Art Therapy in the United States* (Springfield, Ill.: Charles C. Thomas, 2010), p. 19.
11 From 1950 to 1957 Edith Kramer created and directed an art-therapy program for children in New York, an outline of which was published in 1958 as *Art Therapy in a Children's Community* (it has since been republished by Schocken Books in 1977), and from 1959 to 1973 taught at the New School for Social Research. Her book *Art in Therapy with Children* (New York: Schocken Books, 1971), a classic in the field, has been published in seven languages. Her quote about Dicker comes from an interview in the film *Black and White Is Full of Colors* (1994).

Children and the Spanish Civil War
1 By 1937 some thirteen thousand new teachers had been trained and more than fourteen thousand new schools had been built.
2 Lorenzo Luzuriaga was also editor of the journal *Revista de pedagogía*, established in 1922. When the Republic fell, in 1939, he went into exile in Britain and later Argentina. His book *La escuela única* (The unique school), published in 1931 by *Revista de pedagogía*, was a foundational text for the Republican government's education policy. See M. del Mar del Pozo Andres and J. F. A. Braster, "The Reinvention of the New Education Movement in the Franco Dictatorship," *Paedagogica Historica* 42, nos. 1/2 (2006): 109–11.
3 The frontispiece to *La escuela única* shows the motto "Escuela única, activa, pública y laica."
4 Ernest Hemingway was the best-known foreign journalist writing regular articles for publications in the United States throughout 1938.
5 George Orwell, *Homage to Catalonia* (London: Secker and Warburg, 1938), p. 5.
6 See Anthony Geist and Peter N. Carroll, *They Still Draw Pictures: Children's Art in Wartime from the Spanish Civil War to Kosovo* (Champaign: University of Illinois Press, 2002).
7 Dorothy Parker, "No Axe to Grind," *Volunteer for Liberty* (Madrid) 1, no. 23 (November 15, 1937). Quoted in ibid., p. 46.

Growing Up in the Shadow of World War II: Children's Books and Games
1 Richard Minear, *Dr. Seuss Goes to War: The World War II Editorial Cartoons of Theodor Seuss Geisel* (New York: The New Press, 1999).
2 Marcia Blitz, *Donald Duck* (New York: Harmony Books, 1979), p. 133.
3 Donald Sturrock, *Storyteller: The Authorized Biography of Roald Dahl* (New York: Simon and Schuster, 2010).
4 "Birthday Bios: Munro Leaf," Children's Literature Network, www.childrensliterature network.org/birthbios/brthpage/12dec/12-04leaf.html; Philip Nel, "Children's Literature Goes to War: Dr. Seuss, P. D. Eastman, Munro Leaf, and the *Private SNAFU* Films (1943–46)," *Journal of Popular Culture* 40, no. 3 (June 2007): 468–87; and Lee Bennett Hopkins, "Munro Leaf," in *Pauses: Autobiographical Reflections of 101 Creators of Children's Books* (New York: Harper Collins, 1995), p. 117.
5 Yukio Sugiura and Fukujiro Yokoi, *Imoncho no Tsukurikata* (Tokyo: Rikugun Juppei-bu, 1943).

Processing Trauma
1 Bert I. Beverly, M.D., "Effect of War upon the Minds of Children," *American Journal of Public Health and the Nation's Health* 33, no. 7 (July 1943): 796, www.ncbi.nlm.nih.gov/pmc/articles/PMC1527649/pdf/amjphnation00697-0039.pdf.
2 Henri Storck, *The Entertainment Film for Juvenile Audiences* (Paris: UNESCO, 1950), p. 102.
3 See Jørgen Gaare and Øystein Sjaastad, *Pippi og Socrates: Filosofiske vandringer i Astrid Lindgrens verden* (Oslo: Huitfeldt, 2000).
4 Tove Jansson's drawings were first published when she was fourteen, in the children's section of the magazine *Allas Krönika*. See "Tove Jansson," Design Forum Finland, www.designforum.fi/tove_jansson_en.
5 MoMA press release, "Museum of Modern Art Opens Competition for Designs to Be Used in Therapy for Disabled Soldiers and Sailors," October 14, 1942. The Museum of Modern Art Archives, New York.
6 The Committee on Art in American Education was formed in October under MoMA's sponsorship and was led by Victor D'Amico, the Museum's first director of education. For this exhibition D'Amico helped prepare a continuously projected film illustrating the use of free media in creative therapy and psychotherapy.
7 MoMA press release, "Museum of Modern Art Opens Exhibition of Arts in Therapy for Disabled Soldiers and Sailors," February 1, 1943. The Museum of Modern Art Archives, New York.

REGENERATION

Introduction
1 The full text of Van Eyck's 1962 study was published in Vincent Ligtelijn and Francis Strauven, eds., *The Child, the City, the Artist* (Amsterdam: SUN, 2008). Van Eyck had used the quote on an exhibition panel in 1953.
2 Charles Eames, "Language of Vision," introduction to *Mathematica*, an interactive exhibition he designed with Ray for the Exploratorium in San Francisco in 1961. Quoted in Pat Kirkham, *Charles and Ray Eames: Designers of the Twentieth Century* (Cambridge, Mass.: MIT Press, 1995), p. 297.

"Children Asking Questions": Regeneration by Design
1 The group's name derived from the opening letters of the words Copenhagen, Brussels, and Amsterdam. Issue no. 4 of *CoBrA*, the group's magazine, from 1949, set out a vision of cultural regeneration and featured paintings by children.
2 United Nations Educational, Scientific, and Cultural Organization, *The Children of Europe*, no. 403 (Paris: UNESCO, 1949), p. 5.
3 For an English-language discussion of Borg's career, see Renja Suominen-Kokkonen, *The Fringe of a Profession: Women as Architects in Finland from the 1890's to the 1950's* (Helsinki: Muinaismuistoyhdistyksen aikakauskirja, 1992).
4 Birch-Lindgren's doctoral thesis of 1934 was on hospital design. See Astri Andresen, "'Never was there a more beautiful war memorial': The Children's Hospital in Bergen," *Lars Cultura y Ciudad*, no. 15 (2009): 26–31.
5 Herbert Matter had a personal commitment to this subject. The boy on the poster is his son Alex, who had suffered from polio.
6 United Nations Education and Scientific Organisation, *The Children of Europe*, no. 403 (Paris: UNESCO, 1949), p. 10.
7 Francis Strauven, "Aldo van Eyck and the City," in Vincent Ligtelijn, ed., *Aldo van Eyck: Works* (Basel: Birkhäuser, 1999), p. 31.
8 Aldo van Eyck, quoted in Vincent Ligtelijn, "Orphanage, Amsterdam," in ibid., p. 89.
9 Kauffmann, quoted in Galia Bar-Or and Yuval Yasky, eds., *Kibbutz: Architecture Without Precedents*, Israeli Pavilion, 12th International Architecture Exhibition, Venice Biennale (Tel Aviv: Top-Print, 2010), p. 129.
10 In some cases, children between the ages of twelve and eighteen were sent to a regional "institution" planned as a sort of miniature kibbutz providing for all of the children's needs. See ibid., p. 216.

New Starts: Japan and Poland
1 John W. Dower, *Embracing Defeat: Japan in the Wake of World War II* (New York: W. W. Norton & Co., 1999), p. 28.
2 Some 6.5 million Poles, out of a population of around 35 million in 1939, died in the war. Poland did not regain its prewar population levels until the 1970s. See Norman Davies, *Europe: A History* (Oxford: Oxford University Press, 1996). By 1945 almost eighty-five percent of the buildings in Warsaw had been destroyed.
3 For a further discussion of these designers and the general cultural context, see Czesława Frejlich, ed., *Out of the Ordinary: Polish Designers of the 20th Century* (Warsaw: Adam Mickiewicz Institute, 2011).
4 *Toys*, film directed by Andrzej Wolski and produced by the Adam Mickiewicz Institute, Warsaw, 2011.

Reclaiming the City: Children and the New Urbanism
1 Interview recorded in the film *Toys* directed by Andrzej Wolski and produced by the Adam Mickiewicz Institute, Warsaw, 2011.

2 See, for example, the 1947 British film *Hue and Cry*, directed by Charles Crichton, the first of the Ealing comedies.
3 Lady Allen of Hurtwood, "Why Not Use Our Bomb Sites Like This?," *Picture Post*, November 16, 1946.
4 Alison and Peter Smithson, "The 'As Found' and the 'Found,'" in David Robbins, ed., *The Independent Group: Postwar Britain and the Aesthetics of Plenty* (Cambridge, Mass.: MIT Press, 1990), pp. 201–02.
5 I am grateful to Tess van Eyck for sharing these panels with me.
6 Petr Skácel, "MVB + STM," *Blok* (special issue titled *Mládez Vede Blok* [The young lead Blok]) 3, no. 8 (1949): 286–88.
7 Arvid Bengtsson, *Environmental Planning for Children's Play* (New York: Praeger, 1970), p. 7.
8 Lady Allen of Hurtwood, "Symposium on Play in Different Settings," typescript of unpublished lecture, Paul and Marjorie Abbatt Archive, Victoria and Albert Museum of Childhood, London.

Back to School
1 "A Good Neighborhood Has an Elementary School" was the title of one of twelve didactic panels that were displayed at MoMA in the 1944 exhibition *Look at Your Neighborhood*. From 1944–50 the Museum's Department of Circulating Exhibitions traveled the exhibition throughout the country as a practical inspiration for postwar planning. MoMA promoted modern school design in traveling exhibitions that originated at the Museum, especially *Modern Architecture for the Modern School* (1942) and *Built in USA* (1953).

Good Toys
1 Lady Allen of Hurtwood, a founding president of OMEP, stated, "Play is not a trivial thing; it is the business of childhood. It is the means by which they learn to think and to feel. It is the basis of all later learning and living." Lady Allen of Hurtwood, "Symposium on Play in Different Settings," typescript of unpublished lecture, Paul and Marjorie Abbatt Archive, Victoria and Albert Museum of Childhood, London.
2 Alva Myrdal, *Riktiga Leksaker* (Stockholm: Kooperativa föbundets bokfölag, 1936).
3 MoMA's series of exhibitions titled *Good Design*, which ran from 1950 to 1955, encouraged consumers to scrutinize home furnishings and everyday objects—including toys—based on the modernist precepts of functionalism, simplicity, and truth to materials.

The Modern Playroom
1 This criticism was widely echoed in responses to the presentation. See, for example, Frederick Gutheim, "Museum House Is Romantic but Has Its Flaws," *New York Herald Tribune*, April 17, 1949; and Eleanor Roosevelt, "Museum Model Home Is New but Expensive," *New York World-Telegram*, June 24, 1949.
2 "An Interior to Come," *Interiors* (January 1949): 104.
3 "Space and Saucer House: Oklahoma family lives in suspension in a new unique structure," *Life* 39, no. 12 (September 19, 1955): 155.

"Developing Creativeness in Children": Victor D'Amico at MoMA
1 D'Amico's influence extended far beyond the Museum's walls. In 1942 he founded the National Committee on Art Education. This avant-garde group, whose membership grew from a dozen to more than one thousand over just a few years, met annually and garnered influential guest speakers such as Margaret Mead and Walter Gropius. The committee was originally intended to promote art education during the war years but continued to organize exhibitions and teaching conferences until it dissolved in 1963.
2 Dewey became a faculty member at Columbia University Teachers College in 1904, the year D'Amico was born, and he was still teaching there in the 1920s when D'Amico attended and received a B.S. and M.A. in Fine Arts and Art Education.
3 "Modern Art for Children: The Educational Project," *Bulletin of The Museum of Modern Art* 9, no. 1 (October 1941): 3.
4 Victor D'Amico, *Experiments in Creative Art Teaching: A Progress Report on the Dept. of Education, 1937–1960* (New York: The Museum of Modern Art, 1960), p. 9.
5 MoMA press release, "Exhibition of Toys at Museum of Modern Art," October 14, 1953. The Museum of Modern Art Archives, New York.
6 MoMA press release, "Art for the Family," 1954. The Museum of Modern Art Archives, New York.
7 D'Amico, *Experiments in Creative Art Teaching*, p. 35.
8 MoMA press release, "Materials for Children's Creative Center at U.S. Pavilion Shipped This Week to Belgium for World's Fair 1958," January 31, 1958. The Museum of Modern Art Archives, New York.
9 The project was directed by assistant design curator Greta Daniel and cosponsored by Creative Playthings and *Parents* magazine. The other jurors were Frank Caplan (Creative Playthings founder), Edith Mitchell (Delaware State Director of Art), Penelope Pinson (*Parents* magazine), and George Butler (National Recreation Association).
10 MoMA press release, "New Kinds of Playground Equipment on View at Museum of Modern Art," June 30, 1954. The Museum of Modern Art Archives, New York.

POWER PLAY

Introduction
1 Daniel Thomas Cook, "The Other 'Child Study': Figuring Children as Consumers in Market Research, 1910s–1990s," *Sociological Quarterly* 41, no. 3 (Summer 2000): 501.
2 James U. McNeal, "The Child as Consumer," *Journal of Retailing* 45 (1969): 16.
3 John Palfrey and Urs Gasser, *Born Digital: Understanding the First Generation of Digital Natives* (New York: Basic Books, 2008).
4 Cook cites McNeal, *Kids as Customers: A Handbook of Marketing to Children* (New York: Lexington Books, 1992); Ellen Seiter, *Sold Separately: Parents and Children in Consumer Culture* (New Brunswick, N.J.: Rutgers University Press, 1993); Selina S. Guber and Jon Berry, *Marketing to and through Kids* (New York: McGraw-Hill, 1993); and Dan S. Acuff, *What Kids Buy and Why: The Psychology of Marketing to Kids* (New York: Free Press, 1997).
5 Paco Underhill, *Why We Buy: The Science of Shopping* (New York: Simon and Schuster, 1999), p. 142.

Space Wars
1 The three Disney films aired in 1955–57. See Mike Wright, "The Disney-von Braun Collaboration and Its Influence on Space Exploration," Marshall Space Flight Center, history.msfc.nasa.gov/vonbraun/disney_article.html.
2 See Thomas Hine, *Populuxe* (New York: Overlook Press, 2007).
3 "Playgrounds Take a Space-Age Spin," *Life*, March 15, 1963, p. 97.
4 Alastair Best, "Imaginative Toys," *Design Journal*, no. 243 (March 1969): 36–39.
5 On the design and history of robots in media and popular culture, see Michael Webb, "The Robots Are Here! The Robots Are Here!" *Design Quarterly*, no. 121 (1983): 4–21.
6 "Cheerios/V-8 (1960)," Prelinger Archives, www.archive.org/details/Cheerios1960.
7 Ieuan Hopkins, "Space Hoppers and Skeelers (with a Whizz Bang to Boot)," Victoria and Albert Museum of Childhood, British Toy Making Blog, April 23, 2010, www.vam.ac.uk/things-to-do/blogs/british-toy-making-blog/space-hoppers-and-skeelers-whizz-bang-boot.
8 Shirley Moore, "How to Be a Space-Age Santa," *Science News-Letter* 76, no. 20 (November 14, 1959): 326.
9 Ibid.
10 Yoshiyasu Ishii, "The Development of Capsela–Formation Toy," in "The World of Children," special issue, *Industrial Design: The Journal of Japan Industrial Designers Association*, no. 87 (May 1977): 27–32.

Disneyland
1 Beth Dunlop, *Building a Dream: The Art of Disney Architecture* (New York: Harry N. Abrams, 1996); and Karal Ann Marling, ed., *Designing Disney's Theme Parks: The Architecture of Reassurance* (Montreal: Centre Canadien d'Architecture/Canadian Centre for Architecture; Paris: Flammarion, 1997).
2 Eric Smoodin, ed., *Disney Discourse: Producing the Magic Kingdom* (London: Routledge, 1994); and Henry A. Giroux, *The Mouse That Roared: Disney and the End of Innocence* (New York: Rowman and Littlefield, 1999).

Pop and Play
1 Anna Campbell Bliss, "Children's Furniture," *Design Quarterly*, no. 57 (1963): 1.
2 "1966 Was a Happening," *New York Times*, January 8, 1967.
3 Gilles de Bure, "Production Plastics from France," *Design*, no. 256 (April 1970): 52–55.
4 Various formations of Stephan Gip's Fun on Wheels are illustrated in Bliss, "Children's Furniture," pp. 15–18.
5 In 2011 there were two exhibitions devoted to Libuše Niklová's work: *200 dm3 of Breath*, at the Museum of Decorative Arts in Prague (organized by Niklová's son, the artist Petr Nikl) and *Plastique ludique* (Playful plastic), at the Musée des Arts Décoratifs in Paris.
6 Tereza Bruthansová and Nikl, *Libuše Niklová*, trans. Lawrence Wells (Prague: Arbor vitae, 2010), pp. 10–11.

Italy: A New Domestic Landscape for Children
1 The Saul Steinberg drawings for the Children's Labyrinth are at The Saul Steinberg Foundation, New York.
2 MoMA press release, *Italy: The New Domestic Landscape*, May 26, 1972. The Museum of Modern Art Archives, New York.
3 Bruno Munari, "Abitacolo," in *Codice ovvio* (1971; Turin: G. Einaudi, 1993), p. 124. Published in English in Claude Lichtenstein and Alfredo W. Häberli, eds., *Far vedere l'aria/Air Made Visible: A Visual Reader on Bruno Munari* (Zurich: Lars Müller, 2000), p. 14.

Retail Fantasies
1 See Jan Whitaker, *Service and Style: How the American Department Store Fashioned the Middle Class* (New York: St. Martin's Press, 2006).
2 Ladislav Sutnar, *Design for Point of Sale* (New York: Pellegrini and Cudahy, 1952), case 23.
3 Ibid.
4 Ibid.
5 Ibid.
6 Joan Cook, "A Toy Store Designed So That Children Can Play in It," *New York Times*, October 21, 1969.
7 A description and color photographs of the store from around 1969 are available at the website of architect Lester Walker, www.lesterwalkerarchitect.com/commercial/creative_pts/index.html.

Marketplace Modern
1 Judy Attfield, "Barbie and Action Man: Adult Toys for Girls and Boys, 1959–93," in Pat Kirkham, ed., *The Gendered Object* (Manchester, U.K.: Manchester University Press, 1996), p. 83.
2 Eugenio Perazza , "Magis and the Furniture Fair," Magis Me Too, www.magismetoo.com/history/perazza_eng.pdf.
3 Julia Flyyn and Lori Bongiorno, "Ikea's New Game Plan," *BusinessWeek*, October 6, 1997.
4 Ibid.

McDonald's
1 James L. Watson, ed., *Golden Arches East: McDonald's in East Asia* (Palo Alto, Calif.: Stanford University Press, 1997).
2 Eric Schlosser, *Fast Food Nation: The Dark Side of the All-American Meal* (Boston: Houghton Mifflin, 2001), pp. 47–48.
3 Ibid., p. 41.
4 Joe L. Kinchloe, "McDonald's, Power, and Children: Ronald McDonald/Ray Kroc Does It All for You," in Shirley R. Steinberg and Kincheloe, eds., *Kinderculture: The Corporate Construction of Childhood*, 2nd ed. (1997; Boulder: Westview Press, 2004).

Pee-wee's Playhouse
1 Constance Penley, *The Future of an Illusion: Film, Feminism, and Psychoanalysis* (Minneapolis: University of Minnesota Press, 1989), p. 153.
2 Paul Reubens, quoted in T. Gertler, "The Pee-wee Perplex," *Rolling Stone*, February 12, 1987, p. 36.
3 The remarkable diversity and unstereotyped characterization of the recurring human characters have been widely observed. They include Captain Carl (Phil Hartman), Miss Yvonne (Lynne Marie Stewart), Jambi the Genie (John Paragon), Cowboy Curtis (Laurence Fishburne), the King of Cartoons (Gilbert Lewis, subsequently William H. Marshall), Reba the Mail Lady (S. Epatha Merkerson), Dixie (Johann Carlo), Opal (Natasha Lyonne), Mrs. Steve (Shirley Stoler), Mrs. Rene (Suzanne Kent), Tito the lifeguard (Roland Rodriguez), and Ricardo (Vic Trevino), many of whom went on to become quite famous in film and television.
4 Gertler, "The Pee-wee Perplex," p. 38.
5 Henry Jenkins III, " 'Going Bonkers!': Children, Play and Pee-wee," *Camera Obscura*, May 1988, pp. 180–81.

Less Is More: Technology and Toys
1 Nick Monfort and Ian Bogost, *Racing the Beam: The Atari Video Computer System* (Cambridge, Mass.: MIT Press, 2009), p. 2.
2 Ibid., p. 15.
3 "A Brief History of Handheld Video Games," Endgaget, www.engadget.com/2006/03/03/a-brief-history-of-handheld-video-games; and Damien McFerran, "Game Boy," in "The Making of Game Boy," special issue, *Retro Gamer Magazine*, no. 9 (2004): 42–47.
4 "History of Game Boy," Gamer Fit Nation, gamerfitnation.com/2011/07/history-of-gameboy; and Benj Edwards, "Happy 20th B-Day Game Boy—Here Are 6 Reasons Why You're #1," Ars Technica, arstechnica.com/gaming/news/2009/04/game-boy-20th-anniversary.ars.
5 Kevin Slavin, "Reality Is Plenty, Thanks: Twelve Arguments for Keeping the Naked Eye Naked," in Paola Antonelli, ed., *Talk to Me: Design and the Communication between People and Objects* (New York: The Museum of Modern Art, 2011), p. 170.

Japanese Youth Culture and Childhood
1 Massimo Alvito and Giulia Reali, "Small Hands on Tokyo: Urban Icons in Contemporary Japan," in Alexander von Vegesack, Jutta Oldiges, and Lucy Bullivant, eds., *Kid Size: The Material World of Childhood*, (Milan: Skira; Weil am Rhein, Germany: Vitra Design Museum, 1997), pp. 211–21.

2 Yuniya Kawamura, "Japanese Fashion Subcultures," in Valerie Steele et al., *Japan Fashion Now* (New Haven: Yale University Press, 2010), p. 212.
3 Bruce Grenville, "Mr.," in Grenville et al., *KRAZY: The Delirious world of Anime + Comics + Video Games + Art* (Vancouver, Canada: Vancouver Art Gallery and Douglas & McIntyre; Berkeley: University of California Press, 2008), p. 257.
4 Steele, "Is Japan Still the Future?," in Steele et al., *Japan Fashion Now*, p. 58.
5 Craig Norris, "Manga, Anime and Visual Art Culture," in Yoshio Sugimoto, ed., *The Cambridge Companion to Modern Japanese Culture* (Cambridge: Cambridge University Press, 2009), pp. 239–43.
6 Ibid., p. 243.
7 Brian Camp and Julie Davis, *Anime Classics: ZETTAI!* (Berkeley: Stone Bridge Press, 2007), p. 39.
8 Steele, "Is Japan Still the Future?," pp. 64, 68.
9 Woodrow Phoenix, "The Toy as Art," in *Plastic Culture: How Japanese Toys Conquered the World* (Tokyo: Kodansha International, 2006), p. 80.
10 Norris, "Manga, Anime and Visual Art Culture," p. 244.
11 Steele, "Is Japan Still the Future?," pp. 27–28.
12 Ibid., p. 29; and R. J. Preece, "Mariko Mori at the Brooklyn Museum of Art 1999," *World Sculpture News* 5, no. 4 (Fall 1999): 81–82.
13 Brian J. McVeigh, *Wearing Ideology: State, Schooling and Self-Presentation in Japan* (Oxford: Berg, 2000). Cited in Steele, "Is Japan Still the Future?," p. 48.
14 Kawamura, "Japanese Fashion Subcultures," p. 222.

DESIGNING BETTER WORLDS

Introduction
1 Nelson Mandela, "A Society's Soul," speech at the launch of the Nelson Mandela Children's Fund, Pretoria, May 8, 1995. Reprinted in *Nelson Mandela: In His Own Words* (New York: Little, Brown, 2003), pp. 421–23.
2 Joel Bakan, "The Kids Are Not All Right," *New York Times*, August 21, 2011, p. A19.

Deschooling Society
1 *Whole Earth Catalog*, Spring 1970, p. 80.
2 Stewart Brand, *The Last Whole Earth Catalog: Access to Tools* (Menlo Park, Calif.: Portola Institute, 1971), p. 439.
3 Brand, "How to Do a Whole Earth Catalog," in ibid., pp. 435–44.
4 Ivan Illich, *Deschooling Society* (London: Calder & Boyars, 1971), p. 77.

Every Child Should Have a Hundred Parents
1 Bodil Graae, "Børn skal have hundrede forældre," *Politiken*, April 9, 1967. Translation by Russell L. Dees.
2 Ibid.
3 Ibid.
4 Jan Gudmand-Høyer, "Det manglende led mellem utopi og det foraeldede enfamiliehus," *Information*, June 26, 1968. In contemporary Denmark a small percentage of the population occupies true cohousing settlements (known today as *bofællesskaber*, or "living communities")—about one percent according to the Cohousing Association, www.cohousing.org/cm/article/europe, and other sources. But the model's broader legacy has been in influencing other types of housing, including subsidized, multifamily, and single-family dwellings in new and old developments.
5 On postwar modernism in Denmark, see Vibeke Andersson Møller, "Factsheet Denmark: Architecture," January 2008, Ministry of Foreign Affairs of Denmark, www.netpublikationer.dk/um/8582/pdf/Architecture.pdf. On the *tæt-lav* building style, see Erik B. Jantzen and Hans Kaaris, "Danish Low Rise Housing," *Scandinavian Housing and Planning Research* 1, no. 1 (1984): 27–42.
6 Sherry Ahrentzen, a professor and housing expert, has reported that Danish cohousers consist largely of married couples with children (forty-five percent) and single parent families (twenty-nine percent), with single residents (sixteen percent) and couples without children (one percent) in the minority. George C. Hemmens, Charles J. Hoch, and Jana Carp, eds., *Under One Roof: Issues and Innovations in Shared Housing* (Albany: State University of New York Press, 1996), p. 57.

Dismantling the Museum
1 Robert Smithson likened museums to asylums and jails, where the function of the "warden-curator" is to separate art from public society. Smithson, "Cultural Confinement," *Artforum* 11, no. 2 (October 1972). Reprinted in Jack Flam, ed., *Robert Smithson: The Collected Writings* (Berkeley: University of California Press, 1996), pp. 154–55. See also Brian O'Doherty, *Inside the White Cube: The Ideology of the Gallery Space*, rev. ed. (Berkeley: University of California Press, 1986).
2 Palle Nielsen, quoted in Lars Bang Larsen, "The Mass Utopia of Art Activism: Palle Nielsen's *The Model for a Qualitative Society*," in Larsen, ed., *Palle Nielsen, The Model: A Model for a Qualitative Society (1968)* (Barcelona: MACBA, 2010), p. 70.
3 See Josh MacPhee, *Realizing the Impossible: Art Against Authority* (Oakland, Calif.: AK Press, 2007), p. 132.
4 Larsen, "The Mass Utopia of Art Activism," p. 49.
5 Ibid., p. 95.
6 Ibid., p. 31.
7 "Planetengetriebe," *Frankfurter Allgemeine Zeitung*, no. 170 (July 26, 1972).
8 The exhibition's titular declaration of children as "a people" made prominent an idea that had roots in earlier scholarship. The British-American curator Douglas Newton called children "the greatest of savage tribes, and the only one which shows no sign of dying out." Newton, quoted in Iona and Peter Opie, *The Lore and Language of Schoolchildren* (1959; New York: New York Review of Books, 2001), p. 2.
9 "The situation of children in society" was the exhibition's publicized subject. Pernille Stensgaard, *Da Louisiana stjal billedet* (Oslo: Gyldendal N.F., 2008), p. 195. Translation by the author.
10 In May 2008, inspired by the *Modellen* and *Kinderplanet* experiments, the Frankfurt Kunstverein transformed its entire exhibition space into a playground for children, adolescents, and adults. The project was called *The Great Game to Come* and was organized with the help of both Nielsen and Thomas Bayrle.

Reggio Emilia Children
1 Carla Rinaldi, "A Metaproject," *RE Child*, April 2007, zerosei.comune.re.it/pdfs/rechild08.pdf.
2 Loris Malaguzzi, "Una carta per tre diritti," January 1993, Istituzione del Comune di Reggio Emilia website, www.scuolenidi.re.it/allegati/cartaper3diritti.pdf. Translation by the author.
3 Malaguzzi, "The Hundred Languages of Childhood," Reggio Kids website, www.reggiokids.com/about/hundred_languages.php; and Howard Gardner, "The Wonder of Learning and the Construction of Knowledge," in Ilaria Cavallini et al., eds., *The Wonder of Learning: The Hundred Languages of Children* (Reggio Emilia: Reggio Children, 2011), p. 12.
4 Giulio Ceppi and Michele Zini, eds., *Children, Spaces, Relations: Metaproject for an Environment for Young Children* (Reggio Emilia: Reggio Children, 1998), p. 38.
5 Malaguzzi, quoted in Carolyn Edwards, Lella Gandini, and George Forman, eds., *The Hundred Languages of Children: The Reggio Emilia Approach—Advanced Reflections*, 2nd ed. (Westport, Conn.: Praeger, 1998), p. 57.

Design for the Real World
1 Victor Papanek, a UNESCO-appointed International Design Expert, was born in Vienna, educated in England, and studied at Cooper Union, New York; Frank Lloyd Wright's Taliesin West, in Scottsdale, Arizona; and MIT. He worked and taught in the United States, Canada, Sweden, England, Yugoslavia, Switzerland, Finland, and Australia.
2 Papanek, *Design for the Real World: Human Ecology and Social Change* (New York: Pantheon Books, 1971), p. xxi. More than forty years later it is still read by design students and regarded as an inspirational text. Design critic Alice Rawsthorn recently examined the history and lasting relevance of the text in "An Early Champion of Good Sense," *New York Times*, May 15, 2011.
3 The Fingermajig was designed by Jorma Vennola, a student of Papanek, and first produced and sold in Finland by Kaija Aarikka before being marketed and distributed in the United States by Creative Playthings.
4 Papanek, *Design for the Real World: Human Ecology and Social Change*, 2nd ed. (Chicago: Academy Chicago Publishers, 1985), p. 107.
5 Ibid., pp. 124–25.
6 For photographs and diagrams of Ken Isaacs's structures, including contemporary images from *Life* magazine, see Leslie Coburn, "Nice Quads," *Dwell* 7, no. 6 (May 2007): 141–48.
7 Isaacs, *How to Build Your Own Living Structures* (New York: Harmony Books, 1974), p. 43.
8 Ibid.
9 Ibid.
10 Ibid., p. 44.
11 Mohamed Sharif, "Six for a City: Craig Hodgetts; Playmaker," *Constructs: Yale Architecture*, Spring 2012, p. 12, www.architecture.yale.edu/drupal/sites/default/files/pdf/constructs/Constructs%202010_spr.pdf.
12 "Industrial-Environmental-Product Design Conference (HDL 1968)," Helsinki Design Lab website, www.hdl1968.org/program.php.
13 Marianne Aav, *Marimekko: Fabrics, Fashion, Architecture* (New Haven: Yale University Press, 2003), p. 116.
14 In 1975, stimulated by Katsuji Wakisaka's still-popular Bo Boo pattern of colorful vehicles, Marimekko produced an entire range of Little People items, with clothing, tableware, and paper products.
15 Papanek, *Design for the Real World: Human Ecology and Social Change*, 2nd ed., p. 154.
16 Papanek and James Hennessey, *Nomadic Furniture* (New York: Pantheon Books, 1973), p. 87.
17 Ibid., p. 130.

Classroom Without Walls
1 Marshall McLuhan, quoted in "Playboy Interview: Marshall McLuhan—A Candid Conversation with the High Priest of Popcult and Metaphysician of Media," *Playboy* 16, no. 3 (March 1969): 55–56.
2 McLuhan, *Understanding Media: The Extensions of Man* (New York: McGraw-Hill, 1964), p. 248.
3 Edmund Carpenter and McLuhan, "The New Languages," *Chicago Review* 10, no. 1 (Spring 1956): 46.
4 Ibid., p. 51.
5 McLuhan with Carpenter, "Classrooms Without Walls," *Explorations*, no. 7 (1957): 22.
6 Jane Howard, "Oracle of the Electric Age," *Life* 60, no. 8 (February 25, 1966): 92, 96.
7 "You must remember that the TV child has been relentlessly exposed to all the 'adult' news of the modern world—war, racial discrimination, rioting, crime, inflation, sexual revolution. The war in Vietnam has written its bloody message on his skin; he has witnessed the assassinations and funerals of the nation's leaders; he's been orbited through the TV screen into the astronaut's dance in space, been inundated by information transmitted via radio, telephone, films, recordings and other people. His parents plopped him down in front of a TV set at the age of two to tranquilize him, and by the time he enters kindergarten, he's clocked as much as 4,000 hours of television. As an IBM executive told me, 'My children had lived several lifetimes compared to their grandparents when they began grade one.'" McLuhan, "Playboy Interview," pp. 55–56.
8 Kit Laybourne, ed., *Doing the Media: A Portfolio of Activities and Resources* (New York, Center for Understanding Media, 1972), pp. 5–8.
9 Ibid.

Inclusive, Therapeutic, and Assistive Design for Children
1 Universal design, conceived in the 1980s by Ronald L. Mace, an architect, designer, and educator, was based on the principle that optimal products and environments could be designed for and used by all people, without adaptation or specialization. This generally requires a design to be equitable, flexible, and intuitive in use; to require little physical effort; and to allow for error. See the website of the R. L. Mace Universal Design Institute, www.udinstitute.org/principles.php and www.udinstitute.org/history.php. The interpretation and practice of universal design has been expanded in recent years, in response to the difficulty of designing for all potential users; such a task is indeed often impractical or impossible and may neglect the needs of individuals for the sake of the group. Smart design espouses the idea that "the true basis of Universal Design is not 'one product for everyone.' It is about treating people equally." Daniel Formosa, "Social Responsibility through Design," www.smartdesignworldwide.com/pdf/Social_Responsibility_Through_Design.pdf.
2 The first large-scale efforts to accommodate people with disabilities were made in the barrier-free movement of the 1950s, which was organized to respond to the needs of World War II veterans with disabilities.
3 The Education for All Handicapped Children Act has been known since 1990 as the Individuals with Disabilities Education Act, or IDEA. See "A Guide to Disability Rights Laws," September 2005, U.S. Department of Justice website, www.ada.gov/cguide.htm.
4 MoMA press release, "Designs for Independent Living," February 1988. The Museum of Modern Art Archives, New York.
5 See Czesława Frejlich, ed., *Out of the Ordinary: Polish Designers of the 20th Century* (Warsaw: Instytut Adama Mickiewicz, 2011).
6 Ibid.
7 Sonneberg is in the region of Thuringia, Germany, which was also home to Friedrich Froebel.
8 Renate Müller studied at the Fachschule für Spielzeug under Helene Haeusler, an advocate for therapeutic play with a special interest in burlap.
9 Evan Snyderman and Zesty Meyers, eds., *Renate Müller: Toys + Design* (New York: R 20th Century Gallery, 2010), p. 11.

10 Müller reclaimed the rights to her designs after the reunification of Germany in 1990 and has continued to produce her vintage designs by hand. Her work has been featured in solo exhibitions at the Deutsches Spielzeugmuseum in Sonneberg in 1996 and the R 20th Century gallery in New York in 2010.
11 See Usha Goswami, ed., *The Wiley-Blackwell Handbook of Childhood Cognitive Development*, 2nd ed. (Malden, Mass.: Wiley-Blackwell, 2011). Jean Piaget's *The Origins of Intelligence in Children* (New York: International University Press, 1952) is still relevant in therapeutic circles; Piaget identified a "sensorimotor stage" of development, from birth to twenty-four months. Sensory Integration (SI) therapy, a model of treatment for developmental disorders that relies on sensory stimulation, is based on the work of Dr. A. Jean Ayres, which focuses on "the neurological processing of sensory information as a foundation for learning of higher-level (motor or academic skills)." Grace T. Baranek, "Efficacy of Sensory and Motor Interventions for Children with Autism," *Journal of Autism and Developmental Disorders* 32, no. 5 (October 2002): 406; see also Ayres, *Sensory Integration and the Child: Understanding Hidden Sensory Challenges*, twenty-fifth anniversary ed. (1979; Los Angeles: Western Psychological Services, 2005). Ayres's work appears to remain influential, although Baranek has reported that some of the neurological assumptions that underlie SI have been deemed outdated and similar therapies reconceptualized. Baranek, "Efficacy of Sensory and Motor Interventions for Children with Autism," p. 406.
12 Another recent example of design for emotional therapy is the Kimochis. Designed by Nina Rappaport-Rowan in California and named for the Japanese word for "feeling," these pillow-characters (Cloud and Huggtopus, among others) encourage children to identify and manage their feelings by selecting smaller cushions corresponding to different emotions for each doll's storage pouch. Kimochis are being used to help children express themselves in classrooms, hospitals, and therapy.
13 Mariana Uchoa, "The Importance of Play," Prosthetics Project website, design.sva.edu/prosthetics/project_mariana.php.
14 "Case Study: Blink Twice Tango!," Frog Design website, www.frogdesign.com/pdf/frog_design_blinktwice.pdf.
15 Krabat was founded in 2006 by colleagues and engineers Tom-Arne Solhaug and Fredrik Brodtkorb. When Solhaug's son Kasper was born with cerebral palsy, both he and Brodtkorb left their jobs and started a new business to create alternatives to the ugly, poorly functioning, intimidating, and stigmatizing equipment that was available; their first work was the Pilot, a crawling aid for babies and toddlers. Jockey, an adjustable active chair for children with various disabilities, for everyday activities such as eating, playing, and watching television, was acquired by The Museum of Modern Art, New York, in 2010. Krabat also produces Sherrif, a wheelchair. According to Solhaug, only about ten companies in the world focus on the design of pediatric technical aids. Conversation with the author, Hvalstad, Norway, October 19, 2009.

Design and the Universal Child
1 Charles Stubblefield, "The Child That Went Forth," *The English Journal* 54, no. 2 (February 1965): 12.
2 Eckhardt Fuchs, "Children's Rights and Global Civil Society," *Comparative Education* 43, no. 3 (August 2007): 393.
3 The Declaration of the Rights of the Child, United Nations website, www.un.org/cyberschoolbus/humanrights/resources/child.asp.

4 *Every Child* is available on the National Film Board of Canada website, at www.nfb.ca/film/every_child.
5 The provisions of the Declaration of the Rights of the Child (in fifty-four articles and two optional protocols) were integrated into UNICEF's mission in 1996.
6 "Convention on the Rights of the Child," UNICEF website, www.unicef.org/crc.
7 Marian Wright Edelman, founder and president of the Children's Defense Fund, has written numerous articles and books on children's rights and well-being, including, with James D. Weill, "Investing in our Children," *Yale Law & Policy Review* 4, no. 2 (Spring–Summer 1986): 331–63; *Stand for Children* (New York: Hyperion Books for Children, 1998); and *The State of America's Children: A Report from the Children's Defense Fund* (Boston: Beacon Press, 2000).
8 "SOS Kinderdorf Poster Design, Germany," *Graphis: International Journal for Graphic and Applied Arts*, no. 318 (1998): 150–51. On *Children's Games*, see Sandra Hindman, "Pieter Bruegel's Children's Games, Folly, and Chance," *The Art Bulletin* 63, no. 3 (September 1981): 447–75.
9 "Bracelet of Life," Doctors Without Borders, www.doctorswithoutborders.co.nz/education/activities/braceletoflife/braceletoflife-print.html.
10 See Milton Tectonidis, M.D. "Crisis in Niger: Outpatient Care for Severe Acute Malnutrition," *New England Journal of Medicine* 354, no. 3 (January 19, 2006): 224–27.
11 The term "digital divide" was coined in 1996 by Lloyd Morrisett, a founder of the Children's Television Workshop, to describe "the chasm that purportedly separates information technology…haves from have-nots in U.S. society." Virginia Eubanks, *Digital Dead End: Fighting for Social Justice in the Information Age* (Cambridge, Mass.: MIT Press, 2011), p. 35.
12 Fuseproject website, www.fuseproject.com/pdf/OLPC%20Case%20Study.pdf.
13 "Sugata Mitra shows how kids teach themselves," lecture, 2007, TED website, www.ted.com/talks/sugata_mitra_shows_how_kids_teach_themselves.html.

The Playground Revolution
1 "Fears concerning children's safety in adventure playgrounds are largely unwarranted. In general, their safety record is significantly better than that of traditional playgrounds." Arlene Brett, Robin C. Moore, and Eugene F. Provenzo, Jr., *The Complete Playground Book* (Syracuse, N.Y.: Syracuse University Press, 1993), p. 14.
2 J. M. Richards, "Art in Use," *Architectural Review* 116 (August 1954): 121–23.
3 Egon Møller-Nielsen's Ägget was featured on the cover of *Architectural Review* in August 1954; other publications covering play sculpture included *Art and Architecture* and *School Executive*, both in August 1954; *Interiors*, in February 1954; and *The Rotarian*, in September 1956.
4 Lady Allen of Hurtwood believed that children quickly tire of "over-slick" play sculpture, which "being immobile is useless to the energetic young." Lady Allen, quoted in Tania Long, "Briton Criticizes U.S. Playgrounds," *New York Times*, May 16, 1965.
5 "Newest Thing in Playgrounds Opens in Brooklyn," *New York Times*, May 19, 1967.
6 Cypress Hills was featured on the cover of "Playground Revolution," a booklet put out by the Park Association in 1966, and in Alfred Ledermann and Alfred Trachsel's landmark survey of postwar playgrounds, *Creative Playgrounds and Recreation Centers* (1959; New York: Frederick A. Praeger, 1968), pp. 62–63.
7 Jay Jacobs, "Projects for Playgrounds," *Art in America* 55, no. 6 (November–December 1967): 41.
8 "Colin Greenly: Public Art," Leaning Post Productions website, www.leaningpost.com/PublicArt.html.

9 Over the course of his tenure, from 1934 to 1960, Robert Moses oversaw the construction of more than seven hundred new playgrounds, including nineteen fenced-in playgrounds on the perimeter of Central Park, deliberately placed to intercept children upon entrance and minimize their impact on the park's original design.
10 Jacobs, "Projects for Playgrounds," pp. 44–45.
11 Lady Allen, quoted in Long, "Briton Criticizes U.S. Playgrounds."
12 Richard Dattner's other adventure playgrounds in Central Park are the Water Playground and Heckscher Playground near West Fifty-ninth Street, the Seventy- second Street Playground, and the Wild West Playground at West Ninety-first Street.
13 Dattner's Central Park playgrounds were supported by the Estée and Joseph Lauder Foundation.
14 Lisa Hammel, "Two Playground Designers Who Used to Be 'Rebels,'" *New York Times*, November 29, 1972.
15 Lina Bo Bardi was born and trained in Italy and started her career with Gio Ponti. She moved to Brazil in 1946. Her husband, Pietro Maria Bardi, was the founding curator of MASP.
16 "I believe that Lina painted this watercolour when the building was almost ready in May 1968, just a few months before the museum opened. Therefore it cannot be a drawing intended to explain the building to the client. It suggests another use for the building, in addition to its functional role, another way to think of it — as one of these games." Olivia de Oliveira, *Subtle Substances: The Architecture of Lina Bo Bardi* (São Paulo: Romano Guerrra; Barcelona: Gustavo Gili, 2006), p. 348.
17 Andreas Luescher, "Experience Field for the Senses: Hugo Kükelhaus' Phenomenology of Consciousness," *Jade* 25, no. 1 (2006): 69. The German company Richter Spielgeräte continues to produce Play Stations for Developing the Senses, which include rotating optical discs, singing stones, wind harps, prisms, and pendulums and are based on the collaboration between Kükelhaus and designer Wolfram Graubner. www.richter-spielgeraete.de/h-kuekelhaus-504.html?.
18 The artists connected with the Zalaegerszeg project were also involved in innovative educational programming at the Hungarian National Gallery, in which children were permitted to engage with more cutting-edge contemporary art than their elders, and at the Fészek Artists' Club in Budapest, where Ildikó Várnagy ran free, interdisciplinary art classes for children in the late 1970s.
19 See Rebecca Mead, "State of Play," *The New Yorker*, July 5, 2010, pp. 32–37; Diane Cardwell, "New York Tries to Think Outside the Sandbox," *New York Times*, January 10, 2007; and Kaomi Goetz, "Rockwell's Imagination Playground Is a Cutting-Edge Learning Experiment," Co.Design, July 27, 2010, www.fastcodesign.com/1661987/rockwells-imagination-playground-is-a-cutting-edge-learning-experiment.
20 See Susan Solomon, *American Playgrounds: Revitalizing Community Space* (Lebanon, N.H.: University Press of New England, 2005).
21 One such activist is Roger A. Hart, codirector of the Children's Environments Research Group and a professor of environmental psychology at the Graduate Center of the City University of New York. See "The Right to Play" (with Alfhild Petrén), in James Himes and Petrén, eds., *Children's Rights: Turning Principles into Practice* (Stockholm: Save the Children Sweden; Kathmandu: UNICEF ROSA, 2000); and *Children's Experience of Place: A Developmental Study* (New York: Irvington Publishers, 1978).

For a more extensive bibliography, please visit the exhibition's website, at www.moma.org/centuryofthechild.

Adamovič, Ivan, and Tomáš Pospiszyl, eds. *Svět zítřka v socialistickém Československu, 1948–1978*. Prague: Arbor vitae, 2010.

Ariès, Philippe. *Centuries of Childhood: A Social History of Family Life*. Translated by Robert Baldick. New York: Vintage, 1962.

Atkins, Jacqueline, ed. *Wearing Propaganda: Textiles on the Home Front in Japan, Britain, and the United States, 1931–1945*. New Haven: Yale University Press, in association with the Bard Graduate Center for Studies in the Decorative Arts, Design, and Culture, New York, 2005.

Bachrach, Julia Sniderman. *The City in a Garden: A Photographic History of Chicago's Parks*. Santa Fe: The Center for American Places, 2001.

Bar-Or, Galia, and Yuval Yasky, eds. *Kibbutz: Architecture Without Precedents*. Tel Aviv: Top-Print, 2010.

Bengtsson, Arvid. *Environmental Planning for Children's Play*. New York: Praeger Publishers, 1970.

Benson, Timothy O., ed. *Expressionist Utopias: Paradise, Metropolis, Architectural Fantasy*. Berkeley: University of California Press, 1994.

Bergdoll, Barry, and Leah Dickerman, eds. *Bauhaus 1919–1933: Workshops for Modernity*. New York: The Museum of Modern Art, 2009.

Brosterman, Norman. *Inventing Kindergarten*. New York: Harry N. Abrams, 1997.

Bruthansová, Tereza, and Petr Nikl. *Libuše Niklová*. Prague: Arbor vitae, 2010.

Büren, Charles von, ed. *Kurt Naef: Der Spielzeugmacher/The Toymaker*. Basel: Birkhäuser, 2006.

Caldwell, John Thornton. *Televisuality: Style, Crisis, and Authority in American Television*. New Brunswick, N.J.: Rutgers University Press, 1995.

Canadian Centre for Architecture. *L'Architecture en jeux: Jeux de construction du CCA / Buildings in Boxes: Architectural Toys from the CCA*. Montreal: Canadian Centre for Architecture, 1990.

Carlin, John. "Graphic Poetry: Lyonel Feininger's Brief and Curious Comic-Strip Career." In Barbara Haskell, ed. *Lyonel Feininger: At the Edge of the World*. New Haven: Yale University Press, 2011.

Cavallini, Ilaria, et al., eds. *The Wonder of Learning: The Hundred Languages of Children*. Reggio Emilia, Italy: Reggio Children, 2011.

Châtelet, Anne-Marie, Dominique Lerch, and Jean-Noël Luc, eds. *L'Ecole de plein air: Une expérience pédagogique et architecturale dans l'Europe du XXᵉ siècle/ Open-air Schools: An Educational and Architectural Venture in Twentieth-Century Europe*. Paris : Éditions Recherches, 2003.

Council on Museums and Education in the Visual Arts. *The Art Museum as Educator: A Collection of Studies as Guides to Practice*. Edited by Barbara Y. Newsom

and Adele Z. Silver. Berkeley: University of California Press, 1978.

Cross, Gary, and Gregory Smits. "Japan, the U.S., and the Globalization of Children's Consumer Culture." "Globalization and Childhood," special issue, *Journal of Social History* 38, no. 4 (Summer 2005): 873–90.

Daprey, Carole. *Mobilier design pour enfants*. Paris: L'As de pique, 2009.

Dower, John W. *Embracing Defeat: Japan in the Wake of World War II*. New York: W. W. Norton, 1999.

Druin, Allison, ed. *The Design of Children's Technology*. San Francisco: Morgan Kaufmann Publishers, 1999.

Dudek, Mark. *Kindergarten Architecture: Space for the Imagination*. London: Chapman and Hall, 1996.

———, ed. *Children's Spaces*. Oxford: Architectural Press, 2005.

Earle, Joe. *Buriki: Japanese Tin Toys from the Golden Age of the American Automobile: The Yoku Tanaka Collection*. New York: Japan Society, 2009.

Fairfield, Richard. *The Modern Utopian: Alternative Communities of the '60s and '70s*. Port Townsend, Wash.: Process Media, 2010.

Fass, Paula S., ed. *Encyclopedia of Children and Childhood in History and Society*, vols. 1–3. New York: Macmillan, 2003–04.

Fineberg, Jonathan. *The Innocent Eye: Children's Art and the Modern Artist*. Princeton: Princeton University Press, 1997.

———, ed. *Discovering Child Art: Essays on Childhood, Primitivism and Modernism*. Princeton: Princeton University Press, 1998.

Frejlich, Czesława, ed. *Out of the Ordinary: Polish Designers of the 20th Century*. Warsaw: Adam Mickiewicz Institute, 2011.

Froebel, Friedrich. *Friedrich Froebel's Pedagogics of the Kindergarten; or, His Ideas Concerning the Play and Playthings of the Child*. Translated by Josephine Jarvis. New York: D. Appleton, 1895.

Fuchs, Eckhardt. "Children's Rights and Global Civil Society." *Comparative Education* 43, no. 3 (August 2007): 393–412.

Gellér, Katalin. *The Art Colony of Gödöllő (1901–1920)*. Translated by Judit Pokoly. Gödöllő, Hungary: Gödöllő Municipal Museum, 2001.

Grant, Julia. *Raising Baby by the Book: The Education of American Mothers*. New Haven: Yale University Press, 1998.

Gutman, Marta, and Ning de Coninck-Smith, eds. *Designing Modern Childhoods: History, Space, and the Material Culture of Children*. New Brunswick, N.J.: Rutgers University Press, 2008.

Haas, Malka. "Children in the Junkyard." *Childhood Education* 73, no. 6 (1996): 345–51.

Heuvel, Dirk van den, and Max Risselada, eds. *Alison and Peter Smithson: From a House of the Future to a House of Today*. Rotterdam: 010 Publishers, 2004.

Hewitt, Karen, and Henry Petroski. *Toying with Architecture: The Building Toy in the Arena of Play, 1800 to the*

Present. Katonah, N.Y.: Katonah Museum of Art, 1997.

Hilty, Greg, and Alona Pardo, eds. *Watch Me Move: The Animation Show*. London: Merrell, in association with the Barbican Art Gallery, London, 2011.

Hollein, Max, and Gunda Luyken. *Kunst— ein Kinderspiel*. Frankfurt am Main: Revolver Verlag, 2004.

Hurtwood, Lady Allen of. *Planning for Play*. London: Thames & Hudson, 1968.

Isaacs, Ken. *How to Build Your Own Living Structures*. New York: Harmony Books, 1974.

Janáková, Iva, et al. *Ladislav Sutnar: Prague—New York—Design in Action*. Prague: Argo, 2003.

Kane, Pat. *The Play Ethic: A Manifesto for a Different Way of Living*. London: Macmillan, 2004.

Kaplan, Wendy, ed. *Charles Rennie Mackintosh*. New York: Abbeville Press, 1996.

Kelly, Catriona. *Children's World: Growing Up in Russia, 1890–1991*. New Haven: Yale University Press, 2007.

Key, Ellen. *The Century of the Child*. New York: G. P. Putnam, 1909.

Kinchin, Juliet. "Hungary: Shaping a National Consciousness." In Wendy Kaplan, ed. *The Arts and Crafts Movement in Europe and America: Design for the Modern World*, pp. 142–77. London: Thames & Hudson, 2004.

Koon, Tracy H. *Believe, Obey, Fight: Political Socialization of Youth in Fascist Italy, 1922–1943*. Chapel Hill: University of North Carolina Press, 1985.

Kries, Mateo, and Alexander von Vegesack, eds. *Rudolf Steiner: Alchemy of the Everyday*. Weil am Rhein, Germany: Vitra Design Museum, 2007.

Küper, Marijke, and Ida van Zijl, eds. *Gerrit Th. Rietveld: 1888–1964: The Complete Works*. Utrecht: Centraal Museum, 1992.

Lacqueur, Walter. *Young Germany: A History of the German Youth Movement*. New York: Basic Books, 1962.

Larsen, Lars Bang. *Palle Nielsen: The Model: A Model for a Qualitative Society (1968)*. Barcelona: Museu d'Art Contemporani de Barcelona, 2010.

Ledermann, Alfred, and Alfred Trachsel. *Creative Playgrounds and Recreation Centers*. 1959. Revised ed., New York: Frederick A. Praeger, 1968.

Lefaivre, Liane, and Ingeborg de Roode. *Aldo van Eyck: The Playgrounds and the City*. Amsterdam: Stedelijk Museum; Rotterdam: NAi, 2002.

Lichtenstein, Claude, and Alfredo W. Häberli, eds. *Far vedere l'aria/Air Made Visible: A Visual Reader on Bruno Munari*. Zurich: Lars Müller, 2000.

Ligtelijn, Vincent, ed. *Aldo van Eyck Works*. Basel: Birkhäuser, 1999.

Lindgren, Astrid. "Pippi Can Lift a Horse: The Importance of Children's Books." *Quarterly Journal of the Library of Congress* 40 (Summer 1983): 188–201.

Lindley, Betty, and Ernest K. Lindley. *A New Deal for Youth: The Story of the National Youth Administration*. New York: Viking Press, 1938.

Lloyd, Jill, and Christian Witt-Dörring, eds. *Birth of the Modern: Style and Identity in Vienna, 1900*. Munich: Hirmer; New York: Neue Galerie, 2011.

Maino, Maria Paola. *A misura di bambino: Cent'anni di mobili per l'infanzia in Italia (1870–1970)*. Rome: Laterza, 2003.

Makarova, Elena. *Friedl Dicker-Brandeis, Vienna 1898–Auschwitz 1944: The Artist Who Inspired the Children's Drawings of Terezin*. Los Angeles: Tallfellow/Every Picture Press, 2001.

Marling, Karal Ann, ed. *Designing Disney's Theme Parks: The Architecture of Reassurance*. Montreal: Centre Canadien d'Architecture/Canadian Centre for Architecture; Paris: Flammarion, 1997.

Marshall, David, ed. *Understanding Children as Consumers*. London: SAGE Publications, 2010.

Martino, Stefano de, and Alex Wall. *Cities of Childhood: Italian Colonies of the 1930s*. London: Architectural Association, 1988.

McCamant, Kathryn, and Charles Durrett. "Cohousing in Denmark." In Karen A. Franck and Sherry Ahrentzen, eds. *New Households, New Housing*, pp. 100–26. New York: Van Nostrand Reinhold, 1989.

Montessori, Maria. *The Montessori Method: Scientific Pedagogy as Applied to Child Education in the Children's Houses with Additions and Revisions by the Author*. New York: Stokes, 1912.

Montgomery, Kathryn C. "Children's Media Culture in the New Millennium: Mapping the Digital Landscape." "Children and Computer Technology," special issue, *The Future of Children* 10, no. 2 (Fall–Winter 2000): 145–67.

Müller, Thomas, and Romana Schneider. *Das Klassenzimmer vom Ende des 19. Jahrhunderts bis heute/The Classroom from the Late 19th Century until the Present Day*. Tübingen: Ernst Wasmuth Verlag, 2010.

Mumford, Eric. *The CIAM Discourse on Urbanism, 1928–1960*. Cambridge, Mass.: MIT Press, 2000.

Noever, Peter, ed. *Margarete Schütte-Lihotzky: Soziale Architektur; Zeitzeugin eines Jahrhunderts*. Vienna: MAK Wien, 1993.

———, ed. *Jugendschatz und Wunderscherlein. Buchkunst für Kinder in Wien/ Book Art for Children in Vienna, 1890–1938*. Vienna: MAK Wien; Nuremberg: Verlag für Moderne Kunst Nürnberg, 2009.

Ogata, Amy F. "Creative Playthings: Educational Toys and Postwar American Culture." *Winterthur Portfolio* 39, nos. 2/3 (Summer/Fall 2004): 129–56.

———, "Building for Learning in Postwar American Elementary Schools." *Journal of the Society of Architectural Historians* 67, no. 4 (December 2008): 562–91.

Opsvik, Peter. *Rethinking Sitting*. Oslo: Gaidaros Forlag, 2008.

Overy, Paul. *Light, Air and Openness: Modern Architecture Between the Wars*. London: Thames & Hudson, 2007.

Papanek, Victor. *Design for the Real World: Human Ecology and Social Change*. New York: Pantheon Books, 1971.

Pérez, Carlos. *Aladdin Toys: Los juguetes de Torres-García*. Valencia: IVAM Centre Julio Gonzalez, 1997.

———, et al. *Infancia y arte moderno*. Valencia: IVAM Centre Julio González, 1998.

Postman, Neil. *Amusing Ourselves to Death: Public Discourse in the Age of Show Business*. New York: Penguin, 1985.

———. *The Disappearance of Childhood*. 1982. Reprint, New York: Vintage Books, 1994.

Pullin, Graham. *Design Meets Disability*. Cambridge, Mass.: MIT Press, 2009.

Rasmussen, Briley. "The Laboratory on 53rd Street: Victor D'Amico and the Museum of Modern Art, 1937–1969." *Curator: The Museum Journal* 53, no. 4 (October 2010): 451–64.

Roth, Alfred. *The New School/Das neue Schulhaus/La Nouvelle École*. Zurich: Girsberger, 1950.

Rowell, Margit, and Deborah Wye. *The Russian Avant-Garde Book, 1910–1934*. New York: The Museum of Modern Art, 2002.

Sassoon, Rosemary. *Marion Richardson: Her Life and Her Contribution to Handwriting*. Bristol, U.K.: Intellect, 2011.

Segel, Harold B. *Pinocchio's Progeny: Puppets, Marionettes, Automatons, and Robots in Modernist and Avant-Garde Drama*. Baltimore: The Johns Hopkins University Press, 1995.

Snyderman, Evan, and Zesty Meyers, eds. *Renate Müller: Toys + Design*. New York: R 20th Century Gallery, 2010.

Solomon, Susan G. *American Playgrounds: Revitalizing Community Space*. Lebanon, N.H.: University Press of New England, 2005.

Stals, José Lebrero, and Carlos Pérez, eds. *Toys of the Avant-Garde*. Málaga: Museo Picasso Málaga, 2010.

Starks, Tricia. *The Body Soviet: Propaganda, Hygiene, and the Revolutionary State*. Madison: University of Wisconsin Press, 2009.

Steinberg, Shirley R., and Joe L. Kincheloe, eds. *Kinderculture: The Corporate Construction of Childhood*. London: Open University Press, 1997.

Sutton-Smith, Brian. *Toys as Culture*. New York: Gardner Press, 1986.

Tomlinson, R. R. *Crafts for Children*. London: Studio Publications, 1935.

Vitali, Antonio. *Antonio Vitali: Spielzeugdesigner—Creator of Toys*. Weingarten, Germany: Kunstverlag Weingarten, 1994.

Viola, Wilhelm. *Child Art and Franz Cižek*. Vienna: Austrian Junior Red Cross, 1936.

Vitra Design Museum. *Kid Size: The Material World of Childhood*. Milan: Skira, 1997.

Walker Art Center. *New Learning Spaces and Places: Design Quarterly*, nos. 90/91 (January/March 1974).

Warburton, Nigel. *Ernő Goldfinger: The Life of an Architect*. London: Routledge, 2004.

Ward, Colin. *The Child in the City*. New York: Pantheon Books, 1978.

White, Colin. *The Enchanted World of Jessie M. King*. Edinburgh: Canongate Books, 1989.

White, Michael. *De Stijl and Dutch Modernism*. Manchester, U.K.: Manchester University Press, 2003.

Whyte, Iain Boyd, ed. *The Crystal Chain Letters: Architectural Fantasies by Bruno Taut and His Circle*. Cambridge, Mass.: MIT Press, 1985.

Will, Cornelia K. *Alma Siedhoff-Buscher: Entwürfe für Kinder am Bauhaus in Weimar*. Velbert, Germany: Stadt Velbert, der Stadtdirektor, 1997.

Daddytypes, Washington, DC: 2.24.
Danish National Art Library, Copenhagen: 5.38.
Courtesy Richard Dattner: 7.54; photo Richard Dattner: 7.21.
Dell & Wainwright/RIBA Library Photographs Collection: 3.54.
Design Council/University of Brighton Design Archives www.brighton.ac.uk/designarchives. Photo Timothy Quallington: 6.04.
Design Council Slide Collection at Manchester Metropolitan University: 7.34.
Design Museum Finland, Helsinki. Photo Rauno Träskelin: 7.24, 7.25.
© Disney: 4.45, 6.12, 6.14.
Dixon Ticonderoga Company: page 19.
© Dumfries and Galloway Council: 1.20.
© Dumfries and Galloway Council/Victoria and Albert Museum, London: 1.19.
Photo Charles Eames © 2012 The Eames Foundation: 5.57.
Aldo van Eyck Archive, Loenen aan de Vecht, the Netherlands: 5.24, 6.06.
© Foto Marburg/Art Resource, NY: 2.06.
The Estate of Abram Games: 3.55.
Courtesy Gemeente Amsterdam Stadsarchief, Dienst Ruimtelijke Ordening (DRO): 5.25.
© Gemeente Musea: page 14 (bottom).
© J. Paul Getty Trust. Used with permission. Julius Shulman Photography Archive, Research Library at the Getty Research Institute (2004.R.10): 3.33.
© Glasgow Corporation/Glasgow Mitchell Library: 1.13, 1.17.
The Glasgow School of Art Archives and Collections: 1.21.
Courtesy Gödöllő Town Museum: 1.42, 1.45, 1.47; Photo Rudolf Balogh: 1.46; Photo Elek Koronghi Lippich: 1.41.
gta Archives, ETH Zürich, bequest of Hans Hofmann: 3.47, 3.48; bequest of Hannes Meyer: 3.49, 5.35.
© 2012 Andreas Gursky/Artists Rights Society (ARS), New York/VG Bild-Kunst, Bonn: page 13 (bottom).
© The Estate of Margaretha Hamerschlag/Victoria and Albert Museum, London: 1.49.
Courtesy Helen + Hard. Photo Emile Ashley: 7.59.
Photo courtesy © Herman World, Inc., All Rights Reserved: 6.41, 6.42.
Photo Lucien Hervé: 5.33.
Courtesy HiWEL, New Delhi: 7.49, 7.50.
© 2012 Craig Hodgetts: 7.22.
Courtesy Hubley Studio, Inc.: page 16.
© The Hunterian, University of Glasgow 2012: 1.15, 1.16.
Photo Ingemann: 5.48.
IKEA, Älmhult: 6.37.
Courtesy Jens S. Jensen: Back endpaper, page 25 (bottom), page 27 (bottom).
Jewish Museum in Prague Photo Archive: 4.35.
Photo Petr Karsulin for Dole Vita Magazine, Prague: 6.02.
Mark Kauffman/Time & Life Pictures/Getty Images: 4.52.
Courtesy Imre Kepes and Juliet Kepes Stone, Pelham and Cambridge, Massachusetts. Photo EPW Studio/Maris Hutchinson, 2011: 5.54.
Klassik Stiftung Weimar. Photo Alexander Burzik: 2.33.
Photo Peter Kleeman, Space Age Museum: 6.03, 6.08, 6.09, 6.47.
© Barbara Klemm: 7.15.
Photo © Ton Koene for MSF: 7.47.
© Katsumi Komagata. ONE STROKE co. ltd: 7.38.
Krátky Film Praha, Prague/DILIA: 4.49, 6.06, 6.07.
Courtesy Lambeth Archives department: 5.23.
© Lisa Law: 7.03, 7.06, 7.07; photo John Phillip Law: 7.05.
© 2012 Bart van der Leck/Artists Rights Society (ARS), New York/PICTORIGHT, The Netherlands: 2.22.
Courtesy Jason Liebig, New York: 6.40.

Magis, Torre di Mosto, Italy. Photo Tom Vack: 6.36.
© Enzo Mari, 1961. Courtesy Corraini Edizioni: 6.25.
© Marusan Japan 2012: 5.15.
Courtesy Maurizio Marzadori. Photo Carlos da Silva: 1.10, 1.39, 2.17, 3.17, 6.22, 6.28.
MASP, Museu de Arte de Sao Paulo Assis Chateaubriand: 7.55.
© Mattel Inc.: 6.32.
© Rosalie Thorne McKenna Foundation, Courtesy Center for Creative Photography: 5.36.
© Susanne Mertz, Courtesy Louisiana Museum of Modern Art: 7.16.
Collection of Zesty Meyers and Evan Snyderman/R 20th Century, New York: 7.37.
© Korta Michał/National Museum, Warsaw: 3.18, 5.18, 7.36.
Minneapolis Institute of Arts, Gift of funds from Don and Diana Lee Lucker: 3.07.
Mondo Cane Gallery, New York: 6.35.
© 2012 Mariko Mori/Artists Rights Society (ARS), New York: 6.52.
Ralph Morse/Time & Life Pictures/Getty Images: 5.52, 5.53.
© 2000 Takashi Murakami/Kaikai Kiki Co., Ltd All rights reserved: 6.51.
© Osamu Murai: page 22 (bottom).
Musée National d'Art Moderne, Centre Georges Pompidou, Paris, France: 3.28.
Archivio Fotografico Museo di Arte Moderna e Contemporanea di Trento e Rovereto: 2.12.
Photo © The Museum at FIT: 6.53.
Museum Boijmans van Beuningen, Rotterdam. Photo Tom Haartsen: 2.26.
Courtesy Museum für Gestaltung, Zürich, Kunstgewerbesammlung, photo Franz Xaver Jaggy: 3.20, 4.34, 5.01, 7.44; photo Marlen Perez © ZHdk: 2.07, 2.11.
The Museum of Decorative Arts in Prague: 1.54, 2.46, 2.47, 2.48, 3.03, 3.05, 5.44, 5.45, 6.29.
© Museum of Finnish Architecture: 5.04.
The Museum of Modern Art, New York, Architecture and Design Study Center: 3.30.
The Museum of Modern Art, New York, Department of Imaging Services: front endpaper, page 2, page 13 (bottom left), page 14 (top), page 20, page 21 (bottom), page 24, 1.03, 1.04, 1.08, 1.23, 1.33, 1.50, 2.04, 2.20, 2.27, 2.35, 2.5, 2.39, 3.06, 3.11, 3.14, 3.23, 3.26, 4.02, 4.07, 4.38, 4.39, 5.02, 5.05, 5.20, 5.42, 5.48, 5.56, 6.05, 6.24, 6.50, 7.02, 7.08, 7.35, 7.40, 7.42, 7.47; photo Peter Butler: 1.53, 2.02, 2.35, 2.36, 2.37, 2.38, 2.40, 2.41, 2.42; photo Robert Gerhardt: 1.31, 1.32, 1.51, 2.29, 2.30; photo Thomas Griesel: page 13 (top right), page 17 (right), 1.02, 1.06, 1.07, 2.25, 2.32, 2.34, 2.49, 4.06, 4.09, 5.03, 5.19, 5.26, 5.40, 5.43, 6.11, 6.27, 6.32, 6.33, 6.34, 6.38, 6.39, 6.43, 6.46, 6.48, 6.51, 6.52, 7.01, 7.09, 7.27, page 248; photo Kate Keller: 1.01; photo Jonathan Muzikar: 4.28, 7.04, 0.20, 2.31; photo John Wronn: page 16, page 18, page 27 (top), 1.14, 1.18, 1.27, 1.43, 1.44, 2.28, 3.02, 4.22, 5.06, 5.10, 5.27, 5.28, 5.32, 6.23, 6.36, 6.49, 7.22, 7.26, 7.28, 7.30, 7.48, back endpaper.
The Museum of Modern Art Archives, New York, Department of Circulating Exhibitions Records, Photo Soichi Sunami: 4.53, 5.61, 5.62.
The Museum of Modern Art Film Stills Archive, New York: 1.34.
The Museum of Modern Art Library, New York: 3.29, 3.37.
The Museum of Modern Art Photographic Archives, New York. Photo William Leftwich: 4.36.
Nachlassarchiv SIK-ISEA Zürich. Photo Theo Schäublin: 5.07.
© NAMCO BANDAI Games Inc. 6.45.
Nationaal Archief/Spaarnestad Photo/NFP. Photo Stevens & Magielsen: 5.08.

Nationalmuseum, Sweden. Photo Erik Cornelius: page 10,
Die Neue Sammlung–The International Design Museum Munich. Photo A. Broehan, Munich: 2.19; Photo A. Laurenzo: 2.03; Photo Antonio Vitali. The Museum of Modern Art, New York. Department of Imaging Services. Photo John Wronn: 5.41.
Image courtesy Dion Neutra, architect, for the Neutra Archive: 3.34.
© New Lanark Trust. Licensor: www.scran.ac.uk: 1.05.
© The New York Times/Redux, Photo Michael Evans: Cover, 6.10.
Image courtesy Nintendo: 6.44.
© 2012 The Isamu Noguchi Foundation and Garden Museum, New York/Artists Rights Society (ARS), New York: 3.08.
© Ingrid Vang Nyman/Saltkråkan AB: 4.50.
Photo Aidan O'Connor: 3.31.
Photo Denise Ortiz, founder SharingToLearn.org © Sharing To Learn: 7.41.
Courtesy Alasdair Peebles: 3.04.
Courtesy John and Sue Picton. Photo Ian Cameron: 4.31.
© Ligier Piotr/National Museum, Warsaw: 5.17.
With kind permission from PLAYMOBIL. PLAYMOBIL is a registered trademark of geobra Brandstätter GmbH & Co.KG, Germany: 6.34.
Price Tower Arts Center, Bartlesville, Oklahoma, PTAC 2009.01.2. Photo Cody Johnson: 1.25.
© Primordial LLC, Michael Joaquin Grey: page 21 (top).
Courtesy Archivio Prini: 2.01.
Public Collectors, Gift of the Library of Radiant Optimism for Let's Re-Make the World: 7.13.
Archivio Randone, Roma: 1.35, 1.37.
Image redrawn by Jesse Reed: 1.29.
Photo from the book Advisories © Preschools and Infant Toddler Centres–Istituzione of the Municipality of Reggio Emilia and Reggio Children, Italy www.scuolenidi.re.it and www.reggiochildren.it: 7.18.
Still from the video Everyday Utopias © Preschools and Infant Toddler Centres–Istituzione of the Municipality of Reggio Emilia and Reggio Children, Italy www.scuolenidi.re.it and www.reggiochildren.it: 7.19.
RIBA Library Drawings & Archives Collection: page 22 (top), 3.01, 5.31.
RIBA Library Photographs Collection: 3.43, 3.46.
Art © John Rombola/Licensed by VAGA, New York, NY: page 17 (left).
Michael Rougier/Time & Life Pictures/Getty Images: 5.49.
Courtesy Andrea Schito. Photo Carlo Cichero, Ovada, Italy: 4.15.
SDO–Sitra Archive. Photo Kristian Runeberg: 7.23.
Courtesy Sesame Workshop: 7.29.
© David Seymour/Magnum Photos: 5.16.
© Estate of Ben Shahn/Licensed by VAGA, New York, NY: 5.02, 5.20.
© 2012 David Shrigley: page 24.
© 2012 Estate of Alma Siedhoff-Buscher: 2.33.
Stadt Soest, Stadtarchiv, Nachlass Hugo Kükelhaus: 7.56.
Courtesy Estate of Ralph Steiner: 3.32.
© Rudolf Steiner Archiv, Dornach: 1.11, 1.12.
Courtesy Bruce Sterling. Photo EPW Studio/Maris Hutchinson, 2011: 5.15.
Stokke. Photo of Lars Hjelle and Kjell Heggdal by Dag Lausund: 7.33.
© Ezra Stoller/Esto: 5.51.
© From the book Libuše Niklová by Tereza Bruthansová, published by Arbor vitae societas, 2010. Photo Studio Toast: 6.19, 6.20.
Strüwing Reklamefoto. Photo Jørgen Strüwing: 5.37.
Courtesy Hugo Stüdeli, Otto Morach Estate, Solothurn: 2.11.

© The Ladislav Sutnar Family: 2.49, 2.46, 2.48, 2.50, 3.05, 6.29.
Svensk Form, Stockholm. Photo Carl-Johan Rönn: 6.18.
Tampere Art Museum, Moominvalley. © Moomin Characters TM: 4.51.
Photo courtesy Tange Associates, photo © Chuji Hirayama: 5.12.
© Tezuka Productions: 6.50.
© 2012 Times Wide World Photos: 3.02.
TINKERTOY ® & © 2012 Hasbro Inc.: 5.26.
© UDI Archive (Italian Women's Union), Reggio Emilia, Italy, http://unionedonne.altervista.org. From the book One City, Many Children [page 66], curated by Rolando Baldini, Ilaria Cavallini, Vania Vecchi, Reggio Children Publisher, 2012, Reggio Emilia–Italy www.reggiochildren.it: 7.17.
Courtesy UNICEF Sweden, Stockholm. Photo of Marion by Henrik Halvarson, after an idea by Johan Jäger at Jung von Matt, Stockholm: 7.43.
United Colors of Benetton, New York. Photo Jean-Pierre Laffont: 7.45.
United States Holocaust Memorial Museum: page 23.
Universität für angewandte Kunst Wien, Kunstsammlung und Archiv: page 19, 1.58, 3.12, 3.38, 3.39, 3.40, 3.41, 3.42, 4.32, 4.33.
Special Collections Research Center, University of Chicago Library: 1.28.
Courtesy U.S. Fund for UNICEF: 7.46.
Vandkunsten Architects, Copenhagen: 7.12; photo Jens Thomas Arnfred: 7.10, 7.11; Photo Finn Christoffersen, foto C: 7.13.
Photo Alessandro Vasari: 1.36, 2.15.
© 2012 Twan Verdonck: 7.39.
© Victoria and Albert Museum, London: 1.57, 3.19, 3.44, 3.45.
Vitra Design Museum, Weil am Rhein, Germany: 3.53, 6.01.
Courtesy Walt Disney Imagineering: 6.12, 6.14.
© Todd Webb, Courtesy Evans Gallery and Estate of Todd & Lucille Webb, Portland, Maine: 5.63.
© 2012 William Wegman: 7.28.
Courtesy Margot Weller, New York. The Museum of Modern Art, New York. Department of Imaging Services: 5.46.
The Mitchell Wolfson, Jr. Private Collection, Miami, Florida. Photo Silvia Ros: 3.13.
The Wolfsonian–Florida International University, Miami Beach, Florida, Gift of Pamela K. Harer. Photo David Almeida: 4.41, 4.43, 4.44, 4.45, 4.46, 4.47; Gift of Steven Heller. Photo David Almeida: 4.14.
The Wolfsonian–Florida International University, Miami Beach, Florida, The Mitchell Wolfson, Jr. Collection. Photo David Almeida: 3.51, 4.03, 4.04, 4.10, 4.13, 4.16, 4.17, 4.20, 4.21, 4.23, 4.25, 4.26, 4.42, 4.48, 4.24; Photo Silvia Ros: 3.52, 4.08, 4.12; Long-term loan, The Mitchell Wolfson, Jr. Private Collection, Miami. Photo Silvia Ros: 3.50.
Wolfsoniana–Fondazione regionale per la Cultura e lo Spettacolo, Genoa: 2.18.
Photo The Frank Lloyd Wright Fdn, AZ/Art Resource, NY: 1.26.
© 2012 Frank Lloyd Wright Foundation/Artists Rights Society (ARS), New York: 1.23, 1.26.
Courtesy Yuval Yasky, photo Hanan Bahir: 5.09; photo Galia Bar Or: 7.57.
© 2012 Tadanori Yokoo: page 2.
© Zürich University of the Arts, Archives: 2.09, 2.01.

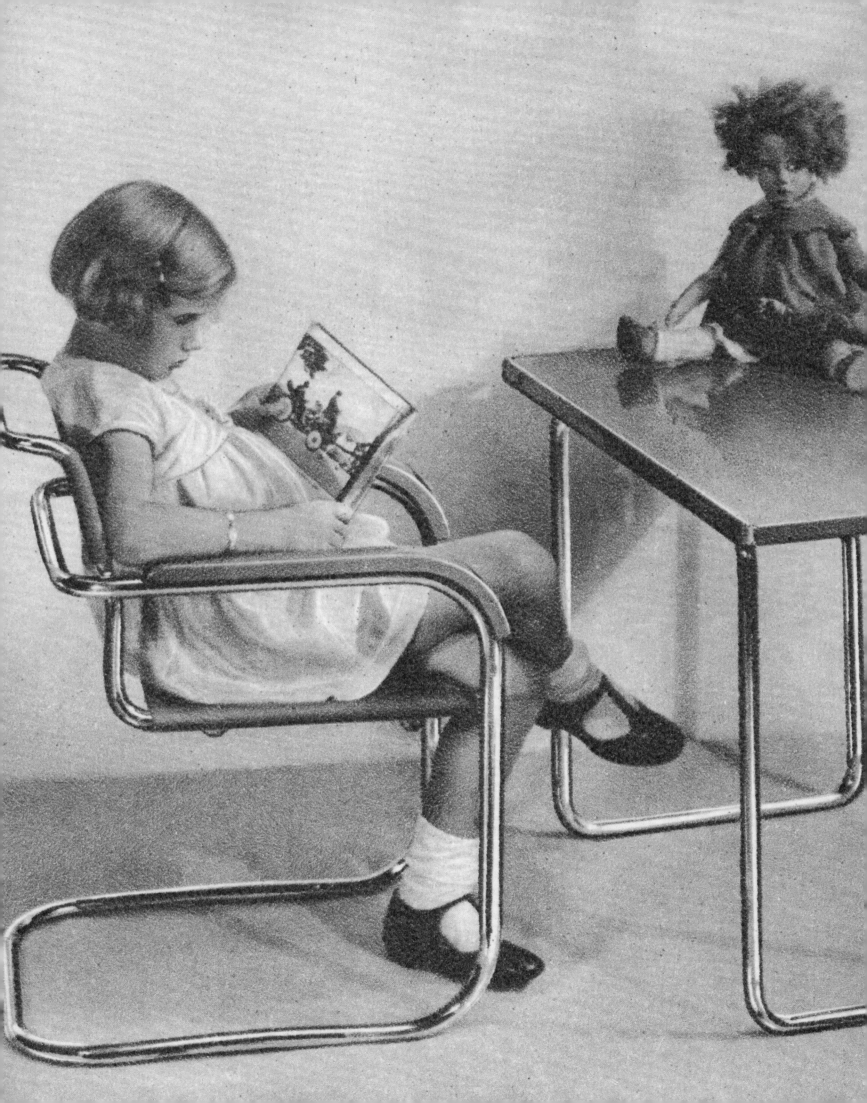